FOUNDATION PRESS

ENVIRONMENTAL LAW AND POLICY

By

JAMES SALZMAN
Professor of Law
Washington College of Law
American University

BARTON H. THOMPSON, JR.
Robert E. Paradise Professor of Natural Resources Law,
and Vice Dean
Stanford Law School

CONCEPTS AND INSIGHTS SERIES

FOUNDATION PRESS
New York, New York
2003

COPYRIGHT © 2003 By FOUNDATION PRESS

395 Hudson Street
New York, NY 10014
Phone Toll Free 1–877–888–1330
Fax (212) 367–6799
fdpress.com

ISBN 1–56662–984–5

TEXT IS PRINTED ON 10% POST
CONSUMER RECYCLED PAPER

To my parents, with gratitude for encouraging me to look beyond the horizon and follow my star.

J.E.S.

To my mother, Lorraine, and in memory of my father, Barton, for everything they taught me.

B.H.T.

*

PREFACE

Environmental law is critically important and endlessly fascinating. To see its importance, just imagine the United States today without federal regulation of air and water quality, pesticide use, and solid waste disposal. No matter how far the nation has come in addressing environmental issues, there remains much to do. Federal and state laws have only begun to address such important environmental issues as global climate change, non-point water pollution, indoor air pollution, groundwater depletion, and fisheries collapse. Scientific uncertainty, risk tradeoffs, cognitive biases, and fundamental policy disagreements, moreover, make it extremely difficult to agree on solutions to many of these remaining problems. Environmental law already has picked the low hanging fruit. The remaining problems continue to challenge even the wisest and most patient policy experts.

In many environmental law books, the important concepts and issues underlying the regulatory schemes can get lost amid a myriad of legal details. The purpose of this book therefore is to provide a conceptual overview of environmental law and policy in a concise, readable style. The book covers all of the major environmental statutes and cases, but from a broader and more policy-oriented perspective than other hornbooks, treatises, and student guides. Our goal is to introduce the reader to the major themes and frameworks of environmental law, not to overburden the reader with minutiae. The book should be useful to law students seeking a readable and stimulating companion to their casebooks, to professors looking for a short yet comprehensive introduction to environmental policy that they can supplement with other materials, and to professionals wishing a quick, user-friendly survey of environmental law.

The book is divided into three sections. Part I introduces the major themes and issues that cross-cut environmental law, such as scientific uncertainty, market failures, and problems of scale. Part I also covers major legal concepts in the environmental field such as standing, citizen suits, takings, the commerce clause, and administrative procedure. Later chapters use the themes and conceptual framework introduced in Part I to integrate the discussions of individual statutes into a broader portrait of the law. Part II offers overviews of each of the major federal pollution statutes. As in the rest of the book, the focus is on the ideas and debates underlying the statutes. International pollution issues such as ozone depletion, climate change, and transboundary waste disposal are integrated with their domestic counterparts. Part III explores the increasingly controversial trade and environment debate, discussing the WTO, GATT and NAFTA, as well as the international trade in hazardous chemicals. Part IV examines the public trust doctrine and the policy and legal issues underlying two of the major natural resource statutes – the Endangered Species Act and section 404 of the Clean Water Act, which regulates wetlands. Part V addresses environmental impact statements, focusing on the National Environmental Policy Act, the model for environmental assessment legislation around the world.

We hope this book conveys the excitement that we feel in teaching in this area. We are grateful for the helpful review of chapters by Craig Oren, John Applebaum, and Bill Cohen, the substantive contributions of Lewis Grossman, Josh Eagle, Durwood Zaelke and David Hunter, the hospitality of Andy Beattie at the Key Centre for Biodiversity and Donna Craig and Michael Jeffery at the Macquarie Centre for Environmental Law, and the creation of diagrams by Robert Starner. We are indebted to our colleagues in law schools throughout the nation, who have helped develop the theories and analysis on which the nation's environmental policy and this book are built, and to our students, who keep the field fresh and alive.

J.E.S.
B.H.T.

TABLE OF CONTENTS

*

ENVIRONMENTAL LAW AND POLICY

*

PART I

Tools of the Trade

CHAPTER 1

An Introduction to Environmental Law and Policy

I. Why Study Environmental Law?

The simplest definition of "environmental law and policy" might read: "the use of governmental authority to protect the natural environment and human health from the impacts of pollution and development." While accurate, this definition suffers from two fatal flaws—(1) it's deadly boring and (2) it fails to capture why environmental law matters.

Instead of laboring over a precise definition, instead pick up today's newspaper and see if you find any of the following types of headlines— "Scientists Say Climate Heating Up," "Endangered Salamander Stops Development," "Environmental Protection Agency To Clamp Down on Benzene Emissions," "Pesticides Found in Local Groundwater." Environmental law and policy are a part of everyday life, no matter where you live. It is more than protecting cuddly pandas or clamping down on Dickensian factories that belch smoke and churn out barrels of waste. Indeed the field cuts a remarkably broad swath—taking in climate change, water pollution, wetlands conservation, wildlife protection, green spaces, ozone depletion, smog alerts, recycling, etc.

While every field jealously claims for itself primacy as "the most important area of the law," environmental law has as good a claim on that title as any. Why should we care about environmental law? Because, taken together, the challenges to environmental quality have a critical influence on where we live, how well we live and, perhaps most important, the kind of world our children and their children will live in. These things matter. Consider how sea level rise will affect a coastal community, what soil erosion means to a farming community, what the collapse of a fishery does to a fishing community, and how long it will take to reverse these impacts, if they even can be reversed.

Not only does environmental law matter, it's also difficult, controversial, and fascinating. Our regulation of endangered species, to take an example, challenges deeply held convictions across the political spectrum.

1

Do endangered species have rights that we should respect? How do we balance the benefits of saving an endangered salamander against the costs of an industrial development that can provide jobs to an economically depressed town? Do some species deserve more legal protection than others? We may be willing to protect a bald eagle, but who really cares about the Delhi Sands flower loving fly?

The annual debates over drilling for oil in the Arctic National Wildlife Refuge are no less challenging. On the one hand are the arguments that drilling could bring much needed economic development to impoverished Eskimo communities, that it will reduce America's dependence on foreign oil and that, with modern technology, it may be possible to drill with little impact on the landscape. Opposed are those who counter that drilling will threaten the Porcupine Caribou Herd and, even with best efforts and technology, despoil one of America's great remaining natural areas. How can the law mediate between these opposing views? And why do opponents of drilling care so much, given the fact that it's unlikely they'll ever meet someone who has ever been to the refuge, much less go themselves?

This is not to suggest that opposition to drilling (a position shared by most Americans) is irrational but, rather, that whatever drives this view resonates widely and defies simple explanation. Indeed it may seem odd to describe the environmental field as contentious at all, given the fact that virtually all Americans consider themselves environmentalists. Poll after poll shows that 80% and more of those surveyed believe that environmental protection should be a high governmental priority. Scratch the surface beneath the pablum that "environmental protection is good," though, and this seeming consensus dissolves into difficult questions of how much environmental harm we should accept, how much we as a society are willing to pay for certain levels of environmental protection, and who should bear these risks and costs. This chapter and the next provide a series of frameworks through which to consider these questions—historical, economic, ethical, equitable, etc. While these perspectives and modes of analysis may not provide definitive solutions, they will explain why so many people find the field exciting and important.

Before proceeding further, it is worth noting that the broad subject of environmental law is often viewed as comprising two quite distinct fields—pollution law and natural resources law. In some respects, these really are different. Laws such as the Clean Air Act and Clean Water Act focus on sources of pollutants, threats to human health, and risk levels, for example, while the Endangered Species Act and wetlands protections concentrate more on land use management and ecological concerns. Hence it's not surprising that many law schools offer separate courses on pollution and natural resources law. As Chapter 2 makes clear, however, despite their differences in emphasis, both fields share fundamental similarities and can usefully be viewed as protecting different aspects of the environment, whether clean air and water or species and their habitat.

II.   A Short History of Environmental Protection in America

One cannot understand current conflicts over allocation and protection of our nation's natural resources—whether water, timber, wilderness, or rangelands—without some grasp of the changing values of those resources over the course of our nation's history. Nor do the approaches taken in our pollution statutes make sense unless understood in their historic context. While the histories of natural resource protection and pollution control are interwoven in places, as the stories below explain they have important differences as well.

A.   *Natural Resources*

Wilderness holds a special place in the American consciousness. The stillness of a remote forest lake or the imposing crags of a mountain peak provide for many both a sense of connection to a larger world and a sense of inner wonder. Wilderness is also big business. It primes our economy through eco-tourists paying top dollar for trips to Antarctica, backpackers buying high-tech gear for trekking in Alaska, families enjoying Disneyworld's Jungle Cruise, and even kids having birthday parties in the Rainforest Café. The environment holds a strong grip in our collective imagination and, as the above examples make clear, the marketplace provides a dizzying number of ways for us to enjoy a range of "wilderness experiences."

Our love affair with things wild, however, is quite recent. To the Europeans who first came to America, eagerly seeking out the wilderness would have been incomprehensible. Indeed for most of the last two millennia, wilderness has been viewed more often with repugnance, as something dangerous and even an affront to civilization. The roots of this view go back to the Bible and earlier. After Adam and Eve have tasted the forbidden fruit, for example, their punishment is exile from the Garden of Eden into the wilderness. This is the same harsh, inhospitable region where Moses and the tribes of Israel must wander for forty years, where Jesus is sorely tempted by the Devil for forty days. The Biblical wilderness is unforgiving, a wasteland of physical hardship and spiritual testing that forges iron faith.

The later folk traditions in Europe reflected this harsh view. In many of the fairy tales of the Brothers Grimm, for example, when the

3

protagonists leave the village bad things surely follow. For Hansel and Gretel, the forest is a place of monstrous beasts and creatures, surely no place for innocent children to wander. In the same manner, William Bradford, the first governor in Plymouth Plantation, described the surrounding forests as "hideous and desolate." To be fair, he had his reasons. The world outside his settlements posed very real threats to survival, hiding wild animals and potentially hostile and, to his eyes, heathen tribes. Faced with this absence of morality and civilization, the Pilgrims and their successors felt both a religious and practical compulsion to "civilize" the wilderness.

This is not to say, however, that the natural environment had no positive characteristics for early Americans. The goal of conquering the wilderness was usually not to convert it into cities but, rather, to a rural, pastoral state—a controlled, managed nature. Thus was wasteland converted to garden. One could have too much civilization as well as too little. The city—a pure civilized state—was viewed equally by many as immoral and disconnected from God. To the degree that the earliest Americans did admire the unspoiled American landscape, these were either areas that reminded them of cultivated landscapes in England, or particular aspects of the landscape—birds, flowers—that could be incorporated into a garden view.

To the early settlers, it seemed that much of Europe had gone too far toward the pole of civilization to achieve the ideal pastoral state. But it wasn't too late for America. Thus early American writers, such as Crevecoeur, despised wild areas but praised the improved, managed nature of the rural landscape. As he described, "I will revert into a state approaching nearer to that of nature, but at the same time sufficiently remote from the brutality of unconnected savage nature." Thomas Jefferson's ideal citizens were those yeoman farmers who labored on the earth (unlike city dwellers and industrial laborers). They were virtuous, close to God, independent—the moral center of democratic society.

In the Westward expansion and development that long accompanied America's growth, the frontier mantra was largely one of taming the environment. Wilderness posed a barrier to progress and prosperity. It was an obstacle, something to be conquered. As naturalist Aldo Leopold later wrote of the 1930s, "A stump was our symbol of progress." But the era of frontier settlement coincided with the rise of a broader appreciation for wilderness. In art and literature, the presence of a grand and ancient wilderness assumed a role as a distinctive source of American identity and superiority. This nationalist embrace of wilderness as a replacement for history was evident in the poetry of William Cullen Bryant, the novels of James Fenimore Cooper, the art of Thomas Cole, Asher Durand, Albert Bierstadt, and, most famously, in the writings of Henry David Thoreau.

The best known of the Transcendentalists, Thoreau's writings sprang from his belief that God could be found in nature through intuitive contemplation. For Thoreau, modern industrial society, by cutting people off from nature, was cutting them off from God. The commercial spirit of civilization kept people from contemplation of the divine. Nature was a source of vigor, inspiration, and strength. It stripped life down to its essentials. As Thoreau simply stated, "In Wildness is the preservation of the world." Yet Thoreau's terrifying account of climbing Mount Katahdin in Maine leaves little doubt that he believed one could experience too much wilderness as well. In fact, Thoreau's ideal was really a middle landscape rather than pure wilderness, a life alternating between wilderness and civilization or residence in "partially cultivated country." This middle landscape is the essence of *Walden*, a subsistence farming existence near a town.

Thoreau was not particularly influential in his day, however, and the notion of preserving wilderness was not a serious option. Indeed the opposite was true. Throughout most of the Nineteenth Century, federal policy was to settle the western wilderness with Jefferson's virtuous yeoman farmers. A series of preemption and donation acts followed by the Homestead Act of 1862 and a variety of other statutes gave successive waves of settlers title to millions of acres of public lands. Often the statutes required some effort to cultivate the land before title would vest. It's important to note, of course, that despite publicizing these lands as "virgin" and "uninhabited," that was rarely the case; rather, the native Americans previously living there were often moved off the land to reservations.

To the extent there was federal supervision of the often chaotic process, it was to assure that wilderness was being tamed, not protected. And if wilderness could not necessarily be turned to farmland, particularly in the arid lands between the 100th Meridian and the Sierra Nevada and Cascade mountain ranges, its natural resources could at least be developed and exploited. Cattle were allowed freely to graze the public grasslands and miners were promised exclusive control of minerals they were able to discover on the public lands. At the same time that public lands were being granted for agriculture, mining, and other development, Congress was granting railroads millions of acres of alternating sections of public lands in an effort to speed the process along.

While this mass transfer of land from public to private ownership was taking place, halting steps toward preserving wilderness began, albeit from very modest beginnings. George Catlin, a painter of native Americans and prairie life, had proposed in 1832 the concept of preserving Indians, buffaloes, and their wilderness home in a park. And there was some early action. In 1832, Arkansas Hot Springs was set aside as a national reservation; in 1864, the federal government granted Yosemite

Valley to California as a park "for public use, resort, recreation"; in 1872, President Grant signed an act creating Yellowstone "as a public park or pleasuring ground for the benefit and enjoyment of the people"; and, in 1885, New York State created a huge forest reserve in the Adirondacks "to be forever as wild lands." Yet few of these acts were motivated by the aesthetic, spiritual, or cultural values of wilderness. The Adirondacks forest reserve was created to ensure clean water for New York City. Arkansas Hot Springs and Yellowstone were given protection primarily to prevent commercial exploitation of curiosities such as geysers. These were museum for freaks of nature.

As the Nineteenth Century drew to a close, though, public attitudes began to change about wilderness preservation. As Frederick Jackson Turner famously observed in 1893, "The frontier has gone, and with its going has closed the first period of American history." To Turner and many others, wilderness in American history had served as a fundamental source of democracy and rugged individualism. Ironically, the success of the frontier movement had raised the fear that wilderness, and the prized social values it had come to represent, might be lost. If the frontier were vanishing, preservation of the remaining wild areas was now a valid public concern.

The dominant personality of the "preservationist" movement was a remarkable Scot named John Muir. Like Thoreau, Muir celebrated the presence of the divine in wilderness. It was not trite for him to proclaim that forests were temples on earth and mountains their steeples. He and other preservationists praised wilderness as a source of toughness and ethical values. Indeed he argued that many of the nation's difficulties could be attributed to *too much* civilization and the effete, corrupt urban culture. Unlike the earlier transcendentalists, however, Muir had no ambivalence about pure wilderness. He was the first great public defender of wilderness for its own sake. When asked what a rattlesnake is good for, Muir famously replied, "It is good for itself." Founder of the Sierra Club, Muir was enough of a pragmatist to realize that the public and politicians needed to be persuaded of the wisdom of preserving wilderness.

An early and important ally of Muir was the equally impressive figure, Gifford Pinchot. The first American professionally trained as a forester in Europe, Pinchot became the consummate Washington insider. He was made the first Chief of the U.S. Forest Service by Teddy Roosevelt and later helped found the Yale School of Forestry, the first of its kind in America. Like Muir, Pinchot opposed the wholesale exploitation of public lands, but for very different reasons. While Muir championed the preservation of the nation's sublime landscapes, Gifford Pinchot's views rested on a philosophy of "wise use"—the view that expert management should ensure the optimal use of natural resources. The key words here are "management" and "use." Pinchot recognized that there would always be competing demands for natural resources, and thus supported the strategy of multiple use. From this "conservationist" perspective, the natural resource expert might manage parts of the public lands for their wilderness values (as Muir would demand) or, equally, for forestry, grazing, hunting, or water power. The guiding principle in this decision was ensuring the greatest good for the greatest number of people.

The great battle that catapulted the preservationist and conservationist movements into national prominence involved the Hetch Hetchy Valley in Yosemite National Park. From 1901 through 1913, there were repeated calls for damming the Tuolomne River in Hetch Hetchy Valley to increase San Francisco's water and electricity supply. From a conservationist perspective, there was a pretty good argument in favor of damming the river if one weighed the water needs of a city of 400,000 against the interests of those who would benefit from Hetch Hetchy's preservation. Despite support of the dam by the President, Congress, and Pinchot, however, Muir led a more effective opposition campaign than anyone anticipated. Against the claims of dam supporters praising the beauty and potential recreational uses of a reservoir, Muir and grassroots supporters denounced as wasteful and sinful this "destruction" of a valley they claimed was more sublime than Yosemite. In response, the pro-dam San Francisco Chronicle ridiculed Muir's supporters as "hoggish and mushy esthetes," setting the tone for the many similar battles that have followed. The preservationists lost and Hetch Hetchy was dammed, but through the process of a sustained political campaign preservationists gained many supporters and popularized the wilderness ethic.

Following World War II, the growth of America's middle class, and construction of the interstate highway system, America's public lands became both more familiar and cherished. While there had been only a handful of conservation groups at the time of the Hetch Hetchy dispute, by the early 1950s there were over 300. Thus when the battle of dams was rejoined, the results were different. In 1954, a dam was proposed at Echo Park that would threaten Dinosaur National Monument on the Colorado–Utah border. This time, the far larger preservation movement enjoyed greater support and created an unprecedented grassroots campaign against development. Mail to Congress was almost eighty-to-one against the dam. After five years, the dam proponents gave up.

The first great preservation victory behind them, environmental groups continued to organize and keep up their pressure on Congress. The 1960s saw passage of landmark laws such as the Wilderness Act of 1964, the Land and Water Conservation Act of 1965, the National Historic Preservation Act of 1966, and the National Wild and Scenic Rivers System in 1968. Totally unlike earlier laws that had encouraged disposal of the public lands, this new wave of legislation took the opposite approach of retention and preservation. Recent conversion of public lands into national monuments is only the latest example of this counter-trend.

In the 1970s, the nation turned its attention to the importance of preserving environmentally valuable lands and waters that are in *private* hands or part of the more general public domain. In 1973, Congress passed the Endangered Species Act, which both constrains those federal actions, such as the construction of dams and highways, that might jeopardize the continued existence of endangered species and restricts private land development that might kill or harm endangered species. This remains the strongest legal protection of biodiversity in the world. Then in 1977, Congress amended the Clean Water Act to strengthen protections of privately held wetlands. Unlike prior federal laws that focused on the spectacular (e.g., national parks such as Yellowstone) and the special (e.g., wilderness areas), these laws recognized that even lands that appear to many humans to be relatively "ordinary" can provide valuable habitat for biodiversity and other important ecosystem services such as water purification and flood control.

Application of these laws has proven controversial, often pitting environmentalists against property rights advocates who argue that restrictions on the use of their property should be compensated. Nor has passage of these laws resolved the conflict between conservationists and preservationists. The decade–long debates over oil drilling in the Arctic National Wildlife Refuge and logging in private, old growth forests are proof of that.

Today our natural resource policies must continue to ford the raging confluence of distinct historical perspectives—the view of wilderness and nature as obstacles to human welfare and resources to be shaped and managed for society's benefit, in one stream, and the role of wilderness and nature as sacred, essential to defining what we are as a people, and supportive of important ecosystem services, in the other. As Wallace Stegner succinctly described, our position is unique. "No other nation on Earth so swiftly wasted its birthright; no other, in time, made such an effort to save what was left."

B.   *Pollution*

Ever since the rise of farming and settled populations, pollution has been a concern. The classic method of managing waste was one of dilution. Population densities were low and the environment could generally assimilate the largely organic wastes. As city populations rose, however, the harms from pollution and its links to public health became clearer in the public's eye. Thus a proclamation in London in 1306 threatened those responsible for air pollution from coal burning with "grievous ransoms." Forty years later, Londoners could be fined two shillings if they did not remove waste from outside their homes. It's fair to say, though, that even up to the turn of the 20th century, despite the construction of city sewers and early attempts at controlling air and water pollution, London still had "killer fogs" and Chicago's rivers still congealed from the run-off of its slaughterhouses. As a practical matter, pollution regulation simply didn't exist.

Instead, legal responses to pollution relied on the common law doctrines of trespass and nuisance. As described in Chapter 3, however, these legal remedies were retrospective, compensated only property losses, and required proof of specific causation, often difficult to come by in pollution cases. Despite the obvious weaknesses of relying on the common law to protect the environment, there was very little national political concern over pollution through the first half of the 20th century. Following World War II, though, the nature of pollution began to change. In particular, the field of organic chemistry took off, with mass distribution and use of synthetic compounds such as plastics and many modern pesticides. Viewed as technological wonders (which these new compounds truly were), there was little understanding of their impacts on the environment or human health. While worth a chuckle when viewed in retrospect, there were serious proposals in the late 1940s to use (small) nuclear bombs to build canals. If a single event can be linked to triggering the erosion of this naïve acceptance, it would be the publication and uproar that surrounded publication of Rachel Carson's book, *Silent Spring*, in 1962.

Known for her wonderful writings about the natural history of the ocean and seashore, Carson, a marine biologist with the U.S. Fish and Wildlife Service, was an unlikely pioneer of the environmental movement. Knowing that attacking a popular chemical product would be controversial, Carson spent four years of research prior to publication of *Silent Spring* carefully documenting the health and environmental effects of the pesticide DDT. The magazine, the *New Yorker,* published *Silent Spring* in a three–part series. Even prior to publication, the chemical industry mounted a high-profile attack on the book and its author, dismissing Carson as a nature-nut and unscientific. Ironically, the strength of the attacks on *Silent Spring* caught the interest of President Kennedy, who formed an advisory group to investigate the use and control of pesticides. This, in turn, spurred Congressional studies on pesticide regulation. Suffering from breast cancer at the time her book was published, Carson died in 1964, but the concerns aroused by *Silent Spring* continued to grow, spawning new advocacy-based organizations.

The group Scenic Hudson, for example, was formed in 1963 and, in an early grassroots victory, successfully opposed plans to develop Storm King Mountain in the Hudson Valley into the world's largest pumped-storage hydroelectric plant. The case, *Scenic Hudson Preservation Conference v. Federal Power Commission*,[1] marked the first time environmental groups had been granted standing. Environmental Defense (formerly known as the Environmental Defense Fund), another grassroots organization, was founded in 1967 to ban use of the pesticide DDT in Long Island.

Over 20 million people participated in the first Earth Day in 1970, and pollution control was firmly set on the national political scene. Creation of the Environmental Protection Agency and enactment of the Clean Air Act in 1970 was closely followed by the Clean Water Act in 1972, as President Richard Nixon and Senator Edmund Muskie competed with one another for the newly important environmental vote. The Resource Conservation and Recovery Act followed in 1976 and Superfund in 1980. Events such as Love Canal (described at page 197) and the nuclear accident at Three Mile Island ensured that the public interest in environmental issues remained high. Taken together, these laws and those that have followed are known as the era of "modern environmental law." In contrast to earlier regulation of pollution, all of these laws established uniform, tough, national standards.

When looking back to 1970 from today's vantage, it is easy to point out flaws in these laws. Congress was consistently over-ambitious, setting goals that could not be met, such as clean water or air within a decade, and shifting pollution from one medium to another (e.g., burning solid waste to reduce landfill pressure but increasing air pollution). Nonetheless, overall the modern era of environmental law stands out as a stunning success. Despite a larger population and greatly increased levels of economic activity, most of our nation's air and water are cleaner than three decades ago. Moreover, public opinion polls today routinely show that upwards of 80% of respondents consider themselves "environmentalists."

1. 407 U.S. 926 (1972).

CHAPTER 2

Perspectives on Environmental Law and Policy

I. Basic Themes of Environmental Law

In seeking to provide client counsel, all too often environmental lawyers look first to the law rather than to the problem itself. To be sure, the law creates the framework within which environmental problems are resolved. But one cannot intelligently apply the law without also understanding the forces that created the problem in the first place. Consider, for example, the seemingly different threats posed in the newspaper headlines described in the introduction to Chapter 1—climate change, development in an endangered species habitat, factory emissions, polluted drinking water. All of these stories share a similar trait, of course, since they directly relate to environmental protection. But the similarities run far deeper. While the actors, the location, and the nature of the concerns are quite different in the particulars, the *underlying* causes of the environmental problems may be understood as simple variants on common themes.

This section introduces the basic themes that run throughout environmental law and policy—the themes of scientific uncertainty, market failure, mismatched scale, cognitive biases, sustainable development, and nontraditional interests. It is no exaggeration to say that these resonate throughout the entire field of environmental law and policy, irrespective of the particular issue. Understanding their implications is a critical first step in understanding the field and resolving environmental conflicts.

A. Scientific Uncertainty

In many respects scientific uncertainty is *the* defining feature of environmental policy. Most environmental problems involve complex technical and economic issues. But lawmakers rarely have anything approaching perfect knowledge when asked to make specific decisions. Certainty may come too late, if ever, to design optimal legal and policy responses.

In the context of climate change, for example, the detailed mechanisms of global warming are still only partly understood. Will increases in the earth's temperature lead to greater cloud formation, acting as a negative feedback to warming? Are measured temperature increases over the last century due to increased carbon in the atmosphere, the onset of an unrelated global warming trend, or a combination of the two? If atmospheric carbon dioxide concentrations continue to increase, what will the mean global temperature be in 20, 30, and 40 years, and what costs will this impose?

All of these questions bear directly on our decisions *today* to regulate emissions of greenhouse gases or introduce carbon taxes. The UN's Intergovernmental Panel on Climate Change has provided estimates based on the best judgment of over 2,000 scientists researching these issues from around the globe, but no one can claim these conclusions are correct. They are simply the best estimates we have.

Similarly in the case of benzene emissions, experiments may show that exposing mice to very high levels of this compound causes cancer. But we have no baseline data to understand what happens to humans exposed to benzene at everyday levels, orders of magnitude lower than those that harmed the mice. And mice, of course, aren't people, so perhaps the effects observed in mice would not occur in larger mammals.

Troubling levels of uncertainty are present when conserving natural resources, as well. Perhaps developers have proposed setting aside an acre beside a new mall to provide habitat for an endangered salamander population. Will an acre provide sufficient habitat for its survival? Is the main reason for the salamander population's collapse not loss of habitat but, rather, predation by cats? We do not know enough about the salamander's life history or recent population declines to be certain, yet such information is critical to designing an effective policy response.

Another source of uncertainty is the complex interrelations among causes of environmental harms. Rather than resulting from a single, identifiable action, many environmental harms are caused by cumulative, multiple actions. Addressing one cause may have little effect or, even worse, exacerbate another problem. Acid rain is an obvious example. Did the emissions of a particular coal-fired plant in the Ohio Valley contribute to the acidification of a mountain lake in the Catskills? Most likely yes, but good luck figuring out *how much* harm it contributed. Or take the example of endangered salmon in the Pacific Northwest. Why are so many stocks collapsing? One can point to overfishing, damming of rivers, logging practices that lead to erosion and silt in the rivers, coastal pollution, and over-reliance on hatchery fish. To conserve and restore salmon populations, we must address most, if not all, of these causes, yet there is enormous debate over which particular action will be most effective. And solving one problem may cause another to appear somewhere else.

In fact, uncertainties over the magnitude of environmental problems, their causes, and future impacts bedevil law and policy. What we would like to know as policy makers rarely approaches our actual knowledge. But if we do not understand well the current situation, then how can we predict the future impacts of our laws and policies? Does prudence dictate waiting until we have better information or taking early action in the face of potentially serious threats?

In the climate change debate, for example, industry-sponsored trade groups argue that scientific uncertainty counsels prudence. The "problem" of global warming has not been rigorously established, they argue, and our limited knowledge of atmospheric physics severely restricts our ability to predict future temperatures or climates. And even if global warming is happening, there are enormous unknowns over how much warming will occur and at what rate. If the threat of global warming turns out to have been an exaggerated threat, then actions taken today to reduce fossil fuel consumption will have been an overreaction. Spending money to reduce fossil fuel use, it follows, may cause more harm than good because of increased unemployment and diversion of resources away from other worthy causes. The best response is more research and development. After all, how can one craft an effective policy without clearly understanding the problem we're trying to solve?

The obvious response to such arguments is that waiting for more scientific certainty, if it ever comes, imposes costs of its own. In the face of a credible and significant threat, the opposing argument goes, we must act today so as to avoid the present and future harms (which may well be greater) imposed by delay. To employ a nautical metaphor, we should be bailing water out of our sinking ship as fast as possible, not standing on the deck studying the angle and rate of descent.

The exact same dynamic is at work in the examples of benzene and the endangered salamander. Delay while we study the toxicology of benzene may result in an increase in cancers that could have been prevented. Delay in the case of the salamander may lead to greater understanding, but of a now extinct species. Yet, as the voices of caution warn, overreaction imposes its own real costs in the form of higher prices and scarce public monies that could have been better spent elsewhere. In these and countless other examples, there are good reasons to wait and reduce the uncertainty, and good reasons to avoid potential future costs by acting now. Thus perhaps the first question of environmental law and policy is how to act in the face of uncertainty.

There are two basic strategies to address this intractable problem. The first is to develop better information. As we shall see later in the book, many environmental statutes require generation of considerable information to provide a surer basis on which to create policy. A second strategy is known as the *precautionary principle*. Influential in the field of international environmental law, in its simplest form the principle counsels caution in the face of significant but uncertain threats. It's hard to argue against such an obvious rule of conduct but people differ significantly over how the principle should be applied in practice. In its most extreme form, the principle would forbid any activity that potentially could produce significant harms, regardless of the likelihood that these harms may occur. The problem, though, is that such a view counsels inaction in the face of uncertainty, no matter what the cost. The strategy, moreover, is paralyzing in the context of risk-risk choices, where every alternative poses significant risks and one must choose among them. Such risk-risk choices arise commonly in the environmental field, such as deciding whether to build a nuclear power plant or a coal-fired plant. Each option poses environmental concerns and potential harms.

In the international context, the precautionary principle generally has been viewed as shifting the burden of proof from those who would challenge an offending activity to those who wish to commence or continue the activity. This shift in burden could shorten the time period between when a threat to the environment is recognized and a legal response is developed. In the climate change context, for example, the burden would fall on oil companies to establish that global warming is not a serious and credible threat. In the salamander example, the developer would shoulder the burden of proving that the loss of habitat will not threaten the salamander's survival. Chemical manufacturers would bear the responsibility of justifying that current emission levels of benzene pose no significant health risks.

This shift in burden changes the tenor and nature of the debate over *how well understood* the problem must be before taking action. But it does not shed light on an equally important question—*how serious* the problem must be before taking action (i.e., which risks are worth addressing), much less the appropriate action to take. As we shall see below, these are fundamentally political, not scientific, questions, and they pose additional levels of uncertainty.

B.   *Market Failures*

Misaligned incentives underlie most environmental conflicts. While protecting the environment often provides a net benefit to society, the economic interests of individual parties involved often can encourage harmful activities. Thus a basic challenge to an environmental lawyer lies in understanding the reward structures of the parties and then changing incentives so that environmental protection reinforces rather than collides with the parties' self-interest. In the following examples, consider how costs and benefits are allocated.

In the case of climate change, a company may choose voluntarily to reduce its greenhouse gas emissions, but it may end up raising its operating costs and losing market share if its competitors do not reduce their emissions as well. A neighbor of a factory may be having constant sore throats because of particulate emissions, but the bother isn't worth the cost of bringing a lawsuit. All of her neighbors have sore throats, too, but they can't seem to get together to negotiate with or sue the factory.

On its face, one might think that the market would automatically promote environmental protection. The most basic principle of economics, after all, is supply and demand. As the supply of a valuable good becomes scarce, its price rises. Since clean air and water are clearly valuable, one would expect that as they become scarcer their price should also rise, making it more expensive to pollute. Yet this clearly does not happen in real life. The market has somehow failed, as it does when the company fails to reduce its greenhouse gas emissions and the factory's neighbors can't agree to sue the factory. To correct these market failures and craft an effective legal response, we first need to understand the distortions at play.

1.   Public Goods

Try to buy some clean air. Sure, you can buy real estate in the wilds of Alaska where the air is clean, but you own the land there, not the air. In fact, your neighbor can breathe it right after it blows through. It turns out that many environmental amenities, such as clean air and scenic vistas, are called *public goods*. Their benefits can be shared by everyone, but owned by no one. No one owns the air. No one can sell it or prevent others from using it.

The same is true for *ecosystem services*. Largely taken for granted, healthy ecosystems provide a variety of critical services. Created by the interactions of living organisms with their environment, these ecosystem services provide both the conditions and processes that sustain human life—purifying air and water, detoxifying and decomposing waste, renewing soil fertility, regulating climate, mitigating droughts and floods, controlling pests, and pollinating plants. Not surprisingly, recent research has demonstrated the extremely high costs to replace many of these services if they were to fail. Looking at just one ecosystem service that soil provides, the provision of nitrogen to plants, serves as an example. Nitrogen is supplied to plants through both nitrogen-fixing organisms and recycling of nutrients in the soil. If nitrogen were provided by commercial fertilizer rather than natural processes, the lowest cost estimate for crops in the U.S. would be $45 billion; the figure for all land plants would be $320 billion.

The value of $320 billion is estimated by calculating replacement costs—what we'd have to pay to replace the ecosystem service of nitrogen fixing by other means. But what are these natural goods and services *really* worth? Perhaps surprisingly, in the eyes of the market they are not worth anything. We have no shortage of markets for ecosystem goods (such as clean water and apples), but the services underpinning these goods (such as water purification and pollination) are free. Make no mistake, these environmental amenities are valuable— just ask yourself how much it's worth to you to breathe unpolluted air— but they have no *market value*. There is no market to exchange public goods such as ecosystem services and, as a result, they have no price. This explains the riddle of why pollution does not become expensive as clean air is "used up." Because there's no market for clean air or climate stability, there are no direct price mechanisms to signal the scarcity or degradation of these public goods until they fail. Hence, despite their obvious importance to our well being, ecosystem services largely have been ignored in environmental law and policy. Partly as a result, ecosystems are degraded.

2. The Tragedy of the Commons

Imagine you are a shepherd who grazes twenty sheep on a village common. Along with your pan pipes and bag lunch, you herd your flock to the common every day. So long as the number of sheep on the common remains small, the grass in the common remains plentiful. Assume, though, that shepherds from over the mountain have heard of the wonderful grass in the common and bring their flocks. With each hour these sheep graze, there is less grass available for future grazing. In fact, you realize that this increased level of grazing will soon nibble the grass down to the roots, with the result of not enough forage in the future for anyone's flock, including your own. Yet you and the other shepherds will likely continue to allow your sheep to overgraze. Why?

The answer lies in the economic incentives. The more the sheep graze the fatter and more valuable they will be when they come to market. You could stop your flock's grazing, of course, to try and preserve the pasture for other days; but there is no guarantee your fellow shepherds will be similarly conscientious. As a result, you well may encourage your sheep to graze as much as possible, and your neighbors will do the same. "Might as well get the grass in my sheep's tummies before it disappears in others'," you think. The result is individually rational in the short term—if the resource will be depleted, you might as well ensure you get your fair share—but collectively disastrous in the long term. It would be far better for each shepherd to restrain her flock's grazing, but seeking to maximize immediate economic gain ensures long term economic—and environmental—collapse.

This same phenomenon, known as *the tragedy of the commons*, can be identified in many open access resources, as farmers race to pump water from an underground aquifer, fishing boats with ever larger nets chase fewer and fewer fish, and wildcat drillers race to pump out oil as fast as they can. In each case, individually rational behavior is collectively deficient. Individuals' personal incentives work *against* the best long-term solution.

3.   Collective Action and Free Riders

So what is to be done? Perhaps you could negotiate with all the shepherds and collectively agree to graze less. This may work when there are a handful of shepherds who all come from the same village. But it becomes increasingly difficult to reach agreement as the number of shepherds increases (and more difficult still if they come from different places without shared cultural norms and informal means of enforcement). This obstacle is known as a *collective action problem* and is due to the increased transaction costs in negotiating solutions as the number of parties increases. At a certain point, it's simply too expensive and difficult to reach consensus agreement. To see this in action, try to decide on which movie to see or settle a restaurant check with more than four friends.

Perhaps, as a last resort, in frustration at the inability to agree on a common solution, some of you decide to stop grazing your flock so that the grass on the common can grow back. Noble intent, no doubt, but there is a risk that other shepherds will take advantage of your generosity and keep their sheep on the common. More food for their flocks, they may smirk. These shepherds benefiting from your sacrifice are known as *free riders*. A similar phenomenon might occur even if all the shepherds agreed to graze less. New shepherds might come in and start grazing all the time, free-riding off of your sacrifice. Thus any solution to commons problems must overcome both the high transaction costs in reaching agreement among many parties (collective action) and counterproductive behavior by parties outside the agreement (free riders).

4.   Externalities

Assume you have sold your sheep, moved on from the now trampled and scraggly common, and own a chemical factory. When you balance your firm's financial books, you notice something odd. In figuring out your bottom line, you subtract your costs to operate (such as labor, materials, utilities, and so on) from the revenue you earn from selling your chemicals. But the pollution from your smokestacks does not reduce your bottom line. Make no mistake; your factory *is* causing real costs in the form of acid rain, smog, and reduced air visibility. But, as described above, because clean air is a public good you do not have to pay as you "use up" the clean air. It acts as a sink for your pollution at no cost. As a result, in seeking to maximize short-term economic gain, you do not consider the cost of your pollution. You can "overuse" the air and continue polluting. The costs from damage to forests, increased respiratory ailments, and reduced pleasure in clear vistas from your pollution are very real, but they are *external* to the costs you currently pay to operate. These costs are borne by the public and known as *externalities*.

If, on the other hand, your factory has to pay for the external harm it causes, then it will reduce its pollution. The process for forcing the factory to recognize environmental and social costs is known as *internalizing externalities* and reflects a basic lesson of economics—when we have to pay more for something, we use less of it than if it is free. By internalizing externalities, we correct the market failure by charging for environmental harms and providing more accurate price signals to buyers.

This works both ways. Assume that you own a wetland beside your factory. The wetland provides a nursery for young fish to spend their first few months in relative safety before entering the adjacent river. The outdoors enthusiasts who fish along the river and the sporting good stores who sell fishing tackle all benefit from the services your wetland provides, but they don't pay you for them. While your factory's pollution generates *negative externalities*, your wetland provides *positive externalities*. Just as the fact that you don't have to pay for the costs caused by your pollution removes any incentive to reduce pollution so, too, does the fact that you are not paid for the benefits provided by the wetland remove any incentive to conserve rather than pave it over for a parking lot.

If all negative externalities were internalized—if all costs imposed on the environment were borne by the polluting party—then environmentally harmful products and processes would be relatively more costly and the market would reinforce environmental protection. Equally, if positive externalities were internalized—if benefits generated by ecosystem services such as flood control and water purification were paid for by the recipients—then habitat conservation would be truly valued in the marketplace. A central problem, of course, is "getting the prices right." Even if we had the authority to charge a factory for the damage its pollution caused, how much would that be? As with clean air, there are no markets for environmental harms, either; thus their costs must be estimated. But even rough estimates would be an improvement over the current situation where negative externalities are costless to polluters and positive externalities are not rewarded. One of the key goals of environmental law is to bring environmental externalities into the marketplace; we discuss policy instruments to internalize externalities later in the chapter.

C.   *Mismatched Scales*

Natural boundaries rarely track political boundaries. A map of the western United States shows states and counties with straight lines and right angles. Map the region's watersheds, ecosystems, or forests, however, and nary a straight line will appear. Ecological concerns were, not surprisingly, far from the politicians' and surveyors' minds when these political jurisdictions were created, but the mismatch of natural and political scales poses difficult challenges for environmental management. Air pollution, water pollution, and wildlife certainly pay no heed to state (or national) borders, with the result that often the generator of the pollution is politically distinct from those harmed.

Acid rain was hard to control in the 1970s and 1980s because of political jurisdictions. The costs of reducing emissions downwind were borne by those who received no benefit and, similarly, those benefiting from reduced pollution upwind did not have to pay for it. Midwestern power plants were far removed from the polluted lakes and forests of the Northeast and Canada. New York, Vermont, and certainly Canadian voters couldn't vote in Ohio or Pennsylvania. Thus those with the greatest cause for concern did not live in the areas where their concerns could be most effectively expressed. Similar problems of scale are evident in wildlife protection, where draining or filling prairie potholes in the Great Plains, for example, may benefit the local farmers but imperils migratory birds from Mexico to Canada. Pumping carbon dioxide in the air may not seem significant to someone driving an SUV in Montana, but to an islander on a low-lying Pacific atoll the prospects of sea-level rise are a good deal more unsettling.

As a result of these *geographical spillovers* across jurisdictions, transboundary environmental problems often pose the challenges of collective action (the high transaction costs to bring differing parties together), equity (ensuring that the parties enjoying the benefits of environmental protection also bear a share of the costs), and enforcement (monitoring compliance at a distance from the source of authority). This is as true with national laws as with international.

Mismatched political and natural boundaries also pose challenges of management authority. This is often expressed as a problem of federalism. Who should control pollution and natural resource management: local or national authorities? Locals are closer to the problems, often understand them better, and have to live with the consequences of the environmental policy. At the same time, if the problem is one of transboundary pollution, the locals don't live with the consequences of their pollution. Those downstream do.

With natural resources, locals may well feel an entitlement. Their parents and grandparents may have grazed their herds on the same government land that some bureaucrat in Washington now wants to fence off from cattle. But public lands belong to the nation as a whole, so shouldn't they be managed at the national level? If public lands are being degraded by locals' over-use, then the federal government must restrict use, the argument goes, regardless of local tradition or expectations. This conflict has no simple solution, and has led in the past to violent intimidation of federal officials and broad political movements such as "the sagebrush rebellion" in the 1970s and the "wise use" movement today.

In another variant of this problem, political and economic scales can be mismatched as markets encompass multiple political jurisdictions. Imagine, for example, that in order to attract business Arkansas decides to lower its standards for air pollution. This not only poses a transboundary concern for the border states of Louisiana and Alabama; it also pressures states with similar industries, such as North Carolina, to lower their standards as well, in order to prevent industry relocation. The dynamic of local jurisdictions competing with one another by lowering environmental standards to attract industry is known as the *race-to-the-bottom*. Realize, as well, that concerns over the race-to-the-bottom can not only pressure jurisdictions to lower their standards but can also chill efforts in states seeking to strengthen standards (because industry will threaten to relocate if their costs of regulatory compliance are increased). If this is the case, then nationwide standards seem necessary. The same phenomenon can occur in the international context as well, as nations compete with one another for business investment.

The fact that companies choose their locations based in part on costs of doing business is indisputable. There is a strong debate, however, over the extent to which a race-to-the-bottom really occurs in the environmental field. For one thing, states can compete on many grounds, perhaps lowering tax rates or workplace safety requirements to attract business. Hence it's not a given that they would reduce environmental standards to attract industry. More important, because environmental quality is an important amenity, there's an argument that local jurisdictions are more likely to engage in a "race-to-the-top," competing for industry by offering *higher* environmental quality. The data on international industry relocation suggest that stringency of environmental regulation is less important to companies than proximity to markets, labor costs, raw material costs, political stability, etc. And this makes sense, since environmental costs are usually a small percentage of total business costs. In those industries where environmental costs are relatively high, though, such as in the chemicals sector, there is evidence that companies have relocated with environmental compliance costs in mind.

20

Perhaps more important, though, is the fact that many regulators believe the race-to-the-bottom occurs, whether that is borne out in fact or not, and act accordingly.

Problems of scale occur in time as well as in space. Decisions must be made today that may prevent harm ten or twenty years from now or, indeed, in generations not yet born. Ozone depletion and climate change are two examples. CFCs (which are the major cause of stratospheric ozone depletion) and greenhouse gases we emit today will cause impacts over the next 50 years or longer. The same distributional asymmetry is at play here as with physical scale. The costs of refraining from an action fall on us today, while the benefits are enjoyed (most likely by others) far later. Yet these future beneficiaries can't express their preferences in today's voting booth or courtroom. Indeed, the temporal scale of many environmental problems makes it difficult even to hold current elected officials accountable, since many of their actions will not cause harms until they are no longer in office. Supporting overfishing today may keep a local politician in office, for example, while the stark impacts may not be evident until years later when the stock has collapsed. As a result, many environmental advocates claim to be acting on behalf of the interests of future generations, but deciding what the proper sacrifice today should be for future benefits that may or may not be appreciated is easier said than done.

D.   *Cognitive Biases*

To complicate matters further, people do not think about environmental options in the way that an economist would predict a "rational" person would. Everyone suffers from cognitive limitations and biases that affect our views about the environment and environmental policy. In some cases, these limitations and biases undercut efforts to reduce pollution and to protect the environment. In other cases, these limitations and biases lead us to overestimate environmental risks and to demand policy measures that may not economically be justified.

Part of the problem is that people just are not very good with numbers. Start with probabilities. Assume, incorrectly, that the federal government requires all new chemicals to be tested to see if the chemicals are carcinogenic (i.e., cause cancer). And assume, again incorrectly, that the federal government has developed a new toxicity test that is highly reliable in testing for carcinogens: if a chemical is carcinogenic, the test will be positive 95 percent of the time, while if a chemical is not a carcinogen, the test will be negative 95 percent of the time. If a chemical tests positive, what is the probability that it really is a carcinogen? Most people would estimate that the odds are very high (probably 95%) and urge that the chemical be regulated immediately. But the probability depends on the distribution of carcinogens within the universe of all chemicals. If there are 10,500 chemicals in total, and only 500 are carcinogens, for example, a chemical that tests positive has less than a 50–50 chance of being a carcinogen. If only 100 of the chemicals are carcinogens, a chemical that tests positive has about a 15 percent chance of causing cancer.[1]

People also are not very good at evaluating environmental tradeoffs, particularly when the tradeoffs require them to compare costs and benefits across time. During the energy crisis of the late 1970s, economists examined how much more people would pay to buy energy-efficient appliances that would reduce the buyers' future energy bills. The surprising answer was "not much," even when the future savings were substantial. The average consumer bought cheaper, energy-guzzling appliances even when the future "returns" on the energy-efficient appliances, depending on the appliance, would have been equivalent to a 17% to 243% return on a bank account! Although customers received information about the energy savings, buyers had a hard time figuring out the exact amount of money they would save in the future and then comparing those savings with the difference in purchase prices. Buyers therefore focused on the one piece of information that was undeniably obvious—the energy-efficient appliance cost more today than the energy guzzler.

The problems go far beyond being bad at numbers, though. Consider how people evaluate potential risks from pollutants and toxic substances. People may reach very different conclusions based solely on how information is conveyed. Psychologists, for example, have found that people are less likely to be concerned if told that a substance is 95 percent likely to be safe than if told that the same substance poses a five percent risk of causing cancer. In psychology terminology, this is known as a *framing effect*. People also find it difficult to evaluate very small risks, so that a one-in-a-thousand risk sounds bigger to most people than a purely numerical analysis would suggest. Familiarity plays a role in risk perception, as well, with people underestimating the risk of familiar events (e.g., driving or breathing polluted air). More importantly, we tend to overestimate unfamiliar risks about which we have read or heard recent stories. Psychologists attribute this to an *availability heuristic* in which the availability of examples makes people believe that something is more likely to occur. Where stories about a potential risk get told and retold,

---

1. For those readers who need numbers to be convinced of this point, if 500 chemicals are carcinogens, 500 of the non-carcinogens (5% of 10,000) would test positive, while only 475 of the carcinogens (95% of 500) would test positive, so a chemical that tests positive is more than likely not a carcinogen. If only 100 chemicals are carcinogens, 520 of the non-carcinogens (5% of 10,400) would test positive, while 95 of the carcinogens (95% of 100) would test positive, so the odds that a chemical that tests positive is a carcinogen is 95/615 or 15.4%.

and perhaps even highlighted by the press or others, an *availability cascade* may lead to mass public concerns about relatively small risks (hence the widespread concern over an asteroid hitting the earth or flesh eating diseases). Finally, once people decide that something is risky, an *anchoring effect* makes it very difficult to change their minds, even by showing them contrary evidence. These psychological heuristics can lead the public to demand that even insignificant risks be regulated.

Other cognitive biases, however, can undermine efforts to regulate significant environmental risks. People, for example, tend to be overly optimistic about their ability to overcome environmental risks that they voluntarily confront. Fishermen rarely believe that overfishing will lead to the collapse of their fisheries; most sun lovers are convinced that they can bake for days under the sun without contracting skin cancer. As a result of what psychologists call *self-enhancing attributional biases*, moreover, few people believe that they are to blame for environmental problems. It always is the other guy's fault. Car drivers believe that factories are to blame for smog; farmers believe that they are better at conserving water than city residents. When it comes time to decide how to solve an environmental problem, people similarly believe that others should bear most of the burden of the solution. Developing nations believe that the industrialized world should solve the problem of global climate change, while the United States argues that developing nations also must do their "fair share." To use the technical terminology, people (and nations) suffer from *egocentric interpretations of fairness*.

E.   *Sustainable Development*

Economic development has long been a defining goal of governments. Economic expansion has been considered fundamental to ending poverty in the developing world and raising standards of living worldwide. For decades, international institutions, foreign aid programs from developed countries, and non-profit organizations have expended tremendous resources to develop the energy, transportation, education, and institutional infrastructure necessary to fuel economic growth in the developing world. At the same time, most developed countries have sought to maximize economic growth within their own borders. And why not? Ever-expanding global and national economies have meant more wealth to go around, and ideally, ever higher standards of living for everyone, from the very poor to the very rich.

As global warming, loss of biodiversity, crashing fisheries, ozone depletion, and other recent environmental crises make clear, however, the current pace and manner of economic expansion may be incompatible with environmental protection. The development goal cannot, however, be abandoned. Poverty still must be reduced and standards of living raised throughout the developing world, as well as in the poorest sections of industrialized nations. Development cannot simply be subordinated to environmental protection. Instead, development and environmental protection must be integrated, and this process of integration lies at the core of the concept of *sustainable development*.

The principle of sustainable development provided the core message for the 1992 Earth Summit in Rio de Janeiro (the largest international governmental meeting ever held). Sustainable development was defined as "development that meets the needs of the present without compromising the ability of future generations to meet their own needs." Sustainable development provides an important overarching theme for three reasons. First, in historical terms, sustainable development tied together two disparate fields—development and environmental protection. Prior to the 1990s, those working in the development world saw their goal primarily as poverty alleviation and those in the environmental field as environmental protection, with little overlap between the two. As a result, development projects often had unnecessarily destructive environmental impacts and environmental protection efforts too often took little heed of economic impacts. Creating a park in a developing country might be viewed as a conservation success, for example, despite the potentially adverse economic consequences for the local community. Gandhi is said to have remarked that poverty is the greatest threat to the environment. By linking environmental protection and poverty alleviation to economic development, sustainable development forged the key insight that development and environmental protection efforts must be mutually reinforcing.

Second, sustainable development focuses both on *intragenerational equity* (allowing members of the present generation to meet their needs) and on *intergenerational equity* (the interests of future generations). Thus sustainable development lengthens the geographic and time horizons of decisions, ensuring that both long and short-term interests are considered. What this means for foreign aid policies and nonrenewable resources remains contentious, as does the matter of deciding what future generations would want us to do, but these are important policy debates that might otherwise not have occurred.

Third, sustainable development contradicts the common assumption that growth is good. Importantly, "growth" is not the same thing as "development." In order to create a sustainable economy—one that provides goods and services to ensure a positive quality of life into the future—the model cannot be one of growth, for the simple reason that our natural systems cannot continue to assimilate the impacts of growth. Climate change provides a case in point. Thus, central to the concept of sustainable development is the importance of limits—that we must develop within the constraints of natural systems. Hence to many

24

environmental policy experts, the greatest challenge posed by sustainable development is that of re-orienting our economies so they develop (providing greater value and standards of living) while not physically growing (in terms of resource consumption and pollution).

F.   *Protected Interests*

As should be evident by the examples provided above, environmental protection inevitably causes a clash of competing interests. In addition, the protected interests frequently do not have a voice of their own. We already have discussed the importance of future generation' interests. Endangered species litigation is brought technically on behalf of an affected person (perhaps a researcher of the species) but in reality is brought on behalf of the species as well. It goes without saying, of course, that these entities cannot bring a lawsuit on their own behalf, much less appear in court. (Well, perhaps one could carry a bird or a fish into court for dramatic effect, but what are you supposed to do with future generations?) Proxies therefore must bring the litigation on their behalf. It is no surprise then that the most significant standing cases over the last three decades have been environmental cases. The injury-in-fact requirement for standing traditionally has required physical or economic injury to the plaintiff. Should it be extended to include recreational or aesthetic injuries as well? *Sierra Club v. Morton*[2] and subsequent cases say it should. Thirty years ago, Professor Chris Stone provocatively asked, "should trees have standing?"[3] In environmental law, in some contexts they really can.

This innovative inclusion of interests, however, poses its own challenges. To paraphrase the Lorax of Dr. Seuss, who should speak for the trees? And how should nonhuman interests be balanced against those of flesh and blood people. The Spotted Owl conflict in the Pacific Northwest often pitted environmentalists against logging communities, with loggers complaining that environmental groups cared more about animals than people. While "win-win" compromises can often be found, so long as environmental protection extends beyond peoples' immediate health and wallets, such conflicts will be inevitable.

Thus to someone new to environmental law, it may seem odd that our wildlife conservation laws protect endangered species that most people would squash if found crawling in our kitchens. It may give pause to realize that our natural resource management laws protect parks and refuges that no one you know will ever visit. The simplest explanation of these observations is that there clearly is something at stake in the

---

2.   405 U.S. 727 (1972).

3.   Christopher D. Stone, Should Trees Have Standing: Toward Legal Rights for Natural Objects (1974).

environmental field beyond classic protection of human health and economic interests. The underlying perspectives that drive environmental attitudes are explored in the next section.

II. Three Analytical Frameworks

Imagine that the government is trying to decide whether to permit a new pesticide to be manufactured and sold in the United States. What criteria would you use to make this decision? Should the United States ever permit the sale of a pesticide that would injure human health? What if the pesticide would not injure humans but might harm wild animals that come into contact with the substance? Would you consider the benefits of the pesticide? Should it matter, for example, if the pesticide would increase crop yields? Reduce the costs of producing crops? Assuming that the pesticide could harm human health, does the distribution of the harm among individuals matter? Should harm to farmworkers, many of whom are poor and Hispanic, be viewed differently than harm to consumers?

In evaluating environmental decisions such as this, most policymakers and analysts use one of three general frameworks. Some policymakers and analysts focus on ethical rights. Others take a utilitarian approach and balance the risks posed by environmental problems against the cost of controlling them. Yet others look to see whether the costs and other burdens of environmental harms and solutions are equitably distributed among individuals and groups throughout our society. In the pesticide hypothetical, the "ethicist" would want to know whether the pesticide would injure humans, in violation of their "right" to a healthy environment, and perhaps whether it would harm other animals and plants. The "utilitarian" would want to know whether and how the pesticide would benefit society and then weigh those benefits against the health costs. Those individuals concerned with distributional equity would be interested in whether the harms from the pesticide use would fall primarily on minorities or less powerful members of society, such as farmworkers.

These three frameworks do not exhaust all of the potential modes for analyzing environmental issues, nor are they necessarily mutually exclusive. Some environmental writers, for example, have suggested that the law should follow a "pragmatic" philosophy that borrows and balances among all three of these frameworks. Yet other writers have urged an "ecological economics" approach that evaluates the long-term sustainability of activities such as pesticide use or irrigated agriculture, as well as the sustainability of the overall scale of the economy. Virtually every argument found in contemporary environmental debates, however, builds off of one or more of the three basic frameworks outlined above.

Whenever you hear or read an environmental argument, you should ask yourself what policy framework is being used. Disagreements over environmental policy often stem more from disagreements over the correct framework than from disagreements over the facts or how the facts should be applied under a framework. For example, in deciding whether to reduce the airborne emissions of a pollutant, environmental groups may stress the right of people to a healthy environment, while businesses may emphasize the high economic costs of the emission-control equipment compared to the health risks. To complicate matters, most policymakers and analysts do not say what framework they are using, let alone explain why they are using one framework rather than another. Instead, the policymakers and analysts simply assume that everyone agrees with their framework. As a result, they fail to confront the real source of their disagreement with others. Even worse, some policymakers and analysts use multiple and even inconsistent frameworks, using one and then another as best befits their goals.

A. *Environmental Rights*

Environmental law often reflects a strong, if not well elaborated, view that humans have a right to environmental protection. Even before the first Earth Day, Senator Gaylord Nelson of Wisconsin proposed an amendment to the United States Constitution in 1968 that would have recognized an "inalienable right to a decent environment" and required both the federal and state governments to "guarantee" that right. Nelson's proposal, as well as numerous other efforts to add an environmental right to the United States Constitution, have failed. Yet both international law and the constitutions of a handful of states now acknowledge rights to various environmental amenities. At the international level, the 1972 Stockholm Declaration of the United Nations Conference on the Human Environment states the "common conviction" that people have a "fundamental right to freedom, equality, and adequate conditions of life, in an environment of a quality that permits a life of dignity and wellbeing," as well as a "solemn responsibility to protect and improve the environment for present and future generations."[4] At the state level, the Hawaiian constitution proclaims that every person has the "right to a clean and healthful environment."[5] The constitutions of Massachusetts, Montana, and Pennsylvania set out similar rights.

Both judicial opinions and statutes also often speak in the language of rights. The Ninth Circuit has written that is "difficult to conceive of a

---

4. Report of the United Nations Conference on the Human Environment, U.N. Doc. A/CONF. 48/14/rev. 1, U.N. Pub. No. E.73.IIA14, at 4, Principle 1 (1974).

5. Haw. Const. art. XI, § 9.

more absolute and enduring concern than the preservation and, increasingly, the restoration of a decent and livable environment. Human life, itself a fundamental right, will vanish if we continue our heedless exploitation of this planet's natural resources."[6] The environmental advocates who pushed for new federal environmental legislation in the late 1960s and 1970s often unabashedly compared environmental protection to civil rights and the constitutional proscription of cruel and unusual punishment. The idea of environmental rights proved very powerful and helped encourage Congress to address environmental problems aggressively.

The concept of environmental rights tends to push policy toward absolute positions. If the population has a right to a healthy environment, for example, the cost of eliminating health risks would seem irrelevant. Because environmental-rights arguments drove passage of many of the major federal environmental statutes, these laws often appear to call for complete protection of human health without consideration of costs. The Clean Air Act, for example, mandates ambient air quality standards that are "requisite to protect the human health."[7] The original goal of the Clean Water Act was to eliminate the discharge of all pollutants into the nation's waterways by 1985.[8]

Although environmental-rights arguments have encouraged the passage of environmental statutes that often seem to call for absolute protections, reality has tempered what the government has been willing to do in practice. Consider, for example, the proposition that every person has a right to be free from air pollution that could harm his or her health. Although this might sound reasonable, even small levels of exposure to most major air pollutants will injure a small population of sensitive individuals. Only a zero pollution standard would ensure everyone a safe environment. Because that could seriously undermine the economy, the federal EPA establishes ambient air quality standards that protect most, but not all people. Similarly, although the Clean Water Act talked of eliminating all pollutants by 1985, the nation has come nowhere close to meeting this goal. As explained in Chapter 5, most facilities that discharge effluent into the nations' waterways need only reduce their discharges to the degree technologically feasible, and some pollution sources such as farms enjoy broad exemptions from the Act.

The earliest proposals for a constitutional guarantee of environmental rights typically stressed the rights of current humans to a healthy environment. But claims to environmental rights go considerably farther. For example, philosophers and ethicists have argued that future generations of humans also have rights to a livable environment and an

---

6. Stop H–3 Ass'n v. Dole, 870 F.2d 1419, 1430 (9th Cir.1989).

7. 42 U.S.C. § 7409(b)(1).

8. 33 U.S.C. § 1251(1)(a).

equitable share of the Earth's natural resources. Such rights would call for limiting the current exploitation of groundwater, petroleum, hard minerals, and other scarce resources and for regulating actions, like the emission of greenhouse gases or the storage of nuclear waste, that could have serious impacts in decades to come. Few people would disagree that public policy should take into account the needs and interests of future generations. The tough questions are how and to what degree. How should an exhaustible resource be allocated among current and future generations? Is the current generation free to use up a natural resource if they use the resource to produce capital amenities, such as roads and factories, of value to future generations? How can we even determine the preferences of future generations?

The rights discussed so far are all *anthropocentric*. They address the rights of current and future generations of humans to a healthy and livable environment, however that might be defined. Some philosophers and ethicists have suggested that other living organisms, and perhaps nature more generally, enjoy independent rights. *Biocentric* rights concern the rights of plants and animals other than humans. In passing the Endangered Species Act, Congress took a primarily anthropocentric view of the importance of protecting plants and animals. According to Congress, threatened species often "are of esthetic, ecological, educational, historical, recreational, and scientific value to the Nation and its people."[9] To protect these human interests, the Endangered Species Act protects threatened species; individual members of a species are protected only when necessary to preserve the species. But many environmentalists argue that species, and individual animals and plants, have a right to preservation even if the animals and plants are of no practical importance whatsoever to humans. The influential wildlife ecologist, Aldo Leopold, for example, believed that humans are not separate from the other animals and plants, but part of a community with them. As part of this community, humans should respect a "land ethic" based on the notion that a "thing is right when it tends to preserve the integrity, stability, and beauty of the biotic community. It is wrong when it tends otherwise."

Taking an even broader *ecocentric* perspective, some environmentalists argue that nature as a whole has a right to protection. Under this view, strip mining of a mountainside raises much the same concerns as clear cutting a forest or extirpating the last known population of an endangered animal species. In all these cases, humans are interfering unethically with natural processes and creations.

To other people, discussion of biocentric and ecocentric rights is mere silliness. In their view, humans are different from most other

---

9.   16 U.S.C. § 1531(a)(3).

animals (and certainly from plants and rocks). Humans are intelligent, sentient creatures. Because animals, plants, and rocks cannot talk, moreover, their interests and preferences remain unknown. In the view of such critics, people who assert that biota and the rest of the physical world have "rights" are merely expressing their own policy preferences for conservation—giving their own preferences an extra push by claiming that they are protecting the moral rights of entities that cannot communicate. Critics also question why, given the constant change in the world through extinction and speciation, the existing geological configuration and assortment of species have any special claim to preservation. Finally, critics observe that people do not think or act as if most animals, plants, or rocks have broad rights to existence and preservation. While most people would oppose cruelty to animals, only a few would oppose fishing a non-threatened stock of fish, killing a marauding coyote, exterminating household "pests," or weeding the garden.

Rights arguments, moreover, do not always favor greater environmental protection. While environmental proponents argue that regulation is needed to protect people's right to a healthy and livable environment or to protect biocentric or ecocentric rights, landowners often assert that regulations of their land use intrude on their property "rights." Businesses, unions, and other economic interests argue that proposed regulations will interfere with "rights" of employment or the "rights" of a local community to determine for itself how to use local resources and determine its own future. Some of these "rights" have taken on international or constitutional dimensions. After announcing the fundamental environmental right quote earlier, the Stockholm Declaration of the United Nations Conference on the Human Environment also affirms the "sovereign right" of all nations to "exploit their own resources pursuant to their own environmental policies."[10] As discussed in Chapter 3, environmental regulations that conflict with existing property rights might be considered unconstitutional takings. In whatever context the rights are raised, however, legislators, judges, and other policymakers must decide how to balance the varied rights that are asserted.

B. *Utilitarianism and Cost–Benefit Analysis*

Neo-classical economists have long advocated a very different approach that balances the costs and benefits of contemplated environmental policies. In the eyes of economists, environmental problems are the result of market failures, and the goal of the law should be to correct the

---

10. Report of the United Nations Conference on the Human Environment, supra note 4, at Principle 21.

market. No rational person would pay more for a product than the product is worth to her. Neither should the government regulate an environmental problem if the cost of the regulation exceeds the benefits to society. Such a regulation would unjustifiably waste society's resources even though some people might benefit from the regulation. In the economist's view, the government should regulate the environment up to the point where the value to society of the last unit of regulation just exceeds its cost, but no further.

The government compares the costs and benefits of regulations in several different ways. In a full cost-benefit analysis, the government uses market prices, surveys, and other devices to place a monetary value on the environmental benefits that the regulation hopes to achieve—e.g., avoided medical costs, lives or species saved, the aesthetic value of cleaner air or preserved wetlands. The government then compares these benefits against the costs of the regulation—e.g., employment loss, reduced industrial production or land development, the cost of needed pollution control equipment. Under traditional economic logic, the government should proceed with the regulation only if the expected monetary value of the benefits exceeds the monetary costs.

Where a regulation is designed primarily to save human lives, the government sometimes conducts a simpler analysis that calculates the cost of the regulation per life saved. The government again calculates the costs of the regulation, but rather than placing a monetary value on the benefits, the government merely estimates the likely number of lives saved. By dividing the costs by the expected number of lives saved, the government obtains the cost per life saved. The government then can compare this cost to the price of similar regulations or to economic estimates of the value of a human life to decide whether to pursue the contemplated regulation.

The executive branch of the federal government has long touted cost-benefit analyses as a means of choosing among alternative environmental policies. Every president since Richard Nixon has required EPA and other regulatory agencies to conduct cost-benefit analyses before adopting major regulations that could impose a significant cost on the economy. Under an executive order originally issued by President Bill Clinton, federal agencies currently must quantify, "to the extent feasible," both the benefits and costs of potential regulatory actions and, to the extent the law gives the agencies any discretion, "propose or adopt a regulation only upon a reasoned determination that the benefits of the intended regulation justify its costs." Agencies also must adopt the most "cost-effective" approach where different regulations could accomplish the same goals but at different costs.[11]

11. Executive Order 12,866, 58 Fed. Reg. 51,735 (1993).

Congress, by contrast, has not been as receptive to arguments for cost-benefit analysis. A handful of federal environmental statutes call for explicit cost-benefit comparisons. Thus the two major federal environmental statutes regulating direct human exposure to toxic products—the Federal Insecticide, Fungicide, and Rodenticide Act, which regulates agricultural chemicals, and the Toxic Substances Control Act, which regulates other toxics—both require EPA to balance the benefits that a product would provide against the human and environmental risks that the product would pose. A number of other statutes permit EPA and other regulatory agencies to give at least some consideration to cost in regulating the environment. The Clean Water Act, for example, allows costs to be considered in deciding whether to permit the filling of a wetland and in setting limits on the discharge of pollutants into a waterway. In many important instances, however, Congress has forbidden agencies from considering cost to any degree. EPA cannot consider cost in setting national ambient air quality standards. Nor can a federal agency consider cost in deciding whether to move forward with an action that might jeopardize the continued existence of an endangered or threatened species. Congress repeatedly has rejected proposed legislation mandating cost-benefit analysis for all environmental regulation.

Why has Congress been reticent to embrace cost-benefit analysis in the environmental field? Part of the reason may be that Congress believes that people have a moral right to a clean environment. As emphasized earlier, where rights are at stake, the costs of enforcing those rights has little, if any, role to play. But part of the reason is also the conceptual and practical problems that plague the application of cost-benefit analysis to environmental issues.

Start with the question of fairness. Most people are not troubled when individuals voluntarily choose to make a tradeoff between their health and other goals of importance to them, so long as the choice does not harm someone else. Professional hockey and football players risk their necks and future health every game in exchange for money, fame, and love of their sport. When the government is deciding whether to regulate an environmentally risky activity, however, one group of people generally bears the risk, while a different segment of society enjoys the benefits of the activity. Is it fair to compare the risks and benefits to these separate groups and to tolerate the risks if the benefits to the latter group are large? Imagine, for example, that a factory emits a toxic pollutant that kills one person each year from the local population. The only way to eliminate the pollution is to shut down the factory, but the product that it ships to other parts of the country produces $100 million dollars in social value. Even if you believed that the $100 million outweighs the "value" of the life saved (a difficult calculation to which we will return in a minute), is it ethically permissible to let one person die so that *other* people can economically benefit?

Although it might be tempting to conclude that such tradeoffs are never permissible, consider the implications of that conclusion. What if an air pollution regulation would slightly reduce the number of asthma incidents in one region of the United States but cost several billion dollars? Given that some people are sensitive to even low levels of pollutants, the only way to avoid *any* environmental injuries or damage might be to shut down industry entirely. Most people would find this solution unacceptable because the cost of the solution would seem too great for the benefits received. Such logic, however, inevitably pulls us back toward weighing the costs and benefits of proposed regulations even when the costs and benefits involve different people.

Tradeoffs are often inevitable within environmental policy. The nation can decide to lower sulfur dioxide emissions from power plants to reduce acid rain, but at some point this will raise electricity bills. The government can ban or restrict the use of certain chemicals, but this may raise the costs of production and consumer prices. Increased costs and prices will mean less money to spend on other socially worthwhile needs. While environmental law provides many examples of "win-win" situations, in which environmental protection efforts actually can increase both efficiency and social wealth, we live in a world of limited resources and tradeoffs often are unavoidable. Cost-benefit analyses are one obvious means of choosing among such tradeoffs.

Assuming that cost-benefit analysis is ethically acceptable, however, practical problems of implementation still loom large. To begin with, to what degree are the costs and benefits involved in environmental regulation *commensurate*—i.e., readily comparable? To many people, environmental risks such as the death of a person or the loss of a species cannot be quantified in the same dollar terms as the costs of installing pollution-control equipment or preserving land from development. Nor can such risks be directly compared to the costs.

Even if placing a dollar figure on these risks is theoretically acceptable, how does one determine the value of a life, an endangered species, or an old-growth forest? Economists have developed techniques for trying to determine such values. To measure the value of a life, for example, economists sometimes use the salary premium that employees demand for working in a particularly risky occupation. But most of the techniques are controversial and often generate a wide range of numbers depending on the assumptions used. As a result, many environmental benefits do not get quantified in cost-benefit analyses, but are discussed in the analyses only on a qualitative or descriptive basis. Although the cost-benefit analysis might go to great length to detail and highlight such benefits, psychological studies suggest that decision makers do not pay as much attention to qualitatively described benefits as they do to hard costs.

To illustrate the problems involved in applying formal cost-benefit analysis to environmental issues, imagine that the government is trying to decide whether to prevent the development of several thousand acres of land in order to preserve an endangered species. The government probably will find it easy to put a cost on the lost development opportunity. But placing a value on the endangered species will be a very different manner because of both scientific and economic uncertainties. On the scientific side, conservation biology is still in its infancy. Scientists often do not know the exact role that a species plays in an ecosystem or what medical, industrial, or ecological value might be lost if the species goes extinct.

Even where the value of a species is scientifically known, placing an economic price tag on that value is difficult. Where the species provides a natural service, such as pollination, that is not bought and sold in the marketplace, economists must try to calculate the service's value indirectly—for example, by looking at what people pay for similar services (e.g., bee keepers) or what would be lost if the service disappeared (e.g., lost crops). Often, a species' most significant values are its *nonuse* values: the values that people gain not from using the species or its services today but from having the option to use the species or its services in the future (*option value*), simply knowing that the species exists in the world (*existence value*), or knowing that their kids and grandkids will be able to enjoy the species (*bequest value*). Economists try to determine nonuse value by *contingent valuation methodology* ("CVM"), in which surveyors ask a random sample of people how much they would pay to save a species. Although CVM generates a dollar value, the reliability of that value is open to challenge on numerous grounds. The phrasing of questions in the survey often dramatically affects the value that people report. People also may overstate the value they place on species, both to sound altruistic and because they do not need to back up their answer with an actual contribution toward saving the species. The survey answers, moreover, often are inconsistent with basic economic theory: people, for example, often report that they would pay the same amount to save one member of a species as they would to save several thousand members.

The intertemporal quality of many environmental issues further complicates cost-benefit analyses. As noted earlier, the costs of environmental regulation are often immediate while at least some of the benefits typically accrue in the future. Reducing emissions of carbon or chlorofluorocarbons, for example, costs money today but may generate climate and ozone benefits for decades to come. Standard economic analysis

34

states that these future benefits should be *discounted*—i.e., given a reduced value compared to current costs and benefits—because (1) most people would prefer a dollar today over a dollar next year and (2) any monies saved today by not adopting a regulation can be invested to generate a larger dollar sum in the future. Economists, however, disagree on the appropriate discount rate for environmental analyses. Some economists argue for the *private discount rate* that individuals and companies use to decide whether to make an investment with a future return. Other economists argue for a lower *social discount rate* that would not reduce the value of future benefits by as much. Some analysts argue that any discounting is inconsistent with society's obligation to future generations: while discounting might be useful to an individual deciding whether to save money for a vacation next year, one generation does not have the right to discount the benefits or costs to another generation. Other analysts, while acknowledging the appropriateness of discounting traditional costs and benefits, object to the discounting of lives that a regulation will save in the future. Why, they argue, should society care more about saving lives today than saving lives in the future? Whether a regulation saves five lives today or five lives in twenty years should not matter in their view.

Scientific uncertainty also makes cost-benefit analyses more problematic. As already discussed, scientific uncertainty plagues environmental issues. Scientists typically cannot tell us with any degree of certainty how many people will die or become sick after being exposed to a hazardous substance or the likelihood that an endangered species will go extinct if a particular tract of habitat is developed. Economists try to address such uncertainties in several ways. First, they calculate *expected values* for those costs and benefits subject to uncertainty: all of the potential values are weighted by their probabilities and then summed to obtain a mid-range estimate. Economists also conduct *sensitivity analyses* in which they see how various changes in the assumed costs and benefits would affect the ultimate conclusion of whether the benefits of the regulation outweigh the costs. Economists similarly perform *worst-case scenarios* in which they assume that a pollutant or activity will have the worst possible impact on health and the environment. None of these approaches, however, eliminates the underlying uncertainty.

The practical problems involved in cost-benefit analyses do not mean that the government should ignore the costs of regulation. Many individuals who oppose using formal cost-benefit analyses to decide environmental policy still believe that cost is relevant: the resources that society is willing to spend on environmental issues are scarce, and the government therefore should focus on environmental goals that have the greatest benefit and on the regulatory policies that accomplish these goals at the lowest cost. The practical problems of cost-benefit analysis, however, suggest that cost-benefit analysis is not a precise tool and, where used, must be interpreted with appropriate caution.

C. Environmental Justice

A third framework is environmental justice. Here the focus is on how the burdens of environmental harms and regulations are allocated among individuals and groups within our society. Environmental law historically ignored distributive issues. Supporters of strong environmental laws emphasized environmental rights, while those more sympathetic to economic concerns argued for greater consideration of costs; virtually no one asked how burdens were distributed. This began to change in 1978 when Governor James Hunt of North Carolina proposed disposing of soil tainted with polychlorinated biphenyls (PCBs) in a new waste dump to be opened in Warren County, a poor region in the northeastern part of the state with a population that was sixty–four percent African American and Native American. Joined by national civil rights leaders, local residents blocked the entrance to the dump site for over two weeks, arguing that the county had been chosen for the site because it was a minority community with little political power. Although the demonstration ultimately failed to keep the PCB-laced soils from the site, the demonstration attracted national attention to the issue of environmental justice and forced the governor to support state legislation prohibiting additional landfills in Warren County.

Data developed since the Warren County demonstrations indicates that poor and minority communities bear a disproportionate share of environmental burdens. For example, African Americans and Hispanics disproportionately populate communities that are host to treatment, storage, and disposal facilities for hazardous waste. Minority communities disproportionately suffer from substandard air quality and are home to a higher number of Superfund sites that are contaminated by hazardous substances. Minorities also suffer environmental injuries, such as lead poisoning and pesticide exposure, to a greater degree than do Caucasians. Although the statistical reliability of a number of the studies is questionable, the sheer number of studies, and the consistency of their results, suggests a disturbing maldistribution of environmental burdens in the United States.

The key questions are why the burdens are not equally distributed and how, if at all, the maldistribution can be corrected. Much of the debate over environmental justice in the United States has focused on the siting in minority communities of waste dumps and industrial facilities that could adversely affect the health of local residents. Many residents of minority communities believe that racism is at work and have fought efforts to locate facilities in their communities, labeling such

36

efforts *environmental racism.* Regardless of whether the governmental agencies that oversee the siting and permitting of such facilities intentionally discriminate, minority communities frequently have less political power and may be at a number of procedural disadvantages. Local residents may find it difficult to attend relevant hearings, which may be held in state or county capitals that are hundreds or thousands of miles away from the affected community; the governmental agency might not publish notices and other materials in Spanish and other locally spoken languages or provide interpreters for hearings; few minority communities have the resources to hire scientists and other experts needed to rebut the claims of the facility owners.

In response to such concerns, the federal government has taken a number of steps to improve environmental equity. In 1994, President Bill Clinton issued an executive order, still in effect, that requires all federal agencies to incorporate environmental justice into their decision making "by identifying and addressing, as appropriate, disproportionately high and adverse human health or environmental effects."[12] Some governmental agencies also have adopted their own policies designed to reduce the chances that their decisions will impact minority communities on a disproportionate basis. In licensing nuclear facilities, for example, the Nuclear Regulatory Commission prepares an environmental equity analysis designed to identify and avoid both intentional discrimination and disproportionate burdens. In 1997, the Commission rejected an application to build a uranium enrichment plant in the African American community of Homer, Louisiana, because the Commission's staff had not adequately examined whether racial discrimination had played a role in the site selection process.

Community members seeking to keep an environmentally hazardous facility out of their neighborhoods increasingly have tried to use Title VI of the Civil Rights Act of 1964 to address issues of environmental racism. Title VI prohibits any program or activity that receives federal funds from discriminating on the basis of race, color, or national origin; most state and local environmental programs receive some federal funding and thus are subject to Title VI. Although a plaintiff who sues in court under Title VI must prove intentional discrimination, federal agencies may adopt a lower burden of proof for administrative proceedings. EPA prohibits disproportionate impacts, whether or not caused by intentional discrimination, in programs receiving EPA funding. In 1998, faced by an increasing number of Title VI complaints, EPA issued an Interim Guidance for investigating administrative complaints alleging violations of Title VI. The interim guidance, however, proved so controversial with

12. Executive Order 12,898, 59 Fed. Reg. 7629 (1994).

state and local governments that EPA has yet to adopt a final guidance document.

Discriminatory siting decisions may not be the only or even the principal reason why environmentally dangerous facilities end up located disproportionately in minority communities. Although virtually all studies agree that minority and poor communities host a disproportionate share of industrial and waste facilities, they disagree as to why. The most comprehensive national study of hazardous waste facilities found that original siting decisions placed the facilities disproportionately in Hispanic communities but not in African American communities; the siting decisions, moreover, were less likely, not more likely, to place facilities in poor communities.[13] A number of other regional studies have concluded that original siting decisions for industrial and waste facilities did not have a disproportionate impact on either minority or poor communities. Some, but not all, of these studies have suggested that housing dynamics are instead at fault: after a facility is located in a community, those who can relocate to other neighborhoods move out of the area and housing prices fall, making the community more attractive to minorities and poorer individuals who previously could not afford to live there. To the degree that more systemic problems such as housing underlie the greater exposure of minorities and the poor to industrial and waste facilities, changes in environmental policies by themselves unfortunately will not eliminate distributional inequities.

Although environmental justice discussions have focused on the siting of industrial and waste facilities, environmental justice also provides a framework for addressing environmental policy more broadly. Many advocates of environmental justice, for example, observe that the United States provides for strong protection of environmental amenities such as biodiversity that have little immediate importance to the urban and rural poor while taking a more relaxed stance on issues such as pesticide poisoning that are of immediate importance to these populations. The Endangered Species Act thus does not consider cost in protected endangered species, but the Federal Insecticide, Fungicide, and Rodenticide Act does permit cost to be considered in deciding whether to permit pesticides to be used in the United States.

Environmental justice advocates also suggest that the government should consider distributional impacts in choosing and designing its regulatory tools. As discussed later in this book, for example, the government has experimented with tradable emission credits under the Clean Air Act. Under the trading program, a factory that finds it

13. See Vicki Been and Francis Gupta, Coming to the Nuisance or Going to the Barrios? A Longitudinal Analysis of Environmental Justice Claims, 24 Ecology L.Q. 1 (1997).

relatively inexpensive to reduce its air emissions can reduce its emission by more than the regulations require and then sell its "excess credits" to a factory that finds it more expensive to reduce emissions; the second factory can then use the credits to help meet its regulatory requirements. Emissions trading can achieve the same overall emission reduction at a lower cost and is thus economically efficient. But if the trading system is not carefully designed and implemented, factories in poorer areas of a region might become net purchasers of the pollution credits— resulting in more pollution in the poorer areas at the same time as the air becomes cleaner in other areas.

Environmental justice focuses not only on the distribution of environmental burdens and policies but also on the process by which environmental decisions are made in the United States. In the view of most advocates of environmental justice, local communities should have a significant, if not controlling voice in decisions and activities that impact their residents' lives. Decision making processes in turn should be open to all residents, who should have access to the scientific and other resources needed to understand and assess policy proposals. Environmental justice advocates thus push for decisions to be made at the local level through democratic processes. This runs counter to the modern emphasis in American environmental policy on *federal* decision making by *expert* agencies. Environmental justice advocates also typically have little faith in the traditional environmental organizations, which tend to have few minority employees and accomplish much of their work in the courts and the halls of Congress rather than in local communities.

CHAPTER 3

The Practice of Environmental Protection

I. Instrument Choice

Americans believe they are environmentalists. As noted already, polls show up to 80% or more of Americans agreeing with the statement that environmental protection should be a high priority. The Environmental Protection Agency (EPA) estimates that we spend about 2.5% of gross national product on environmental protection. If this is such a high priority, though, why not spend more? The obvious answer is that there are other important pressing needs, as well, and a finite pool of resources to draw from. This public policy trade-off is sometimes described as the "choice between guns and butter." Should a country spend more of its resources on social services or on the military? Should a country spend more of its resources on environmental protection or economic development? Depending on their situations and values, different countries choose very different allocations.

Determining the proper level of environmental protection is *not solely* a scientific decision. In a world of competing resource needs, the key question for policy-makers is the "socially best" level of protection. Setting the appropriate level of environmental protection is expressly a political decision for the simple reason that there are other competing needs. We could bring Los Angeles quickly into compliance with the Clean Air Act, for example, by drastically reducing the use of cars but this is not a trade-off citizens currently are willing to accept.

In choosing the "right" level of environmental protection, many consider the key issue to be what level of risk we are willing to accept, and at what cost. There are precious few risk-free activities in life. And though we surely can reduce the risks to us and to nature from industrial activities or development, these can come at a cost. We may well decide to bear these costs, either based on a hard-nosed cost-benefit assessment or on an ethical judgment that our national parks should have clear vistas or that the impacts of air pollution should not fall disproportionately on inner-city children, but these decisions are ultimately judgments over what we should protect and how much. How "safe" is safe enough? How "clean" is clean enough? Because these questions are so value-laden, environmental law and policy are deeply contested areas. Indeed, in order to make such judgments it is hard to see how the field could be any other way.

Determining the level of resources we should commit to environmental protection (versus other pressing social needs) and the levels of protection we should set (e.g., whether in the case of air pollution we should seek to protect the average person, asthmatics, or severe asthmatics) will never be easy. Regardless of how these determinations are ultimately made, however, everyone would agree that we should achieve a particular level of environmental protection at lowest social cost. But *how* to do this? Reliance on the common law? Regulations? Market instruments? Implementing environmental policy is where the rubber meets the road and it has provided some of the most innovative regulatory instruments in all of American law.

A.   *Common Law Versus Regulation*

As described in the history section of Chapter 1, prior to the rise of the "modern era" of environmental law in the 1970s, the traditional response to pollution had relied on the common law doctrines of trespass and nuisance. In the 1904 *Madison v. Ducktown Sulphur, Copper & Iron Co.* case,[1] for example, Georgia farmers filed suit against a nearby copper smelter in Tennessee. The farmers claimed that air pollution from the smelter had ruined their crops and made worthless their timber. For its part, the smelter responded that it had already spent close to $200,000 to reduce its emissions. Added to the mix was the fact that the smelter served as the economic linchpin for the community, supporting growth of the surrounding areas from 200 to 12,000 people. Given the farmers' loss, the court found the smelter liable for the nuisance, but refused to issue an injunction. Balancing the equities, the court ordered the smelter to pay the farmers $1,000 for their damage suffered. Given the setting, how could the result have been any different? Would any court have been willing to destroy half of the taxable value of the county in a nuisance suit brought by some out-of-state farmers?

Whether or not one agrees with the result in *Madison*, upon reflection the limits of such nuisance actions are clear. First, what about future damages? Under this type of retrospective remedy, those suffering injury must bring a lawsuit every time *after* they have been harmed. There is no direct prospective protection. Although courts can try to address this problem by awarding *permanent damages* that cover both past and future expected harm, courts must guess at the future harm, so the permanent damages ultimately are likely to prove either too low or too high. Second, imagine there is not only a smelter but also a textile factory and ironworks upwind of the farmers as well. The farmers may still suffer the same amount of damages, if not worse, but whom should

1.   83 S.W. 658 (Tenn.1904).

they sue? Can they prove it was the pollution from the smelter that caused the damage rather than that from the other factories? And if the damage came from all three, how can the farmers demonstrate the relative culpability. When there are multiple sources of pollution, establishing proximate cause becomes difficult. Finally, private nuisance actions may only be brought to remedy damage to private property. Remedies for damage to common resources, such as the fish in a river or trees in a public forest, can be sought only by bringing a *public* nuisance action, and that generally can be brought only by the state. Thus fishermen could not bring a nuisance suit against a factory polluting the river, even if it led to mass fish kills and threatened their livelihood.

Through this vantage, the advantages of a regulatory approach become clear. First, regulating conduct provides prospective rather than retrospective protection. Regulations limiting air or water emissions, for example, prohibit certain activities *before* they can cause significant harm. Thus, in principle, injured parties need not sue afterwards for compensation because they won't be harmed in the first place. Second, a regulatory approach makes unnecessary the need to show causation. Because pollution is regulated as it occurs at the source, there is no need to determine which factory's emissions caused specific harms. Again, if the regulatory limits are well set, there will be no harms that need to be compensated. Regulations also make irrelevant the distinction between harm to public or private resources, since regulation occurs prospectively at the source, regardless of the status of the downwind and downstream properties. Finally, regulations limiting pollution avoid tort debates over whether the polluting parties acted negligently or exercised due care. With regulation, they must meet the standards, period. Given these relative advantages, it should be no surprise why the era of modern environmental law ushered in uniform national pollution control standards.

Simply choosing a regulatory approach over reliance on the common law, however, still leaves fundamental questions unanswered. The most fundamental of these is what type of regulatory instrument to use. To explore the range of possible instruments, let's return to the classic environmental problem—the tragedy of the commons.

Imagine again that you have a herd of sheep that grazes on the public common. The common, though, is an open access resource. This means that anyone can graze as many sheep as he likes. So long as the resource is under little pressure (i.e., few sheep are grazing) there is no need for regulatory intervention because there is no problem of scarcity. Once significant competing uses of the resource develop, however, then the need for state action arises. In the context of the common, once more and more people graze more and more sheep, the common is in danger of becoming overgrazed and denuded. So we need to do something, but how should we best overcome the tragedy currently in the making?

B.   Property Rights

The classic solution to the tragedy of the commons is reliance on private property rights. Assume the state carves up the common into square parcels of land and grants fee simple title to the individual shepherds using the common, including you. Are you still as eager to overgraze as before? All of a sudden, your previous incentive to use up the resource as fast as possible (before everyone else does) is no longer relevant. Instead, your interests are best served by carefully tending your part of the common so it remains fertile long into the future—so it is *sustainably managed*. In a variant of the privatization approach, assume the entire common now belongs to you. What would you do? You may well charge other shepherds to use the common, or even let them on for free, but you would do so only to the extent that the resource base remains intact and productive—i.e., so long as the common is not over-grazed. In financial terms, to maximize profits you will safeguard your asset over the longer term.

Implicit in a property rights approach is the importance of technology. To enforce your rights, you need both to know someone is making use of your resource (an issue of monitoring capacity) and to have the ability to exclude others' use. As an example, consider the history of the American West. It was only with the invention of barbed wire that settlers could effectively exclude cattle from grazing on their lands. Prior to this technology, there was no affordable way to keep cattle from grazing wherever they wanted. In a more modern context, decoders have allowed satellite television channels to privatize the airwave common. Unless satellite channel providers could exclude other's use of their signals, there would be no way for them to sell their product (since people could use it for free).

Reliance on property rights has proven effective in the case of trading systems, discussed below, where rights to emit a ton of pollution or catch a ton of fish are allocated and traded on an open market. Indeed, some commentators have called for far greater reliance on property rights approaches to environmental protection. Sometimes called "Free Market Environmentalism," this strategy would privatize as many environmental resources as possible, in the belief that markets are better mechanisms for allocation of goods than governmental regulators.

Despite the increasing interest and application of property rights approaches to environmental protection, there are some significant obstacles. The first is that many environmental resources are not easily amenable to commodification. Consider endangered species, for example. One might privatize their habitat, but what if the species is mobile? There may be normative concerns, as well, that rub against privatization of national parks or other environmental amenities in the public domain. For example, the government could try to "privatize" wildlife by equipping each animal with a collar or tag that identifies its "owner." Yet wildlife in the process would lose part of their "wildness," which is one of the qualities that gives them a unique and valuable identity. Practically, there also are difficult allocation issues for the initial privatization of environmental resources. Using the commons as an example, assume that the government has divided up the land into 50 separate parcels. Who should be given title? Should the land be auctioned to the highest bidder? This could favor wealthier newcomers and corporate interests. Giving more respect for traditional users, perhaps the allocation should be based on historic use or current levels of consumption. Yet this puts newcomers at a disadvantage and favors those who have been the most profligate in the past. If we can't decide among these competing users, should we just have a random drawing? Any allocation mechanism will tend to favor some groups at the expense of others. Whom should be favored comes down to a contentious policy decision.

Nor, finally, is it clear that privatization will lead to the socially most beneficial use of the land. Private property owners typically value only those uses that provide monetary remuneration. This may ignore environmental values or other important public benefits. Perhaps the new owners of the common wish to use it for mini-golf while the sheep starve. If the government wants to ensure the important public goals of a secure food supply or supporting the agricultural sector, it will need to step in. Property rights advocates would approve of this course of action, so long as the government paid off the property holders. Another approach, though, would involve direct regulation.

C. *Prescriptive Regulation*

In relying on prescriptive regulation, the government mandates how a resource may be used. This strategy explicitly directs behavior of regulated parties and is the most typical regulatory approach in environmental law. In the case of the commons, for example, the government might limit access, perhaps restricting the number of sheep that may graze or the amount of time or season the sheep may graze. The government may set aside areas for re-vegetation, etc. Such prescriptive regulation, also referred to as *command-and-control regulation*, can be very effective but there is considerable debate over its efficiency, as discussed below.

D.   Market Instruments

Hoping to make compliance with environmental laws less costly and reduce the extent of government intervention, there has been growing interest in market instruments. Taxes or fees are one category of market instruments. Using the commons example again, the government may charge an entrance fee to graze on the common or, more effectively, tax use of the common (for instance on the number of sheep or time spent grazing). Such market instruments are attractive because they lead to self-regulation of use. If the fees and taxes are set correctly, these instruments quite literally internalize externalities and provide a direct incentive to modify behavior, aligning environmental and economic interests.

A more popular market instrument in the United States is the tradable permit or credit. To date, the government has used trading systems to reduce emissions of a wide range of pollutants, manage fisheries and lobster harvests, and channel habitat development. Trading systems use the market to make prescriptive regulation more efficient. The government decides how much of a harmful activity (like pollution) to permit, awards private rights to engage in the activity up to the regulatory cap, and then permits those rights to be traded. The market thus does not play a role in determining the level of environmental protection; that is the role of the regulatory regime. The market simply permits those who can most easily avoid the environmental harm (and thus have the least need for their permits) to trade their rights to those who would find it most expensive or difficult to avoid the environmental harm—reducing the total economic costs of the regulation.

To make this more concrete, imagine how a trading program would work with grazing on the common. Government policy makers decide that the common can sustain no more than 400 sheep grazing. The government therefore creates 400 permits. Each permit entitles the holder to graze one sheep for the calendar year listed on the permit. Unless the shepherd has a separate permit for each sheep grazing on the common, he is breaking the law. The government then allocates the permits in some fashion and lets trading commence. In theory, those for whom grazing is most valuable will pay the highest price to buy the permits, ensuring that the common is dedicated to the most valuable use.

E.   Information

If the common law, prescriptive regulation, and market instruments represent "hard" regulatory approaches, then a softer approach may be found in laws requiring information production and dissemination.

Sometimes described as *reflexive laws*, the theory behind such approaches is that the government can change people's behavior by forcing people to think about the harm they are causing and by publicizing that harm. In the context of the commons, the government might require shepherds to record and publish the number of sheep they graze or the amount of forage the sheep eat. The government also may try to educate the shepherds with brochures or presentations on the causes and dangers of overgrazing. In general, information approaches are used when there is either inadequate political support to impose market or regulatory instruments or such instruments are ill suited to the problem. In a number of cases, particularly in the case of pollution, requirements to collect and disseminate information have led to significant change in the behavior of regulated parties, even in the absence of overt prescriptive regulation.

F. The Regulatory Toolkit

While the examples above have all related to the tragedy of the commons, one can apply this toolkit of regulatory instruments to virtually any environmental problem. Taking the example of climate change, for example, consider the range of legal instruments you could use to reduce greenhouse gas emissions as well as their potential shortcomings. If you were head of the EPA, what would your proposed greenhouse gas law look like?

Reliance on the common law would prove difficult because causation—the link between discrete emissions and harm (whether in the form of sea level rise or aberrant weather patterns)—could not be established easily. It's hard to see how nuisance or trespass doctrines would work with such attenuated causation and multiple sources.

Prescriptive regulation seems more workable. In the greenhouse gas context, regulation could take the form of emission controls, limiting the amount of pollution a source may emit. Regulations might mandate the use of certain pollution control technologies or other process design requirements (often referred to as best available technology or BAT). While effective, reliance on a technological approach has been criticized as overly rigid because, unless the technology standards regularly change, there exists little incentive for a facility to reduce pollution beyond the BAT requirements. "So long as the regulations require use of Filter X, we've bought Filter X and it's working properly; there's no reason to go further."

Market instruments seem a good potential fit, as well. One could levy emission fees based on the amount of greenhouse gases emitted. Also known as *Pigouvian taxes*, these encourage each actor to look for ways to reduce his emissions and to regulate his behavior according to how valuable the polluting activities are. Needless to say, this approach also has shortcomings. Setting the correct level of the tax is difficult to do. After all, environmental protection officials care about the *overall* effect of many polluting sources or resource users. What level should the tax or fee be set at to reach the desired pollution or resource extraction level? More practically, there is strong public and political opposition to significant taxes. President Clinton proposed a carbon tax at the start of his presidency, but the proposal quickly died in a hailstorm of political opposition. In most cases, when pollution taxes have been set, they've been more intended for revenue raising than serious behavior modification.

There also has been serious interest in establishing a trading market for greenhouse gases. In the typical *cap and trade program* for pollution, policymakers establish a socially desirable level of aggregate emissions for a given pollutant. Regulators then determine a formula for initial allocation of emissions among sources and issue permits to members of the regulated community that entitle each bearer to emit a given quantity of that pollutant. In sum, the total quantity of emissions allowed by those permits should equal the aggregate level set by policymakers. Proponents of trading programs argue that such arrangements increase efficiencies. In the case of greenhouse gas trades, for example, by letting the market rather than regulators determine individual actors' reductions, profit-motivated agents who can control pollution at low cost will reduce emissions more than needed to comply with permit limits. They can then sell surplus allowances at a profit to higher-cost agents. Thus, the greatest share of reductions will come from agents who can do so at the cheapest cost, allowing each polluter to weigh the marginal cost of abatement against the cost of buying credits and make an efficient individual decision. If the cap is set appropriately, marketable permits achieve the same level of protection as command-and-control alternatives at a lower cost. The net result allows the regulated community to select appropriate control strategies and encourages innovative practices and technologies.

One downside of trading is similar to that for private property approaches—the difficulty of initially allocating permits. Moreover, constructing smoothly functioning markets is not simple. There must be a sufficient and well-defined marketplace and a community of market participants. There also must be a refined currency of trade, one that is fungible and reflects the desired environmental quality. For example, it would be a stretch to consider allowing coastal developers in Florida to "trade" wetland values they eliminate for reductions in phosphorous emissions in Oregon. But where the environmental good (or bad, so to speak) can be captured in a measurable unit (whether that be tons of pollutant or kilos of fish) and market service areas and participants are well-defined, trading programs have had demonstrable success in a variety of contexts, increasing the efficiency and flexibility of prescriptive instruments.

Finally, information disclosure also might work well. One could, for example, require firms to collect and publish over the web data on their greenhouse gas emissions. Perhaps not surprisingly, such proposals have been strongly opposed by many in industry. Similarly, one might create an *eco-labeling* program, providing a seal of approval for those companies or goods that achieve significant greenhouse gas reductions. The theory behind such programs is to provide green consumers with reliable information on which to base their purchases and favor environmentally friendlier companies in the marketplace.

G. Instrument Design Issues

In the context of instrument choice, there are three longstanding issues worth keeping in mind. The first is the debate over relative efficiency. As noted above, there has been longstanding criticism of prescriptive regulations as inefficient both because the government (rather than the market) generally determines the best available technology and because there is little incentive for a firm to reduce its pollution beyond what the government requires. In place of prescriptive regulation, critics contend, there should be greater reliance on market instruments because these allow the regulated parties to choose the most economically efficient means of compliance.

While this is an important debate, the way it has been described above is both misleading and incomplete. It's misleading because many market instruments necessarily rely on prescriptive regulation. For example, tradable permits can increase efficiency, but they often require prescriptive regulation to protect the environment. Trading programs work only because regulated parties are forbidden from engaging in certain activities unless they have an adequate number of permits, whether that be grazing sheep or emitting greenhouse gases. The description above is incomplete because it considers only costs to the regulated community. There are costs of administration to consider, as well.

The second major issue in instrument design—the relevance of administrative costs—has played out most clearly within the category of prescriptive regulations and the choice between technology-based and health-based standards. Assume, for example, you are crafting a regulation that will limit emissions of dimethyl terrible. Should the standard mandate use of best available technology (perhaps a particular filter the company places on its smokestack) or a health-based standard? The health-based standard might mandate, for example, that a facility's emissions of dimethyl terrible cannot increase the risks of cancer above one in a one million (i.e., a chance that one person in a population of one million will contract cancer because of the dimethyl emissions). From a pure efficiency perspective, the health approach is appealing. Why mandate uniform emission controls when we know that in many cases such standards will be over-protective? Take the example of a chemical plant on an ocean peninsula with a strong steady breeze out to sea. If this plant's emissions will not come into contact with people (and assuming it is not toxic to ocean life), then why force it to pay for control technology that provides no benefit?

The classic response to this argument is that, while a health-based standard may theoretically be economically more efficient, in practice a technological standard is not only more protective but much easier for EPA to administer and enforce. A health-based standard necessarily relies on modeling. What level of exposure will people downwind of the plant experience? Based on toxicological studies (generally done on mice), how many cancers is this exposure likely to cause? Needless to say, there are a lot of assumptions and extrapolations necessary in such a calculation and therefore, environmental critics charge, lots of room for fudging results to favor industry interests and lower levels of protection. Moreover, EPA often can monitor whether a company is using required technology more easily than it can monitor a company's emissions and the effect of those emissions. As described above, so long as the regulations require use of Filter X, if the company has bought Filter X and it's working properly, neither the company nor EPA has any worries.

This conflict between health-based and technology-based standards occurs throughout pollution control legislation and is a theme we will revisit often (e.g., in the land ban discussion under RCRA at pages 179–181). When crafting its regulations, EPA typically faces a fundamental trade-off between regulatory strategies that are inflexible but relatively easy to administer (e.g., technology-based requirements) and those that are more complex but flexible (e.g., risk-based).

A third issue worth noting is that, in some respects, the choice of regulatory target is as important as choice of instrument. To illustrate why, assume you are charged to come up with a brand new regulatory strategy to address the potential harms from pesticide use. In approaching this problem, before choosing to rely on prescriptive commands, market instruments, or information, you must first determine the appropriate entity to regulate since this will, in turn, determine which instruments work best. Which potential parties should you regulate? If focusing on the chemicals used in pesticides, should you direct your regulations against manufacturers of these goods or their suppliers (those who sell the chemicals on the market)? Large suppliers often have a great deal of power over manufacturers, so perhaps they are best suited to act as a filter, refusing to purchase goods that are not "environmentally friendly" or shown to be "safe" in use. At the same time, manufacturers know their chemicals better than anyone, so perhaps they should be directly regulated so they can shoulder direct responsibility for re-formulating their pesticides. In a more indirect approach, perhaps the best regulatory target would be farmers. An information disclosure requirement could require them to inform buyers of the chemicals applied to their crops. Finally, one could focus on agricultural produce buyers. By directing their purchasing behavior, they would drive changes throughout the system. Superfund, discussed in Chapter 7, takes a similar approach by holding land owners responsible for the safe disposal of hazardous waste on their property. As the above example makes clear, there are pressure points throughout the product chain to influence pesticide design and use, and selection of the regulatory target partly prejudges which instruments will be most effective.

In any complicated problem, which environmental issues surely pose, potential contributors may have to be left out of the regulatory scheme for sheer practicality. The government simply can't regulate everyone. But this raises political problems—charges of favoring one group over another. Indeed environmental law offers clear examples of such political picking-and-choosing. As Chapter 5 on the Clean Water Act explains, most nutrients in water pollution come from agriculture (as "nonpoint source" pollution). Yet, because of the agricultural lobby's political clout, farm runoff is effectively unregulated.

H. Where to Go from Here?

Environmental protection has progressed from reliance on the common law, to reliance on prescriptive regulatory commands, to reliance on market instruments and information. In comparison to other areas of the law such as torts, property, or even corporate law, however, environmental law is still a very young field, just over 30 years old. While the current structure and approach to environmental protection offers clear advantages over its predecessors, the entire field remains remarkably dynamic and in flux, with major reforms proposed in Congress virtually every year. Environmental law is surely contentious, as well, and widespread criticism has prompted many of these proposed reforms.

The major criticism of environmental law is inefficiency. Environmental law's requirements are too rigid, critics charge, and its rules too restrictive, resulting in protection that could be achieved at less cost or should not be required at all. In 1990, EPA's Scientific Advisory Board ranked major threats to the environment and human health. In its report on "Reducing Risk," the board found little connection between EPA's budget priorities and the scientists' risk rankings (indeed it was close to an inverse correlation).[2] EPA spent large sums on risks that the board ranked as comparatively low and small amounts on risks ranked as comparatively higher. EPA's largest budget item, treatment of contaminated land, for example, was rated as a low priority while high priorities, such as radon exposure and ecosystem protection, received much less funding. "Reducing Risk" and similar studies have led many people to call for stronger reliance on cost-benefit analysis and risk assessment when drafting and implementing environmental laws. Defenders of EPA's priorities have responded that scientific risk estimates do not take into account all of the characteristics of risk that are important to the public (e.g., whether businesses cause the risk or the risk naturally occurs) and that EPA's expenditures closely parallel the public's ranking of risks.

Another cause of inefficiency can be the laws themselves. A number of environmental laws could be described as "management by crisis." Following public outcry over an event, Congress rushes to address the problem and enacts hastily drafted legislation. The clearest example of this is in the Superfund law governing the remediation of contaminated land. Following media coverage of widespread contamination from chemical barrels buried beneath the homes in Love Canal in upstate New York, Congress drafted Superfund in a matter of months. The bill's passage was even more hurried because it was adopted in the lame duck Congress between the election of Ronald Reagan over Jimmy Carter and Reagan's inauguration.

Moreover, as many environmental law students find in their first few classes, environmental law can be quite complex and ambiguous. In some areas, particularly the field of hazardous waste law, the regulations can be dauntingly opaque. To be sure, many of these criticisms represent industry lobbying for more lenient treatment or weaker standards, but simply dismissing such critiques as industry whining misses the point that the system of environmental law raises compliance barriers all on its own. Consider, for example, that there are over 11,000 pages of federal environmental law, not to mention state and local laws, and the number of environmental provisions is growing.

Another major concern raised by environmental law is that of unintended consequences. The simplistic ecological maxim that "everything is connected" has a grain of truth. Actions taken to resolve one problem often may exacerbate or create another problem. Thus restrict-

2. Environmental Protection Agency, Reducing Risk: Setting Priorities and Strat-   egies for Environmental Protection (1990).

ing land disposal of hazardous waste in the 1980s reduced that problem but created a new one. In an example of "media shifting," greater volumes of hazardous waste were burned in incinerators instead of being buried, and the danger from air toxics increased. Another classic case of an unintended impact is Superfund's expansive liability regime for contaminated land sites discouraging development of downtown industrial sites (known as "brownfield sites") and, instead, driving businesses to so-called "greenfield sites" in the suburbs, exacerbating the problems of urban sprawl. Such cases present examples of *risk/risk problems*. Reducing one risk often increases another risk. Given that we live in a closed system and that everything goes somewhere, it's crucial that we manage risk/risk decisions more intelligently since they are inevitable. One way to do so involves taking more of a *life-cycle approach*, identifying where the pollution or resource goes, straight from its creation all the way to its ultimate disposal.

A final major criticism of environmental law is that of fairness. As described earlier, determining who should bear the burden of environmental protection is a controversial subject. Why should a company that complied fully with environmental laws at the time it disposed of its waste be potentially liable under Superfund for cleaning up an entire site that was mismanaged and largely contaminated by others? Is it fair that private landowners should be uncompensated if they cannot develop their land because of the presence of an endangered species?

In response to these concerns and others, the last decade has seen a flood of "reinvention" projects. In the Clinton Administration's Common Sense Initiative, for example, EPA invited a broad range of stakeholders (from federal, state, and local governments, community-based and national environmental groups, environmental justice groups, labor, and industry) to review the environmental requirements in six industries (including automobile manufacturing, computers and electronics, and iron and steel). The goal was to identify complicated and inconsistent environmental regulations and develop a comprehensive reform strategy with broad-based support. In the Project XL initiative, started in the Clinton and continued in the Bush administration, state and local governments, businesses, and federal facilities may propose new strategies that provide better and cost-effective ways of achieving environmental and public health protection. In exchange, EPA provides more flexible regulatory oversight while the new approach is implemented.

In its brief three decades, environmental law has been a fertile seedbed for regulatory innovations, trading programs, environmental taxes, and performance-based regulation, not to mention the most recent flexible approaches described above.

II. The Administration of Environmental Protection

In order to understand the practice of environmental law one must first grasp the broader legal framework within which it operates. While media-specific statutes such as the Clean Air Act or resource-specific laws such as the Endangered Species Act determine what regulated parties may or may not do, these operate within more general constraints on what the government is allowed to do. Administrative law sets the parameters for how agencies may implement these statutes and constitutional law sets the limits of governmental authority. Vast subjects in themselves, the remaining sections of this chapter provide a brief primer on the roles of administrative and constitutional law in environmental protection, as well as the unique role of non-state actors in the environmental field and their use of citizen suits to shape environmental law.

A. *Basics of Administrative Law*

Administrative law is held up as one of the great inventions of the American experience and, in many respects, it truly is. Administrative law makes government activity more open, accountable, and responsive to the public than in any other country. Administrative law concerns *how agencies operate*—the processes and procedures they use to perform their functions—and the *separation of powers*—the competitive relationship and respective powers between the legislative and executive branches of government and the role of courts in refereeing this constant battle. Writ large, the field is about government, what government does, and what it can and can't do. In some ways, administrative law represents the flip side of corporate law. Just as corporate law regulates the conduct of private organizations, administrative law serves as the law of public organizations.

Why is understanding the law of agencies crucial to understanding environmental law? As a short answer, one cannot identify an environmental issue that is *not* managed by an agency. Air and water pollution? Look to EPA. Wetlands? The Department of Defense (through the Army Corps of Engineers). Forests? Department of Agriculture (Forest Service). Endangered Species? Department of Interior (Fish & Wildlife Service). Marine fisheries? Department of Commerce (National Marine Fisheries Service). The list could, and does, go on and on and on. Agency action is where environmental protection happens.

Hardly a new creation, the first three administrative departments were established in 1789 (State, Treasury, and War). Along the way, other well-known departments such as Interior, Treasury, Justice, Commerce, and Labor have been added with growth spurts during the New Deal in the 1930s and the Great Society in the 1960s. President Richard Nixon created the Environmental Protection Agency in 1970 in response to growing interest in the environment. Hard to believe, but the Code of Federal Regulations' Alphabetical List of Agencies now runs over nine pages of fine print!

This alphabet soup of government agencies plays many different roles. Agencies can issue rules, conduct inspections, award licenses, adjudicate disputes, demand information, hold hearings, and give and take money, just to name a few activities. As a result of these varied roles, agencies maintain an uneasy position within the three branches of government. As we all learned in high school, the Executive Branch faithfully executes the laws, the Legislative Branch creates laws and controls the purse strings, and the Judicial Branch interprets the law and applies the Constitution. So where in this scheme do agencies fit in? All agency actions must be authorized by Congress, which effectively delegates some of its authorities. But, from the brief description above, it seems that agencies fit in all three branches—making rules, investigating compliance, punishing violations, and hearing appeals. This combination of tasks leads to tension within the Executive and Legislative branches as they compete with one another to influence agency behavior.

The judiciary is supposed to act as a referee in this turf war, determining if agencies (generally located within the Executive branch) have followed Congressional intent closely enough. Making this determination depends critically on the court's vision of the agency itself. Consider two very different models of administrative agencies. In one model, which is called *scientific expertise*, technocrats in white jackets populate the agency. These agency personnel are experts in what they do, faithfully carrying out the will of Congress by relying on their best professional judgment. This model views agencies as efficiently implementing the mandates of government.

The contrasting model, known as *interest group representation,* views agencies as mini-legislatures. As in Congress, special interests battle it out to influence the implementation of laws. In this model, agencies are simply a microcosm of the larger political debate, with the same political processes taking place within agencies. This is not necessarily a bad thing, but raises the specter of two dangers. The first is known as *agency capture*. Agencies may so closely align themselves with the industries they're supposed to regulate that the public interest is lost in the process. Perhaps the clearest example of this was the decision by the U.S. Forest Service that the best "multiple use" of the Tongass National Forest, given the competing interests of recreation, wildlife protection, preservation, and logging, was to dedicate *100%* of the forest to logging.[3] Such one-sided decisions can be explained by *public choice theory*, which predicts that the efforts of concentrated interests (e.g., timber companies) will more effectively influence the political process than more diffuse, though larger, interests (such as the general public).

A second danger is that of agency self-interest. In order to increase its power and perpetuate itself, the argument goes, agencies may act more out of bureaucratic self-interest than in the public interest. This charge is often levied against the Army Corps of Engineers, for example, for pushing environmentally harmful, expensive construction projects that are popular in Congressional members' home districts.

Which model one believes best describes agency action has a huge influence on the appropriate judicial role in administrative law. If scientific expertise is the accurate model, then judicial review should be deferential since, after all, the agency officials are the real experts. If, however, interest group representation better exemplifies agency action, then little deference should be granted by judges and strict review should be used to uncover hidden deals, rent seeking, and self-interested decisionmaking.

The last broad point to note about agencies is the importance of the Administrative Procedure Act (APA).[4] Passed in 1946, the APA operates for agencies in some respects the way the rules of civil procedure do for trial judges. For our purposes, the APA sets out procedures agencies must follow when promulgating rules and adjudicating conflicts. It also establishes the standard of judicial review (which varies depending on the type of action) when agency actions are challenged in court. The next two subsections briefly explain the APA requirements and case law governing (1) agency rulemaking and (2) adjudication. Understanding these two common types of agency action is important because the main line of attack against agency action is just as often procedural (e.g., the proper notice requirements for rulemaking were not complied with) as substantive (e.g., the Clean Air Act forbids this agency action).

1. Rulemaking

As just noted, the APA breaks most agency actions into two broad categories—rulemaking and adjudication. As its name suggests, rulemaking describes agency decisions that affect general classes of people. Rulemaking concerns prospective policy decisions and produces rules of general applicability. Adjudication, by contrast, concerns agency decisions over claims of disputed facts that require particularized application

---

3. Sierra Club v. Hardin, 325 F.Supp. 99 (D.Alaska 1971), rev'd sub nom. Sierra Club v. Butz, 3 Envtl. L. Rep. 20292 (9th Cir. 1973).

4. 5 U.S.C. §§ 551 et seq.

and produces what are called "orders." An agency decision, for example, to establish the level of sulfur dioxide that oil-fired power plants may emit would be rulemaking. If a particular plant challenged the rule's applicability to its operations, the agency decision would be an adjudication. In general, differentiating between rulemaking and adjudication is straightforward, but it's an important distinction because the APA's requirements for the two procedures are significantly different.

Where do agency rules come from? Usually they come from statutory mandates. In most environmental laws Congress simply passes broad framework legislation, leaving it up to the agency to fill in the (often extensive) details. As described in Chapter 4, when the Clean Air Act requires EPA to protect the public health with an adequate margin of safety, EPA must decide which pollutants to regulate and their permissible levels of emission. In RCRA, Congress leaves it up to EPA to determine which substances should be regulated as solid hazardous waste. These are technical decisions with immense practical impact. Not all agency rulemaking is statutorily driven, though. Some rules may come from public petition; some may result from political pressure from Congress or the White House. All are published in the Code of Federal Regulations.

In reaching these decisions, the agency must comply with the APA's procedural requirements for rulemaking. In the environmental context, we need only concern ourselves with the APA's requirements for what is known as *informal rulemaking* (sometimes referred to as *notice and comment* rulemaking). The term *informal*, though, can be misleading. Informal rulemaking is still a rigorous procedure, not just Bob and Sue sitting around an office saying, "You want to make a rule?" "Sure. You go ahead and write it. I'm going to get some donuts."

Section 553 of the APA requires agencies to provide notice of a proposed rule in the Federal Register, including the agency's source of authority to issue the rule, a description of the proposed rule, notice to interested persons of the location and time of public hearings, as well as opportunity to submit comments. The agency also must publish the final rule in the Federal Register, including responses to the categories of submitted comments, justifying the rule's final form. This is a far more rigorous process for agency action than in any other country in the world and seeks to ensure that agency rules are well crafted and consider the views of affected parties.

When final rules are challenged (as many of EPA's are), the key question for the courts is what the standard of review should be. The APA states that courts must ensure informal rulemaking is not arbitrary and capricious or an abuse of discretion. Although this standard might sound very deferential to agencies, federal courts in the 1970s used it to take a "hard look" at agency actions. In *Citizens to Preserve Overton Park v. Volpe*,[5] the Secretary of Transportation provided no justification for approving the construction of a highway through a park in Memphis, despite the fact that the relevant law forbade use of public funds to construct highways through public parks if a "reasonable and prudent" alternative route was available. In remanding the case back to the agency, the D.C. Circuit Court of Appeals held that it could not determine if the agency's action was arbitrary and capricious absent evidence that the agency's decision had resulted from a thorough, probing, in-depth review. This and similar decisions forced agencies to create more thorough records of decision in anticipation of judicial review.

In its 1978 decision in *Vermont Yankee Nuclear Power Corporation v. Natural Resources Defense Council*,[6] the United States Supreme Court put an end to this trend and announced that courts generally should not add new procedural requirements. In challenging an action by the Atomic Energy Agency, the Natural Resources Defense Council argued that it should have been able to engage in cross-examination, discovery, and other procedures prior to issuance of the rule. The D.C. Circuit agreed, holding that the agency's procedures had been inadequate. On appeal, the Supreme Court told lower courts to knock it off. Courts, the Supreme Court held, cannot impose procedural requirements that are not required by statute unless there are extremely compelling circumstances or constitutional constraints.

The United States Supreme Court appeared to further limit judicial oversight of agency actions a few years later in the classic administrative law case of *Chevron U.S.A., Inc. v. Natural Resources Defense Council*.[7] *Chevron* concerned EPA's interpretation of the term "stationary source" under the Clean Air Act. In simple terms, the Clean Air Act requires "new or modified major stationary sources" to meet stringent new air pollution standards. EPA, however, decided that states could permit industrial plants to install or modify pollution-emitting devices without meeting these standards if total emissions from the plant as a whole did not increase. In essence, EPA decided that states could treat the plant as a whole, rather than the individual smokestacks within the facility, as the "stationary source." (This strategy, known as "bubbling," is discussed further at pages 91–93.) The issue before the Supreme Court was whether this was a permissible interpretation of the Clean Air Act. If Congress gave little guidance over the text's meaning, how much defer-

---

5. 401 U.S. 402 (1971).

6. 435 U.S. 519 (1978).

7. 467 U.S. 837 (1984). It's interesting to note that the most important administrative law cases (*Overton Park, Vermont Yan-* *kee, Chevron, Lujan*) are environmental cases. And a helpful hint—if you're taking ad law, the teacher asks you a question about judicial review, and you have no idea what the answer is ... offer up *"Chevron"* and there's a good chance you'll be right.

ence should be given to the agency's interpretation of the statutory requirement?

The approach to statutory interpretation that the Court adopted in *Chevron*, sometimes referred to as the "*Chevron* two-step," asks two questions. First, has Congress spoken directly to the precise question at issue? If the statutory language is clear or Congress' intent is otherwise clear, then the issue is simple. The court must determine whether the agency action conforms to the unambiguous Congressional mandate. The court exercises a completely independent judgment with no deference to the agency. If, though, as is far more often the case, Congress has not directly addressed the specific question, or is silent, or ambiguous, or has expressly left a gap for the agency to fill, the second step kicks in. In this instance, the court must decide only whether the agency's answer is based on a "permissible" construction of the statute. The agency's interpretation need not be the best or most reasonable in the eyes of the Court; it simply must be reasonable and not arbitrary, capricious, or an abuse of discretion. In *Chevron*, the Supreme Court concluded that the Clean Air Act was ambiguous but that EPA's interpretation of the term "stationary source" was reasonable and thus permissible.

There are, of course, many reasons why Congress might leave issues open by using vague statutory language. It might consciously desire the agency to make a policy choice; it may not have considered the specific issue (as was the case in *Chevron*); it may have been unable to reach a compromise so it passed over the issue. On its face, *Chevron* placed great power in the hands of agencies since it seemed to call for strong deference. This is consistent with arguments that unelected judges should back off and let agencies do what they do best (i.e., apply their expertise) so long as the procedures are followed. In practice, though, *Chevron* has not led to a massive increase in favorable agency decisions. Courts still overturn agency rules, almost always relying on Step One (that Congressional intent was clear and the agency got it wrong) rather than the more deferential Step Two. This practice is more consistent with the interest representation model—because of agency capture and self-interest, agencies may make decisions contrary to the facts or statute and courts must provide the first line of protection against this. We will see these arguments play out in Chapter 9's discussion of *Babbitt v. Sweet Home Chapter of Communities for a Great Oregon*,[8] upholding the Department of Interior's interpretation of the Endangered Species Act.

As a final insight on rulemaking, it is important to note that one class of rules is not subject to the APA requirements for informal rulemaking at all. Known as nonlegislative rules or publication rules,

---

8. 515 U.S. 687 (1995).

these include guidance documents and interpretive rulings (such as tax forms and how to fill them out, or guidance to prosecutors on how various violations should be punished). Such nonlegislative rules are far more voluminous than either the statute or informal rules they support. As an example, there are roughly 20 feet of informal rules for the Clean Air Act. Agencies can issue these rules without any notice or public comment for the simple reason that, technically, these rules are not legally binding. Agencies, however, usually follow such nonlegislative rules, placing regulated parties at the risk of violating regulations that never were published and on which they never had an opportunity to comment.

2. Adjudication

While rulemaking concerns prospective decisions affecting a class of people, adjudication is more often retrospective and covers a broad range of agency actions, from license denials and revocation to the agency's enforcement of its rules. As with rulemaking, the key challenges to adjudication decisions are often procedural, i.e., was the proper process followed?

For most environmental issues, the relevant procedures are set out in the requirements for informal adjudication in section 555 of the APA. Fairly minimal, these requirements include the right to counsel, to appear before the agency, and to receive a decision within a reasonable time. Agencies usually set additional procedures and publish these in the Federal Register. All of these requirements supplement, of course, the Constitutional requirements of the 5th and 14th amendments if there is deprivation of liberty or property.

III. Constitutional Issues in Environmental Policy

The United States Constitution dictates what the federal and state governments can and cannot do in the environmental field. As discussed later in this chapter, the case-or-controversy requirement of Article III limits who can sue to enforce federal environmental laws or to review administrative decisions. In this section, we explore the powers that the federal Congress enjoys to protect the environment, the degree to which Congress and state legislatures can delegate decisions to expert administrative agencies like EPA, and the constitutional "takings" provisions, which restrict the degree to which the federal and state governments can protect the environment by regulating private property.

Two other constitutional issues also loom large in the environmental field and are covered later in this book. First, the supremacy clause of the United States Constitution gives Congress the power to preempt state environmental regulation. Congress has largely eschewed its power to preempt stronger state regulations, leaving states free to go beyond the environmental standards set by the federal government. Congress occasionally has chosen to limit stronger state regulation. As discussed in Chapter 4, for example, most states are not free to set whatever automobile standards they wish. Second, the so-called "dormant commerce clause" restricts the states' authority to ban the importation of hazardous substances from other states. As discussed in Chapter 7, the Supreme Court has concluded that waste is an article of commerce and that its interstate transportation thus is subject only to federal regulation.

A. *Congressional Powers*

In passing environmental laws, Congress has relied primarily on its *commerce power*.[9] For years, this seemed a fairly safe bet because the courts permitted Congress to use this power to regulate virtually any activity that had the remotest possible relationship to interstate commerce. Think of virtually any environmental regulation, and it is easy to imagine some way, no matter how attenuated, that the regulation will affect interstate commerce. In a series of recent non-environmental cases, however, the Supreme Court has suggested that there are limits to Congress' authority, raising new questions about the constitutionality of some federal environmental laws.

Of greatest importance is *United States v. Lopez*.[10] Alphonso Lopez, a high school student, was convicted of violating the federal Gun–Free School Zones Act which banned the possession of firearms within 1000 feet of any school. By a slim 5–4 majority, the Supreme Court reversed the conviction and held that the Act was not within Congress' commerce power. According to the Court, Congress can use its commerce power to regulate only (1) the "use of the channels of intrastate commerce," (2) activities that threaten the "instrumentalities of interstate commerce, or persons or things in interstate commerce," and (3) "activities having a substantial relation to interstate commerce." The third category, moreover, reaches only activities that *substantially* affect interstate commerce; Congress cannot regulate an activity merely because it has some impact on interstate commerce, however remote. The majority refused to "pile inference upon inference in a manner that would bid fair to convert congressional authority under the Commerce Clause to a general police power of the sort retained by the States."[11] In the Court's view, carrying

---

9. Art. I, § 8 ("The Congress shall have Power ... To regulate Commerce ... among the several States....").

10. 514 U.S. 549 (1995).

11. Id. at 567.

a gun near a school does not substantially affect interstate commerce and therefore is not a legitimate subject of federal regulation. As the Court noted, all of its prior decisions upholding Congressional authority under the third category involved the regulation, either directly or indirectly, of commercial enterprises. Those regulations focused on economic activities such as intrastate coal mining, intrastate credit transactions, businesses utilizing substantial interstate supplies, and hotels catering to interstate guests.

Even under *Lopez*, the Commerce Clause provides Congress with very broad authority over the environment. Virtually all of Congress' efforts to regulate pollution or hazardous substances would seem constitutional. The Federal Insecticide, Rodenticide, and Fungicide Act and the Toxic Substances Control Act regulate products such as pesticides and asbestos that are bought and sold in interstate commerce, and thus fall within Congress' authority to regulate the use of the channels of interstate commerce. The traditional pollution statutes, such as the Clean Air Act and Clean Water Act, regulate commercial activities or products, such as automobiles, that again are sold in interstate commerce. Congress' efforts to hold generators of hazardous waste and disposal facilities responsible for the cleanup of contaminated land arguably protects interstate commerce from the dangers of pollution.

However, federal laws that regulate local land uses, such as the Endangered Species Act or the wetlands provisions of the Clean Water Act, have a less certain constitutional footing. There are several reasons. First, land use decisions historically have been the province of local government, making Congress look more like an interloper when it becomes involved. Second, and more importantly, the linkage between land use regulations and interstate commerce often is remote. The connection between interstate commerce and a small seasonal wetland or the habitat of a geographically confined species is far less obvious than the relationship between pesticides and interstate commerce.

To date, however, challenges to federal land use regulations all have failed. Appellate courts repeatedly have rejected constitutional challenges to federal regulation of wetlands under the Clean Water Act. The Supreme Court granted certiorari in *Solid Waste Agency of Northern Cook County v. United States Army Corps of Engineers*[12] to consider whether Congress could regulate isolated wetlands that are not connected to navigable waterways, but ultimately decided that Congress had not intended to regulate such wetlands, avoiding the constitutional issue.

By an extremely fractured vote, a three-judge panel of the D.C. Circuit also rejected a constitutional challenge to the federal government's efforts under the Endangered Species Act to protect the few

12.   531 U.S. 159 (2001).

hundred acres of remaining habitat, all in Southern California, of the Delhi Sands flower loving fly.[13] After a local county found that it could not reconstruct an intersection to meet the needs of a new hospital because the construction might jeopardize the fly, the county sued to challenge Congress' authority over the fly and its habitat. One judge concluded that the federal government could protect the fly both because the fly some day might be found to have genetic value of interstate importance and because, absent federal regulation, states might compete for businesses by lowering their protections of biodiversity. A second judge concluded that Congress had adequate authority because the objects of regulation—the hospital and the traffic intersection—had "an obvious connection with interstate commerce." The third judge dissented, finding no connection with interstate commerce.

Other Congressional powers on occasion also may support particular environmental legislation. For example, the Property Clause, which gives Congress the "Power to dispose of and make all needful Rules and Regulations respecting ... Property belonging to the United States,"[14] justifies laws designed to protect the environment on federal lands, even when the laws regulate activities on nearby private property. Congress also may be able to use its spending power both to pay for environmental amenities and, by conditioning federal funds to states or private parties on various environmental measures, encourage states or private parties to adopt policies that they otherwise might not. Congress, for example, requires states to meet specified ambient air standards if the states wish to receive federal highway funds.

B. Legislative Delegation

As explained in the preceding section, expert administrative agencies like the federal EPA are critical to modern environmental regulation. Congress does not have the expertise, time, or resources to work out all the details of environmental regulation—for example, the appropriate ambient air quality standard for sulfur dioxide, the correct water pollution discharge standards for a factory on Wisconsin's Fox River, or the proper habitat to protect for the endangered snowy plover. Congress unavoidably must rely on EPA and other agencies to determine these regulatory details. As emphasized earlier, moreover, environmental regulation is plagued by uncertainty and beset by change. Even if Congress could establish all the details of a regulatory regime at one point in time, new scientific, economic, and social information would require Congress constantly to revise the details. Congress can best deal with uncertainty

---

13. National Ass'n of Home Builders v. Babbitt, 130 F.3d 1041 (D.C.Cir.1997).   **14.** Art. IV, § 3.

and change by setting out broad policy directives that are not dependent on assumptions that are likely to change and then letting administrative agencies implement the directives on an evolving basis.

The Constitution, however, establishes Congress as the legislative, or policy-making, branch of the government. As Congress provides EPA and other agencies with greater discretion, the question arises whether, at some point, Congress is delegating its legislative authority unconstitutionally to administrative agencies. Every federal environmental statute delegates policy decisions to EPA or other federal agencies. Consider, for example, the Clean Air Act's mandate that EPA set ambient air quality standards at a level "requisite to protect the human health" and allowing for "an adequate margin of safety." At first glance, this Congressional directive might seem relatively specific. But any effort to apply this directive to a particular pollutant raises scores of policy questions. Where even a slight level of pollution would injure a small population of sensitive people, must EPA set a zero standard, or can EPA focus on the average member of the population? How should EPA handle scientific uncertainty: if a minority of scientists believe that a pollutant is more dangerous than the current consensus view, what should EPA assume? What is an "adequate margin of safety"? As an agency's discretion increases, moreover, the agency inherently ends up making even broader policy decisions. Under the Federal Insecticide, Fungicide, and Rodenticide Act, for example, Congress authorizes EPA to license any pesticide that "will not generally cause any unreasonable risk to man or the environment," leaving EPA free to balance a broad set of policy interests.

Does the Constitution require Congress to provide administrative agencies with a minimum level of policy guidance? The temptation is to say "yes." Otherwise, Congress could escape making any controversial policy decisions and delegate to an administrative agency the authority to issue whatever regulations the agency concludes "promotes the public interest." Yet drawing a line between permissible and unconstitutional delegations is exceptionally difficult since any delegation gives an agency some policy discretion. By limiting Congress' authority to delegate regulatory authority, moreover, the courts risk undermining the effectiveness of the modern administrative state.

During the New Deal era, the Supreme Court invalidated a number of statutes for unconstitutionally delegating legislative authority to an administrative agency. In *Yakus v. United States*,[15] however, the Court upheld the Emergency Price Control Act of 1942, even though it gave the federal Office of Price Administration the authority to fix commodity prices at a level which, in the judgment of the Administrator, would be

---

15.   321 U.S. 414 (1944).

"generally fair and equitable and will effectuate the purposes of this Act." Broader delegations are hard to imagine, and the Court has never used the unconstitutional delegation doctrine to invalidate Congressional legislation since. In several cases, Chief Justice Rehnquist has suggested that the Court should use the doctrine to ensure that Congress is facing up to difficult policy decisions in the environmental field and not simply punting politically contentious issues to administrative agencies, but he has yet to convince a majority of the Court to begin policing Congress' judgment. Although the unconstitutional delegation doctrine occasionally rears its head, the doctrine appears dead for all practical purposes at the federal level.

In contrast to the federal courts, approximately a third of the state judiciaries still carefully police legislative delegations under their own constitutions. These courts typically require the state legislature to provide "adequate standards" or an "intelligible principle" to constrain the agency's decisions. Like Chief Justice Rehnquist, these state courts worry that, absent any constraint, legislatures will be tempted to duck tough policy decisions, abdicating their constitutional responsibility.

C. *Regulatory Takings*

The *just compensation provisions* of the United States Constitution, which prohibit the federal and state governments from "taking" private property without the payment of just compensation, also constrain environmental regulation. Although courts could have read the provisions as applying only to physical expropriations of property for highways and other governmental uses, the Supreme Court has held for over a century that regulations may also constitute takings for which compensation must be paid. The difficult trick, as courts have learned, is determining *when* a regulation goes too far and becomes a taking. Perhaps not surprisingly, many of the principal cases addressing this issue have involved environmental regulations.

The question of what constitutes a *regulatory taking* is one of the most difficult legal issues around. Take, for example, the argument that a landowner should be compensated for loss in property value because an endangered species has been listed that lives on her property. She now cannot develop part of her property and sell it. Part of the problem is that neither courts nor academic scholars can agree on *why* the Constitution should require the government to pay compensation for regulations that reduce the value of a landowner's property. Taking an economic approach, some courts and scholars argue that, absent compensation, the government may suffer from what has been labeled *fiscal illusion*. If the government does not have to pay compensation, it mistakenly may conclude that its regulations are costless, even where they destroy significant property value, and therefore over-regulate property. Other courts and scholars, by contrast, argue that compensation is a matter of fairness: a property owner should not have to bear the cost, for example, of preserving the habitat of an endangered species when neighboring landowners bear no cost at all and the habitat will benefit the general public. The arguments for providing compensation are multiple, and each unfortunately points to a different test for identifying regulatory takings.

For every argument in favor of compensation, moreover, there is a counter-argument. In response to the argument that the government will suffer from fiscal illusion if it does not have to pay compensation, other academic scholars have observed that property owners generally enjoy significant political power and are likely to make the cost of a proposed regulation very clear to the legislature. Legislatures thus are more likely to under-regulate property than to over-regulate it. As for the fairness argument, many courts and scholars would respond that property owners do not have the right to develop their land if it would destroy a species' essential habitat. By prohibiting the development, the government is not imposing a cost on the property owner but simply preventing the landowner from injuring the environment in a way that never was permissible.

Even assuming that there is a good argument for providing compensation, one has to worry about the potential costs of providing compensation. Environmentalists, for example, fear that Congress might hesitate to protect the environment if they had to pay every property owner who claimed that their land declined in value as a result. To many conservatives, this simply shows that the benefits of the environmental regulations do not justify their costs. But environmentalists would reply that the legislative process is not always rational and that large compensation payments may deter legislation even when the benefits exceed the costs. The government, moreover, must raise taxes to pay for any compensation, and economic studies have demonstrated that taxes often generate high welfare losses (e.g., by discouraging people from working).

Given these complexities, it should not be surprising that the Supreme Court has had trouble devising an easy test for when a regulation constitutes a taking and requires compensation. Indeed, in the late 1970s, the Court appeared to give up any hope of developing general guidelines for determining when a regulation is a taking. In *Penn Central Transportation Co. v. New York City*,[16] the Court confessed that it had been "unable to develop any 'set formula' for determining when 'justice and fairness' require that economic injured caused by public action be compensated by the government, rather than remain

---

16.   438 U.S. 104 (1978).

disproportionately concentrated on a few persons." The Court concluded that regulatory takings cases should be analyzed instead on an ad hoc, fact-specific basis in which courts balance (1) the extent of interference with "distinct investment-backed expectations," (2) the nature of the interference, and (3) the purposes of the governmental regulation. Over a quarter of a century of experience with the *Penn Central* balancing standard, however, has led to few regulations being overturned. Given the latitude, most courts appear to be unwilling to encumber governmental efforts to protect the environment and other public amenities by requiring the government to pay compensation if it wishes to regulate the actions of property owners.

In an attempt to bring greater certainty to regulatory takings doctrine (and perhaps to add a bit of backbone to the law), the Supreme Court in the late 20th century announced two "categorical takings tests" to supplement the *Penn Central* balancing standard. In several cases, the Court held that regulations constitute takings if they interfere with a property owner's "core" right to exclude others from her land. Thus, regulations that permit members of the public onto someone's property or that otherwise authorize a *permanent physical occupation* of the property are takings for which compensation must be paid. In *Lucas v. South Carolina Coastal Council*,[17] the Court also held that a regulation constitutes a taking if it deprives a landowner of *all* the economically viable use of her property. Because only preservation statutes are likely to deprive a landowner of the total economic use of her property, environmentalists worried that *Lucas* reflected an anti-environmental bias on the part of the Court.

At the turn of the 21st century, however, the Supreme Court does not appear anxious to apply these categorical takings tests to a broad set of regulations. Landowners have challenged a variety of regulations. Tellingly, landowners have never argued that pollution-control statutes such as the Clean Air Act are takings. By restricting the way in which property owners can use their land, pollution-control statutes potentially can reduce the value of some parcels. But no one contends in our society today that a landowner has the right to pollute. Because pollution-control statutes do not take any property right from the landowner, pollution-control statutes do not constitute takings, even if they lower the value of someone's land. By contrast, many landowners do believe that they have the right to develop their land even if it contains wetlands, habitat for endangered or threatened species, or other environmentally valuable resources. In their eyes, governmental protections of these lands therefore do raise takings issues.

17. 505 U.S. 1003 (1992).

Landowners have tried a variety of arguments in favor of compensation in these settings. In challenging federal and state endangered species protections, for example, landowners have argued that the government has authorized an unconstitutional physical occupation of their property by the endangered species. If the government cannot permit people to invade someone's land, landowners reason, how can the government authorize endangered species to do the same? Courts have rejected this argument on the ground that the species are native to the land and thus not the same as marauding members of the public. In theory, however, the cases might turn out differently if the government decided to transplant a species onto land that had not recently served as habitat or perhaps had never been habitat.

More commonly, property owners have challenged regulations as preventing them from developing a portion of their property and thus depriving them of all the economically viable use of that land in violation of *Lucas*. These challenges have raised the so-called "denominator question": how narrowly can a landowner define a parcel of land for purposes of applying *Lucas*. The government seldom prohibits a landowner from developing all of her land; as a result, the landowner retains some value. Unless *Lucas* applies to the specific subparcel of land that cannot be developed, the landowner thus loses.

In *Tahoe–Sierra Preservation Council v. Tahoe Regional Planning Agency*,[18] the Supreme Court reaffirmed that courts should examine the "parcel as a whole" in applying *Lucas*. In *Tahoe–Sierra*, the Tahoe Regional Planning Agency imposed a lengthy moratorium on the development of land near Lake Tahoe while the agency tried to determine how to protect the lake's water quality. The landowners challenged the moratorium, arguing that it temporarily deprived them of all the economically viable use of their land and therefore violated *Lucas*. The Court disagreed, rejecting the view that the land could be "conceptually severed" into different temporal pieces. Because the property retained longterm value, *Lucas* did not apply. In a similar vein, regulations that prohibit development of only a portion of a parcel of land are not categorical takings under *Lucas*. In all such cases, the regulation is a taking only if it fails the multi-factored *Penn Central* standard.

Should it matter in environmental takings cases if landowners purchase their property after the governmental regulatory system is in place? Assume, for example, that a landowner buys land in 1990—long after Congress awarded the Army Corps of Engineers authority to regulate wetlands—and is told in 2000 that she cannot develop any of her property, thus triggering *Lucas*, because it contains valuable wetlands. Is it fair to award her compensation given that she knew or should

---

18.   535 U.S. 302 (2002).

have known of the regulation? On the other hand, is it fair to let the government "off the hook" because the land recently changed hands? In *Palazzolo v. Rhode Island*,[19] the Supreme Court held that landowners who purchase property after a regulatory system is in place are not barred automatically from pursuing a takings claim. In concurring opinions, however, Justices O'Connor and Scalia disagreed on the relevance of the timing of the purchase. Justice O'Connor thought the timing should be relevant but not conclusive, while Justice Scalia argued that timing is totally irrelevant.

IV. How Citizen Groups Shape Environmental Law

Ask what has contributed the most to the development of a strong system of environmental regulation in the United States, and the most knowledgeable people are likely to point to the existence of a dynamic and forceful environmental movement. The United States has hosted an active environmental movement since soon after Henry David Thoreau moved to Walden Pond. When the Audubon Society (a predecessor to today's National Audubon Society) was formed in 1886, almost 40,000 people joined. Within the next fifty years, conservationists formed such important national organizations as the Sierra Club, the Izaak Walton League, and the Wilderness Society. By 1960, over 300,000 Americans belonged to the major conservation organizations. These organizations helped to establish the vast system of national parks, forests, and wilderness areas that grace the United States today and to pass early environmental legislation.

The first Earth Day in 1970, however, saw a major change and expansion in the American environmental movement. The number of environmental organizations increased geometrically. The focus of the environmental movement, moreover, broadened to include pollution and toxic substances. Borrowing from the Civil Rights movement, environmental groups also adopted a more activist stance, filing litigation and aggressively lobbying Congress and administrative agencies. A number of the new environmental organizations specifically emphasized legal change. Among the most prominent were the Environmental Defense Fund (formed in 1967 to get DDT banned), the Natural Resources Defense Council (formed in 1969 to help improve federal pollution laws), and the Sierra Club Legal Defense Fund (organized in 1971 to litigate cases on behalf of the environment).

A. *Lobbying for Legislative and Administrative Action*

The American environmental movement has played an essential role in the passage and implementation of effective environmental laws. Few

---

19.   533 U.S. 606 (2001).

political scientists would have predicted that the federal government would pass as strong laws as it has. Typically industrial opponents of environmental laws are well organized and can afford to invest substantial resources to defeat or weaken legislation. Few members of the general public, by contrast, have a sufficient enough interest in any particular piece of environmental legislation to devote equivalent resources to ensuring the legislation's passage. When asked to participate in a collective lobbying effort, moreover, many member of the public may be tempted to decline, presuming that they can "free ride" on the efforts of other members of the public.

The major environmental organizations in the United States have found effective means of overcoming these "collective action" obstacles. Environmental groups have raised substantial money from the public both by framing environmental issues in moral terms and by perfecting mass mailing campaigns. Although many people still free ride on others' donations, environmental groups have used their limited resources efficiently. Unlike industrial lobbyists, environmental organizations have been able to focus their resources entirely on environmental issues. Through coordinated lobbying campaigns, the organizations have provided Congress and state legislatures with valuable scientific and legal expertise. Through member communications and skilled use of the media, environmental organizations also have mobilized voters. As a result, the imprint of environmental organizations can be found throughout environmental law. The Natural Resources Defense Council, for example, helped pass the Clean Water Act. The Environmental Defense Fund helped devise the acid rain provisions of the 1990 Clean Air Act Amendments, including the provisions establishing a trading program in SO_2 emissions.

B.   *Citizen Suits*

Environmental organizations have played an equally important role through litigation. As explained already, environmental groups can obtain judicial review under the Administrative Procedure Act or underlying substantive statutes when EPA or other federal agencies take administrative actions that are inconsistent with the law or facts. The ability to pursue judicial review provides environmental organizations with considerable power in the administrative process. In deciding how to interpret and apply the law, EPA and other federal agencies recognize that environmental groups will sue if not satisfied with the agency action.

Every major federal environmental law passed since 1970 also has contained a *citizen suit* provision. (The lone exception is the Federal

Insecticide, Fungicide, and Rodenticide Act, which the agricultural committees in Congress, rather than the more receptive environmental committees, drafted.) Under the citizen suit provisions, individuals and organizations can pursue two new categories of lawsuits not authorized by the Administrative Procedure Act. First, they can sue anyone, either public and private, alleged to be in violation of an environmental law, serving in effect as private attorneys general. Environmental groups have used this opportunity actively both to supplement the government's limited enforcement resources and to pursue violations that the government is ignoring. When governmental enforcement efforts declined at the beginning of the Reagan Administration in the early 1980s, groups such as the Natural Resources Defense Council organized enforcement campaigns to take up the slack. Second, individuals or groups can sue the EPA administrator or other relevant governmental officials who are failing to carry out a non-discretionary Congressional obligation, such as the promulgation of a specific regulation. Environmental organizations used this provision frequently in the 1970s and 1980s to enforce deadlines that Congress had set for administrative action.

Although deadline lawsuits are less important today, the opportunity to bring private prosecutions remains extremely important. Statutes in other fields, such as antitrust and securities regulation, long have permitted private individuals to sue for damages where the plaintiffs have been injured by violations. In authorizing citizen suits under the federal environmental statutes, however, Congress for the first time called on private citizens to play a direct public role in enforcing the law. The purpose of citizen suits is not to provide compensation to the plaintiffs for injuries but to ensure more effective enforcement of environmental laws.

In authorizing individual citizens and environmental groups to serve as private prosecutors, Congress has been cautious to avoid making citizen suits into profit-making opportunities. Most of the citizen suit provisions permit citizens and environmental groups to pursue only injunctive relief. A few statutes authorize courts to impose monetary penalties in citizen suits, but the penalties are payable to the United States, not the private prosecutor. In practice, however, plaintiffs often settle their citizen suits on terms that include not only the cessation of violations, but also the payment of monies to the plaintiff or other organizations and agreements to engage in supplemental projects of benefit to the environment.

Citizen suit provisions do not permit private plaintiffs to prosecute every violation of an environmental law. First, for largely political reasons, Congress purposefully has excluded some violations from the purview of citizen suits. The Clean Air Act, for example, does not permit lawsuits to enforce many automobile standards. Second, the Eleventh

Amendment precludes plaintiffs from pursuing citizen suits against states if the suits seek monetary penalties, although purely injunctive actions (which have been far more important) are still permissible. Finally, most of the citizen suit provisions authorize lawsuits against persons "alleged to be in violation" of the underlying act. In *Gwaltney of Smithfield, Ltd. v. Chesapeake Bay Foundation*,[20] the Supreme Court unanimously interpreted this language to preclude citizen suits alleging only past violations; to prevail, a plaintiff ultimately must demonstrate a "state of either continuous or intermittent violation"—that is, "a reasonable likelihood that a past polluter will continue to pollute in the future." In response to *Gwaltney*, Congress in 1990 amended the citizen suit provision in the Clean Air Act to permit citizen suits against defendants "alleged to have violated (if there is evidence that the alleged violation has been repeated) or to be in violation."[21] Most federal environmental statutes, however, retain the original wording interpreted in *Gwaltney*.

In authorizing citizen suits, Congress also was worried about the confusion and conflicts that could result from simultaneous actions by both the government and private plaintiffs involving the same violation. As a result, citizen suit provisions prevent private plaintiffs from filing a lawsuit if the federal or state government has commenced and is "diligently prosecuting" a civil or criminal action or, under some statutes, has initiated at least some forms of administrative enforcement proceeding. To give the government an opportunity to pursue its own enforcement relief, plaintiffs also must provide the federal government, any involved state, and the alleged violator with notice of the alleged violation at least sixty days before filing a citizen suit. Courts are split on what happens if the government does not initiate an enforcement action before a citizen suit is filed, but subsequently enters into a consent decree with the defendant while the citizen suit is pending. Most courts have concluded that the consent decree bars the citizen suit if the decree reasonably ensures that the violation will not recur.

To help promote citizen suits, Congress has authorized courts to order defendants to reimburse prevailing plaintiffs for their litigation costs, including "reasonable" attorney fees. Courts calculate fee awards by taking the reasonable time that the plaintiff's attorney has spent on the citizen suit and then multiplying this figure by a reasonable attorney fee rate to get an amount known as the "lodestar." According to the Supreme Court, moreover, the reasonable rate for a public interest attorney is the rate that he or she would bill if in private practice, not the much lower amount that the attorney is paid by the environmental

20.   484 U.S. 49 (1987).

21.   Clean Air Act § 304(a)(1), 42 U.S.C.
§ 7604(a)(1).

organization. Although courts occasionally award more than the lodestar where the lodestar does not fully reflect the quality or competence of council or the case is particularly novel, the Supreme Court has indicated that such "multipliers" should normally not be awarded.

C. Standing

Whenever an environmental group or individual seeks judicial review or files a citizen suit, one of the first questions that the court will ask is whether the plaintiff has standing to sue. According to the Supreme Court, an individual generally must demonstrate four facts to establish standing. The first three requirements are constitutionally required by Article III of the United States Constitution and thus cannot be waived. First, the plaintiff must demonstrate that the challenged action has or will cause the plaintiff "injury in fact." Second, the plaintiff must show that this injury can be traced to the challenged action. Third, the plaintiff must show that the court, through some form of available relief, can redress the injury. The final requirement for standing is only "prudential," and therefore Congress can eliminate or alter it: the injury must be within the "zone of interests" that the underlying substantive statute is designed to protect. Where an organization sues, the organization must show not only that one or more of its members satisfy these standing requirements but also that the goal in seeking judicial relief is "germane to the organization's purposes." Thus, the Minnesota Elk Breeder's Association might have standing problems suing the National Marine Fisheries Service for failure to list a tuna species as endangered.

Are these multiple standing requirements all truly needed? Some academics have argued not. In their view, the question should be whether Congress has authorized individuals or organizations to seek judicial review or other relief in federal court. For example, where Congress has authorized "any person" to pursue environmental violators, as Congress has done in virtually every citizen suit provision, the courts should not erect roadblocks in the way of potential citizen prosecutors. A majority of the current Supreme Court, however, has suggested that standing rules are important for several reasons. First, standing requirements such as "injury in fact" ensure that there is justification for involving the courts in what otherwise might be a largely academic question. If no one has been hurt, judicial intervention is unnecessary. Second, the standing requirements ensure that the plaintiff has sufficient interest in the matter to provide adequate representation of the public interest. Finally, standing is a means of ensuring the separation of powers; absent injury in fact and the other standing findings, courts would be interfering unnecessarily in the discretion of the executive branch. Whether you agree with these arguments, and each has been challenged, they have led federal courts to throw a number of citizen suits and other cases out of court before any consideration of the merits of the actions. Indeed, environmentalists at times have worried that the courts have been trying to use standing to roll back decades of environmental activism.

Injury in Fact. Most standing disputes focus on the first requirement of injury in fact. The Supreme Court helped to promote environmental litigation in the early 1970s, and thus usher in stronger environmental protection, by adopting a broad view of what constitutes an injury in the environmental field. In *Sierra Club v. Morton,*[22] the Sierra Club challenged the Forest Service's approval of Walt Disney Enterprises' plan to develop a ski resort in the Sequoia National Forest. The Supreme Court held that the Sierra Club had not established standing to sue because it had not alleged that any of its members actually used the area of the proposed development and thus would be affected by Disney's plan. But the Court emphasized that standing did not require a showing of *economic* injury. For standing purposes, injuries can "reflect 'aesthetic, conservational, and recreational' as well as economic values" and can be widely shared among the population. All the Sierra Club needed to do therefore was to allege that its members would suffer aesthetic or recreational injury as a result of the proposed development (and that's exactly what the Sierra Club did on remand). Justice William O. Douglas would have gone further and allowed law suits to be filed "in the name of the inanimate object about to be despoiled, defaced, or invaded by roads and bulldozers and where injury is the subject of public outrage."

For almost two decades after *Sierra Club v. Morton,* the Supreme Court showed no interest in constructing standing barriers to environmental litigation. The so-called *SCRAP* case, decided a year after *Sierra Club v. Morton,* showed how far the Court was willing to go to find standing.[23] In *SCRAP,* a group of law students challenged an order of the Interstate Commerce Commission approving freight rates that they feared would discourage recycling. The students argued that they had standing because they camped, hiked, and fished in the Washington, D.C. metropolitan area and these activities would become less enjoyable if the freight rates went into effect, resulting in less recycling and therefore more litter and greater natural resource consumption. Although the Supreme Court held that "pleadings must be something more than an ingenious academic exercise in the conceivable" and recognized that the students' line of causation was a bit "attenuated," six members of the Court found that the students had standing. "The

22. 405 U.S. 727 (1972).

23. United States v. Students Challenging Regulatory Agency Procedures, 412 U.S. 669 (1973).

basic idea that comes out in numerous cases is that an identifiable trifle is enough for standing to fight out a question of principle; the trifle is the basis for standing and the principle supplies the motivation."

The current Court has not been as generous in granting standing. In *Lujan v. Defenders of Wildlife*,[24] for example, an environmental organization sought review of the Department of the Interior's decision that the Endangered Species Act does not extend to U.S. agency actions that affect endangered species overseas. Two of the organization's members submitted affidavits stating that they had previously traveled to overseas areas in which species were threatened by U.S. agency actions and that they hoped to go again. The Court concluded that such inchoate plans to return to the areas were inadequate to establish standing; only present and definite plans to return would provide the type of "actual or imminent" injury required for standing. The Court also held that a plaintiff could not establish standing simply because he or she had a professional or personal interest in studying or seeing an endangered species.

A critical question in *Lujan v. Defenders of Wildlife* and similar environmental cases is the degree to which Congress can provide standing for parties who traditionally would not have met the injury-in-fact requirement. In *Defenders of Wildlife*, the lower court had held that the plaintiffs had suffered a "procedural injury": the Endangered Species Act required agencies to consult with the Department of the Interior before taking actions that might jeopardize an endangered species, giving all citizens a "procedural right" to insist on a consultation. Four members of the Court concluded that a plaintiff has standing to vindicate such a procedural right only where disregard of that right also has impaired "a separate concrete interest." While agreeing that the plaintiffs had not established standing, Justices Kennedy and Souter suggested that "Congress has the power to define injuries and articulate chains of causation" that otherwise would not provide standing, but "Congress must at the very least identify the injury it seek to vindicate and relate the injury to the class of persons entitled to bring suit."

Redressability. The requirement that injuries be redressable by judicial action occasionally also trips up environmental plaintiffs. The Supreme Court, for example, has held that a plaintiff does not have standing to bring a citizen suit for environmental violations that have occurred entirely in the past, because neither of the remedies potentially available to the plaintiff (an injunction or a civil penalty payable to the government) could remedy any injury that the plaintiff suffered as a result of the past violation.[25] In a subsequent decision, however, the

24. 504 U.S. 555 (1992).

25. Steel Co. v. Citizens for a Better Environment, 523 U.S. 83 (1998).

Court held that an environmental organization has standing to seek civil penalties in the face of ongoing violations, even though any penalties awarded go to the government, because the penalties will deter future violations.[26]

Zone of Interests. The "zone of interests" requirement frequently becomes an issue where an industry group seeks to use the environmental laws to seek economic gain or to thwart governmental actions to improve the environment. In a number of lawsuits, for example, industry groups have tried to block the government from reforming grazing, timber, water, or other resource policies on the ground that the government had not prepared an environmental impact statement under the National Environmental Policy Act (NEPA). Lower federal courts have generally rejected these lawsuits on the ground that NEPA's purpose is to protect the environment, not the economic interest of industry. In other cases, however, courts have concluded that Congress intended to provide standing to industry organizations. In *Bennett v. Spear*,[27] for example, ranchers and irrigation districts, upset by the Department of Interior' decision to reduce their water deliveries because of endangered-species concerns, filed a citizen suit under the Endangered Species Act (ESA) claiming that the department had failed to perform nondiscretionary duties—using the "best scientific data available" and considering the economic impact of designating a particular area as "critical habitat" for a species. Borrowing the logic of the NEPA cases, the lower court held that the ranchers and districts did not have standing because the purpose of the ESA was to protect the environment. The Supreme Court, however, reversed. Noting that the citizen suit provision granted a right to file a citizen suit to "any person," the Court concluded that Congress had not meant to restrict who could bring a citizen suit but contemplated that industry groups might use the provision to avoid "overenforcement" of the law.

26. Friends of the Earth v. Laidlaw Environmental Services, 528 U.S. 167 (2000).

27. 520 U.S. 154 (1997).

*

PART II

Pollution Law

CHAPTER 4

Air Pollution

I. The Clean Air Act

Amidst our many environmental laws, the Clean Air Act Amendments of 1970[1] (the CAA) stand apart. A massive law, the CAA was also historic. Unlike earlier laws passed by Congress, the CAA boasted *uniform, national standards* covering a wide range of pollutants and sources. Passed just one year after we put a man on the Moon, the CAA reflected both the technological optimism of the times and the frustration with poor air quality in our cities (it was joked at the time that Pittsburgh's air was so dirty you had to floss your teeth after breathing).

With the passage of the CAA it was assumed that our nation's clean air problems would be largely solved within the decade. Over three decades and billions of dollars later, however, the CAA presents a curious contradiction. Overall, the air we breathe is cleaner than in 1970. With few exceptions, the concentrations of major air pollutants have dropped despite greatly increased economic activity. Yet many of our largest cities still fail to meet the clean air requirements of the CAA. How have we done so poorly by doing so well?

A review of the CAA provides a fascinating study of cooperative federalism, strategic choice of regulatory targets, and cutting-edge environmental policy instruments. To understand the CAA's structure, however, first requires a basic understanding of the air pollution problem. As with most environmental issues, the air pollution "problem" is actually a combination of many different problems. There are many kinds of air pollutants with varying environmental and health impacts. Some are highly mobile, some highly reactive. Apart from toxic air pollutants such as vinyl chloride, air pollution alone generally does not produce fatalities. More often, air pollution aggravates health problems through chronic exposure, increasing the incidence and severity of respiratory diseases such as bronchitis, pneumonia, and asthma.

---

1. 42 U.S.C. §§ 7401–7671q.

77

In cities, we are most concerned about the health effects from breathing smog (O_3), produced by reactions of nitrogen oxides (NOx) with volatile organic compounds (a broad class of hydrocarbons known as VOCs), from breathing carbon monoxide (CO), and from fine particulate matter. While some might dismiss the health threats from air pollution as a bothersome nuisance, we're not just talking about occasional sore throats and coughs. The American Lung Association reports that lung disease is the third-leading cause of death in the United States every year, killing over 330,000 people. More than 30 million Americans currently suffer from chronic lung disease and, over the last five years, the death rate for lung disease has risen faster than any of the other leading causes of death. Recent studies have also identified a strong correlation between fine particles and premature death.

Other common pollutants such as NOx and sulfur dioxide (SO_2) combine to form "acid rain," as well as contributing to the formation of fine particles. The concern with acid rain is direct harm not to human health but to nature, from acidic compounds formed by pollution that deposit many miles from the original emission source and can seriously injure trees and aquatic ecosystems. The German name for the impacts of acid rain, "Waldsterben," tersely describes the problem—"forest death."

From a regulator's perspective, the air pollution problem is made difficult because these air pollutants (and many others) arise from different sources. Vehicle emissions are responsible for all the CO and about half of NOx and VOCs. Power plants are major emitters of SO_2 and NOx. Incinerators and industrial sources are major sources of hazardous air pollutants but, perhaps surprisingly, so are small sources and motor vehicles. Moreover, these pollutants mix in the atmosphere, moving with the winds subject to local topography and climate but paying no heed to state and county lines.

If one thinks back to 1970, then, the architects of the CAA faced a formidable challenge. In place of the available common law nuisance actions, which necessarily provided only retrospective remedies and required proof of causation and harm, in place of a patchwork of state laws with poor effectiveness, the drafters of the CAA needed to create an overarching national law for an entire class of pollutants from disparate sources. Indeed this would be the *first* truly national pollution law. Congress needed to decide not only how clean we want our air to be, but how much are we willing to pay for clean air and who should pay for it. To clarify this challenge, consider how the law needed to address the policy questions posed by *what, how much, where,* and *how* to regulate.

What to Regulate

As a threshold matter, the CAA needed not only to identify which particular air pollutants to regulate (and therefore which not to regulate)

78

but whether the pollutants should be prioritized, regulating some of the more common pollutants differently, perhaps, than others.

How Much to Regulate

Once the pollutants were identified, the next obvious question was at what levels they should be regulated. Assuming we would not simply ban all air pollutants, which would play havoc with the economy, how much pollution should be allowed? Most people would say at a level that protects the public's health, but this begs the question of who "the public" is. Is the public's health represented best by the reasonable person, a John or Mary Doe, or by more sensitive populations, perhaps their asthmatic children? Protecting the former is surely less costly, but to what extent should we take costs into account when setting national standards to protect the public health? Is clean air an issue of individual rights? Should people have to move because the government in their region chose a low level of air pollution control?

Where to Regulate

Assuming we have decided on a permissible level for an air pollutant (e.g., 5 parts of SO_2 per million parts of air), we need to decide where we are talking about. In the air pollution context, ideally we want to regulate based on units of risk to individual receptors. That is, we want to regulate the harm to each one of us from the actual air we breathe outside (known as "ambient air"). The problem, though, is that we can't directly regulate the air each one of us breathes. Beyond the nuisance of having an EPA official follow you around with an air quality monitor, how would the regulator know how much pollution you can breathe without harm? Individuals have different sensitivities. And even if this were known, how would the pollution be traced back to specific sources? This would simply recreate the problem with reliance on the common law—the difficulty in proving causation. Because airsheds and wind patterns are not uniform, the same emission in some places causes more damage than in other places. If it's technically too difficult to regulate where the air is breathed, then we have to go upwind.

Put another way, regulators must determine the *optimal point* of regulation. In the pollution context, ideally one wants to regulate emissions from a particular power plant based on the pollution's impact on *each* individual. This is technically too difficult and expensive to determine, however. Short of that, we should seek to regulate the level of exposure to classes of people (accepting that individuals have different sensitivities) but this, too, is hard to do. Moving further upstream, the next best site to regulate would be the ambient concentration (realizing that airsheds and wind patterns are not uniform), and finally at the level of particular emission sources (the site we actually do regulate). Recognize that at each step further from the ideal point of regulation, the regulatory target less accurately reflects what we care about as it relies on proxies, moving from the ideal regulation of harm to individual receptors, to populations, to ambient air concentrations, to tons of emissions.

Indeed, environmental law relies almost entirely on proxy measures. In the case of power plant emissions, for example, what we care about is the environmental and consequential social impact of acid deposition, but we do not regulate or trade units of acid rain impact. Technically it is too difficult. While it is clear that combustion of high sulfur coal (primarily by utilities) results in SO_2 emissions that are carried northeast by the prevailing winds, it is not well understood how these emissions mix in the atmosphere, how long they stay in the atmosphere, or where exactly they eventually deposit. More important, the significance of variable local factors on the ecological impact of acid rain, such as a heavy snow pack, soil condition, etc., are not well known. Instead we use the proxy of tons of sulfur emitted at the smokestack, hundreds of miles from where the impact will be felt. This is assumed to be a sufficient indicator of potential impact on social welfare. Regulating at the source of emission is less environmentally meaningful than at the point of impact, the receptor, but cost and technological constraints force our hand.

Note that even though the ultimate point of regulation is quite far downstream from our ultimate concern (in this case the impacts of acid deposition), it still may be optimal once technological limitations and costs are taken into account if a close correlation exists between a source's emissions and the risk to individuals, trees, or aquatic life. In practical terms, the regulated party needs to know if it is in compliance, and this requires some kind of standard set at the source (e.g., a municipal incinerator needs to know how many tons of SO_2 it may emit per year). Since our concern is ambient air quality, though, we're still faced with the challenge of figuring out how each of the many sources' emissions combine and determining the quality of the downwind air when it is breathed. Hence complex modeling is used to justify state implementation plans under the Clean Air Act.

How to Regulate

In part because the CAA was the first modern pollution law and in part because air pollution is such an important problem, the CAA has provided fertile ground for a whole range of policy approaches. Given the many different sources of air pollutants, which mix of regulatory tools will work best? Should mobile sources (e.g., cars and trucks) be regulated differently than stationary sources such as incinerators and power plants? Should new sources be treated differently than sources in operation when the law was passed? Since air pollution pays no heed to state lines, uniform national standards for air pollutants would seem to make a lot of sense, but is treating every location in the country the same economically efficient? In political terms, what role do such national standards leave for the states?

The CAA passed in 1970 (actually amending an earlier CAA from 1963) and, with its subsequent amendments in 1977 and in 1990, had to address all of these challenges, and more. As a result, it is a massive piece of legislation. Indeed some professors spend almost their entire survey course covering *only* the CAA! Much of the CAA can be understood as the product of what might be called "cooperative federalism," as a dynamic balance between federal standard setting and state implementation. Once you understand which areas were reserved purely for federal regulation, the CAA starts to make more sense. The basic structure of the CAA is outlined on page 83.

A.　*National Ambient Air Quality Standards (NAAQS)*

The keystone of the CAA is its treatment of the most common pollutants of concern in the outside air, and most of the CAA's provisions are driven by its regulation of these so-called *criteria pollutants*. Defined as pollutants that are emitted from numerous or diverse sources and that can endanger public health or welfare, criteria pollutants include many of the pollutants mentioned above—O_3, NOx, CO, fine particles, SO_2—as well as lead.[2] The CAA requires that these pollutants not exceed uniform levels at *any* outside point to which the public has access. Thus the standards don't apply indoors or on private land.

These National Ambient Air Quality Standards (NAAQS) are set for each criteria pollutant at a level that must "protect the public health" with an "adequate margin of safety."[3] But what constitutes an adequate margin of safety and *whose* health is the public health? These questions were addressed in the case, *Lead Industries Association v. EPA.*[4] Here, in setting the NAAQS for lead, EPA chose a very vulnerable target population—inner-city children. The court upheld this choice and allowed the agency to err on the side of caution in determining an adequate margin of safety. NAAQS levels must be based solely on health considerations and the agency may not consider economic or technical feasibility (though it is interesting to note that EPA refused to choose the *most* vulnerable population—those inner-city children who had high blood-

---

2. 42 U.S.C. § 7408(a)(1).

3. These are known as "primary air quality standards." As noted below, "secondary air quality standards" must be set at levels that protect property and the environment.

4. Lead Industries Association v. EPA, 647 F.2d 1130 (D.C.Cir.1980), *cert. denied,* 449 U.S. 1042 (1980).

lead levels from other sources, such as paint). The requirement of basing the NAAQS on health and not cost was recently reaffirmed in the *American Trucking Associations v. EPA* case.[5]

5. American Trucking Associations v. EPA, 531 U.S. 457 (2001).

EPA

NAAQS §§108, 109	**NSPS** §111	**NESHAPS** §112	**Mobile Sources** §202	**Acid Rain** §§401-416
Harm-based ambient standards for criteria pollutants	new stationary source requirements	identification and emission standards for hazardous air pollutants	vehicle emissions standards; fuel content / clean fuels	Emissions trading
"protect the public health" with "adequate margin of safety"		"ample margin of safety to protect public health"	technology forcing	

EPA must approve SIP or submit a FIP in its place

STATES

SIPS §110	
state implementation plan to meet the NAAQS based on modelling	state Inspection/Monitoring programs
must include monitoring, enforcement, etc.	

83

There are actually two types of NAAQS. *Primary standards*, described above, protect human health while *secondary standards* protect the public welfare, broadly defined to include effects on animals, wildlife, water, and visibility.[6] EPA is required to review these NAAQS and make appropriate revisions at least every five years. In practice, however, EPA has been very reticent to do so because of the tremendous political and economic costs involved. Indeed there have been only seven NAAQS established. As a result, environmental groups have had to sue EPA on a number of occasions to initiate reviews and, even when the reviews have been initiated, EPA has generally chosen to retain the current standards, notwithstanding the recent EPA decision to propose an NAAQS for smaller particulate matter.

The uniform application of NAAQS to all regions of the nation and EPA's inability to consider their costs and benefits have been criticized by some as inefficient. The health impacts of dirty air clearly vary from place to place, as do the costs of control. Just think of setting the NAAQS for lead emissions based on the target population of inner-city children. By setting a uniform national standard to protect the most vulnerable population (and assuming the standard is accurately set), this will necessarily lead to "overprotection" of people in much of the country. Indeed, it does seem odd to mandate the same level of pollutants in an inner city as in a sparsely inhabited valley (unless, perhaps, that valley happens to be the Grand Canyon). Given this seeming inefficiency, why would Congress choose a uniform approach over air quality standards that vary from region to region?

The NAAQS approach provides a classic example of inflexible but easily-administered standards. Such "one-size-fits-all" standards make it easier for an agency to establish, monitor, and enforce than the more flexible and tailored local standards that vary from place to place. Local standards are also, one would expect, more susceptible to local political pressure than national standards, and some areas would certainly resent having lower air quality standards than others.

From a health perspective, given our uncertainties in epidemiology and growing understanding of the health effects of air pollutants, a standard that seemed overprotective a decade ago may not seem so today. Moreover, despite the prohibition of cost considerations, given the nature of the political process perhaps it is unrealistic to assume that the costs of compliance and its effect on jobs and local economies would not enter into the NAAQS standard setting, even if only indirectly and unofficially.

6. 42 U.S.C. §§ 109(b)(1) & (2).

Another major reason for the uniform NAAQS approach is that it stifles potential interstate competition for industry. A driving force behind the CAA was the historic failure of state programs to control air quality and the consequent fear that, absent national standards, states might be willing to sacrifice air quality for economic growth. In other words, because there existed no national clean air requirements prior to the CAA, each state was free to set standards as it wished. This made it potentially easy for states to become "pollution havens," offering lax environmental standards in exchange for an influx of new industries and jobs. This could encourage an environmental "race-to-the-bottom," much as Delaware has led the race to create a corporate friendly state, sacrificing air quality for economic growth or, worse for industry, the potential of a "race-to-the-top." There has been a vigorous debate over whether environmental races to the bottom actually occur, but national standards made the point moot.

1. State Implementation Plans (SIPs)

In practice, the inflexible and uniform approach of the NAAQS has been tempered in implementation. EPA sets ambient air quality standards nationwide, and each state then has the responsibility of setting emission standards that will result in attainment and maintenance of those standards. Each state is required to submit a State Implementation Plan (SIP) that demonstrates how the NAAQS will be achieved by the deadline dates established in the statute.[7] In principle, the SIP should satisfy the NAAQS while taking into account local conditions, thus allowing a degree of flexible, site-specific standards. In fact, the opportunity for local adaptation is even greater because there are 250 areas in which NAAQS are measured, known as air quality control regions. In simple terms, a state creating a SIP must first inventory the current emissions from sources within a region, choose control strategies for reductions, and then demonstrate through computer modeling that the SIP will satisfy the NAAQS levels.

On its face, this is a broad grant of authority, giving the states a great deal of freedom to allocate emissions. In practice, however, exceptions in the CAA serve to take back to the federal government much of what it had seemed to give away. New Source Performance Standards, described later, establish federal standards for new sources and major modifications of existing sources. Existing sources that do not increase emissions must employ federally-mandated "reasonably achievable control technologies" if located in areas have not met the NAAQS. And emission standards for motor vehicles are set by the federal government (with a narrow exception for California).

7. 42 U.S.C. § 7410.

What's left then for the states to do? Primarily tighten the standards on existing sources through permitting. Any stationary source emitting 100 tons or more of a pollutant, 10 tons per year or more of a hazardous air pollutant, or 25 tons per year or more of combined hazardous air pollutants must have a permit to operate issued by the state. In deciding whether to approve a SIP, EPA may only consider the overall question of whether the SIP will satisfy the NAAQS. As the *Union Electric Company v. EPA* case stated, *how* permits are issued to ensure the SIP satisfies the NAAQS, whether by forcing certain companies to go bankrupt or greatly increasing the emissions for others, may not be considered so long as the CAA is not violated.[8] With few exceptions, EPA can only look at the overall question of whether the NAAQS will be met, not every permit the state issues. Thus states have great discretion to achieve their NAAQS through regulating existing sources. And the differences from state to state can be striking. According to their SIPs, a coal plant in Ohio can emit 20 times more SO_2 than a similarly sized plant in Connecticut.

If EPA believes the SIP will not achieve the NAAQS, EPA may start a process that effectively supplants the SIP and requires the state to comply with a Federal Implementation Plan (FIP) prepared by EPA. A FIP was developed for Los Angeles in the 1970s but was extremely controversial, as any proposed curbs on land use or driving naturally would be. Indeed Congress subsequently took away EPA's authority to impose a FIP on Southern California. Since then there have been occasional threats of other FIPs, but in practice the FIP has largely been a paper tiger because of EPA's budget constraints.

Non-attainment

Unfortunately, for both political and economic reasons many SIPs have been unable to achieve the "clean air" levels required by the NAAQS, and some cities remain out of compliance with the NAAQS. The term for this is *non-attainment* and it has been the most challenging aspect of the CAA's history. Non-attainment has been most serious in Southern California, where smog alerts have become a standard part of the weather forecast. In fact, Los Angeles holds the distinction of *never* having been in attainment for ozone, though a suburb of Houston recently took pride of place as the most polluted city in the country. Students often get confused over the concept of non-attainment. When navigating the CAA universe, remember that for *each criteria pollutant* you are either in a non-attainment area or in an attainment area. Where you live, for example, might be in non-attainment for ozone but in attainment for CO.

8. Union Electric Company v. EPA, 427
U.S. 246 (1976).

EPA's quiver to deal with noncompliance has never had many arrows. The threat of a FIP, as discussed above, is available but rarely used. EPA could deny a state in non-attainment federal highway and sewage treatment funds and, in the past, simply ban new construction. The CAA also requires that new stationary sources in non-attainment areas employ control technologies with the "lowest achievable emissions rates" and that existing sources use "reasonably available control technologies." In practice, though, forcing compliance in the face of state opposition has proven difficult, and throughout the 1970s and 1980s the EPA and the states basically muddled along through strategic delays in quest of the increasingly frustrating goal of attainment for criteria pollutants such as ozone, CO and NOx. The CAA of 1970 had called for states to meet the NAAQS by 1975 (with the possibility of two years in administrative reprieves) and secondary standards within a "reasonable time." The 1977 Amendments pushed the compliance deadlines into the 1980s, and the 1990 Amendments pushed the deadlines out again.

In retrospect, this recurring postponement was inevitable given the economically disruptive, massive efforts required for some areas to move into attainment. As an example, consider EPA's 1988 study of the steps necessary to bring Los Angeles into attainment. The EPA concluded that in order to achieve the NAAQS, the SIP "would have to prohibit most traffic, shut down major business activity . . . [and] destroy the economy of the South Coast, so that most of the population would be forced to resettle elsewhere." Not a politically likely move.

The ad hoc accommodation with failure changed, however, when the 1990 Clean Air Act Amendments broke down the goal of attainment into achievable, intermediate steps. Non-attainment areas were divided into five categories, from Marginal, Moderate and Serious to Severe and Extreme. As the level of non-attainment increases, the requirements become more onerous. Taking the example of ozone non-attainment, those areas in Moderate non-attainment must show 3% emissions reduction per year, establish transport control measures, and institute a clean fuels program to reduce VOCs, among other requirements. Areas that are in Extreme non-attainment (i.e., Los Angeles) must do all of this as well as other steps such as offsetting the growth in vehicle emissions by reducing emissions elsewhere. By breaking down the goal of attainment into discrete requirements, SIPs no longer had to meet the NAAQS in one fell swoop. Instead they must only demonstrate "reasonable further progress" as required by the EPA Administrator.

B. New Source Performance Standards (NSPS) and Grandfathered Sources

In the earlier discussion over *where* to regulate, we set out the dilemma of whether to regulate at the source of pollution (the smokestack) or at the point of impact (where the air is breathed). In fact, the CAA does both. The NAAQS regulate at the point of the air we breathe. But the rest of the CAA regulates the emissions of smokestacks and vehicles as an indirect means of influencing the quality of the ambient air. Presumably the tighter the standards of emissions, the better the quality of the air we breathe.

As we have seen, the SIP process allows states to impose restrictions on emissions from stationary sources such as incinerators, power plants, and industrial sites. Section 111 of the CAA, however, shields many of these sources from state control by requiring EPA to set emission standards for pollutants from new or modified stationary sources. These New Source Performance Standards (NSPS) have now been determined for over 70 categories of facilities and apply to "major sources" or major modifications. These emission limits are technology-based, reflecting the best pollution control technologies currently available in the industry. This indirectly ensures costs will be taken into account, since presumably exorbitant control technologies wouldn't be commercially feasible.

By its very name, the NSPS provision assumes that new and existing stationary sources should be treated differently. But why, given that both cause pollution? One might argue that high standards for new facilities promote technological development, creating a market by forcing new sources to employ the best available technologies commercially available. But this would apply equally well if older facilities were also covered. Part of the reason was clearly political. By limiting federal performance standards to new sources, the CAA carved out an important exemption for classes of facilities that were already operating at the time of the act's passage. These "grandfathered" plants do not have to meet the NSPS requirements unless they undertake major modifications, as defined in the Act. For utilities, grandfathering has allowed older power plants to emit 4 to 10 times more SO_2 and NOx per megawatt–hour than new sources. In this way, the CAA shifted the bulk of pollution control costs from existing businesses onto market entrants.

To be fair, this grandfather exemption seemed quite reasonable at the time, given the high costs of retro-fitting existing plants. And it would not be of longterm importance, it was assumed, since the grandfathered plants would shut down over time to make way for more modern, efficient, and cleaner facilities. At least that was the plan. Consider, though, whether grandfathering can create an incentive to keep older facilities operating as long as possible. What would you do if you owned a major facility that was grandfathered and wanted to increase its capacity while avoiding NSPS requirements? Might you try to use regular maintenance and repairs as an opportunity to gradually rebuild the plant, classifying these as minor improvements rather than major modifications? In recent litigation, the EPA alleged that this is exactly what a number of utilities had done over the last 30 years, violating the spirit and intent of the CAA.

Even if one chooses to regulate new and existing plants differently, why reserve the regulation of major new sources to the federal government rather than to the states through the SIP process? This certainly would give the states more flexibility in achieving the NAAQS. In pure cost terms, national NSPS standards make sense because it is much more efficient for the EPA than for 50 separate states to obtain knowledge of the technical capability of industries to control pollutants. One might imagine, as well, that powerful local industries would have more influence at the state level to lobby for lax standards than at the national level (though this is debatable). Perhaps most important, setting national standards for new sources and major modified sources stifles potential interstate competition for industry. It would seem odd, indeed, to battle the dangers of a race-to-the-bottom by mandating a uniform, national strategy of NAAQS while, at the same time, allowing states eager for economic growth to entice major new facilities with the lure of lax emissions standards.

C.   *Mobile Sources and Technology–Forcing*

Mobile sources, including cars, trucks, buses, etc., are major sources of air pollutants. Vehicle emissions currently contribute to over half of CO, almost half of NOx, and over one–quarter of VOC levels. Most of the areas that are currently not in compliance with ozone and CO standards fail primarily because of automobile emissions. Remove cars from Los Angeles and air quality won't be nearly as big a problem, though getting to the beach and Disneyland may.

Title II of the CAA regulates mobile sources, not only setting standards for tailpipe emissions but, depending on the region of the country, requiring cleaner fuels (such as reformulated gasoline with methanol and ethanol), carpool and fleet vehicle programs for large employers, and the accordion-like pumps you find at gas stations (for fuel vapor recovery). We have done a good job of reducing the levels of pollutants from mobile sources (particularly given that the number of automobiles has gone up over the last three decades). Lead in the air has decreased by over 90% and VOCs are down, as well, so next time you fill up your tank, you should thank Title II! At the same time, however, substantial challenges remain. Some predict that many cities in the U.S. will never be able to meet NAAQS for ozone until mobile emissions are cut drastically.

The CAA could have given states authority to set mobile source standards and therefore more flexibility in meeting the NAAQS. As with the NSPS, though, Congress chose to give this power to EPA. Unlike the NAAQS or NSPS, however, it hardly seems plausible that states would compete for industry through regulating car emissions. Given the weak race-to-the-bottom concerns, why set national standards for mobile sources? It's more economically efficient, since the government is better placed to determine the capability of the auto industry to reduce emissions than individual states, but this is hardly an overwhelming argument. The main reason, it turns out, appears to have been that the auto industry *wanted* national standards enacted into law rather than having to meet a patchwork of state requirements. Manufacturing different cars for different states would wreak havoc with the economies of scale possible through large production lines. In recognition of Southern California's ozone problem, though, Title II provides a limited exemption for California to increase the stringency of its mobile source requirements.

The history of mobile sources provides the classic example of "technology-forcing." The 1970 act required a 90% reduction of VOCs and CO emissions in car exhaust by 1975, and a 90% reduction of NOx by 1976. Strong medicine for Detroit, and stronger still because no technologies were commercially available to achieve these standards. So why did Congress set such tough standards? Part of it was technological optimism, coming just one year after landing a man on the Moon. Part was corporate cynicism, since the Department of Justice had recently settled an antitrust conspiracy case against the "Big Three" auto-makers for working together to suppress emission control technologies. And part was Congress's judgment of what was needed to protect the public health. Unless the standards were met the EPA had authority to shut down the auto industry. Over EPA opposition, Congress extended the deadlines, but by the early 1980s the standards had been met through adoption of the catalytic converter.[9]

This type of approach, called technology-forcing or "aspirational commands," is a regulatory version of high-stakes chicken. Auto-makers surely knew that Congress would never allow EPA to shut down the industry, but were they willing to take that risk? And what kind of treatment would the auto-makers get if Congress did adjust the standards? Technology-forcing approaches provide a powerful means to move beyond incremental technological improvement, but also require strong political support to ensure a credible threat in case the goals are not met. Without credible sanctions, there is a perverse incentive in favor of collective non-compliance and *against* reducing emissions, since those that comply and spend money to reduce emissions on time will be at a competitive disadvantage if others who delay do not have to incur the

---

9. International Harvester Co. v. Ruckelshaus, 478 F.2d 615 (D.C.Cir.1973).

same costs. Perhaps of greater concern, in forcing technology the government may actually force the *wrong* technology. Making use of its Title II exemption, for example, in the 1990s California tried to force the introduction and sale of "zero-emission vehicles" (electric cars). Despite millions of dollars spent by auto-makers to develop these cars and build charging stations around Los Angeles, consumers were not interested and the market seems to be moving on in favor of "hybrid" vehicles that rely on gas.

The regulation of mobile sources demonstrates two other important policy issues—there are often multiple ways of addressing a problem, and tradeoffs are inevitable. Consider, for example, an acronym with which you may be familiar, CAFE, standing for *corporate average fuel economy*. CAFE is not mandated by the CAA but, instead, by the 1975 Energy Policy and Conservation Act. This law requires that manufacturers' vehicle fleets today must average 27.5 miles per gallon in highway driving. That's why you see the sticker on the window of new cars with a miles per gallon number. Environmentalists have been pushing for years for this level to be raised (or even applied to sport utility vehicles, which must meet the much lower standard of 20.7 miles per gallon set for light trucks). Assuming no increase in miles traveled, an improvement in fuel efficiency would cause a clear reduction in greenhouse gases and other vehicle pollutants. To date, however, automotive interests have successfully opposed increasing CAFE stringency.

There is, however, another risk to consider. The least expensive way for car manufacturers to improve a car's fuel efficiency is to make the car lighter, thus requiring less energy to move it. The problem is that this can reduce the crashworthiness. The Institute of Highway Safety finds that more than twice as many people die in accidents in small cars than in large cars. This is hardly surprising, since one would be even safer if driving a tank. The problem is that increasing the CAFE can result in a "risk-risk" tradeoff, trading reduced vehicle pollution for increased severity of auto accidents. An increase in a car's fuel efficiency need not, of course, necessarily reduce crashworthiness, but it is a possibility that regulators cannot ignore.

D. *Trading*

The unceasing pressure over the last three decades to improve our nation's air quality has provided a valuable opportunity for experimentation and fine-tuning the CAA's regulatory approaches. This is most evident in the area of trading, where the experiences under the CAA have truly influenced environmental policy around the globe.

Two key challenges to implementation of the CAA have been how to (1) clean up the nation's air at lowest cost while at the same time (2) allowing increased economic growth and the pollution this will create. Put simply, how can the government minimize the cost of meeting a particular pollution goal? And how can the government reduce the pollution in a non-attainment area while permitting the number of sources to increase? The government has achieved these goals by clever use of market instruments to develop trading mechanisms. In principle, these trading systems achieve the goals of the CAA at a lower cost than direct regulation of each source.

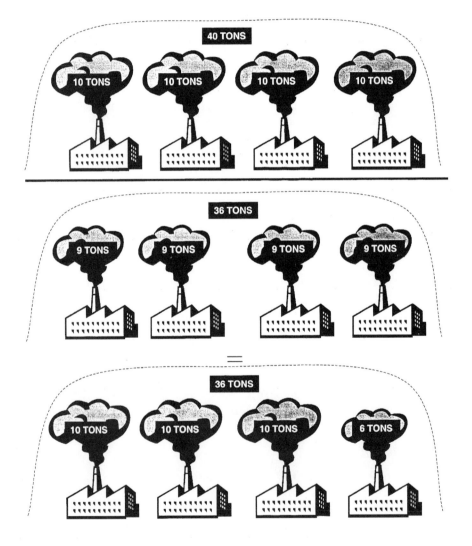

BUBBLING

Bubbling is the simplest form of trading. As shown in the previous figure, imagine that you manage an industrial site with 4 plants, each of which has a smokestack; each smokestack emits 10 tons per year of NOx, for a total of 40 tons $(10+10+10+10)$. The state SIP requires a 10% reduction in emissions. You clearly could comply by now emitting one ton less from each smokestack $(9+9+9+9)$. But if some of the plants are more efficient than others, this uniform approach would be costly. It would be less expensive to reduce emissions from the least efficient plant. If one of your plants was inefficient and could more easily reduce 4 tons, should you be allowed to take all the reductions from this plant and none from the others $(10+10+10+6)$? After all, the total emissions from your site have still been reduced by 10%. By drawing an imaginary bubble over your manufacturing site, and regulating only the total emissions from the bubble, EPA says you can.

And it goes farther. In a similar practice known as *netting*, facilities can increase emissions by one source in the facility but avoid permitting requirements for major modifications by reducing a similar amount of emissions from another on-site source. If, in placing a giant bubble over the facility, the regulator does not see a net increase in emissions then the facility has succeeded in avoiding the costs of permitting requirements while maintaining air quality. Through bubbling and netting, multiple emission sources are treated as a single source. By placing the imaginary bubble over a facility, separate smokestacks underneath can trade with one another and take advantage of the different marginal costs of reduction within the site.

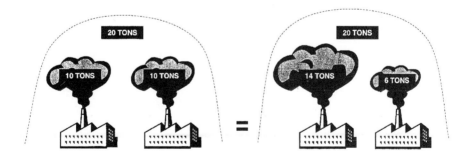

NETTING

More sophisticated trading systems allow separate facilities to trade rights to pollute. The government first decides how much pollution in total to allow. The government next allocates *pollution allowances* among the regulated facilities. Finally, the government establishes a set of rules governing the exchange of pollution allowances among facilities. Facilities that find it relatively expensive to reduce their emissions and need more than their allotted allowances then can purchase additional allowances from facilities that can reduce their emissions more readily. In the end, total emissions will be reduced to the level mandated by the government, but by allowing firms to trade allowances, the government can reduce the overall cost of achieving the reduction.

The CAA's first use of trading (indeed the first use in any environmental law) focused on reducing lead in gasoline. EPA began phasing out lead in gasoline in 1982. To try to reduce the economic cost of the lead phase out, EPA allocated lead content credits among gasoline refiners and allowed refiners to trade the lead content credits or bank them for later use or trading. Refiners were required to have sufficient credits to cover the lead additives in the gasoline they produced. If they did not have enough credits to cover the lead additives they were using, they needed to go on the market and buy more credits from other refiners. The key to this, and all such trading programs, is that the total number of credits available is capped at the desired regulatory level.

Offsets occur within a non-attainment area and rely on both the idea of bubbling and the trading of pollution rights. In simple terms, offsets create a bubble over an air quality region. A new source (or old source with a major modification) may not pollute *unless* it offsets its emissions by reductions from other existing sources in the region. For example, a new source that will emit 10 tons of NOx must offset this amount by paying an existing source in the airshed to reduce its emissions by 10 tons. Thus the reductions from the existing source are offset against the emissions of the new source, resulting in *no net increase* in total emissions within the region. By forcing the source of the new emissions to buy reductions from current sources, offsets permit economic growth in a non-attainment area while maintaining air quality.

The 1990 CAA amendments built on the use of offsets by requiring increasingly stringent offset ratios depending on the level of non-attainment. Thus new sources in marginal non-attainment areas must offset at a ratio of 1.1:1 (e.g., offset 11 tons of current emissions in order to emit 10 tons from the new source) while sources in extreme non-attainment areas must offset at a ratio of 1.5:1 (find 15 tons of current emissions to retire in order to emit 10 tons from the new source). Through this mechanism, new sources end up *reducing* overall emissions in non-attainment areas. States have gotten into the act, as well. Virginia's SIP, for example, required the state Highway Department to decrease usage of a certain type of asphalt, thereby reducing hydrocarbon pollution, by more than enough to offset the expected pollution from a new refinery.[10]

Offsets also provide an example of some of the unexpected problems that can arise when market mechanisms are added to existing regulatory programs. Recall that all of this trading is taking place subject to the requirements of the CAA. Because the CAA effectively bars states from regulating mobile or new stationary sources, in creating its SIP the state eagerly seeks opportunities to reduce criteria pollutants from existing sources. Do you see how offsets might play into the state's hands? Assume your plant could reduce its emissions at low cost and, for the right price, you would be willing to sell these as offsets to a new source in the region. But you have a problem. How will interested buyers know you have offsets to sell? If you make it public knowledge, you may have interested buyers knocking at your door, but don't be surprised if you find state regulators knocking, as well, and informing you that, to meet the new SIP requirements, your permit coincidentally requires you to reduce your emissions by the amount you had planned to sell as offsets. Primarily for this reason, the vast majority of offset trades have been *within* companies rather than arms-length transactions.

The CAA's treatment of acid rain has resulted in the most comprehensive trading program in the world and provides a nice example of clean air politics. The term, "acid rain," describes the atmospheric transport and deposition of sulfur and nitrous oxides, and the resulting ecological damage to forests, lakes and streams. Acid rain has been the subject of a charged political and scientific debate since the 1970s. The basic premise has been that Midwest power plants, burning high sulfur coal, have been primarily responsible for the acidification and forest thinning in the conifer forests of the Northeast and Canada. The history of how to deal with the acid rain problem presents a fascinating regional political battle between "dirty coal" Appalachian states, injured upwind states, and "clean coal" Western states. This is one case where a simple clean air regulation mandating strict smokestack emissions would immediately create big winners and big losers. But politically such a simple result was unacceptable.

Early on, it was recognized that Midwestern coal-burning power utilities would have to be regulated. Their heavy reliance on high-sulfur coal, coming from the Midwest and northern Appalachia, was a prime source of SO_2 emissions. The initial reaction to the NAAQS for SO_2, as well as for some other pollutants, was almost comical—sources built very tall smokestacks. While this eliminated many of the problems for the

10. Citizens Against Refinery's Effects, Inc. v. EPA, 643 F.2d 183 (4th Cir.1981).

SIPs of the polluting states by dispersing the pollution, it made the overall problem of acid rain much worse because it increased long-range transport of the pollutants. The 1977 CAA Amendments forced the SIPs to include emissions from tall smokestacks, but this now raised a political problem. After taller smokestacks, the next cheapest way to cut sulfur emissions would be to burn low-sulfur coal plentiful in the western United States. This, however, would be an economic blow to local communities in the Appalachians where high-sulfur coal is mined (recall that Robert Byrd, a senator from West Virginia, was majority leader in the Senate at the time). In a compromise, rather than imposing a performance-based standard (e.g., X tons of SO_2 emitted per year) the 1977 CAA Amendments mandated a uniform technology-based solution. All utilities had to employ "scrubbers," expensive pollution control technologies that remove sulfur from smokestack emissions.

This uniform requirement of scrubbers seemed absurd for many plants already using low-sulfur coal. One might argue that it was equivalent to a track coach requiring all runners to use crutches, even though only a few of the runners had injuries. In any case, as a political solution, it worked. The PSD program (described *infra*) played a role, as well, since its requirement to use best available control technology for new power plants made it easier for states to justify the use of scrubbers.

Fast forward to 1990. George H.W. Bush is now in office, a president who ran on an environmental platform. The majority leader in the Senate, George Mitchell, is from Maine, an upwind state that has suffered from acid rain for decades. Repealing the uniform requirement of scrubbers, the 1990 CAA Amendments instituted performance-based standards and the first national program of tradable emissions allowances.[11] The program was designed to reduce SO_2 emissions by 10 million tons per year beginning in the year 2000, a more than a 50% reduction compared to 1990. It also provided for NOx reduction of 2 million tons. Starting in 1995, 111 large plants in 21 states were covered. In 2000, all power plants in the country were subject to the program.

How does it work? EPA limits the annual emissions from stationary sources. It also creates a new kind of property right known as an "allowance." One allowance represents an emission of one ton of SO_2 over a year. Thus, for example, a power plant may have a permit allowing it to emit 25 tons of SO_2 per year. Similar to the lead trading program, a power plant may not emit 25 tons of SO_2 without 25 allowances. If the plant's emissions exceed its allowances, it must buy the excess in allowances the next year to "pay back" it debt as well as pay a civil fine per ton exceeded. The total number of allowances available is set at the total level of desired emissions. Thus far fewer

11. 42 U.S.C. § 7651.

allowances were available in the year 2000 than had been at the start of the program. This not only results in a gradual lowering of SO_2 emissions, but it allows market mechanisms to allocate the emissions. Anyone who wants to emit more than their allowances has to buy them from someone else, thus re-allocating the cost of control.

There are three sources of allowances. First, under a formula involving past emissions and fuel consumption, allowances are allocated to existing plants. The CAA also awards "bonus" allowances to particular utilities, including those employing "clean coal" technology or investing in conservation and renewable energy. Plants built after 2000 get no allowances. The practice of granting existing (and often dirtier) plants more allowances than newer (and often cleaner) plants is little different than the grandfathering practice we discussed in connection with the NSPS. Second, new plants that need allowances and existing plants that need more allowances can buy them from other plants. They can do so through bilateral exchanges, simply paying another plant for allowances they do not need, or through a spot market run by the Chicago Board of Trade. You know environmental law has come a long way when you see sulfur allowances sold in the pit alongside pork bellies and orange juice futures! Finally, EPA holds auctions in which it sells new allowances.

As a political side payment, the 1990 Amendments also provided a good deal of money to assist unemployed Appalachian coal miners. This is noteworthy because it is so rare in environmental statutes to compensate the losers.

The acid rain program is far more complex than these simple paragraphs have described, and its proponents had high hopes that creating a market for sulfur dioxide emissions would spur technological developments and efficient operations. The incentive for technological development would depend on how much allowances sold for and the cost of non-technological means of complying (i.e., switching from high to low-sulfur coal). Industry had warned in 1989 that an allowance would cost at least $1,500. EPA responded that this was a gross exaggeration, and that $750 per allowance was more likely. In early trades, though, allowances cost only $250 and are now even less than that.

Why so low? In part, no doubt, industry exaggerated the costs of compliance for advocacy reasons. The low cost is due in part to the unrelated drop in rail freight rates from deregulation of the rail industry, making it cheaper to import low-sulfur coal. But the low cost is also due to an efficient market that ensured low transaction and information costs for exchanges to take place. Moreover, there is strong empirical support that technology has improved. Scrubber technology is now estimated to have reached 90% to 95% efficiency. And one reason for this improvement was the seemingly nonsensical requirement of scrubbers in

the 1977 CAA Amendments, since it gave utilities and scrubber manufacturers an incentive to get the scrubbers to work better. In any case,
reductions in SO_2 have also, in the process, reduced other power plant
pollutants resulting in improved visibility and public health protection.

In theory, trading is preferable to source-specific regulation because
it increases efficiencies. In the case of air pollutant markets, for example,
imagine a source who can reduce more emissions than needed to comply
with its permit limits at a relatively low cost. It now faces a business
decision. Will it make more profit by continuing to emit the full 10 tons
allowed under its permit, for example, or is it better off by selling its
allowances at a profit to higher-cost agents, or perhaps reducing its
emissions but reserving its allowances for future use?

If the market operates, the greatest share of reductions will come
from agents who can do so at the cheapest cost, allowing each polluter to
weigh the marginal cost of abatement against the cost of buying credits
and make an efficient individual decision. The net result allows the
regulated community to select appropriate control strategies and, in so
doing, creates a market incentive for innovative practices and technologies. This is an important point, since technology-based approaches have
been criticized as stifling innovation—so long as you have a control
technology on your smokestack that satisfies the standards, why reduce
emissions further? In a trading system, by contrast, any reduced emissions can be sold on the market to other sources who find it expensive to
reduce their emissions, or banked for later sale (on the bet that prices
will rise). It has been estimated, for example, that the lead trading
program saved about $12 billion compared to the costs of requiring every
refinery to meet the same lead standard. It was very expensive for many
of the smaller refineries to come into compliance, and they took advantage of the trading system.

Flush with the success of the acid rain program, proponents of
trading have been pushing for its adoption in other areas, ranging from
wetlands and endangered species habitat to water pollution and greenhouse gases. The Kyoto Protocol to the Framework Convention on
Climate Change (described *infra*) has taken trading global. The Protocol
allows developed countries to trade greenhouse gas emissions with each
other and, in its Clean Development Mechanism, calls for a variant of
offsets, with carbon sinks such as forests offsetting emissions of greenhouse gases.

Despite these attractive potential benefits, however, trading can
have its drawbacks. Property rights must be secure and costs must be
low or few trades will occur. As described in the offsets example, these
costs include market information costs (identifying buyers and sellers) as
well as transaction costs (the direct costs of doing the deal) and potential

indirect costs such as regulators tightening your permit based on knowledge of your willingness to trade. Most important, however, trading can lead to what are called *hot spots*—areas of concentrated pollution—and environmental justice concerns. As an example, consider the Old Vehicle Scrapping Program that was implemented in Los Angeles. Smog (O_3) is formed when VOCs and NOx react in the presence of still air and sunlight. The trading program sought to reduce VOC levels by allowing VOC emitters to purchase old polluting cars (pre–1982) and scrap them in exchange for VOC reduction credits. The large polluters (primarily oil refineries) were required to reduce emissions, but they could choose between (1) lowering their *actual* emissions or (2) purchasing and retiring enough cars to gain sufficient emission credits. The net result, proponents claimed, would be an overall reduction of VOC emissions in the Los Angeles airshed at least cost, since taking old polluting cars off the road could prove cheaper than pollution control retrofits.

Despite retiring over 17,000 cars, the program was sharply criticized by environmental justice groups. They claimed that the bulk of trades were carried out by only four refineries operating in close proximity to two Latino communities. Their still high emissions formed a pollution hot spot. Moreover, while both the refinery emissions and car exhaust contribute to ozone formation, the refinery emissions were said to be more hazardous than the auto emissions they were replacing. Diffuse vehicular emissions formerly spread across 12,000 square miles had effectively been exchanged for more hazardous refinery emissions concentrated across only twenty square miles.

E. Prevention of Significant Deterioration (PSD)

New sources, no matter where they are located, must employ at least NSPS but, as we have seen, in a non-attainment area they must also purchase offsets and employ lowest achievable emissions rate technology. These requirements are expensive. Wouldn't it make economic sense for a company deciding where to build a plant to set up in a region that is already in attainment? Thanks to the CAA's Prevention of Significant Deterioration (PSD) requirements, not necessarily.[12] One might think that so long as an area is in compliance with the NAAQS there should be no additional requirements beyond NSPS. As a result of a court decision in 1973 and following CAA amendments in 1977, the PSD program says otherwise.[13] The CAA requires EPA to "protect and enhance" air quality, and this was interpreted as ensuring that air

---

12. 42 U.S.C. §§ 7470–7492.

13. Sierra Club v. Ruckelshaus, 344 F.Supp. 253 (D.D.C.), aff'd per curiam without opinion, 2 Envtl. L. Rep. 20656 (D.C.Cir.1972), aff'd by an equally divided Court, 412 U.S. 541 (1973).

quality doesn't drop even in areas that meet or are well below the NAAQS levels. New sources in PSD areas must employ the "best available control technologies," which are at least as, and usually more, stringent than the NSPS.

The PSD program is quite complex. In simple terms, it divides the country into three classes of areas with varying degrees of restriction. Class I areas include national parks such as the Grand Canyon while Class II areas cover most of the rest of the country. The class category determines the amount of development allowed through so-called "growth increments." These increments place an upper limit on the increase in ambient concentration of pollutants in the area. The growth increment for particulates, for example, in Class I areas is 5 micrograms/cubic meter while in Class II it is 19 micrograms/cubic meter. In other words, Class II areas can accept almost four times more increased emissions than Class I areas. When a new source or major modification seeks a permit to pollute, the source must calculate by modeling whether the increased pollution will violate the growth increment. Note that, as with non-attainment, PSD is pollutant-specific. An area can be a non-attainment area for ozone but a PSD area for particulates.

At first glance, the PSD program is puzzling. Presumably there are no health issues involved because the NAAQS are met. The public health is already protected by the NAAQS with an adequate margin of safety. According to the CAA, the air is already "clean." One possible explanation is the importance of preserving clean air in undeveloped regions and national parks. Another possible explanation is political—the PSD program restrains the flight of industry from dirty to clean areas and ensures non-attainment regions remain competitive by making it costly to move into PSD areas.

NEW SOURCES AND MAJOR MODIFICATIONS

Is the area in non-attainment for this pollutant?

only applicable for NAAQS criteria pollutants
SO$_x$, NO$_x$, CO, HCs, particulates, lead, ozone

"yes"

Non-attainment

Do I need a permit?

New major sources
LAER*
Major modifications
RACT*

Can I use a bubble?
net emissions from site

If a net increase in emissions, what offset ration must I achieve?

total allowable emissions in area of non-attainment must be reduced ratio increases according to severity of non-attainment

"no"

PSD

Do I need a permit?

New major sources
BACT*
Major modifications
BART*

Can I use a bubble?
net emissions from site

What is the growth increment? Class I or Class II site?

Visibility protection for Class I sites

*all must be at least as stringent as NSPS

LAER – Lowest Achievable Emissions Rate
RACT – Reasonably Available Control Technology
BACT – Best Available Control Technology
BART – Best Available Retrofit Technology

F. The CAA of Tomorrow

The history of the CAA has been much like the Red Queen in the storybook, *Alice in Wonderland*. Huffing and puffing, the Queen says she has to run faster and faster to stay in the same place. The evolving CAA has faced the same challenge. Despite improved vehicle emissions and CAFE standards, for example, vehicle miles traveled have more than doubled since 1970. Although our city air is much cleaner than three decades ago, we keep struggling to get our cities out of non-attainment and, with better knowledge, adding to our list of what remains to be done.

We can, no doubt, be even stricter in our regulation of stationary sources and provide carrots and sticks for more efficient mobile sources (such as the hybrid car and fuel cells), but this will only get us so far. At the end of the day, to really improve our air quality we may well need to address basic lifestyle issues—such as our ever-stronger reliance on the car or our aversion to adopt strong energy efficiency measures in our everyday activities and where we live. But changing personal habits and preferences is never a popular option and may, in fact, be beyond the power of the law to change. If it can be done, however, the CAA will surely be playing a central role.

II. Ozone Depletion[14]

As of January 2003, the Montreal Protocol had been ratified by 184 countries, including all industrialized countries and most developing countries. While the Protocol and its amendments have not eliminated the dangers of ozone depletion, they have established national commitments that will lessen the threat in years to come. The most important precedent in international law for the management of global environmental harms, the Montreal Protocol provides a useful model for other long-term environmental challenges such as climate change. The difficulties diplomats faced during the negotiation of the Protocol are much the same—genuine scientific uncertainty over the scale of harm, a sharply divided international community, potentially high transition costs, and a global problem requiring a global solution.

The problems posed by ozone depletion were unlike anything international environmental law had ever addressed. With traditional air and water pollution, the harms are generally perceived to be localized and discrete. Even when pollution crosses national borders as acid rain or oil spills, the harm is still confined at worst to a region. The Protocol was

---

14. This section is adapted from material in David Hunter, James Salzman, Durwood Zaelke, International Environmental Law and Policy (2nd ed., 2002).

thus the first treaty to address fully the global nature of a set of pollutants. Moreover, during the initial negotiations and ratification, there was genuine doubt whether ozone depletion had even occurred. Thus the Protocol was also the first "precautionary treaty," instituting tough technology-forcing controls as a safeguard against uncertain future harms.

A. *The Science of Ozone Depletion*

Ozone (O_3) is a simple molecule of three oxygen atoms and occurs naturally as a trace element of the atmosphere. The highest concentration of ozone occurs in the middle of the stratosphere, in a region commonly called the "ozone layer." Although a relatively small part of the atmosphere, ozone performs a critical function. It absorbs certain frequencies of harmful UV–B radiation emitted from the sun, blanketing the planet in a protective shield that effectively protects life on earth from solar radiation. In the stratosphere, as ozone molecules absorb the incoming UV–B radiation, the energy blasts them apart. An equilibrium is maintained, however, by a series of chemical reactions that create ozone as a counterbalance to the ozone destroyed through absorption of UV–B radiation.

Thirty years ago, one would never have suspected that the ubiquitous compounds known as chlorofluorocarbons (CFCs) could cause environmental harm. CFCs had been developed in the 1920s by General Motors' chief chemist, Thomas Midgely, as a safe substitute for the ammonia and sulfur dioxide refrigerants then commonly in use. In place of these explosive and poisonous refrigerants, Midgely synthesized a non-flammable, non-toxic substitute. His invention, CFC–12, was first announced at an American Chemical Society meeting. It is reported he demonstrated the compound's beneficial qualities by inhaling the gas and then exhaling over a fire to extinguish the flame. CFC–12 was quickly adapted to the Frigidaire line and soon became the refrigerant of choice. In a clever commercial strategy, General Motors did not patent the compound, thus speeding up its wide adoption throughout the economy, in uses ranging from air conditioning, refrigeration, and foams to aerosol propellants, cleaning of electronics, and degreasing of parts.

The role of chlorine, bromine, and several other chemicals in the destruction of ozone as part of the natural atmospheric balance was relatively well understood by the early 1970s. It was not until 1974, however, that F. Sherwood Rowland and Mario Molina published the first credible explanation of what happens to CFCs and their potential role in destruction of the ozone layer. They argued that the inert CFCs would be relatively stable in the lower atmosphere, in part because the ozone layer blocks UV–B from penetrating through the stratosphere.

Even though CFCs are heavier than most atmospheric molecules, CFCs emitted on the earth's surface would eventually migrate to the stratosphere because of the constant mixing of the atmosphere. Once in the stratosphere, Rowland and Molina hypothesized that ultraviolet radiation would blast the CFCs apart, releasing highly reactive chlorine (Cl) and chlorine oxide (ClO) molecules. These molecules would then set off a chain-reaction, in which just one reactive chlorine atom could destroy thousands of stratospheric ozone molecules. Thus CFCs would act as a catalyst, upsetting the natural balance of ozone creation and destruction. There would not literally be a "hole" in the ozone layer, but a reduction in the concentration of ozone, and hence its ability to absorb radiation. Over time, the role of CFCs and other ozone depleting substances (ODS) in reducing the ozone layer has been confirmed.

Increases in UV–B radiation have serious impacts on human health, including greater incidence of skin cancers, cataracts and sunburns. More recently, UV–B has been demonstrated to suppress the immune systems in humans with respect to some diseases. Unlike sunburns and skin cancers, the immunosuppression impacts of UV–B affects humans of all skin color pigmentation. Just as disturbing are the potential impacts on agricultural crops. The growth and photosynthesis of certain plants, including strains of commercially valuable plants such as rice, corn, and soybeans, are reduced by relatively low increases in ultraviolet radiation. Increases in UV–B can also reduce the growth of marine phytoplankton, which is the base of the ocean food chain and produces at least as much biomass as all terrestrial ecosystems combined; and UV–B damages midge larvae, the base of many fresh-water ecosystems.

B. International Controls

From today's perspective, gaining broad international support for the strict control of ozone depleting substances perhaps seems inevitable, but in the mid–1980s the likelihood of international controls on CFCs, much less on halons or other substances, appeared slim indeed. To make sense of the Protocol's development, one must keep clearly in mind how little was known with certainty at the time. As noted above, it was not until 1974 that Rowland and Molina first raised the potential role of CFCs in ozone depletion. With the advent of national laws in America and Scandinavia banning CFCs in aerosols, in 1981 the United Nations Environment Program's Governing Council gave approval to develop an international agreement to protect the ozone layer.

Attended by 43 nations (of which 16 were developing countries) and three industry groups, negotiations in Vienna produced the first international agreement to address CFCs. Expectations were low, with minimal public interest and no participation by any environmental organizations.

The result of these initial negotiations, the Vienna Convention for the Protection of the Ozone Layer, was signed by 20 countries.[15] Rather than impose controls on CFC consumption or production, the Convention called for countries to take "appropriate measures" to protect the ozone layer and established an international mechanism for research, monitoring, and exchange of information. With very little known about the scale of CFC production in Soviet bloc and developing countries, it was hoped this data would form the basis for establishing a global production baseline. No chemicals were identified as ozone-depleting substances. At the end of the meeting, despite objections by the European Community, a non-binding resolution was passed calling for the next meeting to work toward a legally binding protocol addressing controls. Nonetheless, with the Vienna Convention's failure to establish controls on production or consumption, the future of CFCs still seemed bright.

In 1985, two months after negotiations ended over the Vienna Convention, British scientists announced an "ozone hole" in the Antarctic, triggering enormous public interest in ozone depletion. The scientists' data showed a 50% springtime reduction in the ozone layer compared to levels in the 1960s. Sharp decreases, however, had only begun in 1979, suggesting the reduction was non-linear. Ironically, because the data showed such a dramatic decline the British team had delayed publication of their findings for three years to confirm the accuracy of the data, and U.S. satellites had automatically rejected accurate data of the depletion as clearly erroneous. While the ozone hole findings were startling and focused nations' attention on the negotiations, the discovery was of little help to diplomats because there was no proof of CFCs' role in creating the hole. Were CFCs to blame, or was there another mechanism at work? Despite uncertainty among scientists, though, media attention linked the ozone hole in the public's mind to CFCs.

Industry played a critical role in the development of international controls, as well. While originally providing a unified front against controls on CFCs, responding to the public clamor over the ozone hole, the chemical giant, DuPont, announced in 1986 that it could develop CFC substitutes within five years provided that regulatory requirements justified such a heavy investment in research and development. Without a legally-fixed phase-out goal to spur the market for CFC alternatives, DuPont feared developing more expensive substitutes for CFCs would prove a poor business decision.

In a compromise between those pushing for ODS controls and those opposed, the Vienna Convention had postponed decisions, calling instead for development of a protocol that would address controls. Discovery of

15. UNEP Doc. IG.53/5, *reprinted in* 26 I.L.M. 1529 (1987).

the ozone hole placed the protocol negotiations on a fast track just two years later. Indeed, the meeting in Montreal could not have shown a greater contrast to the small affair two years earlier in Vienna. With representatives from over 60 countries participating (more than half from developing countries), many industrial and environmental groups, and wide media coverage, the world's attention focused on ODS. The workshops and lobbying since Vienna paid off, for the Montreal Protocol on Substances That Deplete the Ozone Layer was passed by consensus.[16]

In the Vienna Convention, no chemicals had been identified or regulated as ODS. The Protocol, however, not only froze production and consumption levels of CFCs upon ratification (CFCs 11, 12, 113, 114, 115) and of halons three years later (Halons 1211, 1301, 2402), but also set in place a reduction schedule for CFCs. By 1998, a 50% reduction in CFC consumption was to be achieved. Because monitoring consumption of ODS was thought infeasible, a surrogate formula was adopted defining a country's consumption of CFCs or halons as:

$$consumption = production + imports - exports$$

Thus a major CFC producer could satisfy the reduction requirements by decreasing its domestic use but still continuing to export. An importing country would measure its consumption simply by adding domestic production and imports together.

In order to give countries flexibility in their reduction schedules, the Protocol developed a "basket" strategy. Each chemical's ozone-depleting potential (ODP) was compared to that of CFC 11 (arbitrarily given a value of 1). Since CFC 113 is less destructive of the ozone layer than CFC 11, its ODP is 0.8. Using the basket strategy, a country would achieve the same reduction in consumption levels by using either 8 tons less of CFC 11 or 10 tons less of CFC 113 (8 tons x ODP of 1 = 10 tons x ODP of 0.8). This arithmetic was important because CFC 113 was widely used as a solvent in the electronics industry. Countries like Japan, which had opposed CFC 113's inclusion in the Protocol, could now choose to reduce a greater percentage of other CFCs while conserving CFC 113's use.

The reduction schedules and basket strategy not only avoided chemical-by-chemical negotiations but provided clear signals for industrial development by removing uncertainty. CFC producers like DuPont and ICI could now justify heavy research and development spending on CFC alternatives. CFC users like IBM and Toshiba could justify investments for in-process recycling and recovery systems to reduce the need for additional, and certainly more expensive, CFC stocks. For companies in

16.   26 I.L.M. 1550 (1987).

ratifying countries, long-term investments in CFC production or CFC consumption technologies suddenly seemed less attractive.

If the Protocol's only teeth were scheduled phase-outs of controlled substances, countries would have had a strong incentive not to sign in order to gain the newly-freed market share for themselves. To avoid this free rider behavior and as an incentive for countries to join, the Protocol provided tough trade measures.

Regarding imports, parties to the Protocol are prohibited from importing from *non-parties* either controlled substances or certain products containing controlled substances. These products include domestic, commercial, and vehicle air conditioners, refrigerators, and portable fire extinguishers. The parties also decided to ban the import of products produced with controlled substances. The country of origin can avoid these onerous restrictions only if it demonstrates full compliance with the Protocol's reduction schedules. Regarding exports, parties must similarly ban the export of controlled substances to *non-parties* unless the country of destination can demonstrate full compliance with the Protocol's reduction schedules. Exports to non-parties that are in compliance are not counted as exports in the country's consumption calculation, so they must be offset by an equal reduction in production or imports.

As an example, if Country P is a party and Country N is a non-party and not in compliance with the Protocol, there can be no trade in controlled substances between the countries, and Country P cannot import products that are controlled substances, contain controlled substances, or (in some instances) were produced with controlled substances from Country N. If Country N remains a non-party but complies with the Protocol, Country P can export controlled substances to Country N but cannot subtract this amount from imports or production in calculating national consumption. Subject to the reduction schedules, parties may freely trade controlled substances amongst themselves.

Article 5 of the Protocol addressed aid to developing countries. While developing countries' per capita consumption of CFCs in 1987 was much lower than in the developed world, their domestic requirements were steadily growing. Since the manufacture of CFCs is a low-cost, low-tech operation, no practical barriers prevented cottage CFC industries from sprouting around the globe. Thus in part to accept the responsibility for having created most of the ozone depleting substances and in part to encourage broad international participation, developed countries supported a ten–year grace period following ratification for developing countries before the control measures would apply. During this period developing countries were permitted to increase their consumption to 0.3 Kg per capita in order to meet basic domestic needs. Following this period, developing countries would have ten more years to reduce their consumption by 50%. While this allowed growth may seem counterproductive, even if all the developing countries had increased their use of ODS to 0.3 Kg per capita the total consumption would still only have been 25–30% of the 1986 U.S. and EC consumption.

With 24 nations signing in Montreal, the Protocol was universally hailed as a diplomatic triumph. Starting from low or no expectations in Vienna, within eighteen months strict international controls had been negotiated that would be refined and changed over time with the benefit of more knowledge. This flexible, structured evolution marked a new feature of international environmental law and showed great foresight. Because parties were required to assess and review controls periodically, this would ensure that the Protocol's international controls reflected scientists' improved understanding of the mechanisms and causes of ozone depletion. And, in fact, this is exactly what has happened. Not only have the parties met regularly since 1987, but every time parties have sought to tighten reduction schedules and bring new compounds under control, including the widely used compounds carbon tetrachloride and methyl chloroform, which together comprised 16% of industry's total stratospheric chlorine contribution in applications ranging from solvents and pesticides to dry cleaners.

C. Developing Countries

While Article 5 had provided a grace period for developing countries coming into compliance, Montreal had glossed over the terms of financial assistance to developing countries. Some simple facts, however, illustrated the importance of bringing these countries on board by assuring aid. Industrialized countries, with less than 25% of the world's population, were consuming 88% of the CFCs, over twenty times the per capita consumption of developing countries. Ozone depletion, unlike most international issues that had come before it, clearly could not be solved without the full cooperation of all countries, particularly large developing countries. China and India, representing approximately 37% of the global population, were not parties to the Protocol. These countries' large and growing domestic markets made the Protocol's trade restrictions moot. Huge local CFC industries could develop over time and never sell products outside the Chinese or Indian borders. Moreover, products containing CFCs, like refrigerators and air conditioners, were viewed as necessary to improve the standard of living in those countries and, indeed, essential in a number of applications. These facts gave developing countries additional power in the negotiations, requiring innovative compromises to meet their demands.

Developing countries showed keen interest in the emerging global scientific consensus over ozone layer depletion but rejected as unacceptable the options of either going without these products or paying more because of expensive substitutes and retrofitting existing equipment. Indeed, they charged it would be adding insult to injury to actually increase the profits of the multinational chemical industry that had produced the damaging substances in the first place. If the Protocol would produce winners and losers, developing countries wanted guarantees they would not suffer. They sought assurance that if aid proved insufficient they would be relieved from meeting their treaty obligations. They wanted to avoid writing their own check. The developed countries, however, wanted to avoid writing a blank check—providing financial and technical aid with the amounts determined by the recipient country. As a compromise, the parties approved an interim funding source that, in 1992, was permanently established as the Multilateral Fund with funding of $160 million from 1991–1993 and $510 million from 1994–1996. By 2000 the Fund had disbursed over $1 billion supporting 3,300 projects and activities in 121 developing countries.

D. Remaining Challenges

Despite the impressive negotiated agreements, the battle against ozone depletion still faces significant obstacles. One of the most disturbing aspects of ozone depletion is the lag time between when ODS are released and when they stop depleting the ozone layer. The atmospheric lifetimes of some ODS are hundreds of years. Others like methyl bromide may have life times of 2 years or less. This lag time means that we have in fact "banked" a considerable amount of ozone depletion into the next century. In addition, many ODS are currently locked inside products such as automobile air conditioners or refrigerators. If not properly captured at the time of disposal, these banked ODS represent another major source of ozone depletion. Indeed the market for CFCs is still strong, in large part because over 100 million older cars in the U.S. have CFC air conditioning units that need to be re-filled periodically.

Assuming that all countries meet the Protocol's broad reductions in ODS, scientists predict the ozone layer will stabilize by around 2050. In the meantime, however, because of ODS still working their way up in the stratosphere, the situation continues to worsen with record low ozone layer concentrations reported annually over both the Arctic and Antarctic regions. The European Commission reported that the Arctic stratosphere may have lost up to 60% of its ozone during the 1999–2000 winter, for example, and that the average ozone concentrations over Europe were 15% less than those of the early 1970s.

Nonetheless, with nearly universal ratification and coverage of over 90 ozone depleting compounds, the Protocol must be regarded as a triumph of international diplomacy. Based on data submitted by parties, UNEP claims that production and consumption of CFCs has decreased by over 86% since 1986, with one–third of developing countries stopping their consumption of halons and over half ending their consumption of carbon tetrachloride and methyl chloroform.

E. Lessons Learned

The ozone depletion story offers three key lessons. The first is the necessity of international cooperation to deal with international environmental challenges. In practical terms, this means creative "North–South deals." Throughout the negotiations in Montreal and after, developing countries pressed for explicit linkage between financial assistance provisions and any developing country obligations. Fulfillment of their commitment was ultimately made contingent upon the "effective implementation" by developed country parties of the provisions for technology transfer and for financial co-operation. The establishment of the Multilateral Fund to finance the incremental costs of acquiring substitute technologies helped allay developing countries' fears that they might be charged exorbitant prices for new substitute technologies. Without the Fund and technical assistance, the Protocol would almost certainly have been a failure because CFC use in developing countries would eventually have eclipsed use in developed countries.

Second, the participation of non-state actors proved just as important as the participation of developing countries. Scientists' study of the ozone layer laid the foundation for all of the negotiations and persuaded governments of the need for haste. Despite being the target of much criticism, the chemical industry played a critical role, as well. Reacting to mounting evidence of the impacts of ODS, the relative certainty of control measures being adopted, and pressure from ODS consumers for alternatives, ODS manufacturers quickly adapted to rapid marketplace and regulatory changes. For ODS manufacturers, the products under threat of regulation were highly profitable. Any control measures reducing the demand for ODS would hurt their bottom line. Thus the earliest press releases and advertisements from DuPont and other ODS manufacturers had argued forcefully for a "go-slow" approach. Later, however, seeking a competitive edge, certain ODS manufacturers actively led the effort to develop chemical alternatives. Indeed, chemical giants like DuPont had a distinct competitive advantage both because the 1978 U.S. aerosol ban had given them a head start in looking for alternatives and because of their expertise in fluorocarbon chemistry. Ironically, DuPont, the leading CFC producer, would come to be seen as a champion of CFC phase-outs and even make a well-publicized promise to halt the production of CFCs ahead of schedule. The Montreal Protocol, for its part, established clear and certain timetables which gave companies confidence to invest in development of new chemicals.

Third, a precautionary approach to treaty making can work. While the Protocol has not proven a total success, its adoption and implementation did represent a diplomatic breakthrough. In no other treaty have so many disparate actors in international society successfully cooperated and compromised to address a global environmental threat. At the heart of this success is the flexible nature of the Vienna Convention. Despite having only minimal substantive standards, the Vienna Convention provided a framework for the international community to respond through an evolving consensus to the urgency of ozone depletion. The Convention specifically helped to organize scientific reviews, to incorporate new scientific and economic developments, and to ensure that international policy makers had a forum for ongoing negotiation. In addition, the rules of decision set up by the Convention and the Protocol were a unique and powerful departure from the typical international rule requiring unanimous consent prior to moving the international response forward. By moving ahead step-wise, acknowledging that more information was needed but not halting action in the meantime, the ozone treaties provide the best examples of international implementation of the Precautionary Principle.

III. Climate Change[17]

A. *The Science of Climate Change*

Climate change looms as a defining issue of the 21st century, pitting the potential disruption of our global climate system against the future of a fossil fuel-based economy. Policy-makers are the arbiters in this battle, attempting to negotiate among vastly different interests, and challenged by significant uncertainties in science and computer modeling. Climate change refers to the response of the planet's climate system to altered concentrations of "greenhouse gases" such as carbon dioxide (CO_2) in the atmosphere. These gases earn their name because, like a glass greenhouse, these gases allow sunlight to pass through the atmosphere while trapping heat from the earth's surface.

The basic mechanism of how CO_2 and other greenhouse gases warm the planet (i.e. the "greenhouse effect") has been well known for decades. Indeed, over a century ago, in 1896, the Swedish chemist

17. This section is adapted from material in David Hunter, James Salzman, Durwood Zaelke, International Environmental Law and Policy (2nd ed., 2002). We are grateful for the contributions of David Hunter.

Arrhenius first advanced the theory that carbon dioxide emissions from combustion of coal would lead to global warming. Assuming all else is held constant (e.g., cloud cover, capacity of the oceans to absorb carbon dioxide, etc.), increases in greenhouse gases lead to "global warming"— an increase in global average temperatures—as well as other changes in the earth's climate patterns.[18] The debate regarding the science of climate change has not been over the proven warming potential of gases but, rather, over how much, at what rate, and where the planet will warm, and how such warming will affect human health and the environment.

The major man-made (or "anthropogenic") greenhouse gases include carbon dioxide (CO_2), methane (CH_4), nitrous oxide (NOx), and chlorofluorocarbons (CFCs). These gases account for only 3% of the earth's atmosphere, but concentrations have been steadily increasing over the last century. Ice core samples taken from the Antarctic and Greenland ice caps show that atmospheric concentrations of anthropogenic greenhouse gases—carbon dioxide, methane, and nitrous oxide— have increased by about 30%, 145%, and 15%, respectively, in the industrial era. In short, our fossil fuel-based economy is unlocking and releasing greenhouse gases taken out of the atmosphere in prehistoric times.

Carbon dioxide and NOx remain in the atmosphere and contribute to the greenhouse effect for many decades to centuries. This means that we have "banked" substantial amounts of greenhouse gases already, and any reductions taken today will not reduce the overall impact for some time. Despite variations in weather over the short-term, the long-term climate data suggest that the planet's average surface air temperature has increased by about 0.6° C since the late 19th century. In the Northern latitudes, temperatures have risen 0.8° C.

The atmosphere's resiliency in adjusting to variations from the status quo is remarkable, as only about three billion tons of the estimated total 6.5 billion to 8.5 billion metric tons of carbon emitted remains in the atmosphere every year. The additional carbon is assimilated, either through plants and the soil or through increased absorption by the oceans. Thus in addition to emissions of greenhouse gases by burning fossil fuels, many land-use and agricultural practices directly influence climate change. "Carbon sinks" refer to processes that remove a net

18. Often the media and others confuse weather with climate. Weather refers to meteorological conditions at a specific place and time, including temperature, humidity, wind, precipitation, and barometric pressure. Climate refers to weather patterns that prevail over extended periods of time, including both average and extreme weather. Climate change often receives front–page media coverage only during droughts or floods. Unfortunately, this means that as soon as the weather breaks or appears to go back to normal, media coverage wanes and many people are left believing that the climate change stories were a false alarm.

amount of carbon from the atmosphere (e.g. through photosynthesis). Thus, carbon sinks present important opportunities for reducing the overall increase in atmospheric concentrations of greenhouse gases. The critical importance of sinks can be understood by recognizing that only 40% of the estimated man-made emissions of CO_2 over the last century is showing up in the atmosphere; the remaining 60% has been absorbed either by the oceans, forests, or other sinks. "Carbon reservoirs" currently store carbon previously removed from the atmosphere. Carbon reservoirs are in equilibrium with the atmosphere unless disturbed, in which case they can release carbon and add to the concentrations of greenhouse gases in the atmosphere. Forests are perhaps the most well known carbon reservoirs and sinks. Mature forests tend to be carbon reservoirs. The relationship of forests to the global climate system is complex and not completely understood. Forests can act as reservoirs (storing carbon), sinks (sequestering carbon), or sources (emitting carbon) depending on the relative maturity of the forest as well as the human uses of the land. Over time, changes in forest cover, for example through deforestation and conversion to agriculture, have contributed significantly to the level of carbon in the atmosphere.

Anticipating the critical role that scientific consensus would play in building the political will to respond to climate change, the United Nations Environment Program (UNEP) and the World Meteorological Organization (WMO) created the Intergovernmental Panel on Climate Change (IPCC) in 1988. With over 2,000 accomplished natural and social scientists from around the globe, the IPCC was initially charged with assessing the scientific, technical and economic basis of climate change policy in preparation for the 1992 Earth Summit and the negotiations of the Climate Change Convention. After the Convention entered into force, the IPCC continued to provide technical reports to the Conference of the Parties and its scientific advisory body.

Although legitimate and important areas of uncertainty still exist with respect to the ultimate impacts of climate change, the range of uncertainty is narrowing over time. Perhaps most important, a global consensus now exists among the international scientific community that we are witnessing discernible impacts on our climate and natural systems due to human activities. The IPCC's Second Assessment concluded in 1995 that the observed warming trend was "unlikely to be entirely natural in origin" and that the balance of evidence suggested a "discernible human influence" on the Earth's climate.[19] Given the conservative nature of the IPCC, this conclusion was critical for fueling the 1997

---

19. IPCC, Working Group I, The Science of Climate Change, 3–5 (Second Assessment Report, 1995).

Kyoto negotiations. The IPCC compiled and released its Third Assessment in 2001, which concluded that "most of the warming observed over the last 50 years is likely to have been due to the increase in greenhouse gas concentrations" attributable to human activities.

According to the IPCC, failure to mitigate greenhouse gases will result in a projected increase of between 1.4 to 5.8° Celsius by the year 2100. Such a rate of warming is apparently without precedent for at least the last 10,000 years. Temperatures over land and particularly over the northern hemisphere are anticipated to increase even more than these global averages. The expected impacts of climate change include not only an increase in global temperature but a rise in the "energy" of storms and weather patterns, sea level rise, water availability, disease, and loss of biodiversity. The range of possible impacts is so broad and severe that many observers believe climate change to be the most significant long-term environmental problem facing the planet.

Who's to Blame?

Not all greenhouse gases are created equally; different gases have different "global warming potentials" (GWPs). Thus, for example, the global warming potential of methane is 56 times that of CO_2 (which has a GWP of 1.0) or, put another way, methane is 56 times more potent in causing global warming than is CO_2. The global warming potential for nitrous oxide is 280 and the global warming potential is in the thousands for the major CFC replacements (HFCs and PFCs). Thus emitting one ton of these compounds into the atmosphere has dramatically higher impacts than emitting one ton of CO_2 or even methane.

Most greenhouse gas emissions come from industrial activity and thus, not surprisingly, industrialized countries have been the primary contributors to the increase in atmospheric concentration of greenhouse gases over the past century. As shown in the table below, with over 30% of historic carbon dioxide emissions, the United States has been by far the largest contributor to atmospheric levels of carbon dioxide.

Cumulative Carbon Dioxide Emissions (1900–1990)[20]

Country	Percent Cumulative CO_2 Emissions	Country	Percent Cumulative CO_2 Emissions
United States	30.3%	Japan	3.7%
Europe (including EEC)	27.7%	Middle East	2.7%
Former Soviet Union	13.7%	Africa	2.5%
China, Indian and Developing Asia	12.2%	Canada	2.3%
South and Central America	3.8%	Australia	1.1%

20. Adopted from World Resources Institute, Historic CO_2 Emissions by Fossil Fuels, http//www.wri.org (September, 2001).

The United State is also the world's leader in current emissions, as well. With only 4% of the world's population, we now emit an estimated 25% of the world's greenhouse gases each year. China is next at approximately 12%. Although China's emissions grew significantly over most of the last decade, in the past two years their carbon dioxide emissions have been reduced significantly, in part as they have shifted away from a major emphasis on coal.

National totals, however, represent only part of the picture, because they depend on both population size and the level of industrial activity. Per capita emissions provide a better measure for comparing an average individual's contribution to emissions in each country. Again, the United States had the highest per capita emissions—19.4 metric tons per person per year—among the nations that were the major sources of global emissions in 1995 (the oil-rich middle eastern countries generally lead in per capita emissions). By contrast, per capita emissions in India and China were 1.1 and 2.6 metric tons per year. A representative review of other countries also demonstrates the significantly disproportionate amount of CO_2 emitted by the United States—Germany 10.3 metric tons, Japan 9.2, Canada 14.7, Indonesia 1.5, and Brazil 1.5. As developing countries raise their standard of living and industrial activity, however, absent changes in technology these per capita and absolute levels will surely change, dramatically increasing greenhouse gas emissions.

B.   Impacts of Climate Change

But so what if the climate changes? So what if the planet's temperature increases? The ultimate impact, if any, of these changes on human health and the environment is the source of much of the uncertainty that has clouded policymaking with respect to climate change. The impacts from climate are expected to be significantly different across regions, with potentially dramatic environmental and social ramifications.

Global sea level has risen by between 10 and 20 cm over the past century, and this rise is very likely caused by this century's observed global warming. The IPCC estimates a sea-level rise of between 9 cm and 88 cm during the next century, caused in part by the melting of polar ice and in part by thermal expansion of water. Coastal systems are expected to vary widely in their response to changes in climate and sea level. Climate change and sea level rise or changes in storms or storm surges could result in the erosion of shores and associated habitat, increased salinity of estuaries and freshwater aquifers, altered tidal ranges in rivers and bays, and increased coastal flooding. Under different estimates of sea-level rise, the impacts on low-lying areas could, of course, be severe. For example, several countries could be submerged, including the Maldives and the Cook Islands.

Warmer global temperatures introduce more energy into the global weather system and are likely to lead to a more vigorous hydrological cycle; this translates into prospects for more extreme and unpredictable weather events, with more severe droughts, floods, and heat waves in some places. According to the IPCC, changes in the occurrence or geographical distribution of hurricanes and other tropical storms are possible, but still not certain. Changes in the total amount and frequency of precipitation directly affect the magnitude and timing of floods and droughts. Relatively small changes in temperature and precipitation can result in relatively large changes in runoff, especially in arid and semi-arid regions. More intense rainfall would tend to increase runoff and the risk of flooding. A warmer climate could decrease the proportion of precipitation falling as snow, leading to reductions in spring runoff and increases in winter runoff. Satellite data show an estimate 10% loss in the extent of snow cover since the 1960s, as well as a reduction of about two weeks in the annual duration of lake and river ice cover in the mid and high latitudes of the Northern hemisphere during the last century.

The increase in global temperatures may also have significant impacts on public health, particularly in developing countries. The World Health Organization has linked warmer temperatures with the spread of insect-borne diseases, such as malaria, increased illnesses and deaths from heat waves and air pollution, and increased cases of diarrhea and other water-borne diseases that are particularly dangerous in developing countries. The IPCC suggests that under most scenarios both malaria and dengue will expand their geographical and seasonal ranges.

Existing studies suggest that global agricultural production could remain relatively stable in the face of anticipated climate change, but crop yields and changes in productivity could vary considerably across regions and among localities. Productivity is projected to increase in some areas and decrease in others, especially the tropics and subtropics. Many of the world's poorest people—particularly those living in subtropical and tropical areas and semi-arid and arid regions—may face the greatest risk of increased hunger.

As suggested by the preceding discussion of impacts, climate change could also cause quite substantial harm to biodiversity, since forests and other ecosystems might not be able to adapt to the rate of change in temperature. Indeed there is strong evidence that distributions, population sizes, population density, and behavior of wildlife already have been affected directly by climate change.[21]

21. IPCC Working Group II, at 11 (2001).

116

While the concern over climate change stems from the costs described above, it should be kept in mind that there will likely be some beneficial impacts, as well. The IPCC, for example, has identified the prospects of increased crop yields in some regions at mid-latitudes, an increase in global timber supply, increased water availability in some water-scarce regions (e.g., in parts of southeast Asia), reduced cold-weather mortality in mid and high-latitudes, and reduced energy demand due to higher winter temperatures.[22] Nonetheless, the IPCC has also concluded that the costs of climate change will clearly and significantly outweigh the benefits.

C. *Legal Responses*

Concern about climate change and calls for international action began in the 1970s and continued throughout the 1980s. In 1990, the United Nations authorized an Intergovernmental Negotiating Committee on Climate to begin discussions of a global treaty. These negotiations culminated in the 1992 Framework Convention on Climate Change ("the Climate Change Convention") signed at the Earth Summit.[23] The Climate Change Convention established a general framework, but delineated few specific and substantive obligations to curb climate change. While in many ways disappointing to environmentalists, the Convention was nonetheless a positive step in the control of greenhouse gases. Central to the Convention is the objective found in Article 2, requiring that Parties achieve "stabilization of greenhouse gas concentrations in the atmosphere at a level that would prevent dangerous anthropogenic interference with the climate system." The Conference of the Parties is charged with periodically evaluating implementation of the Convention to ensure that commitments are adequate to meet this overall objective. It was just such an evaluation that would ultimately lead to the recognition that binding targets were necessary in the Kyoto Protocol.

Perhaps the most controversial provisions were those that addressed the specific commitments of the Parties. The Parties are essentially divided into three categories: all Parties; "Annex I," which includes all industrialized country Parties; and "Annex II," which includes all industrialized country Parties except those from the former Soviet bloc in a process of economic transition. Article 4(1) places certain information and data collecting requirements on all Parties. Article 4(2) subjects the Annex I countries to additional requirements, including most notably the obligation to "adopt national polices and take corresponding measures on the mitigation of climate change, by limiting anthropogenic emissions of greenhouse gases and protecting and enhancing greenhouse gas sinks

22. IPCC Working Group I, at 5–6.   **23.** 31 I.L.M. 849 (1992).

and reservoirs." This requirement to adopt a national policy is not tied legally to any specific target, but Article 4(2)(b) requires the developed countries to provide detailed information on their policies as well as on their emissions *"with the aim of* returning individually or jointly to their 1990 levels...." Environmentalists argued that these provisions reflected a commitment, albeit a non-binding one, by developed countries to stabilize their emissions at 1990 levels by the year 2000.

As with the Montreal Protocol regime, the Convention vests important policymaking authority in the Conference of the Parties, day-to-day monitoring of implementation in the Secretariat, and advisory obligations in a scientific and technical advisory group. The Convention selected the Global Environment Facility as the interim financial mechanism and established a relatively unique subsidiary body and procedures for facilitating implementation.

In 1995, the IPCC released a report stating for the first time that "the balance of evidence suggests that there is a discernible human influence on global climate."[24] This conclusion sparked considerable debate, pitting the great majority of atmospheric scientists and environmentalists who endorsed the IPCC report, against a small but vocal group of "greenhouse skeptics" funded substantially by the fossil fuel industry. Despite the initial controversy, the IPCC Report provided one of the most important catalysts for the negotiation of the Kyoto Protocol. The scientific consensus that climate change was not only a serious long-term problem but was actually occurring now provided the political leaders with critical support for adopting targets and timetables. On the other hand, global emissions of greenhouse gases had increased dramatically in the years since Rio, making efforts based on a 1990 baseline even more difficult for some countries, including the United States.

In December 1997, the Parties responded by negotiating the Kyoto Protocol to the Climate Change Convention, which established binding reduction targets for the United States and other developed countries.[25] The core of the Kyoto Protocol is targets and timetables, or "quantified emissions limitation and reduction objectives" (QELROs), for industrialized (Annex I) Parties to reduce their net emissions of greenhouse gases. Most European countries agreed to lower their emission 8% below 1990 levels, while the United States agreed to a 7% reduction. Countries in economic transition were allowed to select a baseline year other than 1990, and several countries did so. In addition, all countries had the option of choosing 1995 as the baseline year for three relatively minor but potent greenhouse gases (hydrofluorocarbons, perfluorocarbons, and

---

24. IPCC, Working Group I, The Science of Climate Change 3–5 (Second Assessment Report, 1995).

25. 37 I.L.M. 22 (1998).

sulphur hexafluoride). All of the reduction targets must be met over a five–year commitment period—from 2008 to 2012—which is to be followed by subsequent commitment periods and presumably stricter emission targets. The issue of emission targets for developing countries was hotly contested during negotiations. Based on the reasoning that developed countries have been responsible for the lion's share of emissions to date and are better able to pay for reductions, the Kyoto Protocol does not address emission reduction targets for developing countries. Indeed a proposal that would have established procedures for developing countries to take on *voluntary* commitments for emission limits was not adopted. It is widely assumed, however, that after the first commitment period has ended developing countries may well take on binding targets.

In addition to the targets and timetables, the Kyoto Protocol also sets forth broad and general guidance for various flexibility mechanisms, including emissions trading, joint implementation, and a new initiative called the "Clean Development Mechanism." Parameters are also set for a compliance and monitoring system and for the accounting of certain land-use and forestry activities that could alter carbon reservoirs or sinks. Many of these provisions raise as many questions as they answer, and have set the stage for further negotiations after Kyoto.

Indeed no sooner had the ink dried on the Kyoto Protocol then it became clear that significant ambiguities existed in the text of the Protocol that could lead to vastly different reduction requirements for the United States and other Annex I countries. Several provisions of the Protocol had been deliberately left ambiguous allowing countries to make their own interpretations and thus their own calculations of the costs they faced in meeting their emission reduction targets. With the clock already ticking toward the first reporting period of 2008, however, all of the Parties recognized some urgency in clarifying a unified interpretation of the Protocol.

D.   *Climate Change Policies—No Regrets, Trading, Joint Implementation, and the CDM*

A wide range of policy options are available for curbing the impacts of greenhouse gases, although many of them require significant restructuring of our economies, particularly the energy and transportation sectors. The international negotiations have focused on imposing clear national targets and timetables for overall reduction of greenhouse gases, but ultimately left the policy mix of how to achieve the targets and timetables largely to the national governments.

Generally, policymakers have focused on the "no-regrets" approach to climate change policy, undertaking measures such as improvements in energy efficiency, forest management, and air pollution control that provide economic and environmental benefits additional to any climate benefits that may be achieved. Increased energy efficiency technologies often pay for themselves through lower energy costs. Reduced air emissions may improve local public health conditions more than the cost of the technologies. Thus, these "no-regrets" policies make good sense, and can be pursued even while the extent of harm from climate change remains uncertain. One significant problem, however, is that no low-cost reliable technology exists for removing or sequestering CO_2 from fossil-fuel combustion emissions. Once the carbon is released from oil or coal, little can be done to prevent it from ending up in the atmosphere. Thus, the strategies for reducing CO_2 do not typically include end-of-the-pipe or substitution solutions, making this a far more difficult challenge than phasing out ozone depleting substances.

One of the most controversial and complicated issues in the climate change negotiations has been the extent to which industrialized (Annex I) countries will be allowed to meet their own obligations by financing or undertaking activities in other countries. For example, would Canada be allowed to meet its obligations under the Convention by investing in energy efficiency in China? In some respects, the nature of climate change is ideal for establishing global trading markets in pollution; the reduction of one ton of carbon dioxide emissions anywhere in the world reduces climate change as much as any other ton of reduction. This has led many observers to develop different trading schemes to allow greater flexibility in meeting climate change targets. In theory, at least, such trading schemes can result in lowering the costs of compliance, as explained earlier.

The Protocol contains four trading mechanisms (collectively know as "flexibility mechanisms") that allow parties to meet their commitments jointly. Emissions trading under Article 17 allows an Annex I party to purchase or otherwise transfer part of its assigned amount to another Annex I party, presumably in exchange for payment. For example, assume Country A has excess reductions to meet its goal under Kyoto (e.g., it has reduced its emissions by 200 tons compared to its 1990 emissions, and this is 40 tons more than required to meet its Kyoto reduction target of 160 tons.). It can sell its remaining emissions (up to 40 tons) to Country B. These can then be subtracted from Country B's total emissions in calculating its emissions under Kyoto.

Like emissions trading, joint implementation (JI) under Article 6 may take place only between Annex I countries. JI involves the sale of "reduction units" from one Annex I party, or private enterprise, to another Annex I party or enterprise. Reduction units are generated by specific projects that reduce emissions or increase removals in the selling country. JI may be distinguished from emissions trading in that emissions trading is country-based, while JI is project-based. Emissions trading may also occur before associated emissions reductions are achieved, while JI reduction units can be transferred only after they have accrued. Emissions trading may be government-to-government, while JI may be initiated and undertaken by private sector entities. But in the final analysis, emissions trading and JI are closely linked.

The third approach, joint fulfillment of commitments under Article 4, allows an agreement between two or more parties to meet their combined commitments by reducing their aggregated emissions. Article 4 essentially allows parties to create a bubble around one or more of them to create their own targets and timetables, as long as the aggregate emissions from the parties do not exceed the aggregate allowances under the Protocol. Article 4 allows the European Union, for example, to operate essentially as one entity within the Protocol.

Finally, the Clean Development Mechanism (CDM) allows developing countries to help developed countries meet their emission reduction commitments. Article 12 provides that Annex I parties, or their private entities, may fund activities in non-Annex I countries that result in emissions reductions and, after they are certified, use those reductions to offset their domestic emissions. In principle, a developing country could re-forest an area and ensure it was not logged. It could then sell the calculated amount of carbon sequestered by this forest to an Annex I country, which would subtract this amount from its total emissions in calculating its emissions under Kyoto. The Protocol provides little guidance as to what the CDM would be; it is virtually undefined. Although the G77 as a bloc opposed joint implementation, they readily accepted the CDM. One possible explanation is that developing countries feared that joint implementation would go the way of previous "commodity" agreements, which yielded little profit for sellers. The CDM on the other hand might allow them to coordinate prices—in effect, to create a carbon cartel. Of course, purchasing countries, particularly the United States, worked to oppose such an outcome. Some developing countries, particularly Costa Rica, have jumped on the CDM bandwagon, creating national programs to solicit projects actively from developed countries. The state of New South Wales in Australia has passed a law creating alienable property rights in a land's carbon sequestration.

Many controversies continued beyond Kyoto regarding how the flexibility mechanisms would operate. Among the controversies was whether the use of emissions trading under Article 17 and the other flexibility mechanisms should be capped or not. In other words, would countries be forced to meet most or at least some amount of their emission reduction targets by reducing emissions *at home,* or could they simply purchase all of their needed emissions from Russia or other countries that had emission reduction units to sell because of the collapse of their economies following 1990 (called "hot air" by climate afficianados). The flexibility mechanisms intended to operate in developing countries raise additional questions for ensuring that any emission reduction credits are indeed additional to "business as usual" over the long-term. Beyond the technical issues of calculating the amount of carbon sequestered by CDM projects and monitoring to ensure the projects are properly implemented, CDM raises concerns of "carbon leakage." Leakage refers to the displacement of emissions from one source to another source. Since Kyoto caps total emissions of Annex I nations but not developing countries, it's possible emissions could be reduced in an Annex I nation simply by moving an emissions intensive activity to a developing nation. While perhaps too obvious to mention, the Kyoto Protocol remains a high-stakes work in progress.

E.   The Future of the Climate Regime

The Protocol enters into force after 55 parties, representing at least 55 percent of global carbon emissions, have ratified it. Early after taking office in 2001, President George W. Bush repudiated the Protocol and announced that he would not present it to the Senate for ratification. He first claimed that the science was too uncertain. Following a review by the National Academy of Sciences supporting the IPCC conclusions, the Bush administration changed tack, arguing that the absence of developing country commitments made the Kyoto Protocol "fatally flawed" and that ratifying the Protocol would damage U.S. interests. The Bush administration called for reliance on voluntary measures, instead. This announcement led to an acrimonious split with the European Union and indeed most of the world. The European Union and Japan have announced their intention to seek ratification of the Protocol without the United States. At the World Summit on Sustainable Development in 2002, Russia, Canada, and China effectively announced their intention to ratify the Protocol. Currently, among Annex I countries only the United States and Australia have refused to ratify. This split among the countries most responsible for climate change, and particularly the U.S. recalcitrance in addressing climate change, undoubtedly cannot last. As a result, the climate regime remains a complex and controversial regime— a regime that will evolve substantially in the years to come. What do you think will happen next? Can the Protocol be effective without the United States? Can the United States continue to be isolated on this issue internationally? These issues remain unanswered as this book goes to print, making the future of the climate regime very uncertain.

CHAPTER 5

Water Pollution

Having tackled air pollution in 1970, Congress two years later passed the Clean Water Act (CWA), originally known as the Water Pollution Control Act of 1972.[1] Just as the Clean Air Act has improved air quality, the CWA has reduced significantly the volume of effluents discharged from factories and sewage treatment facilities into the nation's rivers, lakes, estuaries, and other waterways. As a result, our nation's waters are cleaner than when the CWA was passed three decades ago. The CWA still has a long way to go, however, in ensuring good water quality across the nation. In 1996, EPA surveyed nearly three–quarters of the nation's watersheds. EPA was unable to gather sufficient data to determine the water quality of about a quarter of these watersheds. Of the other watersheds, however, only 22 percent enjoyed good water quality; almost half suffered moderate water quality problems, while the remainder experienced serious problems. States surveyed a smaller percentage of waterways in 1998 and found that 29 percent of the river miles and 20 percent of lake acreage did not support swimming part or all of the time. Similarly 30 percent of river miles, 29 percent of lake acreage, and 34 percent of estuary miles were too polluted during some or all of the year to provide adequate support for aquatic life. Only four percent of the Great Lakes shore miles were clean enough to permit local residents to consume any fish caught in the waters.

Environmentalists not surprisingly find much to criticize about the CWA. As discussed in more detail later in this chapter, the CWA focuses primarily on the discharge of pollutants into waterways, while largely ignoring hydrological changes to waterways, such as dams and water withdrawals, that also can harm water quality. More importantly, while reducing pollution from factories and sewage plants, the CWA has done a poor job of reducing effluent from farms, mines, construction sites, and other "nonpoint" sources of pollution.

Economists, by contrast, object that the CWA has required factories and other "point" sources of pollution to adopt pollution control technologies that were more expensive than justified by the benefits to water quality. Economists also complain that the CWA has not taken a "least cost" approach to improving water quality. Rather than focusing on those effluent discharges that produce the greatest damage or that can be reduced most inexpensively, the CWA typically imposes uniform effluent limitations on all companies within an industry. A number of

---

1. 33 U.S.C. §§ 1251 et seq.

studies suggest that Congress could have achieved the same level of water quality at a lower cost by adopting a more flexible regulatory approach.

I. An Overview of Water Pollution

Before examining the CWA's provisions, it is worth getting a better sense of the multiple causes of water pollution. Start with the sources of water pollution, as shown in Figure 5–1. Many factories, commercial facilities, and sewage plants discharge sludge and other effluents directly into waterways. These sources are known as *point sources* because they typically dump pollution into the waterway at a particular point along its shore through a pipe or channel. Other industrial and commercial facilities do not discharge their wastes directly into a waterway but instead empty their wastes into the local sewage system. These facilities are frequently labeled *indirect sources* of water pollution.

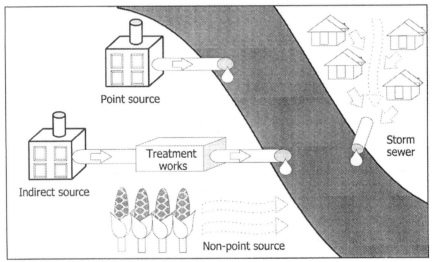

Figure 5-1: Sources of Water Pollution

Much of the pollution found today in the nation's waterways comes from farms, mines, construction sites, parking lots, and other land uses. When a farmer irrigates her crops, for example, much of the water ultimately may run off the land and, laced with various pesticides and other agricultural chemicals, find its way back into a river or other waterway. Rain or snow may pick up oil from parking lots, debris from construction sites, or tailings from mines before flowing into local watercourses. Because such runoff is often diffuse, these sources of pollution generally are called *nonpoint sources. Storm sewers* often collect such runoff from urban land, streets, and parking lots, and then convey the runoff to the waterway.

These are not the only sources of pollution. Air pollutants can blow miles away from their source and then settle into local waterways. Moisture in the atmosphere also can pick up or combine with air pollutants and then deposit the pollution as rain or snow directly into waterways or onto land where it again can runoff into waterways. The problem of acid rain, discussed earlier at pages 94–97, for example, occurs when water combines with airborne sulfates (which in turn arise from sulfur dioxide pollution) to form sulfuric acid. Water pollution also can arise naturally. Many rivers and lakes, for example, are naturally salty. The Colorado River in the western United States gains salinity as it passes over soils and rocks laden with soluble salts; one of its feeder streams, Blue Springs, alone contributes 550,000 tons of salt every year.

Changes to the hydrology of a waterway also can affect water quality. When water is diverted from a river, for example, there is less water to dilute downstream pollutants. Similarly, the creation of a large artificial reservoir along a waterway can increase the evaporation rate and thus increase the concentration of pollutants in the remaining water. Although the Colorado River is naturally salty, diversions and reservoirs have significantly increased the salinity level in downstream stretches. Dams also can change the quality of downstream waters. One early EPA study estimated that 15 percent of the water basins in the nation suffered from dam-related water quality problems. Water releases from dams sometimes are low in dissolved oxygen, reducing the ability of the water to break down organic materials and other pollutants. In other cases, the water released from dams can become "supersaturated" as it mixes with air, leading to significant fish kills. Water released from the lower "hypolimnion" layer of a reservoir can contain overly high concentrations of various minerals and nutrients that can harm fish, reduce the palatability of drinking water, and increase plant growth; this water also can be colder than the natural river, harming or killing fish acclimated to warmer water. Water released from the upper "epilimnion" layer can be warmer than the natural river and injure or kill cold-water fish.

Figure 5–2 shows the leading sources of water quality impairment in the United States for rivers, lakes, and estuaries. Thanks to the Clean Water Act, industrial facilities are no longer one of the leading sources of pollution. Indeed, industrial facilities are not even among the five major sources of pollution for either rivers or lakes and rank fourth as a cause of estuarial pollution. Although municipal sewage discharges remain the major source of estuarial pollution, they are only a secondary contributor of pollution to the nation's lakes and rivers. As Figure 5–2 illustrates, agriculture is the major source of pollution for the nation's rivers and lakes, polluting three times as many river miles as the next most important cause and two times as many lake acres. Thus nonpoint sources are today of greater concern than most point sources—largely because, as we will discuss in a moment, the Clean Water Act has not done a particularly good job of regulating nonpoint pollution.

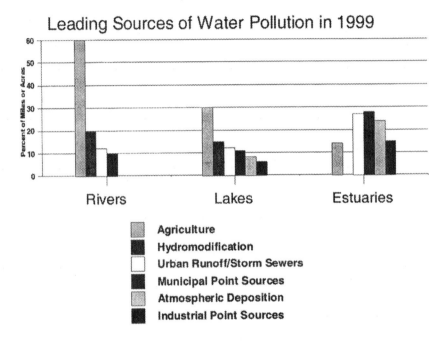

Figure 5-2: Leading Sources of Water Pollution

Source: *U.S. Environmental Protection Agency, National Water Quality Inventory: 1998 Report to Congress (June 2000)*

II. A Brief History of Water Quality Regulation

As in other environmental areas, courts played the primary role in regulating surface water pollution until well into the twentieth century. By the 1930s, most states had adopted administrative programs to control water pollution, but the regulatory measures were generally quite weak. States were reticent to impose the expense of better sewage treatment on local governments and feared driving industry elsewhere if they clamped down on industrial discharges. Nonpoint pollution was not even on the states' radar screens.

Congress first addressed water pollution in the 1965 Water Quality Act. Like many early laws, the 1965 Act relied almost entirely on the states to improve water quality. This law required the states to designate intended uses for interstate waterways within their jurisdiction: a state, for example, could designate that an interstate waterway should be usable for "drinking water supply," "primary contact," "swimming," "aquatic life support," or a number of other potential uses. The 1965 Act also required the states to adopt water quality standards that would ensure that each stretch of interstate water met its intended use and to formulate plans to implement those standards.

The 1965 Act failed to bring water pollution under control for several reasons. States did not have the political willpower to meet those water quality standards that they set. More importantly, the Act's water quality approach proved technically daunting. States typically did not have the scientific information needed to determine the appropriate water quality standards for any particular use such as aquatic life support. And even if a state could determine the correct standards, the state then faced the more complicated task of trying to set effluent standards for individual sources. The available models for translating the overall water quality standards into individual effluent standards were exceedingly complex but still did not come close to representing the actual processes by which effluents mix and influence water quality. In the face of such scientific uncertainty, polluters often argued that their discharges were not the cause of any water quality problems.

By the first Earth Day in 1970, the nation was beset by serious water quality problems. About half of the states still had not promulgated water quality standards under the 1965 Act. Many municipal sewage facilities continued to dump raw, untreated sewage; less than ten percent of the facilities used anything other than filters and settling tanks to treat the sewage. Less than a third of industrial facilities treated their wastes before emptying them into the nation's waterways. The pollution in some water bodies, such as Lake Erie, was so bad that a few scientists feared that the water bodies were beyond restoration. Most dramatically, in 1969 the Cuyahoga River in Cleveland actually caught on fire.

III. The Clean Water Act

Congress responded to these problems in 1972 by passing the Clean Water Act. As with the Clean Air Act, Congress set extremely ambitious goals for its new regulatory regime: the CWA was to "provide for the protection and propagation of fish, shellfish, and wildlife" and for "recreation in and on the water" by July 1, 1983, and to eliminate *all* discharges of pollutants into the nation's waterways by 1985. Although Congress passed the CWA by overwhelming margins, many observers were dumbfounded by Congress' announced goals. Among the critics was the National Water Commission, a bipartisan federal panel of water experts created in the late 1960s by President Lyndon Johnson to study the nation's water problems. To start, the critics noted that the goals were totally infeasible and thus destined to lead to public disappointment. More importantly, the critics observed that the "no discharge" goal implied that clean water was of infinite value and thus worth whatever costs were needed to eliminate all effluent discharges. Or, to quote from the National Water Commission's final report, the "no discharge" goal imputed "an extravagant social value to an abstract concept of water purity."[2]

The CWA in fact has come nowhere close to meeting its goals. No waterway is pristine. Over a third of the waterways surveyed in 1998 still were not fishable and swimmable. When Congress passed the CWA, most of its members recognized that the zero–discharge goal was "quite possibly 'beyond the ability of the American people to absorb the cost.' "[3] Indeed, the regulatory provisions in the CWA do not proscribe all pollution and often permit EPA to consider cost in setting specific discharge limits.

So why did Congress set unattainably aggressive goals? No matter how much Congress realized that costs and political realities would prevent it from eliminating all pollution, Congress may have wanted to make a moral statement that water pollution is bad. As we discussed in Chapter 2, moral outrage, not pragmatic cost-benefit comparisons, motivated the flood of federal environmental legislation in the early 1970s, including the CWA. Congress also may have believed that ambitious goals were needed to keep the government's feet to the fire. As Senator Edmund Muskie commented, a "national commitment" was needed to ensure that the nation developed the necessary new technology. Anticipating that industry and municipalities were likely to fight vigorous implementation of the CWA, Congress may have felt that the fishable–swimmable and "no discharge" goals would provide a valuable counterweight.

The key water quality provisions of the CWA fall into three main categories. Historically the most important set of provisions regulates point sources of pollution through a diverse array of effluent limitations and technological standards. A second, and to date far less consequential, body of provisions requires states to develop plans for the regulation of nonpoint pollution. As discussed in more detail later, the CWA itself does not directly regulate nonpoint pollution but leaves it largely to the

---

2. National Water Commission, Final Report: Water Policies for the Future 70 (1973).

3. National Wildlife Federation v. Gorsuch, 693 F.2d 156, 181 (D.C.Cir.1982) (quoting from the legislative history).

discretion of the states. A final group of provisions, of growing relevance today, requires states to set water quality standards for the waterways within their borders and to limit discharges as needed to achieve those standards. The CWA also contains a number of other regulatory provisions of less direct relevant to water pollution. The most important of these—section 404 of the CWA—restricts the filling of wetlands and is discussed in Chapter 9.

The CWA applies only to "navigable waters," but defines these expansively as "the waters of the United States, including the navigable seas."[4] As discussed at greater length in connection with federal wetlands protection in Chapter 9, courts have concluded that Congress did not intend to limit the reach of the CWA to waterways that would be considered "navigable" either in the dictionary sense of the term or under traditional legal definitions of navigability. The CWA thus applies not only to rivers and streams, but also to man-made canals, dry creek beds, and even the waste streams inside an industrial facility. Courts have concluded that the CWA generally does not apply to groundwater. But the CWA might apply even here if the groundwater feeds a spring or otherwise drains into surface waters.

A. *Regulation of Point Sources*

Congress' principal goal in passing the CWA was to reduce discharges from point sources. Congress could have done this in several ways. Congress could have set water quality standards for the entire nation and then left it to the states to develop plans to meet those standards. As discussed in Chapter 4, Congress took this approach in regulating air pollution under the Clean Air Act (through establishment of NAAQS and the SIP process). But the problems that had arisen in implementing the 1965 Water Quality Act, as discussed earlier, convinced Congress that the states would find it difficult to translate water quality standards into numeric effluent limitations for individual point sources. Congress therefore decided instead to have the United States EPA establish effluent standards for each type of point source, based on what the available technology could accomplish. Rather than figuring out what levels of pollution were consistent with various uses and then using complex models to translate these standards into individual effluent limits, EPA would only need to evaluate the technological opportunities for effluent reduction. States would still play a role in applying the technological standards to each individual point source, but this role would be far more straightforward and involve much less discretion than the states' responsibilities under the 1965 Act. Put another way, the CWA reversed

---

4.   CWA § 502(7), 33 U.S.C. § 1362(7).

the approach of the CAA. Instead of setting ambient air concentrations and working backwards to determine individual emission levels, the CWA starts with individual effluent levels.

1. NPDES Permits

The system that Congress chose to implement these technological standards is the National Pollutant Discharge Elimination System ("NPDES"). Under the CWA, the "discharge of any pollutant by any person" is unlawful without an NPDES permit, and the CWA defines "discharge of a pollutant" as "any *addition* of any *pollutant* to navigable waters from any *point source*."[5] Thus point sources generally must obtain an NPDES permit before discharging their wastes into the nation's waterways. The permits are generally good for five years, after which they must be renewed, and during their life are subject to modification or revocation for cause. States can qualify to issue the NPDES permits if they can show that they have the needed administrative and engineering capability, and about three quarters of the states currently are qualified to issue them. In the other states, the United States EPA issues the permits.

A regulatory system is only as good as its enforcement mechanisms, and the NPDES approach provides for quite effective enforcement. Each point source must report discharges on a regular, usually monthly, basis to EPA and to any state that has been delegated enforcement authority. Anyone wishing to determine whether a point source is violating the CWA can easily compare the effluent limitations contained in its NPDES permit with the reported discharges. The discharge reports, moreover, are admissible as evidence of a violation in court. Because the permits and reports are public records, anyone can check for violations. When the Natural Resources Defense Council feared in the early 1980s that the Reagan Administration would prove reluctant to prosecute CWA violations, it trained a cadre of students and other individuals to compare the permits and discharge reports and began filing citizen suits. Although companies could lie about their actual discharges, any misrepresentation in the discharge reports is subject to severe sanctions.

2. Publicly Owned Treatment Works

The effluent limitations in an NPDES permit depend on whether the permittee is a sewage plant, otherwise known as publicly owned treatment works or "POTWs," or another type of point source. POTWs are passive receivers of pollution, unlike most point sources. While most point sources must comply with numeric limits on their effluent discharges, the CWA requires POTWs simply to use a specific level of

---

5. CWA §§ 301(a) & 592(12), 33 U.S.C. §§ 1311(a) & 1362(12).

technology. A quick overview of the different types of sewage treatment technology is worthwhile in this regard. Engineers often distinguish between three broad categories of technology. In *primary treatment*, POTWs separate out solid waste using filters, screens, and settlement tanks. In *secondary treatment*, POTWs use microorganisms to break down organic matter biologically. The microorganisms, which need oxygen to survive, feed on the organic matter. POTWs can speed up this process by blowing air into the sewage in aeration tanks. These are the round tanks you often see from the air when landing at airports. In *tertiary treatment*, POTWs "polish" any remaining contaminants out of the water through physical methods such as sand filters or membrane microfiltration or by using ultra-violet light to kill bacteria.

Originally, the CWA required all POTWs to use secondary treatment by 1977, and by 1983 to use the "best practicable waste treatment technology over the life of the works." Congress assumed that the latter standard would require secondary and often various forms of tertiary treatment. Because Congress recognized that many municipalities did not have the funds needed to upgrade their POTWs, the CWA also provided significant federal grants to municipalities of up to 85 percent of the cost of installing the needed technology.

Unfortunately, these provisions were singularly unsuccessful. Many cities dragged their feet and were still not using secondary treatment in 1977. The costs of converting to secondary treatment, moreover, were higher than expected. Critics criticized the grants program for undermining the incentive that municipalities might otherwise have to keep down the costs of upgrading their facilities. Many cities used the federal funds to expand their sewage systems to meet growing population needs rather than to improve their effluent quality. And budgetary constraints were making it difficult for Congress to continue to fund the grants program. In light of these problems, Congress amended the CWA to eliminate the stricter 1983 standard and to permit EPA to waive even the secondary treatment standard for POTWs that discharged their sewage sludge into coastal waters. More than fifty POTWs currently enjoy a waiver from secondary treatment. Congress also phased out its grant program and replaced it with a revolving loan program.

3. *Industrial Point Sources*

Point sources other than POTWs must meet technology-based effluent limits. For these sources, the CWA does not require the point sources to use a particular technology. The government instead decides on an appropriate numeric effluent limitation based on what the technology can accomplish. Sources are then free to meet the effluent limitation in whatever manner they wish. Most sources are likely to adopt the technology used by EPA to set the limitation because the sources know that this technology will permit them to meet the effluent limitation. But a source is free to use a different technology if it will be at least as effective in reducing the pollution. This flexibility can be valuable to the firm that figures out a cheaper way to meet the effluent limitations.

In drafting the effluent-limitation provisions, one of the first questions that Congress faced was which technology the government should use in determining the numeric limitations. First, what *types* of technology should be considered? "End-of-pipe" technologies help clean up the harmful byproducts of industrial processes before they are discharged into a waterway. But facilities often can reduce their discharges even more by changing their industrial processes and finding ways of reducing their production of the harmful byproducts in the first place, an approach known as "pollution prevention" and further discussed in Chapter 7. While end-of-pipe technologies merely treat the water pollution, process changes can prevent or reduce all harmful by-products and sometimes even reduce a company's costs by making more efficient use of raw materials and by eliminating disposal costs. Most companies, however, oppose efforts to regulate their processes for a number of reasons: (1) process changes sometime can prove more expensive than end-of-pipe technologies, (2) government regulation of processes intrudes more into business decisions, (3) process changes are generally less certain to meet effluent limits than proven end-of-pipe technologies, and (4) because production processes determine the characteristics and quality of a company's product, process changes can negatively affect product quality and hurt a company's sales and reputation. So although environmentalists have consistently pushed the government to consider process changes, most companies have strongly resisted such interventions.

Second, no matter what types of technologies are considered, how should the government choose the particular technology to use in calculating the effluent limitations? An economist would argue that the government should pick the technology based on a cost-benefit comparison: what is the most exacting technology for which benefits outweigh costs? But there are other options. The government, for example, might pick the best technology that companies can afford, without considering whether its benefits outweigh its cost. The government might believe that balancing the benefits and costs is too difficult, or that pollution reduction is a moral rather than economic issue, and that the only relevant question therefore should be economic feasibility. The government might even conclude that the only question should be whether the technology works; if companies cannot afford the technology and must close down, that's the necessary price of having clean rivers and lakes.

Third, should effluent limitations be determined on a facility-by-facility basis or by industry? Assume, for example, that the government is setting effluent limitations for pulp and paper mills and has decided to select the best technology that is economically feasible. If 80 percent of the mills in the United States can afford a particular technology, but the other 20 percent would be forced out of business if they had to meet effluent limitations based on the technology, what should the government do? Should the government use the technology to set a uniformly high effluent limitation for all mills, recognizing that some mills will cease operating and throw their employees out of work? Alternatively, should the government set lower standards for those facilities that cannot afford the technology, even though water quality will suffer and some mills will be forced to take on a greater burden than others? Or should the government reject the technology because it is economically infeasible for some mills and use a lower effluent limitation for all mills, to the detriment of water quality throughout the nation? Administrative costs can play a major role in whether to make determinations by facility or by industry. While there are tens of thousands of industrial facilities in the United States that discharge effluent into waterways, these facilities can be reduced to just a few score of industry groups.

Name of Standard	Possible Technology	Role of Cost
BPT	"End of the pipe"	Cost compared to benefit
BCT	"End of the pipe"	Cost can be considered
BAT	"End of the pipe"	Cost can be considered
BCT	"End of the pipe," process changes, operation changes	No consideration of cost

Figure 5-3: CWA Technological Standards

The CWA unfortunately does not provide uniform answers to these questions. Instead, Congress chose to take different approaches to the choice of technology depending on whether facilities are new or old and depending on the type of pollution being discharged. The answer to these questions, moreover, has varied over time. Just as it did in the case of POTWs, Congress started out with more rigorous criteria than are found in the CWA today. As industry balked at the initial criteria for selecting the appropriate technology, Congress backed down. The lawyer trying to understand the CWA therefore must master a number of different technological standards, each with its own acronym. This is where environmental law begins to resemble a child playing with a bowl of alphabet soup. To help you through the morass, Figure 5–3 provides a quick summary of the various standards, all of which are discussed in more detail below. The standards are listed in their general order of stringency, with the standards at the top of the table being less stringent than those at the bottom.

4. Existing Point Sources

The CWA originally provided that effluent limitations for existing point sources would generally reflect the "best practicable control technology currently available" ("BPT") by 1977 and the "best available technology economically achievable" ("BAT") by 1983. Although the "best practicable control technology currently available" might sound more stringent than the "best available technology economically achievable," Congress anticipated that BAT would be the more stringent of the two. In choosing BPT, EPA must balance the costs and benefits of alternative technologies. By contrast, EPA can "consider" cost in determining BAT, but is not supposed to directly compare the costs with the benefits. (If you find that difference a bit subtle, you are in good company.) In practice, BAT generally has been the environmentally best technology that is economically feasible. BAT does not require that the technology actually be in use, so long as it can be shown to work. In summary, the 1970 CWA anticipated that the technological standard for existing sources would become more rigorous over time, with the cost of the technology playing less of a role.

In drafting the 1970 CWA, Congress also believed that a technological approach was not appropriate where a point source was discharging toxic pollutants. Here, Congress believed that the effluent limitations should be strict enough to protect human health, no matter how difficult or costly point sources would find it to meet the limitations.

Faced by industry objections, however, Congress backed away from applying the BAT standard on a universal basis to all existing point sources and abandoned entirely its health-based approach to toxic pollutants. The exact technological standard that EPA uses today to determine the effluent limitations for an existing point source depends on whether the pollution being released by the source is "toxic," "conventional," or "nonconventional."

Toxic Pollutants. Toxic pollutants include a list of 126 chemical substances specified by Congress in the CWA, as well as any other pollutants that EPA determines to be toxic based on the pollutant's toxicity, persistence, degradability, and impact on organisms. Because scientists only recently have begun to understand the health effect of various toxic pollutants in waterways, EPA found it virtually impossible to implement Congress' original health-based approach. As a result, Congress abandoned the health-based approach and now requires EPA to use the BAT standard to calculate effluent limitations for these pollutants.

Conventional Pollutants. The CWA defines "conventional pollutants" as those pollutants that commonly pollute waterways, including biological oxygen demand (BOD), suspended solids, pH, fecal coliform, bacteria, oil, and grease. In place of the BAT standard, the CWA now requires EPA to use the "best conventional pollutant control technology" (BCT) to set effluent limitations for these pollutants. Although Congress anticipated that BCT would lie somewhere between BPT and BAT, EPA in most cases has treated BCT as very similar to the BPT standard.

Nonconventional Pollutants. Any pollutants that do not fit within the definitions of toxic or conventional pollutants, including ammonia, chloride, color, iron, and nitrate, are regulated as "nonconventional pollutants." Such pollutants are generally subject to the BAT standard, although the CWA permits EPA to waive or modify the BAT requirement where justified either by cost or by the quality of the receiving water.

5. New Point Sources

Like the Clean Air Act, the CWA singles out new industrial point sources for tighter effluent limitations. Both policy and politics again help explain why. From a policy perspective, new sources do not need to retrofit their facilities, which can be very expensive, to comply. Instead, new sources can build pollution control technology into their design from the outset and thereby achieve low discharge standards for less money than existing facilities would need to pay. Over time, moreover, companies will need to replace old plants with new facilities, so that ultimately all companies will be meeting the tighter standards established for new sources. Politically, existing sources usually are a potent lobbying force against stringent discharge standards, while few companies are as worried about hypothetical future plants. In fact, existing companies often favor saddling new facilities with stricter standards because the stricter standards can make it more difficult for competitors to enter the industry; the stricter standards, in short, act as economic barriers to entry.

The imposition of tighter effluent standards on new point sources also poses potential problems. Because the stricter standards can act as a barrier to entry, for example, they in theory can reduce the number of companies competing in any given industry; the reduced competition, in turn, can lead to higher prices and other forms of monopolistic behavior. By making new facilities more expensive, moreover, stricter standards for new sources may encourage companies to keep their existing facilities in operation as long as possible (as EPA charges has happened with coal-fired power plants avoiding New Source Performance Standards under the Clean Air Act, *see* pages 87–89). Not only may this be economically inefficient, but old facilities tend to have poorer environmental performance across the board. Whatever the possible disadvantages of differentiating between existing and new facilities, however, Congress has found such differentiation to be irresistible time and time again.

Under the CWA, new point sources must meet effluent standards that reflect the "greatest degree of effluent reduction which the Administrator [of EPA] determines to be achievable through application of the best available control technology, processes, operating methods, or other alternatives, including, where practicable, a standard permitting no discharge of pollutants," otherwise known as "BCT." Note that BCT can include not only end-of-pipe technology, but also changes to a facility's processes and operations. Also note that cost does not play any explicit role in the selection of BCT.

6. Industry-by-Industry Determination

The CWA unfortunately does not say whether effluent limitations are to be set on a facility-by-facility basis or by industry. Although one section of the CWA refers to "effluent limitations for *categories and classes* of point sources,"[6] other sections are more ambiguous. In 1977, however, the Supreme Court concluded that EPA could set industry-wide guidelines for effluent limitations.[7] Otherwise, as the Court observed, EPA would need to determine technological standards for tens of thousands of individual permits—a result it did not believe Congress had intended. As a result, EPA now has set technological standards for more than fifty major categories of industrial facilities. If companies within an industry are dissatisfied with the guidelines, they must challenge the guidelines when issued by EPA, not when the government uses the guidelines to set the effluent limitations in individual NPDES permits.

Industrial plants that feel they are different from the bulk of their industry, however, are not without remedy. First, point sources that can show that key assumptions behind the EPA effluent limitation guidelines are inapplicable to them can apply for a "fundamentally different factor" (or "FDF") variance. A point source cannot ask for a FDF variance because of cost factors. Instead, it must show that the applicable technology will not work or achieve the same results because of unique characteristics of the facility (e.g., a fish cannery located on a mountainside instead of by the shore). If EPA grants a FDF variance, the permit writer must develop a site-specific standard based on the

---

6. Clean Water Act § 301(b)(2)(A), 33 U.S.C. § 1311(b)(2)(A) (emphasis added).

7. E.I. du Pont de Nemours & Co. v. Train, 430 U.S. 112 (1977).

statutory criteria for the particular type of pollution. Second, an industrial facility sometimes can obtain a variance from the BCT limits for conventional pollutants either because the national standard is beyond the facility's economic capability or because less stringent limitations will protect water quality conditions adequately. Although variances could play a major role in shaping water discharges, EPA in practice has issued only a very limited number of variances.

7. Indirect Sources

Like playing chess, designing an environmental law requires legislators to think one step ahead of regulated companies. Not only must the legislator design an effective regulation, but the regulator must predict how companies might try to get around the regulation. Faced by expensive effluent limitations, for example, what might a company do to avoid the limitations? One option might be to discharge the waste into the local sewage system rather than directly into the waterway. This can pose at least two problems. First, the secondary treatment required of (most) POTWs does not adequately treat a number of common industrial pollutants. In fact, at one point, over a third of the toxins that polluted the nation's waterways flowed from industrial facilities through POTWs. Second, pollution from industrial facilities can increase the risk of fire or explosion at a POTW and can interfere with the effective operation of the POTW's treatment of other waste.

To address these problems, the CWA also regulates such indirect sources of pollution through both *prohibited discharge standards* and *categorical pretreatment standards*. Under the former, the CWA prohibits indirect sources from discharging wastes into a POTW system that will interfere with the proper operation of the POTW or pass through the POTW untreated. Under the categorical pretreatment standard, the CWA requires indirect sources to meet BAT standards for any discharge of toxic pollutants into a POTW system, unless the POTW has demonstrated that it can treat the pollutant adequately. In addition to these federal standards, most POTWs impose their own restrictions on what forms of industrial wastes can be discharged into the sewer system.

8. Criticism of the Technological Approach

Many economists have been highly critical of the technology-based standards in the CWA because the technology-based standards do not take the most cost-effective route to reducing water pollution. All facilities in the same industry must generally meet the same technological standards, even though the pollution from one facility may not be as harmful as pollution from another facility (because the water is already highly degraded or, alternatively, has a greater assimilative capacity) and even though some facilities may find it more expensive than others to install the technology. Under the CWA's technological standards, moreover, an industry which imposes a minimal impact on water quality might be required to install more expensive equipment than an industry with serious pollution problems. From the economist's perspective, the government should focus on those facilities where the *net* benefits of installing pollution-control equipment (i.e., the benefits from reducing pollution minus the cost of the reduction) are greatest. But the CWA instead generally looks only at technological and, in some cases, economic feasibility and imposes uniform standards across all facilities in an industry. Not surprisingly, economic studies suggest that the technological standards in economic terms may have cost more than they have delivered. One 1990 study estimated that costs through 1985 were between $25 and $30 billion, while benefits were more in the range of $6 to $28 billion.

Environmentalists also have been critical of the technology-based standards, but for other reasons. Because the standards require complex technical studies and judgments, EPA often takes years to develop and adopt individual standards and often has missed statutory deadlines for the issuance of standards. Moreover, rather than studying the effects of pollution on water quality and human and aquatic health, EPA officials have more often focused their attention on engineering questions.

So why then does the CWA continue to focus on technological standards? The simplest answer is that, by and large, this strategy has worked in reducing water pollution in the United States. Determining practicable technologies is much simpler, less costly for EPA, and far less controversial than weighing the costs and benefits of various control measures. Technological standards, moreover, are relatively easy to enforce. Government officials need only check to see if a facility has installed and is using the relevant technology.

B.   The Non–Regulation of Nonpoint Sources

The CWA's highly effective regulation of point sources must be balanced against its lackadaisical approach to nonpoint pollution. The CWA effectively leaves the regulation of nonpoint pollution up to the individual states. Section 208 of the CWA was Congress' original effort to control nonpoint pollution. Section 208 requires states to designate lead agencies to head up pollution control efforts in waterways with "substantial water quality problems" and orders these agencies to prepare "areawide waste treatment management plans," including procedures and methods to control pollution from agriculture, silviculture, mining, and construction "to the extent feasible." Section 208, however, does not require the states to implement these plans. Even the planning requirements, moreover, are toothless. States must submit their management plans to EPA for approval. But if a state fails to submit a plan or submits an inadequate plan, EPA has no authority to make the state submit an adequate plan or to issue a federal management plan. Left to their own discretion and faced with significant opposition by agricultural, mining, and construction lobbies, most states have chosen not to adopt meaningful management plans under section 208.

By the mid–1980s, nonpoint pollution had eclipsed point discharges as the largest contributor to water pollution in the United States. Given the failure of section 208, numerous members of Congress urged a "renewed commitment to the cleanup of nonpoint sources of pollution."[8] The result was the addition to the CWA in 1987 of section 319 which requires states to implement a "nonpoint source management program." Section 319 instructs each state to prepare a report identifying those categories of nonpoint sources that are preventing the state from attaining its designated water quality standards and describing the measures needed to "reduce, to the maximum extent practicable, the level of pollution" from those sources. According to section 319, moreover, states must require nonpoint sources to use "best management practices ['BMPs'] . . . at the earliest practicable date." The Senate Report on section 319 noted that BMPs can include soil conservation programs, such as the terracing of agricultural land, and "simple" changes in agricultural practices, such as the careful scheduling and application of fertilizer and pesticides. Section 319 finally instructs each state to prepare a management plan describing how the state will implement its program.

Although section 319 on paper appears to push states toward greater regulation of nonpoint pollution, Congress again failed to back up its bark with any bite. If a state failed to prepare its first report, which was due in August 1988, section 319 required the United States EPA to prepare a report for the state identifying those categories of nonpoint sources that the state needed to address. But Congress did not authorize EPA to identify control measures or to impose a management plan on any state. The omission, moreover, was intentional. According to then Senator George Mitchell, who was one of the sponsors of the amendment, section 319 does not require a state to control nonpoint pollution. "If a state decides that it does not want a program to control nonpoint pollution, that is it."[9]

Why has Congress been so reticent to adopt measures that will reduce nonpoint pollution firmly and effectively? Nonpoint sources often are more difficult to regulate than point sources. Nonpoint sources far

---

8. 133 Cong. Rec. S744 (Jan. 14, 1987) (comments of Sen. Baucus).

9. 133 Cong. Rec. S1968 (Feb. 4, 1987) (comments of Sen. Mitchell).

outnumber point sources. They are more varied, complicating the effort to determine appropriate technological standards. And they often do not offer a simple means for monitoring performance. The government readily can measure the pollutants flowing out of a pipe, but how do you evaluate the runoff from a construction site? None of these problems, however, is fatal. Without great difficulty, the government could prescribe best management practices for common land uses that contribute sizable amounts of nonpoint pollution. Under a BMP approach, moreover, the government does not necessarily need to monitor pollution. Instead, the government can monitor whether sources are actually using the mandated BMPs. Another possible hurdle to non-point regulation is that land uses have been the traditional province of state and local governments. But the federal government can require states to reduce nonpoint pollution, yet leave the choice of specific BMPs to the states. The problem with the CWA's nonpoint pollution provisions has not been the delegation of authority to the states, but the lack of any effective mechanism to force the states to use that authority to reduce the nonpoint pollution. After analyzing all of the policy considerations, one inevitably is left with the conclusion that politics has driven the CWA's failure to take on nonpoint pollution in any meaningful way. The agricultural lobby, in particular, has been very successful in weakening or killing off proposals to regulate nonpoint pollution more rigorously.

C.   Escaping Regulation as a Point Source

A repeated lesson in environmental regulation is that if the law draws a bright-line distinction between two different types of activities or actions and regulates one far more than the other, the regulated community will fight hard to end up on the less onerous side of the line. Under the CWA, a lot depends on whether a source must apply for an NPDES permit. So not surprisingly, this question generated several hard-fought disputes in the first decade or so after the CWA was passed. As described earlier, the "discharge of any pollutant by any person" is unlawful without an NPDES permit, and the CWA defines "discharge of a pollutant" as "any *addition* of any *pollutant* from any *point source*." To escape NPDES regulation, therefore, a potential regulatory target must argue either that it is not a "point source" or that it is not "adding" a "pollutant" to the water.

One of the most important questions in the early years of the CWA was whether agricultural runoff ever could be considered a point source of pollution. The CWA originally defined a point source as "any discernible, confined and discrete conveyance, including but not limited to any pipe, ditch, channel, tunnel, conduit, well, discrete fissure, container, rolling stock, concentrated animal feeding operation, or vessel or other floating craft, from which pollutants are or may be discharged." Although the runoff from many farms and ranches is diffuse, many farms, ranches, and agricultural districts collect runoff and discharge the runoff into waterways through confined conveyance facilities. In 1973, however, EPA issued a regulation exempting farms of less than 3000 acres, as well as animal feedlots and silviculture, from the NPDES permit requirements, even if a facility satisfied the statutory definition of a point source. As justification for the exemption, EPA argued that it would be infeasible to apply numeric effluent limitations to such agricultural operations. "An effluent limitation must be a precise number in order for it to be an effective regulatory tool; both the discharger and the regulatory agency need to have an identifiable standard upon which to determine whether the facility is in compliance."[10] EPA also argued that the exempted agricultural sources numbered in the hundreds of thousands and, if subject to NPDES requirements, would overwhelm EPA and state permitting agencies.

An environmental organization sued, arguing that EPA did not have the discretion to exempt discharges that met the statutory definition of a point source. In 1977, the D.C. Circuit agreed and invalidated the regulation. In *Natural Resources Defense Council v. Costle*,[11] the court held that Congress had not authorized EPA to grant categorical exemptions from the NPDES requirements. The court, moreover, found EPA's administrative concerns unconvincing: EPA could adjust the permit terms to fit the unique characteristics of agricultural sources and could reduce the sheer numerical burden by issuing general permits for various classes of agricultural polluters.

The court's decision invalidating EPA's exemption was short lived. Only a few months after the D.C. Circuit issued its decision, Congress amended the definition of point source to exclude return flows from irrigated agriculture. Congress also banned EPA from requiring an NPDES permit for "discharges composed entirely of return flow from irrigated agriculture" or, "directly or indirectly, requir[ing] any State to require such a permit." The lobbying power of agriculture once again prevailed over environmental interests. Although a committee of the National Academy of Sciences has recommended that Congress repeal the agricultural exemption, Congress has indicated no interest in doing so.

In 1987, however, Congress did choose to bring some forms of storm water runoff under the NPDES system. Storm water runoff is rainwater that picks up contaminants as it flows across the land and then into a

---

10. The language is from an EPA memorandum quoted in Natural Resources Defense Council v. Costle, 568 F.2d 1369, 1378 (D.C.Cir.1977).

11. 568 F.2d 1369 (D.C.Cir.1977).

waterway. Where municipal storm sewer systems or industrial activities, such as pulp mills or chemical plants, discharge the storm water runoff, section 402 of the CWA requires an NPDES permit.

A question that a number of courts have addressed is whether dams must obtain NPDES permits. As discussed earlier, dams can change both the temperature and oxygen content of downstream water. Dams, moreover, are clearly "point sources" since they release water from confined openings. Courts, however, have uniformly held that dams do not "add" "pollutants." The list of "pollutants" contained in the CWA consists primarily of substances; "heat" is the only water condition included. Courts, moreover, have questioned whether, even if conditions such as low dissolved oxygen, cold, and supersaturation are pollutants, dams "add" such pollutants to the water. Although courts could easily go either way on these definitional questions, courts have concluded that Congress in the CWA did not intend to interfere with state water management. Section 101(g) of the Act supports this view by declaring that it "is the policy that the authority of each State to allocate quantities of water within its jurisdiction shall not be superseded, abrogated, or otherwise impaired by this Act."

Courts also occasionally must determine whether other forms of polluting activities are point sources. In *United States v. Plaza Health Laboratories*,[12] for example, the co-owner of a blood-testing lab dumped vials of human blood into the Hudson River. When the government brought criminal charges under the CWA for discharging pollutants without a permit, the owner defended on the ground that he was not a "point source" (since after all he did not resemble a "pipe, ditch, channel, tunnel, conduit, well, discrete fissure," etc.). Because the "rule of lenity" calls for statutory ambiguities to be resolved against the government in criminal cases, the Court of Appeals agreed with the defendant by a two to one vote. In most cases, however, the courts have adopted a broad interpretation of "point sources." Thus, for example, navy planes dropping bombs into the ocean during training are point sources.[13] If effluent is channelized in any way, the discharge almost certainly is a "point source."

D. Water Quality Standards

As discussed earlier, the 1972 CWA took a largely technological approach to water pollution because of the singular failure of the 1965 Water Quality Act, which had tried to regulate water pollution through

---

12. 3 F.3d 643 (2d Cir.1993).

13. Romero-Barcelo v. Brown, 478 F.Supp. 646 (D.P.R.1979), aff'd sub nom. Romero–Barcelo v. Brown, 643 F.2d 835 (1st Cir.1981), rev'd on other grounds sub nom. Weinberger v. Romero–Barcelo, 456 U.S. 305 (1982).

ambient water quality standards. Given the difficulties under the 1965 Act, the Senate in 1972 proposed abandoning water quality standards entirely. At the House of Representatives' insistence, however, the 1972 CWA retained water quality standards as a backup or safety net to the technology-based effluent limitations outlined above.

Section 303 of the CWA sets out a multi-step regulatory process. First, each state designates specific beneficial uses for each of its waterways. These *designated uses* can include "public water supply," "protection and propagation of fish, shellfish, and wildlife," recreation, agriculture, and industry. Given the CWA's goal of providing fishable–swimmable water by 1983, states typically must provide for water quality that protects and propagates fish, shellfish, and wildlife and that permits recreation in and on the water. However, if a state can demonstrate that the fishable–swimmable standard is unattainable because of naturally occurring pollution, low water flows, or other factors, EPA sometimes can permit the state to "downgrade" the designated use to a lower standard such as agriculture or industry. Once a state has designated the use for a waterway, it must review the designation at least every three years.

Second, states determine *water quality standards* needed to support the designated uses. The standards are typically quantitative (e.g., no more than 8 milligrams of a particular contaminant per liter of water in a river). Standards for toxic pollutants *must* be quantitative. To help states determine necessary standards, EPA uses the latest scientific information to prepare *water quality criteria* that show the minimum physical, chemical, and biological parameters required to support the various designated uses of a waterway. If a state fails to establish adequate quality standards for a waterway, the United States EPA can set standards for the state.

Third, the states must identify *quality-limited waterways*—those waterways where the technology-based effluent limitations imposed under NPDES permits are insufficient to attain the water quality standards. For each quality-limited waterway, a state must determined the *total maximum daily load* (or *"TMDL"*) of pollutants that can be discharged into the waterway and still achieve "the applicable water quality standards with seasonal variations and a margin of safety which takes into account any lack of knowledge concerning the relationship between effluent limitations and water quality." The states must submit a list of both the quality-impaired waterways and associated TMDLs to EPA for approval.

What happens after a state establishes the TMDLs is not entirely clear. If the technology-based effluent limitations for point sources are not sufficient to achieve the water quality standards, section 301 of the

CWA requires that the effluent limitations be lowered to the degree needed to meet the standards. But must a state reduce non-point pollution if needed to achieve the water quality standards? In many cases, a waterway would not meet water quality standards even if point sources discharged no waste whatsoever. The CWA is silent on this question. The Act does not explicitly require states to regulate non-point pollution where needed to achieve water quality standards and does not say what happens if states do not. Section 303 of the Act requires states to engage in a "continuing planning process" (CPP) that includes the TMDLs, and the United States EPA can disapprove the CPP if a state's TMDLs are inadequate. But section 303 does not give EPA the authority to implement a CPP if the state fails to do so.

For the first twenty–five years of the CWA, states did not even prepare TMDLs for their quality-limited waterways. And EPA made no effort to force the states to do so; instead, EPA focused on the Act's technology-based effluent limitations. Congress, moreover, encouraged this neglect. According to Senator Edmund Muskie, who was the principal Senate sponsor of the 1972 CWA, EPA should assign "secondary importance" to the water quality standards. Given the problems implementing the 1965 Water Quality Act, Congress wanted EPA to focus on the provisions of the CWA that appeared to have the greatest chance of success—the technology-based effluent limitations—not the water quality standards. Even if EPA had wanted to implement the water quality standards, it is unclear what EPA could have done. If EPA concludes that a state's list of quality-impaired waterways and TMDLs are inadequate, the CWA authorizes EPA to prepare its own list. But the Act says nothing about what, if anything, EPA can do if a state fails to submit a list at all. As noted already, moreover, the CWA does not grant explicit authority to EPA to implement TMDLs, whether state or federal.

A series of judicial decisions starting in the mid–1980s, however, has put pressure on EPA and states to take TMDLs more seriously. In 1984, a federal court of appeals held that the "prolonged failure" of a state to file a list of quality-impaired waterways could constitute a "constructive submission" of no TMDLs, triggering EPA's duty to prepare its own TMDLs.[14] A decade later, a federal district court found that EPA had acted arbitrarily and capriciously in approving a list of quality-impaired waterways that omitted, without explanation, waterways that the state previously had identified as impaired. States in short can no longer ignore their obligation to prepare lists of quality-impaired waterways and TMDLs, and EPA must analyze the lists carefully before approving

14. See Scott v. City of Hammond, 741 F.2d 992 (7th Cir.1984).

them. The question nonetheless remains: what happens after an adequate list is prepared? Does the CWA require process but no substance?

Some commentators believe that TMDLs offer a great opportunity for pollution trading between point and nonpoint sources. In order for point sources to meet their TMDL requirements, for example, they might pay nonpoint sources such as farms to change their irrigation or fertilizer practices. The reduction in nutrients flowing into the water body, in theory, could be set off against the point source's contributions. Water quality trading programs, however, raise very complex scientific and administrative issues because a reduction in discharges at one point in a waterway is not necessarily equivalent to a reduction somewhere else in the same waterway.

Notice also that the concentration of pollutants in a waterway can be reduced by either reducing the pollution entering the waterway or by increasing the amount of water. In a controversial move, point sources and states occasionally have proposed meeting water quality standards by augmenting the flow of quality-impaired waterways. To some environmentalists, "flow augmentation" merely masks pollution and encourages risky "engineering" of rivers and streams. Section 102(b)(1) of the CWA forbids the federal government from releasing water from federal water projects "as a substitute for adequate treatment or other methods of controlling waste at the source." EPA regulations, however, authorize flow augmentation in other settings where point sources are meeting the technology-based effluent limitations and flow augmentation is "the preferred environmental and economic method to achieve the [water quality] standards."[15]

E. *Always Cleaner, Never Dirtier*

Most federal environmental laws assume that regulations should act like a ratchet: environmental standards should continually be tightened, and they never should be loosened. In line with this theme, the CWA suggests that technology-based limitations should become progressively more stringent over time. The CWA, moreover, generally forbids a state from modifying an NPDES permit to permit an increase in pollution. There are only a few exceptions to this "anti-backsliding" policy. If new information becomes available demonstrating a lower technology-based standard is appropriate, a more lenient permit can be issued. Similarly, if a point source is unable to meet its NPDES requirements despite the installation and operation of appropriate pollution-control equipment, a state can reconsider the standards that it originally set.

The water quality provisions of the CWA also include an "antidegradation" policy. Where waterways are meeting their existing designated

---

15.   40 C.F.R. § 125.3(f).

uses, states must protect that water quality. States, moreover, cannot permit the degradation of "high quality waters," defined as waterways that meet the fishable–swimmable standards, unless they can demonstrate an economic or social justification for the decline in water quality.

F. Interstate Water Pollution

As the Supreme Court has observed, "Interstate waters have been a font of controversy since the founding of the Nation."[16] Interstate pollution, moreover, presents perhaps the strongest case for federal intervention because downstream states have limited options, at best, for protecting themselves from the effluent discharges of upstream states. Yet the CWA surprisingly pays meager attention to the problem of interstate pollution. Section 103 of the CWA requires the Administrator of the national EPA to encourage "cooperative activities by the States ... and so far as practicable, uniform State laws relating to the prevention, reduction, and elimination of pollution." The same section provides advance Congressional authorization for states to regulate interstate pollution through interstate agreements (or "compacts," to use the constitutional term for such agreements).

Recall, however, that point sources cannot discharge effluents in concentrations that would violate water quality standards. EPA has decided by regulation that a state cannot issue an NPDES permit if the effluent discharges would violate the water quality standards of any other states through which the waterway flows. Sections 401 and 402 of the CWA require that a state give notice and an opportunity to be heard to downstream states before issuing an NPDES permit for a discharge into an interstate waterway. If a downstream state believes that the proposed discharge would interfere with the state's water quality standards, it may ask the EPA Administrator to disapprove the permit.

EPA is unlikely to intervene unless the discharge will cause a clear deterioration in water quality in the downstream state. In *Arkansas v. Oklahoma*,[17] Oklahoma objected to EPA's issuance of an NPDES permit to a POTW in Arkansas that planned to discharge sewage effluent into the Illinois River only 39 miles upstream from the Oklahoma border. Noting that the Illinois River already was out of compliance with Oklahoma's water quality standards, Oklahoma argued that the Clean Water Act prohibited any additional discharge that would reach Oklahoma waters. EPA disagreed and looked instead to see if the proposed discharge would cause an "actual detectable or measurable" impairment of Oklahoma's water quality standards. The Supreme Court upheld

16. Arkansas v. Oklahoma, 503 U.S. 91,   **17.** 503 U.S. 91 (1992).
98 (1992).

EPA's approach. The Court concluded that EPA has the authority to consider downstream states' water quality standards in issuing NPDES permits but does not have to ban all discharges where downstream water quality standards are not being met.

Indeed the CWA actually might have left downstream states in a worse position than before the Act's passage. In 1972, immediately before Congress enacted the CWA, the Supreme Court had held that a state could sue under a "federal common law" of nuisance to abate pollution resulting from operations in another state. However, almost a decade later in what has become known as the *Milwaukee II* decision, the Court held that the CWA preempted such federal common law actions.[18] A few years after *Milwaukee II*, the Court further held that a Vermont resident could not invoke Vermont nuisance law to enjoin discharges that occurred in New York. "The inevitable result of such suits would be that Vermont and other States could do indirectly what they could not do directly—regulate the conduct of out-of-state sources." A Vermont resident still presumably can go to a New York court and try to block the discharge under *New York* nuisance law. But New York courts may be unsympathetic to out-of-state plaintiffs, particularly where an injunction might harm New York economic interests.

18. City of Milwaukee v. Illinois, 451 U.S. 304 (1981).

CHAPTER 6

Regulating Toxic Substances

The Clean Air Act and the Clean Water Act both focus on "conventional" pollutants—industrial and other by-products that are discharged in large quantities and pose known health problems. But from the earliest days of the modern environmental movement, "toxic" substances—products and by-products presenting a potential risk of serious harm at even low levels of exposure—often have generated greater attention and concern. Rachel Carson's famous best seller, *Silent Spring*, which helped launch the modern environmental era, dealt not with particulate air pollution or with fecal coliform in the nation's water but with the grave dangers that pesticides such as DDT present to humans and other animals. Most people today are worried far more about the potential risks from toxic substances such as lead and asbestos than they are about the chronic side effects of carbon monoxide or particulates.

Toxic substances differ in a number of key ways from conventional pollutants. First, many toxins are valuable agricultural, industrial, or consumer products. While the Clean Air Act and the Clean Water Act deal primarily with by-products that businesses and individuals happily would do without, farmers, businesses, and consumers each year buy millions of dollars of pesticides and other toxic chemicals. Second, we often are not sure what degree of risks, if any, a suspected toxic actually poses. Third, the probability that a toxin will injure any one individual typically is quite small. Finally, because even low levels of exposure to a toxic substance frequently present a risk, safe levels of human exposure often do not exist. As this chapter will discuss, the unique characteristics of toxins make regulation particularly difficult and controversial.

An eclectic collection of federal environmental statutes addresses toxic substances. As discussed in the last two chapters, the Clean Air Act and the Clean Water Act include special provisions regulating toxic and other "hazardous" pollutants. The Resource Conservation and Recovery Act and the Comprehensive Environmental Response, Compensation, and Liability Act, which are the subjects of the next chapter, focus on the proper disposal of hazardous waste in land-based facilities and the clean-up of land contaminated by hazardous substances. A number of statutes regulate particular categories of substances. For example, the Federal Insecticide, Fungicide, and Rodenticide Act ("FIFRA") governs agricultural chemicals, while the federal Food & Drug Act regulates food additives and drugs and the Atomic Energy Act and related statutes manage radioactive substances. Several statutes also regulate specific routes of exposure. The Occupational Safety and Health Act ("OSHA"), for example, limits worker exposure to unhealthy levels of toxins and other dangerous substances, while the Safe Drinking Water Act limits the amount of toxic substances permitted in drinking water. Finally, the Toxic Substances Control Act ("TSCA") serves as a "catch all" statute that regulates the production, sale, and use of toxic substances not regulated otherwise by federal law.

I. The Difficulties of Regulating Toxic Substances

The regulation of toxic substances has generated tremendous controversy, in large part because it poses some of the most difficult policy questions to be found in the environmental field, or in any regulatory field for that matter. Given that life is not risk free, should the government be concerned about the extremely low levels of risk posed by some toxic substances? If some risks are too small to regulate, what should be the dividing line? How should the law deal with scientific uncertainty? How much money should society invest in getting a better sense of the risks posed by particular substances? And if significant uncertainty remains after all the scientific studies have been conducted, should the government err in favor of the economy or of protecting human health?

If toxic substances were of little or no value to society, these questions would be easy to answer. The government would ban any and all substances that posed a potential health risk. Unfortunately, businesses and consumers view many suspected or known toxins as all but "indispensable." Consider, for example, pesticides and other synthetic organic chemicals. These chemicals have improved many people's lives by boosting agricultural yields, increasing the durability of consumer products, producing life-saving drugs, and decreasing product prices. The chemical industry, moreover, is the largest manufacturing sector in the United States, employing over a million people and contributing 12 percent of the manufacturing gross domestic product. The chemical industry also is one of the few sectors of the United States economy in which the nation enjoys an international trade surplus, exporting almost $70 billion worth of chemical products in 1997.

A. *Is "Tolerable Risk" an Oxymoron?*

Most toxic substances present only a *risk* of injury. For example, of every million people exposed to a specific cancer-causing substance (i.e., a carcinogen), only two ultimately may contract cancer as a result of that exposure. Is that a sufficiently large risk to justify regulating the substance, particularly if the substance is economically valuable? It may be tempting to respond that we should not add any substance to the natural environment that increases the overall risk of cancer or other serious health injury. The natural world, however, is replete with health risks, and people often voluntarily assume additional risks in return for varied benefits. Bruce Ames, a professor of molecular biology at the University of California, observes that the food we eat contains far more naturally occurring carcinogens than synthetic carcinogens in the form of pesticides and other farm chemicals.[1] The average person voluntarily increases their risk of serious injury by driving in cars, flying in airplanes, playing sports, and even traveling to or living at high altitudes. The strength of the ultraviolet rays in Denver, Colorado, the "mile high" city, is twenty five times stronger than at sea level, so residents of Denver sustain a higher risk of skin cancer. Should the government regulate chemicals that pose lower risks than these everyday activities?

Some people say "no—the government should outlaw only those substances that pose greater risks of injury than those risks voluntarily assumed by people in their regular lives." Risks, however, vary in a number of important aspects other than their probability of occurring. First, different risks pose different types of threats, some worse than others. Cancer risks obviously are of greater societal concern than risks of eye irritation. Even risks of death can differ because people dread some forms of death (e.g., death from cancer) more than others (e.g., death from a heart attack). The acceptability of a risk involves a balancing of probability and severity (including dread): the more severe the potential injury, the lower the probability of injury that society should accept, and the less severe the injury, the higher the acceptable probability.

Second, people view voluntary risks very differently than risks that are imposed on them. Although people willingly put their lives at risk when they drive a car, most people would be upset to learn that the fumes from a nearby factory presented them with an equivalent risk of dying from cancer. Third, some risks may seem less equitable than others. Public surveys, for example, have revealed that people are less willing to accept the risk of an accident that could kill 1,000 people in a concentrated geographic area (e.g., a nuclear accident) than a risk that could kill 1,000 people spread out over the entire nation (e.g., pollution from diffuse industrial facilities). Deciding whether a risk is acceptable, in summary, can be a complex determination that depends on a wide variety of factors. In regulating risks in a manner acceptable to society, therefore, it is not enough to know only the probability of harm.

1. See, e.g., Lois Gold et al., Rodent Carcinogens: Setting Priorities, 258 Science 261 (1992); Bruce Ames, Ranking Possible Carcinogenic Hazards, 236 Science 271 (1987).

Congress, as the nation's popularly elected legislature, seems best suited to determine acceptable risk levels, either by regulating substances directly or by setting out clear instructions to regulatory agencies. As discussed below, Congress sometimes has faced up to that challenge. In many cases, however, Congress has ducked the issue and either delegated broad discretion to a regulatory agency or, even worse, provided conflicting cues on how the agency should manage potential toxins. Faced with serious health concerns on the one side and important economic interests on the other, Congress often has proven unable or unwilling to resolve the competing interests and left the ultimate decision to the regulatory agencies and courts.

The Supreme Court addressed the question of "acceptable" risk in *Industrial Union Department, AFL–CIO v. American Petroleum Institute* (commonly known as the *"Benzene Case"*).[2] Under the Occupational Safety and Health Act ("OSHA"), the Secretary of Labor regulates workplace exposure to toxic materials. Section 6(b)(5) of OSHA specifies that, for each toxic substance, the Secretary shall set an exposure standard "which *most adequately assures*, to the extent feasible, on the basis of best available evidence, that *no* employee will suffer material impairment of health or functional capacity" even if exposed to the substance for his or her entire working life (emphasis added). Section 3(8) of OSHA, by contrast, suggests that the Secretary is to set standards that are "*reasonably* necessary or appropriate to provide *safe* or healthful employment and places of employment" (emphasis added again). In the late 1970s, the Department of Labor decided to lower the exposure standard for benzene, a liquid chemical frequently used in manufacturing processes and known to cause leukemia. Concluding that no known level of benzene exposure was safe, the Secretary decided to reduce air exposure in factories from 10 parts per million (ppm) to the lowest level that the Secretary believed was feasible, 1 ppm.

The Supreme Court reversed. Justice Stevens, joined by three other justices, concluded that OSHA authorizes the Department of Labor to ban only those levels of exposure that present a "significant risk of material health impairment." Pointing to the language of section 3(8), Justice Stevens reasoned that OSHA requires only a "safe" work place, not a work place that is "risk free." According to Stevens, people consider many activities, like driving a car, to be "safe" even though they entail some risk.

> Some risks are plainly acceptable while others are plainly unacceptable. If, for example, the odds are one in a billion that a person will die from cancer by taking a drink of chlorinated water, the risk clearly could not be considered significant. On the other hand, if the

2.   448 U.S. 607 (1980).

odds are one in a thousand that regular inhalation of gasoline vapors that are 2% benzene will be fatal, a reasonable person might well consider the risk significant and take appropriate steps to decrease or eliminate it.

Justice Marshall's dissenting opinion responded that Justice Stevens was ignoring the broad discretion given the Secretary of Labor to protect workers' health and instead imposing his own "personal views ... as to the proper allocation of resources for safety in the American workplace."

Justice Rehnquist in a concurring opinion concluded that OSHA was unconstitutional because it improperly delegated to an administrative agency the important legislative decision as to the appropriate level of protection. As discussed in Chapter 3, the Supreme Court has not used the "unconstitutional delegation" doctrine to invalidate a Congressional delegation since early in the 1940s. Rehnquist, however, argued that the doctrine cried out for application here. In Rehnquist's view, "one of the most difficult issues that could confront a decisionmaker" is the acceptability of a risk of future deaths. This is exactly the type of decision that Congress should make. Reading OSHA, it "is difficult to imagine a more obvious example of Congress simply avoiding a choice which was both fundamental for purposes of the statute and yet politically so divisive that the necessary decision or compromise was difficult, if not impossible, to hammer out in the legislative forge."

B. The Problem of Uncertainty

Scientific uncertainty also plagues efforts to regulate toxic materials. Note that *risk* and *uncertainty* are not the same things and that they need not be present simultaneously. Scientists might know with a high degree of certainty that exposure to a certain chemical will lead to cancer in two out of every thousand people. If so, there would be risk but little uncertainty. Alternatively, scientists might suspect that *everyone* who consumes 10 milligrams of a particular substance will contract cancer, but not have enough information to be sure. In that case, there would be scientific uncertainty, but if studies confirmed that the substance was carcinogenic, exposure would pose a certitude rather than a mere risk of injury. In the real world, most toxic substances pose only a risk of injury (and typically a very small risk). Scientists, moreover, often are uncertain whether a substance really poses a risk and, if so, about the size of that risk. Both risk and uncertainty thus combine to make the life of the regulator very tough indeed.

1. A Paucity of Information

Part of the problem is that we have not studied carefully many of the chemicals in regular use. In 1984, a panel of the National Academy of Sciences concluded that toxicity information for most chemicals was "scanty."[3] Indeed, for the "great majority of [toxic] substances, data considered to be essential for conducting a health-hazard assessment [was] lacking." Recent studies suggest little has changed over the last two decades.

Businesses worldwide currently manufacture over ten million chemicals. Researchers, moreover, discover thousands of useful new chemical formulations every year, so that the universe of potential toxins continues to expand. Performing comprehensive safety tests on all of these chemicals would be extremely time consuming and exceptionally expensive. Information comes at a cost, and so the government must decide how much testing is worthwhile. Additional testing and analysis always will provide greater insight into the safety of a product, but at some point the cost of that testing may outweigh the marginal value that society receives from the additional information.

Rather than require manufacturers to engage in extensive safety testing of all new chemicals, the federal government generally settles for requiring manufacturers to test only those categories of chemicals that are of high concern because of either their general characteristics or their proposed use. Pesticides and other agricultural chemicals, for example, are designed to kill living organisms and thus raise automatic toxicity concerns; moreover, farm workers, rural residents, and consumers all are likely to come into frequent contact with these chemicals. As a result, the Federal Insecticide, Fungicide, and Rodenticide Act ("FIFRA") requires producers to conduct extensive toxicology tests in the laboratory and the field before applying to produce and sell new agricultural chemicals. Toxicology tests easily can take over five years to complete and cost $5 million or more. The Federal Food Drug & Cosmetic Act similarly requires comprehensive testing of chemicals that will be added to food or included in cosmetics.

By contrast, the Toxic Substances Control Act ("TSCA"), which regulates chemicals not covered by other more specific statutes like FIFRA, does not automatically require producers to conduct an extensive battery of tests. Before manufacturing a new chemical, a producer must file with EPA a pre-manufacture notification (PMN), along with whatever data the producer believes shows that the chemical "will not present an unreasonable risk."[4] But TSCA does not mandate any specific testing. As a result, most TSCA chemicals have not undergone broad testing. One 1983 study found that no toxicity information accompanied about half of the PMNs, and less than 20 percent of manufacturers submitted

3. National Academy of Sciences, Toxicity Testing: Strategies to Determine Needs and Priorities (1984).

4. TSCA § 5(b)(2)(B)(ii), 15 U.S.C. § 2604(b)(2)(B)(ii).

data on longterm toxicity.[5] Section 4 of TSCA authorizes EPA to require more tests if EPA concludes (1) that it does not have sufficient information with which to determine a chemical's toxicity *and* (2) that the chemical "may present an unreasonable risk of injury to health or the environment," will be produced in substantial quantities, or may result in substantial human exposure.[6] EPA, however, normally does not exercise this authority unless the chemical is similar in structural makeup to a substance already known to be toxic or unless EPA has other good reason to suspect its toxicity.

Even the tests required under statutes such as FIFRA often leave significant gaps in the government's knowledge of the toxicity risks presented by a chemical. FIFRA, for example, requires extensive testing of the carcinogenic (cancer-causing) risks of individual chemicals. But FIFRA currently does not mandate that a chemical be tested for some other significant risks, nor does FIFRA require tests of the potential synergistic effects of exposure to multiple chemicals.[7] Once EPA licenses an agricultural chemical, moreover, FIFRA generally does not require regular retesting of the chemical as testing processes improve. Concerned that early testing of agricultural chemicals might have been inadequate, Congress amended FIFRA in 1988 to require reregistration, and thus additional testing, of the tens of thousands of pesticides registered prior to 1984. Reregistration, however, has proven extremely slow, in part because of the huge number of pesticides involved, and is likely to stretch well into this century.

2. The Difficulty of Determining Cancer Risks

Even if the government required exhaustive tests of every chemical, the exact health risks of many chemicals would remain uncertain. This is true particularly of cancer risks. Historically, the two principal methods of determining the cancer risk of a chemical have been epidemiological studies and animal bioassays. In epidemiological studies, scientists look to see if populations of humans who have been exposed to a substance suffer greater incidences of cancer or other illnesses than the general population. Because humans must have been exposed to a substance in order to conduct an epidemiological study, this approach obviously does not work well where the government is trying to determine whether to permit a new substance even to be produced and sold. Before an epidemiological study can determine the risks of a carcinogen, the substance already must have harmed real people—the very danger that

---

5. Office of Technology Assessment, United States Congress, Information Content of Pre-Manufacture Notices (1983).

6. TSCA § 4, 15 U.S.C. § 2603.

7. In a synergistic effect, the sum of contributors is greater than their individual contributions. Thus two mildly toxic compounds might, when combined, produce a highly toxic effect. In this manner, $2+2$ can equal 8, or even 80.

regulation is trying to avoid. Even if a carcinogen has been on the market for several years, epidemiological studies may not provide an accurate assessment of the risk. Virtually all carcinogens present long-term risks; someone exposed in 2001 to a carcinogen may not manifest any cancer symptoms, for example, until 2021 or 2031. Early epidemiological studies thus may not reveal any risk. In addition, because people are exposed to a variety of different health risks over time, the data in most epidemiological studies are extremely "noisy." An increase in a given form of cancer among the exposed population may be the consequence of the exposure to the studied material or, alternatively, of totally different exposures.

Given the obstacles to effective epidemiological studies, regulators have relied primarily on animal bioassays to determine cancer risks. In an animal bioassay, researchers expose laboratory animals to a substance and then observe whether the exposed animals suffer a higher incidence of cancer than a control group of animals that have not been exposed. Rats and mice are two of the more common animals used in cancer studies.

Although animal bioassays can help identify potential carcinogens, a number of limitations undercut the ability to use bioassays to predict the probability of the risk accurately. First is the problem of determining whether a substance that is carcinogenic for rats, mice, and other laboratory animals is also carcinogenic for humans, and vice-versa. Every animal species has a different predisposition or susceptibility to various forms of cancer. Just because a chemical produces cancer in mice therefore does not mean that it will cause cancer in humans. Similarly, a chemical might be a human carcinogen even though animal bioassays come up negative. There generally is enough correlation between what's carcinogenic to humans and carcinogenic to lab animals that scientists feel comfortable extrapolating from animals to humans, but uncertainty nonetheless remains and conclusions need to be carefully couched.

A second limitation of animal bioassays is the problem of translating animal exposure into human exposure. A basic rule of pharmacology is that "the dose determines the poison." A small amount of chlorine in a cup of water will kill dangerous bacteria, making the water safe to drink. Drink a cup of chlorine, though, and it will kill you. Because of the differences in their sizes, exposing a rat to 2 milligrams of benzene per day is not equivalent to exposing humans to the same amount. Scientists unfortunately disagree on the best way of translating exposure from laboratory animals to humans. Some scientists, for example, believe that relative exposure levels are proportionate to weight; if the average person weighs 120 times the average laboratory rat, exposure of a rat to 2 milligrams is equivalent to exposing a human to 240 milligrams. Other scientists, however, believe that the ratio of surface exposure is more appropriate. Yet other scientists argue for other metrics.

Because researchers cannot wait years to see if the animals contract cancer and must study a limited population of laboratory animals, researchers also must expose the animals to large "mega doses" of the substance under study. No matter how the laboratory exposure is translated into human exposure, humans typically will *never* be exposed to the substance at the levels that the laboratory animals suffer. In predicting human risk, scientists therefore must extrapolate from high levels of exposure to much lower levels of exposure. The resulting risk prediction depends on the assumed relationship between exposure dosage and risk. Under some dose-response models, a chemical might pose no risk of cancer at typical exposure levels even if the risk is significant at higher levels.

Scientists more recently have turned to *in vitro* cell and tissue cultures to examine the potential risks of chemicals. In these tests, scientists look to see the affect of chemical agents on cells and tissues in the laboratory. Such tests are far cheaper and faster than animal bioassays or epidemiological studies. Scientists, however, disagree on the accuracy of such tests.

Even if scientists feel somewhat confident that they understand the risk of a substance at various levels of exposure, the government must determine exposure levels in order to determine the projected risk. Although this might sound easy, it often is not. Risk analysts largely must guess, for example, the level at which farm workers and their families are exposed to various toxic pesticides. In one recent experiment, scientists asked rural families to estimate their children's exposure to various potential toxic pathways and then videotaped the children's actual exposure. There was virtually no correspondence between the two.

3. Regulating Under Uncertainty

The high degree of uncertainty involved in estimating toxicity risks makes burden of proof important. The government is likely to regulate fewer substances if it must prove that a substance is "unsafe," however that might be defined, than if producers must prove that the substance is "safe." This is particularly true because producers are likely to have much better information than the government concerning the risks posed by their products.

The standard of proof also is important. Scientists often demand a high degree of certainty, e.g., a 90 or 95 percent probability, before concluding that a particular substance is carcinogenic or poses some other serious health risk. The law generally is willing to act with far less certainty. In *Reserve Mining Co. v. EPA*,[8] the federal government sought to enjoin the Reserve Mining Company from discharging taconite tailings into Lake Superior, using a provision of the Clean Water Act that authorizes the government to sue to stop discharges that "endanger" public health.[9] Although taconite tailings contain asbestos fibers, which were suspected at the time of causing cancer and other serious health harms, health studies of the risk of ingesting taconite tailings in drinking water were inconclusive. A panel of the Eighth Circuit Court of Appeals ruled that the government had not met its burden of showing endangerment and, given the existing scientific uncertainty, probably could never meet its burden. According to the panel, a mere "medical hypothesis" was insufficient to justify abatement.[10] Rehearing the case en banc, the Eighth Circuit disagreed with the panel and held that the government need show only a "reasonable medical concern for the public health." Given the serious consequences if the medical hypothesis should prove true, courts should not be powerless to act in the face of uncertainty. In the court's view, Congress had "used the term 'endangering' in a precautionary or preventative sense and, therefore, evidence of potential harm as well as actual harm comes within the purview of that term."

A year later, the D.C. Circuit also emphasized the importance of precautionary measures in *Ethyl Corp. v. EPA*.[11] The Clean Air Act authorizes EPA to regulate gasoline additives that "will endanger" public health. The question in *Ethyl Corp.* was whether EPA could use this authority to reduce lead in gasoline. A number of studies suggested that lead presented serious health risks, particularly to children, but the studies were far from conclusive. The D.C. Circuit nonetheless upheld EPA's authority, again emphasizing the precautionary nature of the environmental legislation. The court stressed that administrative agencies need not meet scientific standards of proof before regulating potentially harmful substances. The court also suggested that the appropriate standard of proof might depend on the potential severity of harm. Very serious harms may call for a lower standard of proof, and vice-versa.

Politically, however, truly precautionary regulation can be difficult to sustain in the long run. Under precautionary regulation, the government will regulate some substances that later, on further study, turn out to be safe. Greater levels of precaution lead to an increasing number of safe (as well as unsafe) substances being regulated. Producers and consumers of regulated materials are likely to cite such "false positives" as evidence that the government is over-regulating. In hindsight, the government will appear to have interfered unnecessarily with the mar-

8.   514 F.2d 492 (8th Cir.1975).

9.   33 U.S.C. § 1160(g)(1).

10.   See Reserve Mining Co. v. United States, 498 F.2d 1073 (8th Cir.1974).

11.   541 F.2d 1 (D.C.Cir.1976).

ket, even though ex ante its decisions were sound. Over time, the accumulation of these "errors" may undermine support for a precautionary approach. In practice, however, the federal government has seldom taken as precautionary an approach as environmentalists have urged.

II. Major Regulatory Options

The government has taken a wide variety of approaches toward regulating toxic substances. In deciding how to regulate a potential toxin, the government must choose among a number of options. First, the government must decide whether to ban or limit the production of the toxic substance or to permit production but attempt to control exposure. The government, for example, could ban pesticides that present a significant risk of cancer or instead require farm workers to wear protective clothing and to take other precautions against exposure.

Second, the government must decide the appropriate regulatory standard. The government, for example, could choose a *health based* approach and proscribe either all risks or all significant risks. The government alternatively could take a *feasibility* approach and reduce risks, or significant risks, only to the degree technologically and economically feasible. The government also could engage in *risk-benefit* balancing and regulate substances only when their risks outweigh their societal benefits. Although a zero-risk approach is clearly the toughest possible standard, the other standards cannot be ranked neatly by regulatory rigor. In most cases, risk-benefit analysis will be more lenient than a "significant-risk" or "feasibility" standard because it permits risks to be balanced against benefits. In some cases, however, risk-benefit analysis might be stricter. Imagine, for example, a chemical that presents a relatively insignificant risk but that also has little economic value. The government might choose not to regulate the chemical under a significant-risk standard because the risk is so small. Under a risk-benefit analysis, by contrast, the government might decide to regulate the chemical because the benefit is even smaller than the risk. If banning a pesticide would cause a large number of farms to close down, a feasibility approach might not ban the pesticide, while a risk-benefit analysis would call for banning the pesticide if the health risk is large enough to justify the cost.

A. Pure Health–Based Statutes

Congress has chosen only occasionally to ban all risks in a class of substances. The most famous examples of a zero-risk approach are the so-called Delaney Clauses in the federal Food Drug and Cosmetic Act. The Act prohibits the use of unsafe additives in food, drugs, and cosmetics. The Delaney Clauses, one of which deals with food additives and the other with color additives, require the government to treat additives as unsafe if they are "found . . . to induce cancer in man or animal."[12] If an animal bioassay finds that an additive causes cancer in laboratory animals, the Delaney Clauses prohibit the additive's use, whether or not there is any direct evidence that the additive causes cancer in humans and no matter how minuscule the risk at actual levels of human exposure.[13]

Given Congress' clear and unyielding intent to eliminate all risks, courts have refused to let administrative agencies create a "de minimis" exception to the Delaney Clauses. In *Public Citizen v. Young*,[14] for example, the Food and Drug Administration (FDA) refused to ban the use of two color additives in cosmetics even though studies showed that they caused cancer in laboratory animals. Noting that the color additives presented lifetime cancer risks of only one in nine million for one of the additives and one in 19 billion for the other, the FDA concluded that the risks were "so trivial as to be effectively no risk." The D.C. Circuit Court of Appeals disagreed, concluding that Congress clearly intended to ban such additives. In *Les v. Reilly*,[15] the Ninth Circuit Court of Appeals rejected a similar effort by EPA to affix a de minimis exception to the food-additive Delaney Clause. According to the court, "Congress intended to ban all carcinogenic food additives, regardless of amount or significance of risk, as the only safe alternative."

Many people find the Delaney Clauses mulish and irrational. Echoing Justice Steven's observation in the *Benzene Case* that "safe" is not the same thing as "risk free," critics see no reason to ban substances that present only trivial risks. Critics, moreover, fear that, by imposing such an extreme regulatory requirement, Congress may drive federal agencies to ignore or avoid the statute and thus pervert the regulatory process. Critics also argue that the Delaney Clauses could backfire by regulating rigidly some but not all risks. Unable to use a color additive that presents a one in 19 billion cancer risk, for example, cosmetic manufacturers might turn to an alternative color additive that presents no known cancer risk but a very high risk of other injury. According to critics, the government should engage in a risk-risk comparison of additives and their alternatives rather than simply banning substances that present a cancer risk.

So was Congress insane when it passed the Delaney Clauses? And why has Congress never chosen to repeal the Delaney Clauses in the face

---

12. Food Drug & Cosmetic Act §§ 409 & 706, 21 U.S.C. §§ 348(c)(3)(A) & 379e(b)(5)(B).

13. The Delaney Clauses focus only on additives. Thus, they do not ban naturally occurring carcinogens, no matter what the human risk.

14. 831 F.2d 1108 (D.C.Cir.1987).

15. 968 F.2d 985 (9th Cir.1992).

of these criticisms? Defenders of the Delaney Clauses make a number of arguments in response to the critics. Defenders first argue that the scientific uncertainty surrounding cancer risks calls for a precautionary approach. Although scientists currently might believe that a color additive presents only a one in 19 billion risk, additional studies might find that the risk is far greater. Indeed, defenders of the Delaney Clauses charge that most risks have turned out worse than scientists originally thought.[16] Defenders also argue that few, if any, additives are of significant economic or societal value, so banning those that pose a cancer risk is typically costless. Although this is not always true, most consumers can get along fine without most color or food additives. Finally, defenders of the Delaney Clauses note that the public places a high value on eliminating even small risks of cancer. Indeed, psychologists have found that people attach far greater importance to eliminating the last vestiges of a risk than to making more sizable risk reductions that still leave some risk remaining. Although reducing a risk from ten to two percent is valuable, people appear to care even more about reducing risk from two percent to zero.

By singling out additives for special regulatory treatment, the Delaney Clauses, like all bright-line rules, can lead to illogical distinctions. Until 1996, for example, the food-additive Delaney Clause applied to pesticide residues in processed foods (e.g., canned corn) but not in raw foods (e.g., fresh corn). Thus people who bought fresh fruits and vegetables believing the fresh foods were better and healthier actually enjoyed less protection than people getting their essential food groups out of cans. In 1996, Congress finally extended protection to raw foods as part of a political compromise that also lowered the standard of protection for pesticide residues in processed foods. The Food Quality Protection Act of 1996 (FQPA), rather than the food-additive Delaney Clause, now regulates pesticide residues in all foods, whether processed or raw. Unlike the Delaney Clause, the FQPA does not ban all pesticide residues that cause cancer. Instead, it requires only that there be a "reasonable certainty that no harm will result from aggregate exposure to the pesticide chemical residue."[17] The legislative history of the FQPA indicates that extremely low lifetime cancer risks of less than one in a million may be acceptable under this new standard.

B. Feasibility Statutes

In other statutes, Congress requires regulatory agencies to reduce toxic health risks, but only to the degree "feasible." The federal Occupa-

---

16. We are unaware of any convincing empirical evidence one way or the other as to this assertion. Although scientists have conducted occasional retrospective studies on the risks of particular substances, the jury is still out on whether scientists tend on the whole to underestimate or overestimate risks at early stages of study. Of course, one might conclude that only the underestimates are troublesome.

17. 21 U.S.C. § 346a(b)(2)(A)(ii).

tional Health and Safety Act ("OSHA") takes this approach in regulating work place exposures. As noted earlier in connection with the *Benzene Case*, OSHA requires the Secretary of Labor to ensure a "safe" work place but only "to the extent feasible."[18] A major question under such feasibility statutes is the meaning of the term "feasible," which Congress often does not define. In the case of OSHA, courts have concluded that exposure standards must be both technologically and economically feasible. The Secretary of Labor thus cannot set an exposure standard that engineers have no idea how to meet. Nor can the Secretary set an exposure standard that would destroy an entire industry or undermine the industry's competitive structure, although a standard that bankrupts a few marginal firms would be okay.

The Safe Drinking Water Act ("SDWA") also takes a feasibility approach toward reducing toxins in the nation's drinking water. EPA starts by identifying contaminants that, in its judgment, "may have [an] adverse effect on the health of persons and which is known or anticipated to occur in public water systems."[19] Next, EPA sets "maximum contaminant level goals" or "MCGLs" for each contaminant that it has identified. The MCGLs are purely health based. Under the SDWA, EPA must sets MCGLs "at the level at which no known or anticipated adverse effects on the health of persons occur and which allows an adequate margin of safety."[20] Because scientists do not know whether there is a safe threshold of ingestion for most carcinogens, EPA often sets MCGLs of zero. Rather than force water suppliers to meet such "goals," however, OSHA requires EPA also to establish "maximum contaminant levels" or "MCLs" that are "as close to the maximum contaminant level goal as is feasible."[21] It is these MCLs, rather than the MCGLs, that water suppliers must meet. A standard is "feasible" under the SDWA if EPA, after seeing if the necessary technology works "under field conditions," concludes that the technology is "available (taking cost into consideration)."[22]

Although Congress understandably does not want to impose regulations that would put an industry out of business, feasibility standards can lead sometimes to disturbingly arbitrary distinctions. Under OSHA, for example, workers in economically strapped industries could be subjected to relatively high risks because the industries cannot afford to reduce the risks, while workers in economically flush industries might

---

18. OSHA §§ 3(8) & 6(b)(5), 29 U.S.C. §§ 652(8) & 655(b)(5).

19. 42 U.S.C. § 300g–1(b)(3)(A).

20. 42 U.S.C. § 300g–1(b)(4).

21. 42 U.S.C. §§ 300g–1(b)(4)–(5).

22. 42 U.S.C. § 300g–1(5).

enjoy freedom from even relatively minor risks. If wages are proportional to industry profitability, a feasibility approach thus can expose the poorest employees to the greatest risks.

Feasibility standards also create implementation problems. Regulatory agencies must spend valuable time determining whether each individual standard is technologically and economically feasible. In 1989, OSHA estimated that the feasibility review for each new exposure standard took at least a year and cost an average of $500,000. Much of the information needed to determine feasibility, moreover, is in the hands of the regulated industry, which has every reason to overstate the costs and problems of implementing stricter standards.

Economists, moreover, remain troubled that feasibility requirements do not ensure that the benefits from regulation are "worth" the costs. Assuming that it is "feasible" to rid drinking water of a contaminant that poses a very low risk, but that the cost of the needed filtering technology would raise national water bills by 20 percent or more, is it sensible to ban the contaminant? "Feasible" does not necessarily mean "optimal" or "ideal." Faced with growing concerns over the costs of reducing lead and other contaminants in drinking water, Congress chose to amend the SDWA in 1996 to permit EPA to relax MCLs if it believed that the risks of a contaminant did not justify the costs of regulation. If EPA concludes that the benefits of a MCL "would not justify the costs of complying," EPA now may set a MCL that "maximizes health risk reduction benefits at a cost that is justified by the benefits."[23]

C.   Risk–Benefit Statutes

1.   Federal Insecticide, Fungicide, and Rodenticide Act

A number of statutes require EPA to balance the risks and benefits of a product in determining the appropriate level of regulation. Under the Federal Insecticide, Fungicide, and Rodenticide Act ("FIFRA"), the manufacturer of a new pesticide or agricultural chemical must register it with EPA before producing and selling it. Before registering the pesticide EPA must determine both that the pesticide will do what the manufacturer says (truth in advertising) and also that the pesticide "when used in accordance with widespread and commonly recognized practice" will not pose an "unreasonable risk to man or the environment, taking into account the economic, social, and environmental costs and benefits of the pesticide."[24] EPA thus must balance risks and benefits in determining whether a pesticide presents an "unreasonable risk." If the pesticide

23.   42 U.S.C. § 300g–1(b)(6).

24.   FIFRA §§ 2(bb) & 3(c)(5), 7 U.S.C. §§ 136(bb) & 136a(c)(5).

does, EPA can address the problem either by refusing to register the pesticide or by imposing conditions on how the pesticide is used. To date, the federal government has registered over 50,000 agricultural chemicals under FIFRA.

Over time, scientists learn more and more about toxic risks and how to measure them. As a result, pesticides that originally looked safe may become suspect later. FIFRA therefore requires EPA periodically to reevaluate and reregister existing pesticides. FIFRA also authorizes EPA to cancel a registration or to change a pesticide's use conditions if EPA determines that the pesticide presents an unreasonable risk, although EPA must jump through significant administrative hoops, including scientific reviews and a full adjudicatory hearing, before taking action. FIFRA originally required EPA to reimburse both the manufacturer and users of a pesticide for the costs of canceling the pesticide, perhaps intentionally deterring EPA from taking such actions. In 1988, however, Congress amended FIFRA to eliminate the requirement that manufacturers be indemnified. Consumers of a cancelled pesticide, however, are still entitled to compensation.

2.   Toxic Substances Control Act

The Toxic Substances Control Act ("TSCA") also requires EPA to balance the risks and benefits of chemical products. The manufacturer of a chemical substance that is not regulated under another federal law such as FIFRA must file a Pre–Manufacturing Notice ("PPM") before producing and selling the chemical. Because TSCA chemicals generally are less suspect than pesticides, TSCA does not require EPA to evaluate the risks of every chemical for which a PPM is filed. EPA, however, can ban or restrict the use of a chemical if there is a "reasonable basis to conclude" that the chemical "presents or will present an unreasonable risk of injury to health or the environment."[25] Like FIFRA, TSCA requires EPA to balance the risks of a substance against its benefits in determining whether the risks are "unreasonable."[26]

3.   "Paralysis By Analysis"

Many environmentalists worry that statutes like FIFRA and TSCA, by requiring EPA to balance risks and benefits, may lead to "paralysis by analysis." Once EPA starts down the road of trying to evaluate and compare risks and benefits, EPA might find that it never gets to its destination but instead gets bogged down in the details of the analysis or has an inadequate budget to carry out the analysis. Perhaps in fear of

---

25.   TSCA § 6(a), 15 U.S.C. § 2605(a).

26.   The export of banned chemicals to foreign nations, and TSCA's regulation of this practice, is discussed *infra* at p. 234.

this danger, Congress occasionally has emphasized that it does not expect EPA to complete formal, quantified risk-benefit analyses. A rough, qualitative comparison often should be enough. But FIFRA and TSCA inevitably have drawn EPA into quantitative comparisons.

The Fifth Circuit Court of Appeal's decision in *Corrosion Proof Fittings v. Environmental Protection Agency*[27] demonstrates the dangers of paralysis by analysis. The case dealt with EPA's efforts under TSCA to regulate the use of asbestos in a variety of products such as pipes, shingles, and brake pads. Scientists know perhaps more about asbestos than any other toxic substance, and none of that knowledge is positive. Asbestos is one of the most dangerous substances around. Exposure, sometimes at very low levels, can lead to asbestosis, lung cancer, and mesothelioma (a particularly deadly cancer of the chest cavity). Despite the serious health risks, EPA decided to be deliberate and thorough in its evaluation of the asbestos products. TSCA was a relatively untried weapon in EPA's arsenal, so EPA wanted to get things right. As a result, EPA spent almost ten years reviewing the asbestos products and building the case for banning the asbestos. By the time EPA was finished, it had amassed a 45,000–page administrative record.

Based on this record, EPA decided that only a total ban could avoid the known health risks of asbestos. Attempts to limit exposure of particular groups, such as workers or consumers, would leave other persons unprotected. In EPA's view, moreover, the risks justified a total ban. When it reached its decision in the late 1980s, EPA conservatively estimated that, from 1988 to 2000, a ban would save the lives of 202 people who otherwise would die from lung cancer or mesothelioma. EPA calculated that, assuming the price of substitutes for asbestos declined over time, the cost of the ban would be $459 million—or $3.1 million per death avoided. (If both the costs and the lives saved were "discounted" to the present, EPA estimated that the cost per death avoided would be only $2.4 million.) In EPA's view, this cost was more than acceptable.

The Fifth Circuit reversed. The Fifth Circuit began by criticizing the methodology that EPA used as incomplete and inadequate. First, EPA had compared the risks and benefits of only two options: no regulation, and a complete ban on using asbestos in the products. The Fifth Circuit held that EPA should have performed a marginal analysis in which it compared the reduced risks and benefits of successively tighter restrictions. As the Fifth Circuit noted, a restriction somewhere in the middle might provide a better balance of risks and benefits. Second, the Fifth Circuit criticized EPA's failure to quantify risks and benefits beyond the year 2000, despite EPA's belief that uncertainty would plague any effort to quantify the risks and benefits that far into the future. Although the

27.   947 F.2d 1201 (5th Cir.1991).

court recognized that EPA must use some finite time frame, the court believed that 13 years was "unreasonably" short. Third, the court decided that EPA should have weighed the potential harms of any substitutes that manufacturers might use in place of asbestos. Finally, the court ruled that EPA should have preformed separate risk-benefit comparisons for each product, rather than on an aggregate basis.

The Fifth Circuit's opinion assumes that EPA should and can perform a perfect risk-benefit analysis. The Fifth Circuit is correct that a risk-benefit analysis in theory should examine the marginal benefit and cost of each incremental regulatory step, quantify all the possible risks and benefits far into the future, and make decisions for each product individually. But these "improvements" would increase geometrically the difficulty of implementing TSCA and immerse EPA in a sea of scientific and economic uncertainty. As noted, EPA spent ten years completing the relatively complex analysis that the Fifth Circuit found wanting. At some point, the cost of additional analysis and quantification is not worth the increased understanding and analysis.

Corrosion Proof Fittings also raises the question of the appropriate role of courts and administrative agencies in determining the appropriate level of risk. Looked at product by product, EPA's ban on asbestos would have cost as much as $74 million per life saved (in the case of asbestos pipe, where only three lives would have been saved at a cost as high as $277 million). The Fifth Circuit concluded that this was unreasonably high. The court was unclear whether it believed that the acceptability of the cost was a legal issue or a factual question. Nor did the court discuss whether it should defer to EPA's "expertise" in risk analysis. EPA, however, would seem the better body to make such judgments for reasons of both uniformity and democratic accountability. Frequent judicial intervention could lead to considerable regulatory uncertainty, as the level of acceptable risk varied from court to court. EPA, moreover, is more responsible to the electorate for such decisions than the federal judiciary.

4.   Criticisms

Risk-benefit analysis has many critics. One concern, illustrated by *Corrosion Proof Fittings*, is that risk-benefit analysis slows down government regulation and makes it more difficult and thus less likely that the government will restrict harmful toxins. Under FIFRA, it took EPA 17 years to conduct a special review of Alar, 9 years for a review of Captan, and 12 years to review EBCD. Critics also worry that risk-benefit analyses imply greater certainty than actually exists. As highlighted earlier, considerable uncertainty plagues virtually all elements of the risk-benefit analysis, in particular the risk calculations. By quantifying the risk and developing an estimate of the "cost per life saved," however,

EPA suggests that it can compare the risks and costs with a high degree of precision and reduces the apparent need for a precautionary approach. In a similar vein, critics sometimes worry that the government too easily can cook the books under the guise of scientific risk assessment. Given the many judgments that go into a risk-benefit analysis and the underlying uncertainty, an agency can reach a wide range of conclusions based on any given data. What an agency decides may depend more on policy inclinations than science.

Critics also raise the traditional concerns with using economic efficiency to guide environmental policy that Chapter 2 discussed. Is the appropriate level of toxic exposure an economic question or a moral one? As a society, are we willing (and do we have the right) to expose people to harmful substances if it means more jobs, more consumer products, and a higher gross domestic product? Even if we believe that the goal of environmental policy should be to maximize societal utility, can society impose a health risk on one individual in order to make others better off? Although each of us trades off risk and wealth every day (e.g., by buying a cheaper car that is not as safe), that is a very different decision than choosing as a society to accept interpersonal tradeoffs. How, moreover, can the government determine the overall utility of permitting farmers to use a pesticide that can cause cancer in humans? To many, health risks are incommensurate with economic benefits; there is no common metric with which to compare costs and benefits.

Yet despite all of these concerns, risk-benefit analysis still tempts. As emphasized earlier, the modern industrial world is not risk free and never will be. Reducing risks, moreover, can be economically costly. So long as that's the case, the government inevitably will ask itself whether various regulations are "worth" the cost—the inquiry that is at the heart of risk-benefit statutes.

D. *Informational Approaches*

A final approach to toxins is to provide the public with information regarding toxic exposure and let public pressure and market choices address the problem. Few companies want to be known as the toxic leader of their community or industry. Armed with information about a company's toxic releases, members of the public may be able to pressure a company to reduce its emissions. Similarly, few people want to buy products that include toxic ingredients. If the government requires companies to reveal toxic substances in their products, producers may reformulate their products to remove the offending ingredients.

1. *The Toxic Release Inventory*

The Emergency Planning and Community Right-to-Know Act of 1986 (EPCRA) takes such an informational approach to toxic releases.

Under EPCRA, EPA maintains a list of over 650 hazardous substances. Any company that releases more than a specified threshold amount of each substance in any calendar year must report the releases to both EPA and the state. EPA then compiles this data into a national toxic release inventory ("TRI"), which it posts on its public website. The TRI data is picked up and reported by journalists and by other popular websites, such as Environmental Defense's "Scorecard," which combines the data with information about the potential health risks of each of the substances.[28]

The TRI has become an important weapon in reducing toxic releases. Numerous companies have worked to reduce their releases rather than place high on the TRI rankings—and for good reason. Bad publicity can hurt sales and poison local community relations. Studies even show that companies with high toxic releases, as reported in the TRI, have poorer stock market performances. Perhaps the best evidence of the effectiveness of the TRI, however, is industry's opposition to any expansion of the TRI and industry's efforts to get Congress to cut back on the existing TRI.

EPA has used the TRI to help promote other voluntary efforts to reduce toxic releases. In what became known as the 33/50 Program, EPA in 1989 asked 600 large dischargers to reduce voluntarily their emissions of 17 of the most dangerous TRI toxins. EPA set a goal of a 33% reduction by 1992 and a 50% reduction by 1995, measured against a 1989 baseline. According to EPA, the 33/50 Program achieved its goal one year ahead of schedule in 1994. Companies, moreover, have continued to reduce their discharges of the 17 substances since the 33/50 Program ended.

The TRI, however, is not perfect. Some evidence suggests that companies occasionally reduce their reported emissions not by improving their actual environmental performance but by changing their reporting standards or analytical methods. Because material sent for recycling is not counted as a TRI release, moreover, there has been far less pollution prevention (i.e., reduction of waste at the source) than one might expect. EPCRA similarly does not require companies to report on the amount of toxins that they use or that are in their products; companies must report only releases of toxins into the environment. As a result, EPCRA does little to reduce consumer or worker exposure to toxins. Environmental groups have lobbied (unsuccessfully to date) to broaden the TRI either to

28. The Scorecard website (www.score-card.org) provides one of the best examples of how information about environmental releases and performance can be used to try to influence improved corporate behavior.

cover all waste (including waste destined for recycling) or to focus on the amount of toxic substances going into the manufacturing process rather than only the amount coming out as waste. Finally, the TRI covers only a fraction of all toxic chemicals and does not address releases by some significant sources, such as farms.

2. *California's Proposition 65*

In the same year that Congress passed EPCRA, California voters passed Proposition 65, a voter initiative that requires public disclosure of both toxic releases and toxic ingredients in consumer products. Under Proposition 65, the Governor of California publishes a list of those chemicals known to cause cancer or reproductive toxicity; this list currently contains over 500 chemicals. Businesses cannot knowingly discharge or release a listed chemical into water or onto or into land if the chemical probably would travel into a source of drinking water. More importantly, businesses cannot knowingly and intentionally expose someone to a listed chemical without first providing a "clear and reasonable" warning. Thus, if a consumer product contains a listed chemical, the seller must post a notice either on the product or in a location that purchasers will see. Factories emitting toxic air pollutants must warn neighboring residents.

Businesses are exempt from these rules if the amount of chemical at issue is "insignificant." Recognizing that whether a level of exposure is significant or not can be the source of considerable scientific debate, however, Proposition 65 reverses the normal burden of proof. In order to qualify for the exemption, the business has the burden to show that the exposure amount is insignificant. This led businesses to press California in the early days of Proposition 65 to quickly issue regulations specifying what would constitute an insignificant amount. The resulting regulations define an insignificant amount for carcinogens as an amount that presents a risk, assuming lifetime exposure, of less than one in 100,000. For reproductive toxins, an insignificant amount is a quantity that, assuming lifetime exposure at 1000 times that level, would have no observable effect.

Proposition 65 also was one of the first environmental statutes in the United States to include a "bounty" provision. Whoever brings a lawsuit for a violation of Proposition 65 receives 25 percent of any penalty imposed by the court. Courts can assess penalties of up to $2500 per day for each violation. Fearful that the bounty provision might be encouraging frivolous lawsuits, California in 2002 added a requirement that plaintiffs file a "certificate of merit" certifying that the plaintiff believes that there is good cause for the lawsuit.

When Proposition 65 originally passed, some people questioned whether consumers really would pay attention to warning labels and signs. Concern mounted when Proposition 65 warnings began to sprout up virtually everywhere—in liquor stores (potential for birth defects), bars and restaurants (alcohol and, before cigarettes were banned in California bars, second-hand smoke), and in gasoline stations (toxic fumes). Under Proposition 65, moreover, warning signs typically are quite generic. A typical warning reads "Warning: This product contains a chemical known to the State of California to cause cancer." The warnings virtually never provide detailed information about the exact nature and size of the potential risk.

Proposition 65, however, has resulted in significant reductions in toxic exposures. Producers have responded to Proposition 65 by reformulating their products. Producers simply do not want to take a chance on how consumers will respond to warning labels. Wine makers therefore no longer use lead foil for the tops of their bottles, Wite–Out Products removed trichloroethylene (TCE) from their correction fluid, the manufacturers of calcium supplements reduced the lead content in the supplements, and the maker of Progresso tomatoes stopped using lead solder in their cans. Because most manufacturers do not want to manufacture one version of a product for California and another version for the rest of the nation, moreover, these changes generally have benefited consumers nationwide.

CHAPTER 7

Waste Management

I. The Resource Conservation Recovery Act

Americans have a remarkable quality of life, enjoying a range of goods and services that kings and queens in past centuries could only have dreamed of. This material wealth comes at a cost, though, for it also generates a remarkable amount of waste. As with air and water pollutants, wastes come in all shapes and sizes. While some wastes are toxic and highly hazardous, others can be treated to become non-hazardous or are easily assimilated by the environment. To get a sense of the enormous volumes involved in waste management, consider that we generate the equivalent of 4.6 pounds of municipal solid waste daily for every American man, woman, and child, an almost 70% increase since 1960. This comprises a wide range of different waste streams—from household garbage (55–65% of all waste by weight) and industrial waste to construction and biomedical waste. Of all this household waste generated, only about 1% of it is considered hazardous to health. Most hazardous waste is generated by industrial facilities (just over 20,000 facilities produced over 40 million tons of hazardous waste in 1999).

Why is waste a problem? One concern has been the so-called "landfill crisis," the concern that we're running out of places to dispose of our waste. From 1988 to 1999, almost 70% of the nation's municipal landfills closed. While the closure of these sites has largely been in response to stricter regulations, the lack of *new* landfills is not due to lack of space. Rather, NIMBY (Not In my Back Yard) pressures from communities that do no want to live near a dump have resulted in a lack of landfill permits. Another concern is that waste means inefficiency. By throwing away or burning so much waste, we create the need to extract more virgin materials from the earth. The concerns here are both depletion of natural resources and harmful environmental impacts caused by extraction and synthesis of these materials that are then transformed into wastes. By reducing waste through better product and process design, increased re-use of materials, and greater recycling, we can reduce life-cycle impacts.

The single biggest environmental problem posed by waste (and certainly the biggest public concern), though, is its health effects. Drinking water, for example, can be contaminated by waste "leachate." This is easy to understand if one thinks of a landfill as a giant "Mr. Coffee" filter. As water percolates through the landfill it becomes contaminated

170

with hazardous constituents. This leachate then mixes with groundwater and surface water that may be consumed by humans. Incinerators burning waste are a major source of dioxins, mercury and other hazardous air pollutants. While hard to believe, a study of the Chesapeake Bay found that up to 30 percent of the nitrogen in the Chesapeake Bay comes from atmospheric deposition. Incinerators are the primary source of mercury in the Bay, as well.

Prior to the 1970s there were poor and, in some cases, no requirements for waste disposal. The precursor to the Resource Conservation and Recovery Act, the 1965 Solid Waste Disposal Act, merely encouraged states to develop waste management programs. The tougher Clean Air Act and Clean Water Act had required installation of pollution control devices on smokestacks and pipes throughout the nation, but where was the *waste* collected in these end of pipe controls supposed to go? Many landfills were simply holes in the ground that were compacted by bulldozers until full, and then covered over by topsoil and turned into golf courses or commercial developments. Nor were there stringent record keeping requirements to identify where the waste had come from (a failure that would curse the Superfund program, described later in this chapter). The Resource Conservation and Recovery Act (RCRA)[1] was drafted in this regulatory void.

RCRA is an amendment to the earlier Solid Waste Disposal Act and accomplishes four basic goals. It (1) creates definitions to determine the classes of wastes coming under its authority; (2) creates a tracking system for hazardous waste from its creation to its disposal (the first environmental law to take such a life-cycle approach); (3) establishes handling standards for the waste from its generation to its disposal; and (4) provides authority for mandatory clean-up of polluted treatment, storage, and disposal sites.

The key provisions in RCRA deal with the disposal of solid waste (regulated in Subtitle D of the act) and the treatment and disposal of hazardous waste (regulated in Subtitle C). Because Subtitle C makes it much more expensive to dispose of hazardous waste, much of RCRA's legal history can be read as a "great escape" story of industry attempts to avoid having its waste considered hazardous waste and, once within the grips of Subtitle C's coverage, to avoid being classified as a treatment, storage, or disposal facility. As with every other federal environmental law, it goes without saying, at the time of RCRA's passage Congress greatly underestimated the size and complexity of the problem.

For many students, studying RCRA quickly becomes a voyage into Alice's Wonderland, a statutory dreamscape where "solid" includes liquid and gas, where "hazardous" may not look hazardous, and where

---

1. 42 U.S.C. §§ 6901–6992k.

the King Midas fable is reversed with certain wastes turning everything they touch into even more waste. To understand RCRA, then, one must accept at the outset that it is internally consistent and relies on bright-line distinctions, but many of the critical terms have specific, often counterintuitive meanings within the statutory structure. To wind one's way through RCRA, there are three existential questions to keep in mind—"what is it?", "where is it?", and "who am I?".

A. *What is It?*

Because RCRA's requirements for handling solid hazardous waste are very expensive, companies want to avoid their waste being character-ized as either solid or hazardous waste. Thus the first practical questions in any RCRA analysis are (1) is it "solid" waste, and (2) is it solid "hazardous" waste?

1. *Solid Waste and Strategic Behavior*

RCRA regulates only the disposal of "solid waste." If your waste is not considered solid waste under RCRA's regulatory definitions, you can laugh at the statute with impunity. The term "solid," however, is far broader than everyday usage, and covers virtually every form of matter except uncontained gases.[2] This broad definition was necessary to pre-vent parties from converting their wastes to avoid coverage. Add enough water and mix, and most solid wastes become liquid.

The coverage of solid waste is not as extensive as the overbroad definition might suggest, though, because there are a number of impor-tant, gaping exemptions. Some wastes are exempt because they are regulated by other statutes. Thus RCRA does not cover wastes in sewage that passes through a public water treatment plant, wastewater dis-charges regulated by a Clean Water Act permit, mining wastes or nuclear wastes, just to name some of the largest exceptions. Municipal garbage, a very large waste stream that may contain small amounts of hazardous materials, such as batteries and insecticide aerosols, is exempt for practical reasons because of its sheer size. And other wastes, such as irrigation return flows, are exempt for political reasons because of the farm lobby's clout (recall that Congress exempted these from the Clean Water Act's coverage, as well).

While a case can be made to justify every one of these exemptions, the net result encourages strategic behavior by the regulated communi-ty. The more onerous and expensive RCRA regulation of waste becomes, the stronger the incentive to fall out of its coverage entirely and into another statute. And rest assured that there are often significant differ-

---

2. 42 U.S.C. § 6903(27).

ences over how statutes treat the same wastes. Some laws are far more rigorous than others, depending on the politics of the area and the time when the statutes were passed. The less demanding treatment of waste water under the Clean Water Act, for example, explains the large percentage of hazardous waste that is disposed through either the public sewage system or direct emissions into a waterway.

While it may seem a stupid point to make, RCRA only covers solid wastes that are waste products. This seemingly redundant statement becomes important because waste can also resemble products and raw materials. Imagine, for example, that you run a farm and mix large vats of pesticides for application on crops. Under FIFRA, these pesticides can legally be sprayed onto fields, only to wash off into streams and drinking water supplies. But, under RCRA, the same pesticides that remain in the barrel cannot be disposed of in landfills without extensive and expensive pre-treatment. They have now become RCRA hazardous waste.

Consider, too, the challenge posed by recycling. One of RCRA's goals is to encourage recycling. This not only reduces the amount of waste destined for disposal but the amount of raw materials needed for production, as well. Because recycling turns waste into a raw material for the manufacturing process, this avoids the environmental impacts from synthesis and production of virgin materials. Set against this, though, are the legislative goals of protecting the environment from hazardous substances and not interfering with the production process. While often held out as a wonderful and blessedly green activity, recycling can be a dirty business, creating significant wastes itself. Indeed a number of recycling sites later transformed into Superfund sites. How, then, to create regulations that define solid waste in a manner that can be meaningfully applied and enforced, that encourage recycling, and that prevent dangerous or sham recycling? Two cases, *American Mining Congress v. EPA I* and *II* addressed this very challenge.

RCRA's definition of solid waste includes a number of waste streams, such as garbage, liquid material, solid material, "and other discarded material" resulting from certain activities. In *American Mining Congress v. EPA* (known as *AMC I*), the American Mining Congress argued that wastes produced in its manufacturing processes should not be considered solid waste if they would later be used again in the processes—for the simple reason that they were not being "discarded."[3] They were, instead, being recycled. To make this clearer, consider the diagram below of a hypothetical production process. The process turns squares into circles, and in so doing produces a by-product of triangles. If the triangles can be re-inserted back into the manufacturing process, are they discarded wastes (and therefore subject to RCRA) or raw materials?

3. American Mining Congress v. United States EPA, 824 F.2d 1177 (D.C.Cir.1987).

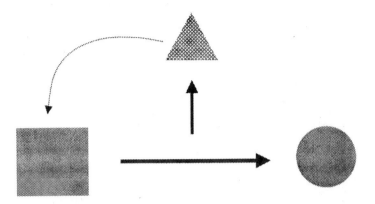

The D.C. Circuit agreed with the American Mining Congress that waste should not be considered discarded if it would later be used in an ongoing manufacturing process. The court held that the materials had "not yet become part of the waste disposal problem; rather, they are destined for beneficial reuse or recycling in a continuous process by the generating industry itself." The dissent took a more functional view. Promoting recycling is surely a goal of RCRA, but its overarching goal is environmental protection. Thus the main issue is whether the waste material creates the opportunity to cause environmental harm by spilling or leaking, even if it eventually will be recycled. If so, then EPA should be able to regulate it as a solid waste. After this decision, RCRA's definition of solid waste depended as much on the owner's plans for the materials as on the nature of the materials. Did the owner plan to sell the materials (in which case they were covered by RCRA) or re-use them in the process? As you might expect, this created an incentive for "sham recycling," stating you would re-use the materials in the manufacturing process but really just storing them on-site indefinitely.

These problems were addressed in a subsequent case with the same parties, *American Mining Congress v. EPA* (known as *AMC II*).[4] Here, plaintiffs argued that sludge stored in a surface impoundment (a holding pond) should not be considered RCRA solid waste because it was being held for potential re-use (despite the fact that in the meantime the wastes might overflow or leak into other bodies of water). Cutting back on its earlier holding, the court stated that the recycling exemption only applies to wastes that are safely stored for immediate re-use in an ongoing process. Otherwise, the materials become part of the waste disposal problem and must be regulated as solid waste. In practice, "immediate" has been interpreted to mean use within 90 days and "on-going

4.   907 F.2d 1179 (D.C.Cir.1990).

process" to mean the same process. As a result of these cases and subsequent decisions, the by-products of a production process destined for recycling are not considered solid wastes if stored safely and used within 90 days in the same process (a practice known as closed-loop recycling). If any of these conditions are not met, these materials are regulated as solid waste.

A final example of how the same materials can receive different regulatory treatment may be found in *American Petroleum Institute v. EPA*.[5] Building off the logic of the *American Mining Congress* cases, plaintiffs argued that the by-products of a manufacturing process should not be considered solid waste once they arrive at a reclamation facility for recycling. Further distancing itself from the *AMC I* holding, however, the court declared that once waste arrives at a reclamation facility it remains solid waste because it has already become part of the waste disposal problem. In other words, the materials cannot shed their label of solid waste once they enter the reclamation facility gates, even though they clearly will be recycled. Unlike the children's game of Tag, RCRA doesn't provide a safe "base."

Taken together, these cases provide stark examples of the difficulties in drafting regulations. By-products processed on-site at a plant for re-use within 90 days are unregulated by RCRA, yet the identical treatment at an off-site reclamation facility is highly regulated. This different treatment of the same activities is perhaps an inevitable result of trying to develop regulations that encourage recycling while, at the same time, closing loopholes. Indeed, the greatest challenge in drafting regulations can lie in trying to fulfill the statute's intent while knowing full well that the regulated community will act strategically to take advantage of any possibility of favorable treatment. In this regard, it's instructive to note that EPA convened a task force in the early 1990s to create a better definition of "solid waste," one that promoted genuine rather than sham recycling. In its 1994 report, the task force proposed a comprehensive four–part classification for regulating different types of recycling. Due to its complexity, the proposal was never adopted.

2. Solid Hazardous Waste and Closing Loopholes

For any regulatory scheme to work, the regulated business has to know clearly what is required of it and the regulator needs to know how to verify this. Imagine, for a moment, that you were the EPA official in charge of identifying and defining the wastes that will be covered by RCRA. Intuitively, given the range of toxicity among various wastes it might seem most effective to distinguish among separate categories of waste, subjecting the most hazardous wastes to the most stringent

---

5.   906 F.2d 729 (D.C.Cir.1990).

controls. But this is easier said than done. Should the mere presence of a hazardous substance in a waste stream make the entire stream hazardous, or should there be some kind of assessment to determine the overall hazard it poses? Realize, as well, that there are tens of thousands of types of waste streams. Precision has a cost.

RCRA distinguishes between two broad categories of covered wastes. If a material is considered a solid waste, it is covered by Subtitle D. If it a solid waste *and* hazardous it falls under the much more onerous, and costly, coverage of Subtitle C. So the regulated community cares a great deal about the definition of "hazardous waste." In contrast to determining whether or not materials are "solid waste" under RCRA or fall under the various exemptions, however, defining a material as a solid "hazardous waste" is relatively straightforward.

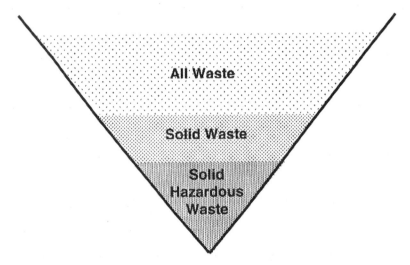

RCRA identifies two categories of hazardous waste—"listed wastes" and "characteristic wastes."[6] Listed wastes are, as the name suggests, substances that EPA has determined routinely contain hazardous constituents or exhibit hazardous qualities. These are listed in the Code of Federal Regulations. If a company produces a listed waste but believes that it should not be treated as hazardous waste, it may petition EPA to delist the waste but this is an expensive and lengthy process.

It would be nice, of course, if EPA produced a comprehensive list of all hazardous wastes, but given the fact that over 50,000 chemicals are now used in commerce EPA is lucky to list even a fraction of the possible

---

6. 40 C.F.R. 261.

waste streams. Thus the second category identifies hazardous wastes by their characteristics. If a waste is not a listed waste but has the characteristics of being ignitable (i.e., products that are capable of causing fire during routine transportation, storage, or disposal), corrosive, reactive, or toxic (set at levels 100 times more protective than the Safe Drinking Water Act) then it is treated as a hazardous waste. While the burden of identifying listed wastes falls on EPA (since, after all, it creates the list), the burden of identifying characteristic wastes falls on the waste generators who must determine through standard tests whether their waste is ignitable, corrosive, reactive, or toxic. Hence the need for rigorous compliance monitoring by EPA.

Recall the previous discussion on how companies producing solid waste could avoid RCRA coverage if they satisfied the recycling exemption. Companies producing hazardous waste would clearly like to avoid Subtitle C coverage, as well. But how? As described above, they could petition for delisting of specific waste but this is an expensive process. They could also try to modify their waste so that it no longer had the characteristics of a hazardous waste. What happens when waste is transformed, either through mixing with other wastes, dilution, or synthesis into another compound? Should EPA regulate it as a hazardous waste (once a waste, always a waste), or has it escaped the coverage of Subtitle C? And with the thousands of sites using hazardous wastes in all kinds of processes, how can EPA ensure credible enforcement?

RCRA regulates treated wastes very differently depending on whether they are listed or characteristic wastes. If characteristic wastes no longer exhibit their hazardous characteristics, they are treated simply as solid waste and fall out of Subtitle C's coverage. Listed wastes, though, are subject to two rules. The *mixture rule* states that any mixture of a listed waste with another solid waste is *still* considered a hazardous waste (with an exemption for municipal solid waste).[7] The *derived from rule* requires that wastes derived from the treatment of a hazardous waste also be treated as hazardous wastes, including contaminated soil and water.[8] As a consequence, EPA has created a perverse variation on King Midas' tragic gift. Whereas everything Midas touched turned to gold, everything listed hazardous waste touches turns to more listed waste. The related *contained-in policy* holds that contaminated media (generally soil) becomes a hazardous waste. This has important consequences for CERCLA (discussed below), since contaminated soil at Superfund sites must often be treated as hazardous waste.

In combination with RCRA's broad exemptions, the mixture and derived from rules have created a bizarre situation. The rules require

---

7.   40 C.F.R. 261.3(a)(2).   **8.**   40 C.F.R. 261.3(c).

strict treatment of many wastes that are significantly less hazardous than wastes that are not covered *at all* because of the broad exemptions for wastewater discharges, mining wastes, etc. The increasingly quixotic dilemma of creating precise, clear, and fair definitions of solid and hazardous waste remains unresolved after more than two decades, frustrated by strategic behavior by firms seeking to avoid having their waste fall under these definitions.

B. Who am I?

1. Generators, Transporters and TSDs

Just as RCRA divides the waste world into solid waste and solid hazardous waste (listed and characteristic) with very different requirements for each, RCRA divides the world of actors into three categories—generators, transporters, and "treatment, storage, and disposal facilities" (TSDs). While each class of actor faces differing responsibilities, all must comply with the tracking requirements. RCRA follows the disposal of waste by establishing a "cradle-to-grave" tracking scheme from the generators of waste to transporters through to disposal facilities. In principle, if we know where the waste is at all times and ensure that people handling the waste at each stage act responsibly, then no worries. To this end, when a generator produces a threshold amount of hazardous waste it must obtain an identification number for the waste from EPA and fill out a "manifest." This sheet accompanies the waste shipment to its final disposal and, at each stage it changes hands, the manifest stays with the shipment while a copy is sent back to the generator. When the TSD finally receives the waste, it must inspect it to check that the contents match the manifest. This cradle-to-grave tracking ensures that the problem of unidentified wastes at contaminated sites, regulated by CERCLA and described later in this chapter, is not repeated.

In addition to the manifest requirements, generators are subject to a variety of requirements. Generators must determine if their waste is a listed or characteristic hazardous waste. They must also ensure proper storage and labeling of wastes, keep records of waste generation and test results, and submit periodic reports. For small companies, these requirements can prove quite resource intensive. Indeed, RCRA was drafted primarily to regulate facilities routinely generating large amounts of the same small number of waste streams. In some relatively new sectors such as the biomedical industry, however, scores of different waste streams are infrequently produced. RCRA's requirements have come to be seen as so ill-fitting that the state of California created a special task force to reform its regulation of laboratory wastes. As the economy continues its trend toward custom manufacturing and biotech, the regulatory fit of RCRA will continue to be challenged.

Transporters face fewer requirements, but must comply with EPA and Department of Transportation requirements for the transportation of hazardous materials (identified as "hazmat" on highway signs), including proper packaging and labeling, reporting, record keeping, and the manifest. These requirements take on added significance when one realizes that more than 3 billion tons of hazardous materials are transported each year, with over 800,000 shipments of these materials every day.

RCRA's requirements are *much* more onerous on TSDs than on generators or transporters. Many Superfund site were formerly TSDs, and RCRA seeks to ensure not only clean operation but clean shut down at the end of the TSD's life. To operate, a TSD must obtain a permit from EPA or an authorized state agency. The permit process often lasts from two to four and the permit is good for ten years. TSDs must satisfy a range of operating requirements that include personnel training, record keeping, groundwater monitoring, security, and technical standards. The technical standards are rigorous and require, for example, that landfills have 2 or more impermeable liners and a leachate collection system. With the problem of contaminated sites in mind, TSDs must also create comprehensive plans for closure. These address not only the closing of the facility but maintaining and monitoring the facility for a period of 30 years after closure. In addition, TSDs must provide financial assurance (through insurance, bonds, or other means) that they will have enough money to pay for closure as well as any consequent liability. While seemingly onerous, in light of the many TSDs that shut down with no resources, leaving only contaminated land beneath them, these requirements are important in ensuring companies do not strategically plan bankruptcy.

Amendments to RCRA in 1984 by the Hazardous and Solid Waste Amendments (HSWA)[9] provided another important tool to ensure that TSDs did not become Superfund sites. EPA was given authority to require that TSDs clean up present or past contamination on their sites if deemed necessary to protect human health or the environment. Known as "corrective actions," these clean-ups may be enforced through a civil action or by suspending operating permits, and represent a clear example of CERCLA and RCRA moving closer together.

2. *The Land Ban and Regulatory Hammers*

HSWA also took aim at landfills. By the mid–1980s, Subtitle C's requirements for generators, transporters, and TSDs had clearly succeeded in at least one area—raising the cost of waste disposal. By making waste disposal more expensive, one would expect waste produc-

---

9. Pub. L. No. 98–616 (1984).

tion to go down. And if waste was produced then EPA had clear preferences for its disposal. This was reflected in the so-called "waste hierarchy," the accepted rule of thumb in managing waste.

first **reduce**

    then **re-use**

        then **recycle**

            then **landfill**

Raising the cost of waste disposal would certainly promote waste reduction, re-use, and recycling, but how to minimize landfill and the fear of groundwater contamination? HSWA greatly restricted the land disposal of wastes, requiring EPA to prohibit disposal of waste in landfills unless "there will be no migration of hazardous constituents" from the landfill. Although Congress could have stopped here, essentially banning the disposal of hazardous waste in landfills, it created an exception for wastes that had been treated to "substantially diminish the toxicity of the waste" or the migration of hazardous constituents. RCRA's "land ban," then, effectively prohibits the disposal only of *untreated* hazardous wastes. Fearful of the Reagan administration delaying implementation, Congress also included a unique "hammer" provision. It shifted the burden of regulatory delay from the agency to industry by providing that if pretreatment regulations were not issued for a particular waste by a particular date, there would be no land-based disposal of that waste *at all*. Needless to say, spurred on by industry interests EPA moved on the issue quickly.

The interesting question that Congress did not clearly answer, though, was how to determine the pre-treatment standards for hazardous waste. RCRA provides that pre-treatment standards must "substantially diminish the toxicity of the waste or substantially reduce the likelihood of migration of hazardous constituents from the waste so that short-term and long-term threats to human health and the environment are minimized." Does this mean that the standards should try to minimize the chances that any waste will ever migrate from landfills, pushing EPA to require the maximum treatment technologically possible? Or should the standards require pre-treatment only to the degree deemed sufficient to ensure that the waste is no longer hazardous to human health and the environment, even if greater treatment is feasible?

Put in simple terms, EPA was faced with two different approaches to protecting groundwater from landfilled waste. One approach would require pre-treatment based on *best available technology*—perhaps over-treating the waste to levels far below any proven health risk. The other would rely on *risk assessment*—treating the waste to a level with acceptable risks to health. This choice of regulatory strategies poses unavoidable trade-offs—technology-based regulations that are inflexible but relatively easy to administer versus more complex but more flexible (and arguably economically efficient) risk-based standards. We saw this very same conflict between technology-based and risk-based standards in our discussion of NAAQS in the Clean Air Act and technological standards in the Clean Water Act. In fact, it occurs throughout environmental law. At the end of the day, the "correct" implementation strategy depends on the regulator's priority, whether it be low cost of administration, impetus to force technological development, desire for potential over-treatment to reflect scientific uncertainty over health effects, or high cost of compliance to drive out marginal TSDs and create barriers to entry for new participants. EPA's final decision to go with a technology-based standard was largely upheld in the case, *Hazardous Waste Treatment Council v. EPA.*[10]

In navigating this regulatory shoal, EPA commenced with a hybrid approach, requiring pre-treatment by the best demonstrated available technology, but only to the degree necessary to move below the maximum concentration of a hazardous constituent that posed health concerns. In response to outrage by environmentalists and Congress (who basically argued that "no migration" means just that, and that a risk approach was inappropriate), EPA later moved to a pure technological approach. In so doing, however, it incurred the wrath of economists at the Office of Management and Budget, who estimated that the cost of the land ban exceeded $4 billion for each life saved.

While making good copy for columnists to decry yet another bone-headed decision by EPA, such monetary estimates warrant careful consideration. How did OMB treat uncertainties? Did they only consider lives saved through reduced cancer deaths? Did they value the benefit of avoided Superfund clean-ups in the future? What about the general impacts on waste reduction? Did they consider the possibility that treatment costs might drop in the future? While it's easy to pick apart the OMB estimate, it's equally worth noting that EPA's scientists have stated that groundwater contamination poses a relatively low health risk compared to other environmental hazards. Public polls, however, consistently rate groundwater contamination quite high on their list of environmental concerns. RCRA reflects the public perception but not, perhaps, the scientific community's. In a democracy, is this the appropriate result?

10. Hazardous Waste Treatment Council v. EPA, 886 F.2d 355 (D.C.Cir.1989).

A final consequence of the land ban worth nothing is the problem of media shifting. EPA's pre-treatment requirements increased the cost of landfill disposal of hazardous waste. Because waste disposal is a market, generators sought the cheapest disposal option and many settled on incineration. Following the land ban, there was a decline in waste sent to landfills and a significant increase in the amount of waste incinerated. Did the waste disappear? Of course not. It simply shifted form, from solid and liquid wastes to gaseous waste. It may be that environmentally this was a good thing, but only if incinerators release fewer contaminants than landfills. And that's far from clear, given that incinerators are major sources of heavy metals, dioxins, and furans in the environment.

C. Subtitle D

Despite the importance of RCRA in regulating solid hazardous waste, the regulation of solid non-hazardous waste has largely remained the responsibility of state and local governments. And it's a *lot* of waste. In 1999, municipal solid waste accounted for 230 million tons of waste. As might be expected, although exempted from Subtitle C, municipal waste still contains some hazardous waste (e.g., from batteries). Subtitle D requires states to create plans that ensure responsible management of these wastes, from collection to disposal. EPA has also created regulations for the design and operation of landfills, ensuring for example that landfills not discharge pollutants into surface waters or engage in open burning. In a clear example of cooperative federalism, these regulations set minimum standards, and states are free to regulate landfills more strictly as, indeed, Pennsylvania, New York, and several other states have. (Subtitle C delegates permitting authority to states, as well, so long as their programs are "equivalent" to and "consistent" with the federal program and provide for "adequate enforcement.")

D. The Challenge of Pollution Prevention

Despite its broad scope, it is important to note what RCRA does not cover. Consider the solid wastes involved in a typical manufacturing operation. The environmental impacts of the raw material inputs and product outputs are regulated, if at all, by other statutes such as TSCA and FIFRA (discussed in Chapter 6). OSHA regulates occupational exposure to contaminants during the process. RCRA, then, covers only the waste stream, a narrow subset of total manufacturing operations. And not all wastes fall under RCRA. Congress intentionally chose not to regulate manufacturing processes, effectively treating the facility as a black box. Indeed, environmental law as a whole treats factories as giant black boxes, refusing to look at what happens inside. Our pollution statutes only kick in when the waste leaves the facility, whether as air and water pollution or as solid waste.

RCRA Cheat Sheet

Does my activity make me a:

Generator
Transporter
TSD

Is the waste I am dealing with "solid" waste

   Is it exempted

municipal waste
domestic sewage
NPDES permit
recycling exemption
ongoing process
immediate re-use

Is the solid waste "hazardous"

listed waste
characteristic waste

If a characteristic waste:

can the character change
   by mixing
   by synthesis

If a listed waste, am I producing more waste by:

the mixture rule
the derived-from rule
the contained-in rule

If I am a TSD, must I take corrective action?

This "end-of-pipe" approach has certainly succeeded, given the improvements in air and water quality over the last three decades. But this approach also favors, indeed intentionally favors, a business-as-usual attitude known as "pollution control." In a pollution control strategy, the company collects the waste from its processes and then ships them off in compliance with RCRA and other environmental laws. Waste disposal becomes a cost of doing business and the pollution control technologies—the filters, scrubbers and settling ponds—are nonproductive assets (insofar as they don't contribute to the bottom line). To be sure, RCRA has greatly increased the cost of waste disposal and this has provided an incentive for companies to reduce their waste generation. Because of the many exemptions, RCRA has provided an even greater incentive to manage the waste so that the waste falls out of RCRA's coverage, either through the recycling exemption, discharge to sewers, or some other exempted route. Recycling and composting, for example, diverted over 64 million tons of material from landfills and incinerators in 1999, almost double the amount a decade earlier.

Instead of disposing of waste trapped at the end of the pipe, why not simply produce less waste in the first place? This strategy is known as "pollution prevention" (and in Europe as "cleaner production"). Indeed in many cases manufacturing waste is simply valuable raw material down the drain. Pollution prevention focuses on good housekeeping, waste audits, and closing production loops rather than more efficient technologies at the end of the pipe. Such strategies have allowed companies such as 3M, Dow, and Johnson Wax to reduce their waste by over 50%, saving money in the process both through less loss of raw materials and avoided costs of waste disposal. RCRA, though, does little directly to promote a pollution prevention approach. Beyond the recycling exemption, RCRA doesn't care how the waste gets produced. Indeed one might argue that, by failing to go to the heart of the production process, RCRA misses the most important waste disposal issue of all—waste reduction at source. Put simply, RCRA is limited in its ability to solve the hazardous waste problem by the fact that it only deals with the results of the production process. It can only encourage reduction or recycling by making disposal less attractive.

II. The Dormant Commerce Clause and Waste Disposal

Being dirty carries a real cost. Disposal fees for hazardous waste are as high in America as anywhere in the world. This is due in part to the many requirements RCRA imposes on waste disposal facilities and in part to the fact that demand exceeds supply. In recent years, commentators have decried the problem of a "landfill crisis." There surely is a problem, but it's not that we're running out of space for disposal facilities. Rather, the problem is that we can't open new ones as old disposal facilities shut down. Not surprisingly, no one wants to live near a waste disposal facility or accept other peoples' trash. One doesn't often see real estate ads boasting: "Beautiful house! Walking distance to playground, shops, and dump!!" NIMBYism—effective local opposition to the permitting of waste facilities—has made it increasingly difficult to open new waste disposal sites and the shortage of disposal capacity has, in turn, driven up the cost of disposal.

As described in the last section, while RCRA prescribes in detail how wastes should be tracked and treated, and how TSDs and landfills should be operated, the law says nothing about *where* geographically the waste should go. Assume that you are a state that has some disposal capacity right now and wants to preserve it. Can you refuse to accept waste from other states? This would certainly be a politically popular action, since voters don't appreciate trucks filled with hazardous materials driving on their roads, much less leaving their wastes behind. On its face, a ban on waste imports would seem fairly easy to justify since the state interest in protecting the public health is clearly legitimate. Controlling the interstate flow of wastes, though, has proven very difficult to defend legally because of concerns over interstate commerce. The Supreme Court has directly addressed whether states can control the movement of wastes in a series of decisions over the last quarter century.

The core decision, still good law today, is the 1978 case, *Philadelphia v. New Jersey.*[11] The city of Philadelphia challenged a New Jersey law banning the disposal of out-of-state waste. The ban was not absolute, though. Out-of-state waste could still be shipped to New Jersey if the state EPA determined that the waste could be disposed without threat to the health and safety of New Jersey residents. The case, and those that followed, turned on whether the Court should characterize the movement of wastes as commerce.

If you have already studied constitutional law, you'll be familiar with the Commerce Clause (Art. I, § 8), providing that Congress shall have power to regulate commerce among the several states. This is what gives Congress the authority to regulate the treatment, storage, and disposal of hazardous waste under RCRA. Indeed, as discussed in Chapter 3, the Commerce Clause provides the handle for virtually all federal environmental regulation and has become a major issue in the context of wetlands protection. The so-called "Dormant Commerce Clause" acts as a corollary and addresses whether *states* can burden interstate commerce

11.   437 U.S. 617 (1978).

185

without Congressional consent. The Supreme Court has long held that states have only limited power over interstate commerce and has established two relevant tests to review challenged laws. When a state regulates evenhandedly to promote a legitimate state interest and imposes only incidental burdens on interstate commerce, the state action will be upheld unless the burden on commerce outweighs the local benefits (known as the *Pike* test). If, however, the state directly discriminates against interstate commerce, the challenged law is subject to strict scrutiny and is virtually per se unconstitutional. It is important to note that these tests only apply when Congress has not granted states the power to burden interstate commerce (i.e., has remained dormant). In cases where Congress has acted (for example, allowing states to burden the interstate transportation of atomic waste) then the dormant commerce clause is inapplicable.

One can easily see why the Court would create such a rule. As described in Chapter 8 on trade and the environment, in any federal system co-equal jurisdictions will compete with one another for economic advantage. If a state can protect local manufacturers by blocking the flow of goods from other states, it often will. And, given the chance, the injured jurisdiction will respond in kind, raising the specter of a trade war. Only a supervening authority enforcing rules against the imposition of protectionist trade barriers will halt this trend. This is exactly the same concern that led to creation of the GATT and the European Community. Thus the dormant commerce clause establishes a presumption against state burdens on commerce, which must be overridden by Congress.

Despite the New Jersey legislature's insistence that their law was not motivated by protectionist concerns, the Court was unpersuaded. While the Court acknowledged that New Jersey's interests were legitimate, its actions impermissibly distinguished waste solely on the bases of its geographic origin. One cannot look at waste and legitimately distinguish between garbage from Los Angeles, Chicago, or Newark. As the majority declared, "whatever New Jersey's ultimate purpose, it may not be accomplished by discriminating against articles of commerce coming from outside the State unless there is some reason, apart from their origin, to treat them differently ... What is crucial is the attempt by one State to isolate itself from a problem common to many by erecting a barrier against the movement of interstate trade." New Jersey, the Court concluded, was hoarding a valuable resource—i.e., landfills. It may find itself the unhappy recipient of other states' waste today, but in the future it may need to ship its wastes to Pennsylvania or New York. Unless the Court struck down the restriction, the majority reasoned, interstate commerce in waste would be blocked.

That's surely one way to view the issue, but consider the dissent by Justice Rehnquist. He characterized the situation not as hoarding an *economic good* for the greedy benefit of New Jersey residents (i.e., keeping its waste disposal capacity for itself) but, rather, in keeping out a *public health bad*. A line of Supreme Court quarantine cases have permitted states to ban the import of diseased animal carcasses, and is this really any different? Put another way, just because a state has to dispose of its own noxious articles, that doesn't mean they should have to accept noxious items from other states. Doing so would fail to protect the public health and welfare. The Court should have treated the flow control law as environmental protection, not economic protectionism.

The basic holding of *Philadelphia v. New Jersey* has been reaffirmed in a series of cases challenging ingenious measures to slow the flow of out-of-state waste imports. In *Chemical Waste Management v. Hunt*, for example, the Alabama legislature sought to limit the out-of-state waste going to a facility operated by a private company near Emelle, Alabama.[12] In an example often cited by environmental justice advocates, 90% of Emelle's population was African American and the county was one of Alabama's poorest. Remarkably, the Emelle facility accepted *17% of the country's* hazardous waste. Roughly 90% of the waste disposed at Emelle came from out-of-state. Clearly, the legislature was not simply concerned with the operation of a small town dump.

Alabama initially tried a reciprocity approach, banning the import of hazardous waste from states that did not have their own hazardous waste disposal facilities, but this was invalidated by the 11th Circuit. The legislature then took the more indirect route of taxation, passing a law that charged $25 per ton on all waste disposed in the state and an additional $72 per ton for out-of-state waste. It also capped the total waste disposed per year in any site. The law worked. Two years after its passage, there was a 63% reduction in waste sent to Emelle. In an 8–1 decision, however, the Supreme Court held that protectionism resides in means as well as ends. States cannot discriminate against out-of-state goods unless there is a legitimate basis (beyond their origin in another state) to treat them differently. Did it matter that Alabama was merely imposing a special fee, rather than outright banning the disposal? The Supreme Court, not surprisingly, said "no," so long as the special tax on out-of-state hazardous waste bore no relationship to any special costs imposed by the waste.

Following the decisions of *Philadelphia* and *Hunt,* one can just imagine young legislative aides, sitting around a table in the State House, scratching their heads to figure out how to get around the decisions and keep out waste. In the next attempt, Michigan's efforts to

12. Chemical Waste Management v. Hunt, 504 U.S. 334 (1992).

move the ban to the local level were challenged in *Fort Gratiot Sanitary Landfill, Inc. v. Michigan Dept. of Natural Resources.*[13] Michigan's Solid Waste Management Act required each county to adopt a twenty year plan for disposal of its own wastes. No out-of-county waste could be accepted unless authorized by the plan. The policy goal of the statute was seemingly straightforward—each county should have to deal properly with its own waste before accepting others'. The law was challenged by a local landfill that accepted roughly 1,750 tons per day of out-of-state waste. Michigan argued that the statute did not discriminate against out-of-state waste because the law treated out-of-state waste the same as Michigan out-of-county waste. The Court, however, held that discrimination against other Michigan waste did not excuse burdening interstate commerce, and struck down the statute.

In the next gallant effort, in *Oregon Waste Systems, Inc. v. Department of Environmental Quality*, Oregon imposed a $2.25 per ton surcharge on out-of-state solid waste, but—unlike Alabama—argued that the tax was compensatory, based on the costs to the state and residents of disposing of the wastes.[14] Nonetheless, the state still lost. According to the 7–2 majority of the Supreme Court, "even if the surcharge merely recoups the costs of disposing of out-of-state waste in Oregon, the fact remains that the differential charge favors shippers of Oregon waste over their counterparts handling waste generated in other States. In making that geographic distinction, the surcharge patently discriminates against interstate commerce."

So after these cases (and other similar holdings), what policy options remain? Perhaps a state could impose a high uniform fee on all waste disposed of in the state. This could lead to less waste disposal in the state, as waste handlers sought less expensive disposal options elsewhere, but would be politically unpopular since it would raise the local cost of doing business. This concern might be addressed, as Rehnquist has suggested in a dissent, by the state subsidizing local waste producers, indirectly relieving them from high waste costs. Or, a state could impose a road tax on wastes, charging a flat fee per mile traveled in state, to reflect the added risks imposed by waste transport. This, too, would be an evenhanded approach and would likely impact local waste less than out-of-state waste since most local waste would not have to travel as far for disposal. Finally, a state could make an end-run around the dormant commerce clause by acting as a market participant. The Supreme Court has held that states can discriminate against interstate commerce if they are acting as business owners rather than sovereign regulators. Thus, if a city acted as an owner of a TSD, it could refuse to

13.   504 U.S. 353 (1992).

14.   Oregon Waste Systems, Inc. v. Department of Environmental Quality, 511 U.S. 93 (1994).

188

accept outside waste. Though, to be fair, no city in its right mind will likely want to own and operate its own hazardous waste TSD given the potential liabilities. One could continue these mental gymnastics, but the bottom line is clear. Throughout the line of cases, the Court has seemed quite intent on preventing states from directly or indirectly excluding imported waste. Moreover, it is unlikely that Congress will act to change these decisions. But why should trying to reduce waste flows be so difficult?

From the vantage of environmental protection, these decisions might seem crazy. New Jersey, for example, was responsibly dealing with its own wastes by requiring that they be disposed of in proper sites. Why should other states be allowed to export their waste problems by shipping them to New Jersey? As a result of these shipments, there is no question that New Jersey will need to spend resources sooner to supplement its scarce landfill capacity, now being filled up with other states' waste. New Jersey, Alabama, and Oregon residents suffer the added risks of hazardous waste passing through and being disposed of in their state. Why shouldn't they be able to tax the waste imposing these additional risks? And the Michigan law's requirement of developing twenty-year county plans seems an entirely responsible way to address a serious public health and welfare issue. Michigan can't ban the local generation of waste, but it can take the next best option. Much as the RCRA land ban created an incentive for waste reduction, controls such as Michigan's encourage local waste reduction and responsible disposal. Indeed, the law has the opposite effect of economic protectionism. By preventing counties from accepting outside waste, they cannot benefit from the lower disposal costs gained by larger facilities' economies of scale.

In all of these cases and others, Chief Justice Rehnquist has been in the small (and often sole) minority. While it may seem unusual for Rehnquist to take such a strong pro-environment position, his arguments bear careful consideration. From his perspective, states face legitimate local concerns over increasing waste volumes, exhaustion of existing capacity, NIMBY pressures against opening new facilities, and the risks of waste disposal. Thus, his dissents argue, the majority's focus on the Commerce Clause has been misguided. These are not cases of trade barriers protecting in-state TSDs from competition or "hoarding" scarce resources to the detriment of other states. Indeed the whole paradigm is wrong. Rather than regulating economic goods to their selfish benefit, states limiting the flow of wastes are engaged in the straightforward protection of health and environment. Landfill capacity, Rehnquist argues, surely can be viewed as an economic good or a scarce resource, but it makes more sense to consider it a health risk to be managed. In this respect, the quarantine cases are directly on point. Why not think of the exporting state as the offending party? As exporting a public bad, rather than trying to acquire a public good?

To determine whether it makes more sense to think of waste-import bans as health and safety measures or favoritism in the use of natural resources, consider the likely result of prohibiting such restrictions. In the generic natural resource case, the result is likely to be freer trade and more competition. Just think of removing restrictions on the hunting of fish or deer. More fish and deer hunters means more meat on the market and lower prices. In the waste case, though, the result is the opposite—less competition because every state may be tempted to close down its waste disposal sites and rely on sites in other states.

This is even clearer when viewed in economic terms. Through this perspective, it is useful to consider whether states such as New Jersey, Michigan, and Alabama have served as commons. Their tragedy, one might argue, is that by acting responsibly to provide disposal capacity, they have been taken advantage of by states not willing to accept the risks or costs of disposal. Hence other states act as free riders, and make the responsible states their dumping grounds. In that regard, consider that 34 states have *no* hazardous waste facilities. In fact, only one state, Colorado, has sited a hazardous waste facility since 1984, and that took 10 years. As Chief Justice Rehnquist observed in his *Fort Gratiot* dissent, while many are willing to generate waste, few are willing to help dispose of it.

Those states with disposal capacity do seem to be shouldering an unfair burden. Their citizens must accept much of the costs and all of the risks from the transport, facilities operation, and disposal of the wastes. Prohibiting waste-import bans also removes a strong incentive for other states either to reduce their waste production or site their own facilities. After all, why should they? Why cook dinner when you can go next door every night *and* they'll clean up after you?

Despite the arguments raised above, it is important to acknowledge that a number of environmentalists support the flow control decisions. Their concern is that, while striking down flow control laws may result in a few large waste disposal facilities, protection of health and the environment will be stronger because these few TSDs will likely be better monitored and controlled than a large number of smaller TSDs spread throughout the country. As the next section describes, the opposite trend, however, has been followed in the international flow of wastes.

190

III.　The Basel Convention

Wastes generated in both developing and developed countries have increased significantly in recent decades. The UN Environment Program estimates that more than 400 million tons of hazardous waste are generated annually world-wide, an increase of over 60–fold since the end of World War II. Until recently, shipments of this waste to developing countries was common practice. The environmental and human health risks posed by this commerce, however, have led the international community to develop a comprehensive legal regime governing the transboundary movement of hazardous and other wastes.

In relative terms, the volume of hazardous waste that crosses international borders is quite small. Only about 4% of hazardous wastes generated by OECD countries, for example, are shipped across an international border. While the percentage of waste moving across international borders may be small, the overall volume remains significant. This includes a range of materials, from chemical and radioactive wastes to municipal solid waste, asbestos, incinerator ash, and old tires. Perhaps surprisingly, of the waste generated in developed countries and shipped internationally, less than half is shipped for final disposal (42%) with the remainder shipped for recovery (58%). The export of recyclable or recoverable materials—wastes that contain valuable precious metals or other residues that can be reprocessed to generate raw materials— from developed to less developed countries is big business, generating billions of dollars annually. Environmentally sound recycling can provide substantial environmental benefits by reducing the need to exploit natural resources that might otherwise be mined in the absence of recycled materials.

The other major factor spurring the transboundary shipments of waste has been the disparity in disposal costs between developed and developing nations. The high cost of waste disposal in many developed countries is due in part to compliance costs with strict regulation and in part to effective local NIMBY opposition to siting landfills. Exporting waste would not raise concerns if the recycling and disposal operations were carried out in an environmentally safe manner. The problem, unfortunately, is that this is often not the case.

There's a reason why disposal of hazardous waste may cost as much as $2,000 per ton in a developed nation, versus only $40 per ton in Africa. Many developing countries have neither stringent regulatory requirements for waste imports and disposal nor adequate enforcement efforts to ensure safe disposal of imported hazardous waste, much less locally generated waste. Landfills are often found near the poorest communities where retrieving scrap for use and re-sale is a common practice.

Indeed, there have been numerous high-profile environmental tragedies associated with the illegal or improper shipment of hazardous wastes from developed to less developed countries, often in the form of wandering waste-laden ships or people killed as a result of improper waste disposal. In 1986, for example, the city of Philadelphia, unable to dispose of its incinerator ash in America, loaded 15,000 tons of the hazardous ash on board the ship, the *Khian Sea*, headed for the Bahamas. Denied permission by Bahamian authorities to dump its ash the ship sailed to Haiti. There, the ship's captain informed Haitian authorities that the shipment was "fertilizer ash" and dumped 3,000 tons of incinerator ash on the shore before the ruse was discovered. After being forced to leave Haiti with the rest of the ash on board, the ship changed its name to the *Felicia* and then to the *Pelicano* while wandering the high seas for 18 months looking for a port to accept the waste. Eventually the *Khian Sea* reached Singapore with its hold empty, claiming to have found a nation to receive the waste. Subsequently, the ship's operators were indicted by a U.S. grand jury for perjury; it is believed that the ship dumped its waste in the Indian Ocean.

The infamous Koko case in 1988 came to represent one of the worst examples of the international hazardous waste trade, though not unique. In return for paying $100 monthly rent to a Nigerian national for use of his farmland, five ships transported 8,000 barrels of Italian hazardous waste to the small river town of Koko, Nigeria. Some waste leached into the river, causing chemical burns and a number of deaths. Italy was eventually forced, under the spotlight of international media attention and pressure from Nigeria (after the Nigerian seizure of an unrelated Italian ship), to repackage the waste and send it back to Italy for appropriate disposal. On its return trip to Italy, the ship bearing the waste was refused port in Spain, Denmark, the Netherlands, and the United States. As a result of this and similar scandals, Nigeria and Cameroon banned the importation of hazardous waste and instituted the death penalty for anyone found to be violating the ban. With reason, developing countries have denounced such practices as "Toxic Colonialism," raising concerns of environmental justice at the international level.

Responding to public outrage over these and similar incidents, after two years of negotiations 116 countries adopted the Basel Convention on the Control of Transboundary Movements of Hazardous Wastes and their Disposal in 1989.[15] The Basel Convention establishes a global notification and consent system for the transboundary shipments of wastes among Parties. It has provided the impetus for many nations to

---

15. 28 I.L.M. 649 (1989).

enact for the first time or revise laws governing the import and export of hazardous wastes.

Basel establishes a global notice and consent regime for the transboundary movement of wastes. Parties may not initiate the export of wastes without written confirmation of: 1) consent of the importing country, 2) consent of any transit countries, and 3) confirmation from the importing country of a written contract between the exporter and the disposer specifying the environmentally sound management of the waste. The waste shipments must be accompanied by a movement document (similar to a RCRA manifest) from the point at which the movement commences until the point of disposal and must comply with applicable international packaging and labeling requirements.

Under Basel, wastes are broadly defined as "substances or objects which are disposed of or are intended to be disposed of." Importantly, this includes materials intended for recycling or recovery. On its face, this seems an odd restriction given that the acknowledged waste management hierarchy is to reduce, re-use, and recycle waste before landfill or incineration. Why would the negotiators of the Basel Convention require the same prior consent for wastes intended for recycling and reclamation as it does for waste going to landfills and incinerators? Why not make the requirements for recycling less burdensome? The answer lies in the same concern, described earlier, over the definition of "discarded" in RCRA—sham recycling. No trade regime can easily verify what happens to the waste once it passes the border and enters the national stream of commerce. If wastes intended for recycling were exempted, drafters feared, it would be too easy for unscrupulous traders to mischaracterize the end use of their wastes.

Parties are prohibited from trading wastes if the exporting or importing country has reason to believe that the wastes will not be managed in an "environmentally sound manner." Seeking to reduce the overall volume of traded wastes, parties are required to take measures to ensure that transboundary movements are allowed only where: a) the exporting country does not have the technical capacity or facilities to dispose of the wastes in an environmentally sound manner; or b) the wastes being exported are required as a raw material for recycling or recovery in the state of import. If it later turns out that the wastes cannot be management in an environmentally sound manner in the receiving country, Parties are obligated to re-import the wastes.

Similar to CITES and the Montreal Protocol, the Basel Convention relies on trade-related measures to encourage States to become Parties and enforce its provisions. Article 4 of the Basel Convention states that Parties may not trade wastes with non-Parties. The Convention also commits Parties to honor import bans adopted by other Parties. In fact,

as described below, many governments have gone beyond the requirements of the Basel Convention to ban the import of certain hazardous
wastes into their national territory. While the Party to non-Party ban
serves as an important incentive for countries to participate, such
measures may impose both economic and environmental burdens. For
example, many U.S. companies operating in less developed countries
have been barred from exporting hazardous wastes generated by their
facilities back to the United States for disposal because the United States
remains outside of the Basel Convention. These companies in many
instances must decide whether to store the waste on-site, incur the costs
of shipping the waste to another developed country that may be able to
accept the waste, or use local hazardous waste management facilities
that may not provide for safe management and disposal of hazardous
wastes. As further described in the trade chapter (page 224), such
Party/non-Party restrictions may also conflict with WTO trade disciplines.

There is, however, an important exception to the Party/non-Party
trading ban. Article 11 of the Convention allows imports and exports of
covered wastes between Parties and non-Parties where the transboundary movements are subject to *another* appropriate bilateral, multilateral, or regional agreement. The United States is not a Party to Basel and
has entered into a number of such agreements. Fearful that the Basel
Convention's entry into force would disrupt existing trade among industrialized nations in recyclable wastes such as scrap precious metals,
glass, and batteries, the Organization for Economic Cooperation and
Development (OECD) adopted the most commercially significant Article
11 agreement. The OECD Decision establishes a notice and consent
regime governing the transboundary movement of wastes for recovery
among OECD Member States (30 of the world's most economically
developed countries). This allows OECD Member States that are Parties
to the Basel Convention to continue trading in wastes covered by the
OECD Decision with OECD Members who have *not* ratified the Basel
Convention (notably the United States). The Article 11 exception only
applies, though, *so long as* the agreements' provisions are not less
environmentally sound than those provided for by the Basel Convention.
In this manner, Basel creates a floor for environmental safeguards in the
hazardous waste trade.

From this brief description, it should be clear that Basel has not
banned the waste trade. Rather, it has created a global prior informed
consent regime. Commerce in hazardous wastes is banned unless the
importing government is made aware of the proposed trade and agrees.
On its face, this seems eminently sensible. To truly ban trade in
hazardous wastes, many have argued, would be both stupid and paternalistic. Stupid because it would kill the trade that supports a multi-

billion business in materials recovery and recycling. Many of the recovered materials are sold and used in developing countries, providing needed jobs in desperately poor countries. Paternalistic, others argue, because a ban would deny developing countries the opportunity to decide for themselves whether or not to accept hazardous wastes. Surely there are potential risks and harms associated with this trade, but they must be considered in relation to the competing problems of poverty, malnutrition, and other scourges of the poorest countries. This is the same argument, for example, made in favor of selling chemicals banned in the United States to other countries. "Don't presume we know best. Let them conduct their own cost benefit analysis. Let them decide for themselves whether the benefits of the jobs, income, and technology flowing from the waste trade outweigh the potential harms."

The flip side of this argument, though, is also compelling. Simply because developing countries can make good use of the income flowing from the hazardous waste trade does not mean it should be allowed. Governments can make money from selling their citizens into slavery, as well, yet few would justify this on economic or anti-paternalistic terms. The waste trade is exploitation, pure and simple, its opponents contend, taking advantage of developing countries' poverty and unequal bargaining power. This is simply environmental justice at the international level. Indeed, even while signing the Convention, many developing countries harshly criticized it, charging that Basel does not prohibit international trade in hazardous waste but, instead, merely provides a detailed tracking mechanism. They wanted a complete ban on the export of hazardous waste to developing countries. As one commentator described, "the Basel Convention has legitimized the international toxic waste game and proclaimed industrial nations the winners."

In reaction, within two year's of Basel's signing, the 51 member States of the Organization for African Unity adopted the Bamako Convention on the Ban of Import Into Africa and the Control of Transboundary Movement and Management of Hazardous Wastes Within Africa.[16] The Bamako Convention requires all Parties to prohibit the importation of hazardous waste from outside Africa. Sharing the concerns of African nations over the Basel Convention's failure to ban the waste trade, other developing nations sought the protection of an additional multilateral treaty prohibiting the import of waste within their territories. Thus former European colonies in Africa, the Caribbean, and Pacific (known as ACP States) banned the direct and indirect export of any hazardous or radioactive waste from European Union States to ACP States in a treaty known as the Lomé IV Convention.[17] In return, the ACP States agreed not to accept waste imports from any other countries outside the

---

16.   30 I.L.M. 775 (1991).   **17.**   29 I.L.M. 783 (1990).

European Union. This sweeping provision effectively halted developed country waste shipments to ACP states and ensured that European nations had not placed themselves at a competitive disadvantage by unilaterally excluding a destination for its wastes.

Despite the informed consent provisions of Basel, restricting the hazardous waste trade has remained a hot issue, with NGOs working toward the goal of a complete ban between OECD and non-OECD Parties. In 1995, Parties adopted an amendment known as the "Basel Ban." If and when ratified, the amendment will prohibit hazardous waste shipments from Parties that are OECD or EU countries to *non*-OECD/EU countries. Thus exports from developed to developing countries will not be permitted, regardless of local environmental conditions and disposal capacity.

This amendment has been controversial, particularly in the context of materials destined for recycling. The competing concerns are much the same as those sketched above. Against the concerns over the lack of institutional and technical capacity of developing countries to manage and dispose of imported wastes are set the arguments that materials recovery and recycling is a legitimate business and an important source of employment for many developing countries. Simply banning the trade in wastes that supply this industry is Western paternalism at its worst— sacrificing developing country interests to salve the conscience of Western NGOs. Despite the lofty rhetoric accompanying passage of the Basel Ban, it's interesting to note that over five years after its signing, only 32 countries had ratified the amendment. Sixty-two are required for it to enter into force.

The United States has signed the Basel Convention and the Senate has provided its advice and consent but the necessary implementing legislation has not been adopted. Thus the United States is not a Party to the Convention. In particular, RCRA must be amended to create authority for the government to stop transboundary shipments of hazardous waste when it believes the waste will not be managed in an environmentally sound manner, to require re-importation of wastes that cannot be disposed of in accordance with the export contract, to control transboundary movement of household wastes and ash residue from their incineration, and to define the term "environmentally sound manner." On their face, these amendments are not particularly momentous. Given that the United States was among the first countries to require prior written notice and consent procedures for waste exports, it seems odd that Congress has not yet adopted the necessary implementing legislation to ratify the Convention (and is likely attributable to fears over re-opening RCRA to significant amendment).

196

A last point to keep in mind about the Basel Convention is the prominent role played by NGOs in raising the public's awareness of the pervasive and harmful effects of the hazardous waste trade. Greenpeace has taken the highest profile in exposing dangerous hazardous waste shipments all over the world. Following the negotiation of the Basel Convention, NGOs continued to push for a total ban on the hazardous waste trade, urging nations to enact individual or regional bans on waste imports. NGOs were the key drivers behind the Basel Ban, making use of investigative research, media relations to publicize waste trade abuses, alliances with local environmental and political groups, and a reputation for humbling large companies.

IV. The Comprehensive Emergency Response, Compensation and Liability Act

Arguably the most contentious and, certainly for lawyers and consultants, the most profitable environmental law has been the Comprehensive Emergency Response, Compensation and Liability Act (CERCLA, known popularly as "Superfund").[18] While RCRA addresses the issue of current waste disposal through a command-and-control approach, CERCLA responds to prior waste disposal practices and imposes liability to ensure the clean up of contaminated sites. It is this imposition of liability, however, that has sparked remarkably harsh criticism over CERCLA's fairness and cost effectiveness.

To understand the drama surrounding CERCLA, one must go back in time to upstate New York and the amorously named town of Love Canal, near Niagara Falls. In the 1960s and 1970s, a number of Love Canal residents began complaining of a series of medical problems, ranging from chronic headaches and skin rashes to seemingly high incidences of cancer, birth defects, and miscarriages. Soil samples in 1978 revealed high levels of chemical contaminants in the soil and air. Further study uncovered that much of Love Canal had been built on top of a landfill containing over 21,000 tons of chemical wastes. Covered with a layer of clay in 1952, the site had been sold to the Niagara Falls Board of Education for $1 and subsequently developed into houses and schools. The buried wastes, though, had broken through the clay liner and were seeping into the soil and basements. As news of the health threat become a national story, President Jimmy Carter declared a State of Emergency, permanently relocating 239 families in the houses that encircled the landfill area. The toxics had migrated, however, and the next year federal funding was provided for the permanent relocation of all 900 residents of Love Canal.

---

18. 42 U.S.C. §§ 9601–9675.

The tragedy of Love Canal had exposed a gap in the nation's hazardous waste regulation. While FIFRA and TSCA (described in Chapter 6) regulated the manufacture, distribution, and use of commercial chemicals, and RCRA regulated the disposal of hazardous wastes, no law effectively addressed hazardous wastes that had been buried years earlier and mostly forgotten. Responding to public cries for immediate action, Congress moved to pass a law but faced significant uncertainties.

How many potential Love Canals were out there? There was an unknown number of sites leaking toxics into the soil. Some of these likely posed serious threats to drinking water supplies. At some sites, it was possible to identify the waste and where it had come from, but in many cases the nature and origin of the wastes was unknown. Because RCRA had been passed just three years earlier, recordkeeping was spotty. Indeed some sites were likely still buried, providing prime real estate; others were abandoned sites cluttered with rusting barrels, their owners bankrupt or out of business. In the face of such vexing unknowns, to meaningfully address the problem of contaminated sites the draft legislation had to deal with four basic challenges.

The first was how to *identify and prioritize* the problem sites. Clearly the sites posing the greatest risks should be remediated first, but where were these? How could EPA find out about them? The second basic challenge was to decide *who should perform the cleanup*. If government took charge, presumably the cleanups would occur more quickly. But industry claimed that it could manage cleanups more efficiently. If the parties that have contributed to the contamination should clean up the site, moreover, which ones? The landowners, waste generators, transporters, past owners of the site? Third, and related, *who should pay for the cleanup*? One could imagine public funding through general tax revenues or a special tax on hazardous chemicals. If it is desirable to implement the "polluter pays" principle, though, the cost should fall on the potentially responsible parties listed above. But do they all share the same culpability? Finally, EPA needed to decide the question of *how clean is clean*. At what point can the cleanup stop? Should there be national standards or site-by-site determinations? Should the dirt be clean enough to eat?

To place Congress' dilemma in a more domestic setting, imagine you held a big party last night while your parents were out of town. You've just woken up, seen that the house is a mess, and realized your parents return in 45 minutes. You don't have time to clean up everything, but where do you start? The living room, the bathroom, or the kitchen? Is your strategy one of permanent cleanup (mops and bucket) or containment (shove everything in the closet)? And do you clean up yourself or wake up the other responsible partygoers and have them work, as well?

The sections that follow explain the structure of CERCLA, but as you read them it is important to keep in mind the challenges described above. In understanding CERCLA, one needs to consider not only the problems Congress was trying to address but the options they didn't choose, for the law could have looked very different. In this regard, it is interesting to note that, while U.S. environmental laws such as the Clean Air Act and the National Environmental Policy Act (discussed in Chapter 10) have served as a models for laws in many other countries, *no* country has followed the approach set out in CERCLA.

A final insight into CERCLA lies in the nature of its passage. While various contaminated land bills had been considered prior to 1979, CERCLA was passed by Congress and signed into law in a remarkably fast period, during the "lame duck" Congressional session between President Carter's electoral defeat and President Reagan's taking office. As a result, not only is there scant legislative history, but the law itself is not well drafted. And resentful at having a law forced down its throat just prior to taking office, the Reagan administration was both ideologically and politically opposed to CERCLA, obstructing its implementation so aggressively that EPA's reputation was damaged, with high-profile resignations and even a jail term for an EPA official.

A. The Cleanup Process

In many respects, CERCLA is a simple statute. Unlike RCRA or other major environmental laws, CERCLA itself doesn't require anyone to do anything beyond one requirement. Any person who knows of a release of a reportable quantity of hazardous waste must notify EPA. That's it. So much for the command-and-control approach. The rest of the statute creates a process for cleaning up contaminated sites through two basic grants of power. First, it gives the government the power to compel parties to clean up releases of hazardous substances from a facility. Second, it gives government and private parties the authority to recover the costs of cleanup. These simple powers allow parties both to force cleanups and to allocate their costs, with enormous indirect effects on the treatment and disposal of waste.

1. Listing and Prioritization of Sites

To determine which sites should be cleaned up first, EPA created a National Priority List (NPL) of the most seriously contaminated sites.[19] Those sites presenting the greatest danger to public health, welfare, or the environment are ranked higher, according to their score based on the Hazard Ranking System, a formula that takes into account a site's

---

19. 42 U.S.C. § 9605(1)(8)(A).

toxicity, proximity to local population, potential to contaminate drinking water, etc. The NPL has grown substantially every year since 1985 and, as of 2002, 1221 sites were listed. It is important to note, of course, that many more sites are proposed for listing than actually are placed on the NPL. By the end of 2000, for example, EPA had conducted assessments of over 41,000 sites.

2. *Responses*

CERCLA kicks in whenever there has been a "release" or a "substantial threat" of a release of a "hazardous substance" into the environment from a "facility."[20] As with all of CERCLA's provisions, these terms have been broadly defined and interpreted. "Release", for example, has been defined to include "any spilling, leaking, pumping, pouring, emitting, emptying, discharging, injecting, escaping, leaching, dumping, or disposing into the environment"[21]—in sum, virtually any event where a hazardous substance could be released from its container (indeed, the definition calls to mind a young Capitol Hill staffer eagerly copying from a thesaurus). A "substantial threat of release" is even broader, covering hazardous substances still contained in corroding tanks or abandoned drums. While there are exemptions from this definition, including workplace releases and emissions from autos and other vehicles, they have been narrowly interpreted. Consider, for example, the case of *State of Vermont v. Staco*,[22] where workers in a thermometer factory were found to have released hazardous substances by bringing mercury home on their clothes (washing their clothes had contaminated the public sewage system and septic tanks).

The definition of "hazardous substance" is likewise very broad. Going beyond RCRA, it includes almost any substance considered hazardous under another pollution statute as well as substances that EPA determines "may present an imminent and substantial danger to the public health or environment."[23] Of special significance to leaking underground storage tanks, petroleum and natural gas are specifically exempted from coverage.

While a "facility" would obviously include a chemical plant or landfill, its definition under CERCLA is broad, as well, extending to virtually any type of place or structure, including "any building, structure, installation, equipment, pipe or pipeline, well, pit, pond, lagoon, impoundment, ditch, landfill, storage container, motor vehicle, rolling stock, or aircraft" as well as any place where a hazardous substance "has been deposited, stored, disposed of, or placed, or otherwise come to

20. 42 U.S.C. § 9607(1).   **22.** 684 F.Supp. 822, 832 (D.Vt.1988).

21. 42 U.S.C. §9601(22).   **23.** 42 U.S.C. §9601(14).

be located."[24] In fact, except for consumer products in their containers (which are specifically exempted), it's hard to think of anything that wouldn't be considered a facility. The term has even been held to include a North Carolina roadside that had been sprayed with PCB-contaminated oil.[25]

Once the threat of release of a hazardous substance from a facility has been established (which, as noted above, is awfully easy to do), CERCLA authorizes two types of cleanups. A "removal" action is short term, intended to alleviate immediate dangers to the public health or environment.[26] These are the emergency actions you see on the evening news with folks walking around in moon suits working behind chain link fences. EPA generally carries out these actions.

The second, and more common, type of response is known as "remediation." This is a longer-term action, seeking to provide a permanent remedy to the maximum extent practicable.[27] Cleanup approaches can range from the blunt approach of digging up all the contaminated soil and disposing of it as RCRA hazardous waste to pumping clean water into the site through wells and then pumping out now contaminated water (i.e., effectively diluting the waste). There are other common technologies, but all are expensive; indeed many cleanups can easily run into the millions of dollars. All cleanups must follow the requirements set out in the National Contingency Plan (NCP), including provisions for extensive remedial investigations and feasibility studies (known as RI/FS), public consultation requirements, etc. If the NCP "cookbook" of mandatory procedures is not followed, then CERCLA's grant of authority to recover costs will not apply.

B. *Compensation for Response Actions*

There are three types of response actions allowed under CERCLA, all driven by the central premise that the taxpayer should not foot the bill for cleanup costs. First, EPA can carry out the cleanup itself and sue the potentially responsible parties (known as PRPs) later in a cost recovery action. For initial funds to pay for the cleanup, EPA draws from the "Superfund," a big pot funded primarily by chemical and petroleum taxes. CERCLA originally authorized a Superfund of $1.6 billion and the 1986 amendments increased this to $8.5 billion. At the time, this was viewed as a great innovation because the cleanup could go ahead quickly without having to wait for liability to be assessed in the courts. The idea was that the fund would be drawn down from time to time, but would

24. 42 U.S.C. §9601(9).

25. United States v. Ward, 618 F.Supp. 884 (E.D.N.C.1985).

26. 42 U.S.C. § 9601(23).

27. 42 U.S.C. § 9601(24).

replenish itself from private party contributions. Reimbursement, though, has proven more troublesome than anticipated. While cleanups went ahead, the Superfund was quickly drawn down because PRPs more often sued EPA than paid up.

To avoid drawing down the Superfund, EPA's other option is to order PRPs to perform the cleanup. This avoids the problem of delay because CERCLA does not allow any pre-enforcement review of such orders. Thus if EPA orders you to conduct a remediation, you have only two choices. You can disobey, but that risks fines adding up to $25,000 per day plus treble final cleanup costs. More likely, you can comply and then sue to recover costs either from EPA, on the ground that you are not a PRP or that the cleanup order was arbitrary or capricious, or from other PRPs to share the costs in what are known as contribution actions.

A third form of compensation applies to private parties that have cleaned up a site. Recall that a site need not be on the NPL for CERCLA to apply. So long as there has been a release of a hazardous substance from a facility, a private party can clean up the site (in a manner consistent with the NCP) and sue other PRPs to recover costs. Through this route there is no need for prior EPA approval or, for that matter, any government supervision at all.

CERCLA also authorizes the federal and state governments to sue for "natural resource damages" to pay for both the restoration and cost of damaged resources.[28] Estimating such costs requires, in most cases, use of shadow pricing methodologies such as contingent valuation because there are no commercial markets for natural resources such as threatened species or the ecosystem service of nutrient filtering. There is no private right of action to recover natural resource damages.

1. Potentially Responsible Parties (PRPs)

As should be clear from the discussion above, under CERCLA the bill ultimately ends up in the hands of PRPs. CERCLA establishes four broad classes of PRPs: (1) current owners and operators of a facility (even if they were not owners when disposal occurred); (2) prior owners or operators (even if they were owners after disposal occurred); (3) arrangers of disposal or treatment (often called "generators"); and (4) transporters (*if* they selected the facility).[29] As with the rest of the statute, the definitions of PRPs are exceedingly broad. Thus, for example, the category of prior owners and operators could include someone who bought the property *after* the waste had been buried and *before* it was discovered so long as releases occurred (e.g., underground barrels continued to leak). The key question for anyone involved with CERCLA,

28. 42 U.S.C. § 9607(f)(1).   **29.** 42 U.S.C. § 9607(a).

then, quickly dissolves into who's a PRP. For those caught up in Superfund liability, the experience can descend into a tragi-comedy entitled, "why PRPs pay," or, more accurately, "why it pays not to be a PRP."

2. *Liability Standards*

While the categories of PRPs set out who *potentially* might pay, CERCLA's kicker and most controversial provision concerns liability— who actually *does* pay. CERCLA does not explicitly refer to a standard of liability. In an awkward form of legislative drafting, the statute refers to Section 311 of the Clean Water Act's oil spill response program. This, in turn, refers to common law principles which, in turn, the courts have interpreted to be the standard of strict, joint, and several liability. The strict liability provision does away with the need for proof of negligence, intent, or harm. So long as there was a release or threatened release of a hazardous substance from a facility, response costs were incurred, and the party is a PRP, it's on the hook. The thinking behind relaxing the causation requirement was, ironically, that it would avoid disputes over apportionment. By moving away from the need to show proximate responsibility (or, indeed, that a PRP's actions actually caused any harm), the liability net could be cast far wider than under a common law standard of negligence. Effectively the burden of proof has been shifted from the government to PRPs.

The joint and several provision means that, in theory, a single party could be liable for all the costs even if 20 other parties were also PRPs. While helping ensure cleanup costs can be collected, a strict, joint and several liability standard creates significant fairness concerns. A PRP who pays for the government's cleanup costs can bring a contribution action against other PRPs, and courts will use equitable rules to allocate the costs among the PRPs who are parties to the contribution action. But not all PRPs may be available to contribute toward the cleanup costs. Some contributors to the harm, for example, may be bankrupt. Others may be unknown. As a result, current PRPs must shoulder the burden of paying for these "orphan shares." Moreover, by making all PRPs potentially responsible for the cleanup, there is an incentive for PRPs to implicate as many other PRPs as possible. Thus CERCLA's retroactive joint and several liability has unexpectedly hit a wide range of actors, including federal, state, and city governments, manufacturers, financial institutions, charities, and small businesses. While a bonanza for lawyers and engineers, the high transaction costs in locating and negotiating with PRPs have diverted a great deal of money away from actual cleanups. Moreover, a strict, joint and several liability standard can easily lead to a search for "deep pockets," those PRPs who may not bear much responsibility but have the resources to pay for the cleanup.

The biggest concern raised by the retroactive liability standards and broad categories of PRPs, though, is that of fairness. While such general categories of PRPs help ensure that the taxpayer will not end up paying for the cleanup, it is worth considering whether there is a principled reason to hold many of the PRPs liable. Can they all fairly be thought of as polluters? And is it fair to hold them liable for actions taken years ago that were completely legal at the time? Where is the fairness, for example, in holding a chemical company liable today for shipping its waste back in 1950, in full compliance with the law, to an operating landfill facility that was improperly shut down in 1970? What about a landowner who unwittingly bought the contaminated property after the disposal had occurred and sold it before the contamination was discovered, and prior to enactment of RCRA or CERCLA? Where is her culpability? Despite such examples, and there are many others, the SARA amendments to Superfund in 1986[30] left the liability provisions intact. The traditional explanation for these liability provisions has been that owners, operators, generators, and transporters benefited from the low costs associated with waste disposal practices in the past and should bear the cleanup costs when they arise. You reap what you sow.

C. Defenses

Because CERCLA's liability net has been cast extremely wide, there has been an enormous amount of litigation to find defenses for PRPs. CERCLA's text holds out some glimmers of hope but few have proven significant. The key routes for PRPs to escape liability are set out below.

1. Acts of God, War, or a Third Party

CERCLA exempts releases caused by an "act of God," an "act of war," or an act of a third party.[31] Defenses based on the act of God and war exemptions, though, have met with little success since courts have held that so long as unexpected natural events such as heavy rains, floods, earthquakes, pestilence, raining frogs, or other disasters could be anticipated, the exemption only applies to exceedingly rare and unforeseeable circumstances. CERCLA also provides an escape from liability for PRPs who can establish that the release was caused by the act or omission of a third party (other than an employee or agent of the defendant or someone in a contractual relationship with the defendant) and the PRP exercised due care. Soon after CERCLA's passage, this was held out as a significant defense, but note that the defense does not apply where there is any direct or indirect relationship between the defendant and the person or organization responsible for the release. If a

---

30. Pub. L. No. 99–499, 100 Stat. 1613 (1986).   **31.** 42 U.S.C. § 9607(b)(1).

company sends its product to X for fabrication and X disposes of wastes improperly, the company can be liable under CERCLA.[32] Parent companies also can be held liable for their subsidiaries' past activities.

2. *Divisibility*

Joint and several liability can be avoided if a PRP can show its waste is divisible. One might think this would be easy to show. Imagine, for example, that you have records showing you sent 100 barrels of waste to a Superfund site of 1,000 barrels. Yes, you contributed and are willing to help fund the cleanup, but shouldn't you be potentially liable for only 10% of the response costs? After all, you can show that you only contributed one in ten barrels. This might make sense in the abstract, but only if the waste had not leached from the barrels. If the waste has escaped (which is likely since it's a Superfund site), then it has also mixed with the *other* waste in the site. Thus, because of diffusion, to remove your waste from the site you would need to remove *all* of the waste from the site because it has all commingled.[33] Note that EPA does not have to show that a particular PRP's waste leaked (or even that waste like it has leaked). It is sufficient that the PRP's waste was simply present and that response costs were incurred. The burden falls squarely on the PRP to demonstrate that its harm is divisible and capable of apportionment.

3. *Small Contributors*

The real tear jerker in any CERCLA Congressional hearing often comes from the testimony from the owners of Ma and Pa Store, who relate how they spent their life savings in legal fees because they were sued as PRPs for a few barrels they sent to a landfill years ago. If EPA determines that a PRP contributed a minimal amount of hazardous waste compared to other wastes at the site, CERCLA allows EPA to reach an early settlement with the PRP, with complete absolution from additional or future liability, in return for the payment of a premium over what would otherwise be a fair share.[34] If PRPs can show they contributed less than 100 gallons of liquid or less than 200 pounds of solid material, then they can qualify for a "de micromis" exemption.[35] This exemption does not apply if the waste has or could contribute significantly to the response action. In a fee-shifting arrangement to cut down on litigation, if exempt parties are sued by other PRPs, they are entitled to recover costs and attorney fees.[36] A similar exemption has

---

32. *See* United States v. Aceto Agric. Chems. Corp., 872 F.2d 1373 (8th Cir.1989).

33. *See,* O'Neil v. Picillo, 883 F.2d 176, 178 (1st Cir.1989).

34. 42 U.S.C. § 9622(g).

35. 42 U.S.C. § 9607(*o*)(1).

36. 42 U.S.C. § 9607(*o*)(4).

been created for small businesses, residential property owners and operators, and nonprofits who sent municipal solid waste (i.e., household garbage) to NPL sites.[37]

4. Municipalities

Municipalities are an equally good poster child for CERCLA's unfairness. Entirely passive in the reception of waste, towns' and cities' landfills often turn out to have received hazardous wastes, thus potentially qualifying them as CERCLA sites. EPA has long had a policy of not going after municipalities for cost recovery actions. Nothing in the statute, however, prevents PRPs from suing municipalities for private contribution. Indeed, more than 650 municipalities and counties in 12 states have been sued as PRPs for contribution claims.

5. Lenders

CERCLA excludes owners and operators from liability if they hold an "indicia of ownership" in the property primarily as a security interest. The narrow scope of this exemption has proven controversial in the context of banks that foreclose on real estate. In the case of *United States v. Fleet Factors Corp.*, for example, the court sent shivers down the spines of bankers by holding that the bank's foreclosure on a future CERCLA site qualified it as a PRP because it had been actively involved in the property's management.[38] Banks that took over outright ownership would become PRPs, as well. Courts took divergent positions on lender liability, with the 11th Circuit assigning broad liability and the 9th Circuit much narrower. Which position makes for better policy? In favor of making banks liable, recognize that lenders can act as effective gatekeepers (or even surrogate regulators), ensuring that borrowers are environmentally responsible with their waste disposal. Lenders are very careful about the financial solvency of those to whom they lend money, why not make them scrutinize environmental records, as well? This approach leverages the influence of financial institutions over the behavior of their debtors. And if banks are protected after property foreclosures, where is the incentive for them to ensure the waste on the property is properly taken care of? Finally, to be blunt, banks have deep pockets and will be able to fund cleanups.

Nonetheless, it's not clear that these arguments favor unlimited liability. After all, unlike insurance companies, lenders never have served as effective gatekeepers for environmental harms. It's simply not in their area of expertise. Moreover, because of the potential risk involved, making banks liable could dry up credit (or make it exceptionally

---

37. 42 U.S.C. § 9607(p).

38. United States v. Fleet Factors Corp., 901 F.2d 1550, 1557–58 (11th Cir.1990).

expensive) for companies handling waste. Indeed, after the decision in *Fleet Factors*, Fleet announced that it would not lend money unless a borrower had environmental liability insurance. And if companies who handle hazardous waste cannot get financing, they will be more likely to do things on the cheap or won't be able to remedy problems.

In 1996, Congress resolved this debate by passing the Asset Conservation, Lender Liability, and Deposit Insurance Protection Act, adding a new section to CERCLA.[39] Banks can foreclose on property "if the person seeks to sell ... or otherwise divest ... the vessel or facility .. at the earliest practicable, commercially reasonable time, on commercially reasonable terms, taking into account market conditions and legal and regulatory requirements." Importantly, the term "participate in the management" does not include "merely having the capacity to influence." To lose the exemption, a bank must (1) exercise decisionmaking over environmental compliance, or (2) exercise overall management control. As we shall see in the case of brownfields, below, even this level of protection has left banks fearful.

6. Innocent Landowners

As originally drafted, CERCLA imposed liability on all current owners of contaminated property. Responding to complaints over unjust results, in the SARA amendments in 1986 Congress extended the third party defense to "innocent landowners."[40] To qualify, the property owner must have undertaken "all appropriate inquiry" before purchasing the property and have no "actual or constructive knowledge" of the hazardous substances. In principle, this should ensure that prospective purchasers fully inspect the land and history prior to purchase. The "all appropriate inquiry" requirement has been elevated to a high standard in order to ensure that new owners cannot avoid liability simply by sniffing the air or kicking up some dirt prior to purchase. Amendments in 2002 clarified these requirements for owners who acquired title after January 11, 2002.[41] New Jersey imposed greater responsibilities on current landowners in its 1983 law, the Environmental Cleanup Responsibility Act (ECRA).[42] ECRA requires an owner to demonstrate, before selling, transferring, or closing industrial and commercial property, that the property is not contaminated by hazardous substances. Failure to comply with ECRA entitles the buyer to recover damages from the previous owner. This law thus seeks to ensure that sites are remediated before sale by creating a disincentive for sellers to play dumb.

7. Settlement Strategies

As the above brief descriptions make clear, PRPs have few viable defenses when faced with cost recovery or contribution actions. This has

---

39. 42 U.S.C. § 9601(20)(E).

40. 42 U.S.C. § 9601(35).

41. Codified at 42 U.S.C. §§ 9601(40), 9607(r).

42. N.J. Stat. Ann. 13:1K–6 to K–14.

important implications, and not all intended. The most obvious is that EPA holds all the cards. As a result, there is strong pressure on PRPs to enter into early settlement with EPA and gain contribution protection from other PRPs. If PRPs choose to hold out, they face the very real danger of being left holding the bag (and writing the blank check) when the final costs of the cleanup are assessed and there are no remaining PRPs with whom to share the cost. Settlements allocations are not, of course, completely random. The court does have the authority to allocate response costs among parties as appropriate, but this is a discretionary judgment.

A second intentional consequence of restricting liability defenses is that potential PRPs become their brother's keeper. In other words, once a bank or real estate developer or chemical company realizes that the actions of parties it lends to, buys property from, or sends products to for fabrication can result in becoming a PRP, they take a really close look. By driving liability deep into the transaction, formerly remote players are forced to act as surrogate regulators. This way, it becomes in everyone's interest to ensure that waste is disposed of properly so that new Superfund sites do not arise, sucking every related party into a vortex of liability and recrimination. As the next section explains, however, forcing banks and real estate developers to act as gatekeepers comes at a cost and appears in unexpected places.

D. Brownfields

In many cities today, large tracts of downtown real estate sit idle and derelict because no one will develop them. CERCLA unintentionally plays a major role in this. Since many of these sites were former industrial areas, developers are wary of purchasing them because they do not want to become PRPs if the sites are discovered to be contaminated. Even if they do want to develop them, financing from banks will be hard to come by. State law may play a role, as well. In New Jersey, for example, the ECRA law effectively forbids the sale of contaminated property. If a current owner is unwilling to fund a clean-up (and unable to obtain the funds from the prospective buyer), she can't sell the parcel. Such unwanted parcels are known as "brownfields," defined by EPA as "abandoned, idle, or under-used industrial and commercial facilities where expansion or redevelopment is complicated by real or perceived environmental contamination."

In simple terms, then, the "brownfields problem" is that lenders and developers are wary of associating with abandoned sites once used for industrial and commercial purposes. These properties can range from

NPL sites to simply dirty areas with no serious contaminants. Investors, however, fear they may find themselves liable for the clean up of contamination they did not create. As a result, brownfields sit vacant while developers seek clean sites outside the city. These suburban sites are, appropriately enough, known as "greenfields." This trend increases sprawl, takes potential economic development opportunities away from the city, and leaves the inner city sites derelict

The brownfields problem has proven divisive, with community groups battling each other over the proper approach. Leaving urban sites undeveloped, some argue, benefits no one. By working to develop such sites, local jobs are created, the urban tax base is restored, and communities are strengthened. Others, however, contend that this is a case of environmental injustice since, they charge, EPA has been willing to adjust cleanup standards depending on what the site will be used for, with less protection for commercial developments than residential properties. Development on contaminated land is worse than no development at all.

Both federal and state governments have actively been seeking to reduce brownfield problems. Grant have been offered by the Department of Housing and Urban Development and the EPA, and tax breaks are available that allow developers of brownfields to write off their cleanup costs in the year they are incurred rather than over several years. EPA also actively pruned the NPL list of 27,000 potential sites, hoping to remove the taint associated with potential listing. And even for sites on the NPL, EPA has offered "prospective purchaser agreements" where it pledges not to bring a CERCLA action if the prospective purchaser can (1) demonstrate it is not linked to the site's contamination, and (2) show the agreement would produce environmental benefits. Over 35 states also provide for voluntary cleanup programs that act as a shield from enforcement actions. Despite these programs and others,[43] brownfields remain a concern in large part because of the commercial community's desire to stay clear of the long shadow cast by "CERCLA horror stories," whether true or not.

E. How Clean Is Clean?

Environmental justice issues have also arisen over the proper level of remediation at a contaminated site. Imagine, for example, that you are the EPA official in charge of three Superfund sites: one at a nursery school, one in a cornfield 40 miles from the nearest town, and one in a

---

43. Recent amendments provide up to $1.25 billion from 2002–2007 to pay for characterization, assessment, and remediation activities and fund state and tribal response programs. Developers, of course, need similar assurances from the state to ensure they do not force a clean up.

national wildlife refuge in Northern Alaska. Should they be equally clean after remediation? Should the goal even be to make all the sites "clean"? What role should cost play in your decision? And how would your views differ if your child went to that school, the cornfield was on your land, you hiked every summer in the refuge, or, conversely, you were the PRP footing the bill for the cleanup?

The issue of "how clean is clean" was never resolved in CERCLA, with Congress leaving much discretion to EPA. The 1986 SARA amendments require EPA to take into account a variety of factors, including a preference for permanent on-site solutions that significantly reduce hazards (over offsite transport and disposal), remediation that assures the protection of human health and the environment, and the often conflicting standard of a solution that is cost effective.[44] Making EPA's task even more difficult, if there are legally relevant and appropriate standards covering the site's hazardous substance, the level of cleanup must satisfy their requirements. In plain english, these so-called ARARs (Applicable, Relevant and Appropriate Requirements) are intended to harmonize the requirements of CERCLA with those of other environmental laws, allowing their standards to function as CERCLA cleanup standards. But it is not at all clear, critics contend, why a standard from the Safe Drinking Water Act for, say, benzene, should be used as the remediation target in a CERCLA cleanup unless the soil is likely to filter groundwater for drinking. The net effect of these various factors and ARARs is that EPA exercises great discretion in every cleanup. Environmental justice advocates, for example, have argued that cleanups in poor areas often use less stringent ARARs and less permanent solutions.

What arrangement, though, would provide a better solution? One could rely on uniform national goals for residual contamination. This would ensure equitable cleanups among rich and poor areas, but could be economically inefficient since site context factors such as the exposed population and proximity to water supplies would be ignored. One might try to tailor the cleanup standards to local conditions by requiring cleanup to background levels. This, though, takes no consideration of risk or cost. Alternatively, one could take a more complex approach, setting a uniform level of risk. Thus each site might seek to reduce the risk from contamination to, say, 1 death in 1,000,000. This approach would take into account site-specific conditions and future health consequences, though how accurately is another matter. Or one could rely on a site classification approach, assuming that standards should differ from site-to-site. Commercial sites need less cleanup, one could argue, than school playgrounds because there will be less exposure to contaminated soil. This might well be the most nationally cost-effective approach, but

---

44. 42 U.S.C. § 9621.

there would be strong pressure from PRPs at each site for the future use to be an asphalt parking lot.

Closely linked to the issue of "how clean is clean" is the procedural issue of who should decide this. As economist Bob Hahn has observed, everyone wants a Cadillac if someone else is paying for it. Local residents will always want the cleanups to be as rigorous as possible, and for good reason since they live there. Similarly, PRPs will seek to keep down costs.

Consider the Superfund site in the small town of Holden, Missouri, for example, where it would cost $71,000 to effectively isolate an abandoned factory and its hazardous chemicals, but another $3.6 million to clean up the residues and bury them under a layer of clay.[45] In this context, recall the Guns and Butter discussion in Chapter 3 and the problem of finite resources. In practical terms, can it ever be a proper goal to make a site "free of risk"? When is a site worth more than $1 million per acre? There is no "right" answer to the how clean is clean debate because it is, fundamentally, a political decision that pits the goals of efficiency and equity against one another. People surely should not involuntarily be exposed to cancer risks, but there is not enough money to make all NPL sites risk free.

F.   Superfund Reform

In many respects, Superfund has been the victim of high expectations and low performance. Living near contaminated sites is a very emotive issue and public interest in CERCLA has remained high. By any measure, CERCLA has proven an expensive program. The budget for Department of Defense cleanups in 1991, for example, was more than $7 billion, greater than EPA's total budget. Moreover, for much of the law's history, a disturbing amount of money has been spent on lawsuits and studies rather than cleanups. A Rand study in 1988 found that of the $2.6 billion paid out by EPA, almost 40% had been spent on litigation and administration, with an eight year delay between investigation of a site and commencement of remedial work. Other studies have found higher costs.

To be fair, administration of the program has become much more efficient in recent years with less litigation over contribution costs and more pre-settlement negotiation. And the total numbers reported on the EPA website look good. Over 6,400 removal actions have been taken at hazardous waste sites. By 2000, work had been completed at 757 NPL

45. Peter   Passell,   *Experts   Question*   TIMES, Sept. 1, 1991, at 1.
Staggering   Costs   of   Toxic   Cleanups, N.Y.

sites, and was underway at 417 sites. PRPs have paid for about 70% of the cleanup costs, amounting to over $16 billion. And EPA has looked after the little folk, reaching over 430 de minimis settlements with more than 21,000 small waste contributors. All good cause for optimism, except for the fact that it is estimated EPA will need to spend about $1.4 billion every year for the rest of the decade to clean up the remaining NPL sites, and the Superfund will soon run dry.

It is hard to find anyone who doesn't think Superfund could be improved, either in terms of fairness or cost-effectiveness. Indeed every legislative session over the last decade has included Superfund reform bills in the House and Senate. Recently, the Bush administration proposed that the Superfund should be replenished through general revenues rather than taxes on petroleum, chemicals, and corporations. This has been criticized as abandoning the polluter pays principle. Other funding reforms have ranged from eliminating liability-based funding for disposal prior to 1986 and more generous de minimis provisions, to greater protection of municipalities and subsequent land purchasers. One consequence of all of these proposals, however, is that they would let some parties off the hook. And that, in turn, is why, despite widespread criticism, CERCLA has remained largely unchanged. The Small Business Liability Relief and Brownfields Revitalization Act in 2002 provided the largest reforms since the SARA amendments 16 years earlier.[46] The most significant changes, though, consisted of codifying prior EPA practices for small contributors, clarifying the innocent landowner defense, and increasing brownfields funding.

Once the decision is made that taxpayers will not foot the bill for cleanups, then CERCLA reform becomes a zero sum game. Any reform that lessens the potential liability of some PRPs will increase the liability for others. Thus, absent large scale reform, the political dynamic has been one of pushing for reduction of your group's liability while at the same time opposing reforms that would lessen any other group's. You win, I lose, and vice versa, with the result that CERCLA remains much criticized but largely unchanged.

As with the Clean Water and Clean Air Acts, "solving the problem" of contaminated sites has proved far more difficult than Congress anticipated over two decades ago. Despite its flaws, though, CERCLA was, and remains, a groundbreaking law. While the target of constant criticism over its costs and retroactive liability provisions, the assignment of responsibility to virtually all actors associated with the disposal of waste has played a critical role in ensuring that waste is disposed of properly. When tallying the costs of CERCLA, it is important to keep in mind the benefits of avoided future Love Canals, as well.

46. Pub. L. No. 107–118.

PART III
Trade

CHAPTER 8
Trade and Environment

In the late 1980s, over half of the U.S. states either enacted laws or entered into "voluntary agreements" with newspapers to use recycled content in their newsprint, with commitments to reach 50% recycled content by the year 2000. This was seen as an environmentally positive development, since it would reduce solid waste going to landfills. The curious thing is that environmental groups were not the key lobbyists for these requirements. Instead, it turns out that American pulp and paper producers were behind most of these laws and agreements. But it's not cheaper for pulp and paper producers to make recycled paper, nor does it provide a larger profit margin. So why did these companies care about and push for recycled newsprint requirements?

The answer, surprisingly, is trade. Prior to these laws, most of American newspapers' newsprint was supplied by Canadian companies. Because of the recycled newsprint requirements, however, the market shifted. Canada's population is too small to provide enough waste paper to raise the level of its virgin pulp to 50% recycled content. As a result, Canadian pulp and paper firms were put in the bizarre position of having to *import* waste paper from the United States and ship it up north to its paper plants (near where the forests are, of course) and then *ship back* the recycled newsprint to the United States. These added costs were reflected in product prices, raising U.S. pulp and paper companies' market share from 42% to 49%, all at the expense of Canadian companies

Were the American lawmakers motivated primarily by protecting the environment or U.S. companies? Who should decide the law's motivation? How should it be decided? And what are the consequences if the law is found to be primarily protectionist? These questions frame the trade and environment debate, a conflict that has taken center stage on the international scene and with important implications for domestic environmental laws.

213

Conflicts between free trade and environmental protection are not solely international. In any federal system there exists a tension between free commerce among states and legitimate state environmental protection measures that may impede the flow of commerce. This tension is clearly evident in the U.S. Constitution for, in many respects, the early United States was an experiment in creating a large free trade zone among the former colonies. Indeed, the precursor to the Constitutional Convention in Philadelphia was a meeting among Maryland, Virginia, and Pennsylvania over trade on the Chesapeake Bay. You may recall, as well, our discussion in Chapter 7 of the waste cases and the role of the Constitution's "dormant commerce clause" in striking down barriers to interstate commerce.

Most of the media's and public's attention, though, has been on international trade and environment conflicts, and for good reason. The past decade has witnessed an almost blinding pace of economic activity around the planet. In 1999, world exports of goods and commercial services topped $5.5 trillion and $1.3 trillion, respectively. Capital flows have seen a spectacular increase, as well, particularly between developed and developing countries. This rapid growth has been driven in large part by international efforts to remove barriers to the flow of goods, services, and capital (also known as liberalization). The growing economic interdependency among nations created by such liberalization has important consequences for environmental protection, and has become a key concern of the "anti-globalization" movement, as witnessed by the annual protests outside WTO meetings.

I. The Trade Debate

On their face, the arguments for increased international trade and capitals flows are compelling. Perhaps most obvious, trade flows increase wealth. Indeed international commerce has fueled much of the economic growth during the last century, and reduced trade has deepened economic downturns (as happened during the period of spiraling protectionism in the 1930s). Many economists argue that economic growth is an essential first step towards poverty alleviation and development, generating both the political opportunity and capacity for environmental protection in developing countries. If demand for a better environment is "income-elastic" (that is, it increases when income increases) then rising incomes will produce more resources for pollution control and clean-up. Put another way, once the basic needs of food, clothing, and shelter have been met, poor societies can dedicate more money to other pressing needs such as environmental protection and health care.

In theory, free trade can also promote more efficient use of the world's scarce resources. First, liberalized trade encourages nations to concentrate on their production of goods and services. According to the theory of "comparative advantage," each nation will specialize in and export those goods that it produces more efficiently relative to other nations. Thus a resource-rich country might specialize in resource extraction while a country with rich soil would specialize in agriculture. The gains in specialization are realized through trade, which ensures that the strengths of each nation result in maximum productivity for all. The benefits of specialization may be further enhanced by "economies of scale," allowing goods to be produced more economically when the scale of their production is increased. By giving producers access to larger markets, international trade allows production to occur at a volume at which economies of scale are maximized. Finally, trade advocates contend, exposing domestic companies to the discipline of international competition forces them to innovate, to upgrade, and to anticipate demand. The resulting efficiencies and cost-savings benefit consumers by providing them with greater choice at lower prices.

Though often overlooked, liberalized trade serves an important political purpose, as well. Countries that are economically interdependent share greater common interests and are less likely to resolve differences through armed conflict. This was a key motivation, for example, behind the creation of the European Community in the aftermath of World War II. Conflict between Germany and France had served as the flashpoint for both World Wars. The founders of the European Community hoped that forging closer economic links between the two countries (at the outset through common steel and coal markets) would make future armed conflict less likely. The same geopolitical motivation underpinned the founding of the General Agreement on Tariffs and Trade (GATT), as well. And, if one looks back over the last 50 years, conflicts between former enemies such as France and Germany, or the United States and Japan, have been resolved peacefully as these nations have forged ever stronger economic ties. As a result, many free trade advocates unabashedly view themselves as working on the side of angels, liberalizing trade to promote development *and* peace.

On the other hand, while increased trade may well promote efficient use of scarce resources, create wealth, and foster geopolitical stability, there are important qualifications to keep in mind. The most basic criticism against increased trade is from an anti-growth or anti-globalization perspective. Current models of development have proven environmentally destructive, the argument goes, and since free trade will by definition increase commerce and development, increased trade will lead to further environmental degradation. Until we shift meaningfully from a model of economic growth to one of sustainable development, trade liberalization should be opposed. Increasing per capita income, for example, does not automatically lead to environmental improvement across the board. In fact, historically, it has led to greater consumption and generation of solid waste, toxics, and greenhouse gases. This is not surprising when one realizes that traditional measures of wealth exclude natural capital. Thus a country can increase its wealth by cutting down all its forests for timber exports. Moreover, while per capita wealth may be increasing, it is important to consider whether the distribution of the wealth is equitable. In countries with a powerful and small elite class, it may well be the case that the benefits of trade are flowing to a very few. Contrary to the hopes that increased trade would allow developing countries to catch up with the developed world (the so-called "convergence hypothesis"), the gap between the richest and poorest nations has been increasing, not decreasing. According to the UN Human Development Report, in 1960 the income gap between the fifth of the world's people living in the poorest countries and the fifth living in the richest countries was 30 to 1. In 1990 the gap had widened to 60 to 1. And by 1998 it was 74 to 1. While free traders claim that "a rising tide will lift all boats," many environmentalists counter that so far the tide has lifted only the yachts.

Liberalized trade is often seen as a threat to a country's ability to choose worthwhile domestic goals—be they high levels of environmental protection, food security, an agrarian lifestyle, or support to certain domestic industries. These non-economic goals suggest a willingness to forgo some of the economic benefits of free trade in order to attain these other goals. A country may choose to levy tariffs on certain agricultural products to promote self-sufficiency in food, or to prevent more efficient foreign producers from underselling domestic small family farmers.

Similarly, the citizens of a country may want high levels of environmental protection, and fear that liberalized trade will cause a "race to the bottom" as countries relax or fail to enforce environmental standards in an attempt to gain market share. In response to foreign competition, it is feared, domestic producers will lobby for lower standards to maintain competitiveness in the global market and may even threaten to relocate to countries with lower environmental standards. There has been a vigorous debate over the extent to which a race-to-the-bottom actually occurs. While environmental compliance costs are generally a small percentage of overall operational costs, insignificant in comparison with labor and material costs, in some sectors (such as the refining and chemical industries) they can be significant. But even if the race-to-the-bottom does not directly drive down standards, it might still result in "chilling" the development of new environmental law. Governments may be fearful of strengthening environmental standards if doing so harms local industries, i.e., by providing foreign producers with lower environmental standards a cost advantage. Perhaps most important, as we shall see in the next section, environmentalists fear that international trade bodies may effectively "tax" national environmental regulations if found to act as protectionist trade barriers.

In sum, free traders view trade as the engine of economic growth to lift nations out of poverty and provide the means for environmental protection. They are deeply concerned that countries may take protectionist measures under the guise of environmental protection, thereby undermining the international trade system. By contrast, many environmentalists believe current international trade rules encourage competitive pressures to weaken environmental standards. Environmentalists are also concerned that trade rules may override existing environmental law and "chill" development of future efforts towards sustainable development.

II.   The GATT and WTO

Following World War II, the international community established three economic institutions: the World Bank, the International Monetary Fund, and the General Agreement on Tariffs and Trade (GATT). The GATT was originally intended to be a component of a larger agreement establishing an International Trade Organization (ITO). The GATT agreement focused mainly on tariff reduction and the ITO, as initially conceived, would have provided a comprehensive code and an institutional framework governing other aspects of international trade. The GATT came into force on January, 1948.[1] The subsequent ITO negotiations, however, were abandoned when it became clear that the U.S. Congress would not ratify the agreement, leaving the GATT in the unexpected position of a treaty without an administrative structure. The GATT necessarily evolved as an institution (adding a Council, Secretariat, and Committees) over the next few decades through practice and a series of later agreements. Most of the evolution came through eight successive multilateral negotiating "rounds," such as the most recent Uruguay Round that established the successor to the ITO, the World Trade Organization (WTO). The WTO forms the legal and institutional framework for the multilateral trading system, providing a forum for implementing the GATT and other trading agreements, negotiating new agreements, and resolving trade disputes.

The objective of the GATT is the progressive reduction of trade barriers among Member States and to ensure that goods and, more recently, services are not discriminated against on the basis of their national origin. To understand the GATT and its progeny, one must recognize its underlying diplomatic principle: that increased trade ties

---

1. With the creation of the World Trade Organization in 1994, the GATT was amended; *reprinted* in 33 ILM 1154 (1994).

will foster political ties and enhance international security. As described above, it was widely believed by the GATT's architects that the spiraling protectionism of the 1930s had directly contributed to the economic instability accompanying the rise of fascism. Just two years after the bloodiest war in human history, protectionist trade barriers represented far more than mere commercial preferences.

Drafted with full knowledge of the attraction in domestic politics of protecting local industries, the GATT's provisions (known as "disciplines") are almost entirely negative—intentionally designed to protect the free trade system from local protectionist interests. In order to liberalize trade, the GATT limits the scope of national regulatory discretion rather than requiring governments to positively enact regulations. For our purposes, there are four provisions of particular importance: Articles I, III, XI, and XX. Article I creates the "Most Favored Nation" (MFN) obligation. This prevents Member States from discriminating between "like products" from other GATT Member States (e.g., the United States cannot favor products from Uruguay over like products from Venezuela). This obligation keeps countries from playing favorites among their trading partners, ensures equal treatment, and promotes rapid reduction of trade barriers. Article III establishes the "National Treatment" obligation. This prevents Member States from discriminating against Member States imports in favor of domestic like products (e.g., the United States cannot favor U.S. products over like foreign products from Uruguay or Venezuela). Articles I and III generally play out in the setting of tariff levels (essentially border taxes) imposed on imports. Article XI, by contrast, forbids quotas that limit the quantity of imports permitted. In its most extreme form this would be an import ban.

The word "environment" is not included anywhere in the text of the GATT. At the time the GATT was negotiated, the relationship between environment and trade had not been widely considered nor were environmental considerations high on the agenda of the public or governments. The primary concern of GATT negotiators was to develop an agreement that would herald in a post–war era of peace, stability, and prosperity. GATT Article XX does, however, provide for environmental exceptions to the requirements of Articles I, III and XI. Even if trade measures violate GATT disciplines, so long as the measures are not applied in an arbitrary or discriminatory manner, Article XX(b) creates an exception for measures "necessary to protect human, animal or plant life or health" while Article XX(g)'s exception applies to measures "relating to the conservation of exhaustible natural resources."

Under the WTO's dispute settlement system, there are no private rights of action. Only Member State governments may challenge other nations' laws. Initially, disputing parties are asked to enter consultations to seek a consensus solution. If this fails the WTO Dispute Settlement

Body establishes a panel to hear the dispute. After the parties offer submissions on the facts and legal arguments, the three–member panel makes its findings and submits an interim report to the parties for comments. The losing party may appeal to an Appellate Body for review of issues of law. If the losing party's appeal is unsuccessful, the injured party may raise countervailing tariffs against imported products from the losing nation equal in value to the harm it has suffered by the offending trade measure. While the dispute panel cannot strike down the trade measure, the offending country must "pay its way" until it comes into compliance. In the recent transatlantic "Bananas Dispute," for example, the European Union's use of preferential tariffs for former colonies was held by a dispute panel to violate the GATT. As compensation, the United States was allowed to levy countervailing tariffs on any EU products it chose. Presumably to increase political pressure in the EU, the United States selected mostly luxury goods from France.

The power of dispute panels to order effective sanctions makes the WTO the envy of other international agreements. Members of dispute settlement panels operate in their individual capacities and are generally drawn from the trade community. The panelists' trade background has been a cause of concern to many environmentalists who argue that panelists often lack experience in the complexities of the environmental issues implicated in their decisions and consequently often fail to give environmental factors sufficient weight. Environmentalists also believe that the WTO should accept amicus curiae (friend of the court) briefs from public interest non-governmental organizations. In recent decisions the Appellate Body has opened the possibility for WTO panels and the Appellate Body to accept amicus briefs if they so choose, but the dispute proceedings still operate behind closed doors. Unlike most other international organizations, non-governmental organizations are not permitted to observe or participate in WTO meetings.

A.   Like Products and PPMs

Prior to 1991, the field of trade and environment didn't even exist. One dispute, known as the "Tuna/Dolphin Cases," set the debate alight. No one knows exactly why, but bottlenose dolphins in the Eastern Tropical Pacific tend to swim above schools of yellowfin tuna. The fishing fleets knew this and lay nets around dolphins, drawing the bottom in tight like a purse. This often resulted in good tuna catches but, unfortunately, a lot of dead dolphins, as well, who suffocated in the nets. This practice (which killed hundreds of thousands of dolphins) disturbed U.S. environmental and animal rights groups who lobbied Congress for an amendment to the Marine Mammal Protection Act effectively requiring that other countries use "dolphin-friendly" nets (i.e., not encircling dolphins). If the country could not prove its fleet was doing so, the amendment *required* the U.S. Secretary of Commerce to ban the import of their tuna products as well as tuna from countries they sold to (to avoid trans-shipments). After losing a citizen suit, in 1989 the Secretary banned tuna imports from a number of countries, including Mexico. Mexico, in turn, appealed to the GATT dispute panel in Geneva.

Mexico argued that the U.S. ban violated Articles I, III, and XI. Once a product reached the border and the tariffs were paid, it should be treated no differently than "like" domestic products. Mexican cans of tuna were the same as U.S. cans. How the tuna got into the cans, Mexico argued, was irrelevant. The United States responded that Articles I and III had not been violated because the dolphin-friendly tuna and Mexican tuna were not "like products." Put another way, the U.S. trade restriction was based as much on the process and production methods (known as "PPMs") and the product's environmental impacts as on the product itself. True, one could not look at the tuna meat in separate cans and identify which had been caught with purse seine nets and which in a dolphin-friendly manner, but how the tuna got into the cans should matter. And even if Article I, III, or XI had been violated, the United States argued, the law was still valid because of Article XX's exceptions for protection of human, animal or plant life and the conservation of exhaustible natural resources.

In a decision that sent shock waves through the environmental community, the GATT panel found for Mexico.[2] Articles I and III had been violated, the panel found, because a trade restriction may not be based on PPMs. "Likeness" should be determined by reference to a product's *physical* characteristics, not by reference to the *process* by which a product is made. What mattered in terms of GATT law was the tuna itself, not how it got in the can. Moreover, Article XX didn't apply because a country cannot unilaterally suspend trade rules for environmental harms occurring *outside* its borders. Otherwise, the panel feared, it would be too easy to hide protectionism in green clothing.

Mexico ended up dropping the case out of political concerns, as did the European Community after winning the Tuna/Dolphin II case that followed,[3] but the decision clearly represented the prevailing opinion of the trade community. What right did the United States have to impose its dolphin-loving values on other countries? Agreed rules should govern international trade, not sentimental feelings over "Flipper the Dolphin."

2. Panel Report, United States—Restrictions on Imports of Tuna, GATT B.I.S.D. (39th Supp.) at 155 (1993), *reprinted* in 30 I.L.M. 1594 (Aug. 16, 1991) (unadopted).

3. Panel Report, United States—Restrictions on Imports of Tuna, GATT Doc. DS29/R, *reprinted in* 33 I.L.M. 839 (June 16, 1994) (unadopted).

How would the United States feel if a country with a large vegetarian population banned imports of U.S. leather because it didn't like the operations of U.S. slaughterhouses? Moreover, bottlenose dolphins are not even an endangered species. Most likely the ban was simply a pretext to protect U.S. tuna sales from foreign competition.

The decision was also generally supported by developing countries whose lower environmental standards may provide them with cost advantages and export market access. For them, improving export performance is an important means of encouraging development and reducing poverty. They fear that PPMs may be used as pretexts for protectionist measures. This is most apparent, they believe, in calls by American labor unions to ban products made with child labor. Are the unions truly concerned about the welfare of foreign children or, rather, in protecting their local markets and jobs from lower-priced imports? Environmental trade measures, it is feared, are simply a 21st century form of eco-imperialism, with developed countries yet again controlling how poorer nations manage their own affairs.

The reaction from the U.S. environmental community was equally strong. Beyond sweeping away national sovereignty, by focusing on the product and ignoring how it was harvested the dispute panel had deliberately *excluded* the environmental issues. By requiring injury within a country's borders, the decision frustrated any attempt to protect international resources and pressing problems of the global commons such as global warming, ozone depletion, and overfishing. In sum, the Tuna/Dolphin decisions placed in doubt whether countries could use trade restrictions to protect the environment outside their jurisdictions.

Clarifying the PPM issue remains one of the most important and difficult challenges in the trade and environment debate. Environmentalists argue that the existing rules fail to provide policy-makers with sufficient clarity about the kinds of measures governments may take to address environmental impacts. Preventing or limiting countries from distinguishing between goods according to the environmental impact of their production, they argue, gives foreign countries with weak environmental protection standards a competitive edge and places downward pressure on domestic environmental standards. It also forces importing countries to import and consume unsustainably produced goods. Trade theorists respond that differing countries set their own environmental standards, and that different preferences for environmental quality are a valid source of "comparative advantage." Allowing countries to distinguish between products on the basis of how they are produced threatens descent down the "slippery slope" to protectionism and would undermine the very foundations of the international trade system.

221

One might wonder why, given the angry charges of paternalism and eco-imperialism by developing countries, the United States continues to rely on trade sanctions as an environmental policy instrument. The simple answer is that trade sanctions work. They are also costless (at least to us). Banning imports of non dolphin-friendly tuna or non turtle-friendly shrimp may cause prices to rise a little in America, but the costs are mainly borne by foreign fleets who have to change their practices. Moreover, because environmental trade measures may also protect U.S. industries, environmentalists can find powerful political allies to press their case (as has happened with labor unions in the case of PPMs).

While conditioning access to one's markets may look like a carrot to the importing country—granting the privilege of access to its consumers—it sure looks like a stick to the exporter—"change what you're doing or lose trade access." Undoubtedly, multilateral solutions to shared environmental problems are preferable to unilateral ones. Perhaps a better way to deal with differing production processes is to reduce the difference between nations' environmental laws. Harmonization of domestic environmental standards, through agreed international standards, is often suggested as an alternative to trade sanctions for addressing environmentally harmful production processes used by exporting nations. If environmental standards are comparable, then there is less scope for international disputes to arise.

This issue arose in the *Shrimp–Turtle* decision, which involved a U.S. ban on imports of shrimp harvested with gear that traps and suffocates endangered sea turtles.[4] Similar to the facts underlying the Tuna/Dolphin cases, a 1989 U.S. amendment to the Endangered Species Act required foreign nations to certify that their shrimp fisheries do not threaten endangered sea turtles as a prerequisite for access to the U.S. market. In practice the law effectively requires foreign fishing fleets to equip their trawling gear with "turtle excluder devices." Turtle excluder devices, or "TEDs," are a simple metal cage with a trapdoor to allow turtles to escape without significant loss of shrimp. India, Pakistan, Malaysia, and Thailand challenged the U.S. measures, arguing that the trade bans violated the GATT. Among other things, the WTO Appellate Body found that the United States had not negotiated adequately with all the affected States prior to taking unilateral action, resulting in discriminatory treatment of Member States. The case did not decide, however, what lengths a country should go to negotiate with other countries before trade measures become "justifiable" discrimination. If a nation genuinely tries to develop common standards and is unsuccessful, may it then resort to trade sanctions?

4. Appellate Body Report, United States—Import Prohibition of Certain Shrimp and Shrimp Products, WT/ DS58/AB/R (Oct. 12, 1998) (adopted, with modifications, Nov. 6, 1998).

Subsequent cases have weakened the Tuna/Dolphin cases' stark holdings. The WTO's Appellate Body, for example, has taken a slightly more nuanced approach to the "like products" analysis, providing some room for non-trade concerns and moving away from a narrow focus on a product's physical characteristics. The Appellate Body's decision in the *Shrimp/Turtle* case suggests that PPM-based measures may sometimes be justified under Article XX(g). Nonetheless, the only way a government can be *confident* that its environmental protection measures will not violate the GATT is if (1) the trade restrictions focus on the products themselves rather than how they were produced or harvested, (2) the harm is local, and (3) the measure is not unilaterally imposed.

So what does this all mean for U.S. environmental laws? One can divide the laws into three categories. The great majority of U.S. law will be unaffected by international trade rules for the simple reason that they have no significant trade implications. For better or worse, dreams of an entire volume of the Code of Federal Regulations disappearing overnight will remain just a dream. The second category contains laws *likely* to be unaffected by GATT disciplines. These reside in a grey area because they may have significant trade impacts. Consider, for example, a law requiring that cars sold in the United States have a catalytic converter. This effectively bars the sale of imported dirty cars and, in this sense, acts as a a trade barrier. So long as the justification for the barrier, though, addresses a local harm, is aimed at the product rather than its PPM, and is not overtly discriminatory then it should satisfy the GATT.

The last category is a small group—laws based neither on local harms nor international consensus. Protecting dolphins in international waters that aren't endangered species serves as an easy example. These laws will remain problematic because the trade restrictions reflect value judgments and, in that respect, are not dissimilar to child labor. There is no *direct* physical harm to me whether dolphins are killed in the Pacific or if five-year olds work in garment factories, but I may disapprove of these practices and choose to use trade restrictions either to express my disapproval or seek to change the practices. And it may be that the GATT can never accept these types of laws because they provide too much potential for protectionism. Once value judgments can justify a trade barrier, can't one provide a rationale for virtually any protectionism?

This may not be all bad, however, given the dispute settlement process. As described above, if a WTO dispute panel and the Appellate Body find that a law violates the GATT or other WTO agreement, it does not strike down the law, nor is the offending country required to change it. Rather, the injured country is permitted to raise countervailing duties against imported goods from the offending country. Thus, if we choose to use trade sanctions to express our displeasure at the environmental harms caused by a fishery or other practice, the international trade system allows us to do so, so long as we are willing to pay the price.

B. *Multilateral Environmental Agreements*

The relationship between multilateral environmental agreements (MEAs) and the GATT is also the topic of considerable debate. A number of MEAs rely on trade measures to protect the environment, sanction noncompliance by parties, or encourage nonparties to join. As discussed in Chapter 7, the Basel Convention relies on trade-related measures to encourage States to become Parties and enforce its provisions. Thus Parties may not trade hazardous waste with non-Parties unless they have entered into a bilateral or multilateral agreement with provisions that are no less environmentally sound than those provided for by the Basel Convention. Similarly, the Montreal Protocol prohibits trade of listed ozone-depleting substances between Parties and non-Parties. Such restrictions are necessary because they give agreements teeth.

If a Party and non-Party to Basel or the Montreal Protocol are both GATT Member States, however, such trade restrictions could violate GATT Articles I and XI. Following the Tuna/Dolphin decisions, environmental groups became concerned that a number of MEAs could be challenged and might be declared in violation of the GATT. To date, there have been no GATT challenges to MEAs because they represent near international consensus. In the event of a conflict between a WTO Agreement and an MEA, though, which should prevail? Under international law on the interpretation of treaties, the more recent agreement wins, but should the GATT be considered a 1947 treaty or 1995 (revised during the Uruguay Round)? Some have argued that, in any case, the WTO is an inappropriate forum to judge MEAs. Others have argued that the WTO should create a "safe harbor" specifically exempting trade provisions in MEAs. They should be a special case, it follows, because they represent international consensus on how to manage a common environmental problem. Yet this begs the question of what membership represents a consensus. In any event, there have been no challenges to date and are unlikely to be any in the future for the simple reason that the MEAs have so many parties. No country wants to be seen as a bad environmental actor by threatening the viability of an agreement adopted by most of the world's countries.

III. The North American Free Trade Agreement (NAFTA)[5]

In December 1992, the United States, Canada and Mexico concluded the North American Free Trade Agreement (NAFTA), the first major trade agreement to address the environmental effects of free trade in the agreement itself.[6] The NAFTA substantially reduces tariffs and other trade barriers, integrating the markets of the United States, Canada, and Mexico into a single $8.6 trillion free trade area with 390 million consumers and annual trade flows of more than $600 billion. It incorporates provisions protecting domestic health and environmental regulations from the downward pressures caused by free trade, giving precedence to the parties' responsibilities under international environmental agreements when those responsibilities conflict with NAFTA, and shifting the burden of proof away from the defending party when environmental or health regulation is attacked as a trade distortion. In addition, the NAFTA parties concluded an "Environmental Side Agreement," the North American Agreement on Environmental Cooperation, to promote environmental cooperation, increase citizen participation in environmental protection, and ensure that each party effectively enforces its environmental laws.[7] Although subject to significant criticism, NAFTA and its Environmental Side Agreement represent an important step in reconciling the often-conflicting demands of economic integration and environmental protection.

This is particularly important because further integration in the Western Hemisphere is proceeding apace. The original parties designed NAFTA with a view to developing an eventual hemisphere-wide Free Trade Agreement for the Americas (FTAA). Negotiations for the FTAA have been underway since 1998, and are scheduled to conclude by 2004. Meanwhile, NAFTA's southern counterpart, MERCOSUR, is courting new members, with Bolivia and Chile recently becoming associate members.

Despite the potentially massive economic impact of NAFTA, initial drafts of the treaty contained no environmental provisions. As originally drafted, NAFTA was similar to the revised GATT that was emerging simultaneously from the Uruguay Round negotiations. After early re-

---

5. Adapted from David Hunter, James Salzman, Durwood Zaelke, International Environmental Law and Policy (2nd ed., 2002).

6. North American Free Trade Agreement, Dec. 8, 1992, Can.–Mex.–U.S., Art. 104, 32 I.L.M. 289, 297 (1993).

7. North American Agreement on Environmental Cooperation, Sept. 8–14 1993, U.S.–Can.–Mex., art. 10(7), 32 I.L.M. 1484, 1486–487 (1993) (effective Jan. 1, 1994) [hereinafter NAAEC Agreement].

ports of its contents sparked widespread protest among environmental-ists, labor groups, and others, the administration of President George H. W. Bush, which had negotiated the NAFTA in secrecy and without public participation for the first eighteen months, revised the draft treaty to include environmental protections. As a general proposition, environmentalists were concerned that the different levels of protection afforded the environment and human health in the three countries might either chill strengthening of environmental laws or induce indus-try flight. Over the past quarter century, both the United States and Canada have developed sophisticated and relatively stringent regimes for protecting human health and the environment. Despite legal and institu-tional advances in the late 1980s and early 1990s, the level of environ-mental and labor protections in Mexico has remained far lower. The consequences of Mexico's inadequate environmental enforcement efforts were most dramatically apparent in the sixty–mile wide free trade zone along the 2,000–mile United States–Mexico border, known as the Maqui-ladora zone.

"Maquiladoras" are factories owned jointly by U.S. and Mexican corporations and operated on the Mexican side of the U.S.–Mexico border. These factories import raw materials or components tariff-free from U.S. suppliers, usually the parent corporation, then produce fin-ished or semi-finished products that are shipped back into the United States for sale, again tariff-free. Since the Maquiladora program was established in 1965, thousands of factories have opened along the border. Before NAFTA, Mexico's government lacked both the resources and the political will to enforce effectively the country's environmental laws. Thus, the Maquiladora facilities on the southern side of the border have gone essentially unregulated for most of their history. Illegal practices, such as the dumping of hazardous wastes onto the ground or directly into waterways, have been common.

A. *Environmental Provisions*

Supplemented at the last minute to mitigate the more serious environmental effects of free trade, NAFTA has relatively few provisions for environmental protection. Nonetheless, it is characterized by many as the "greenest" trade liberalization treaty ever. The agreement con-tains three important requirements. First, in addressing the potential problem of industrial relocation and investment flight toward less strin-gent environmental standards, Article 1114.2 provides that the three nations "should not waive or otherwise derogate from or offer to waive or otherwise derogate from, such measures as an encouragement for the establishment, acquisition, expansion, or retention in its territory of an investment of an investor." In other words, lowering environmental protection standards is not an acceptable means of encouraging investment and development.

Second, Article 104 addresses the potential conflict between trade measures in MEAs and NAFTA. Citing three MEAs (the Montreal Protocol, Basel Convention, and CITES) and two bilateral agreements, Article 104 states that in the case of a conflict between NAFTA obligations and provisions in the listed agreements, the nation should comply with the agreement in a manner "that is least inconsistent with the other provisions of [the NAFTA]." Put another way, in the face of inconsistencies between NAFTA and MEAs, the MEAs will generally win. If in unanimous agreement, the three nations may add other MEAs to the protected list. Given the uncertainty surrounding MEA trade restrictions in the WTO, this "safe harbor" represents a significant protection.

Third, NAFTA also addresses the potential role of sanitary and phytosanitary measures and other standards in acting as barriers to trade. One could easily imagine, for example, using a health standard as a disguised barrier to trade (e.g., by banning imports of vegetables unless they were irradiated even though other processes could provide the same protection against pathogens). NAFTA provides that parties have the right to determine their own "appropriate levels of protection." So long as its actions are nondiscriminatory, a party can ban a product or service if it determines that the risks are too high. In challenges to such a restriction, the burden falls on the moving party, not the government. This is the opposite of the WTO practice, where a nation must bear the burden of justifying its technical, health, and environmental standards in the face of a trade challenge.

B. Environmental Side Agreement

Even with these provisions, NAFTA faced significant opposition from trade and environmental groups. In his presidential campaign, Bill Clinton promised to add separate side agreements to address trade and environmental concerns. This represented another first in trade agreements. The Environmental Side Agreement is not limited to specific regions, species, media, or types of pollutants, but applies wherever the parties feel environmental protection can be enhanced by cooperative efforts. As a response to popular concerns about trade liberalization and as a mechanism for continent-wide environmental cooperation, the Environmental Side Agreement was considered a landmark treaty.

Clarifying the NAFTA provisions, Article 3 of the Side Agreement recognizes each Party's right to establish its own levels of domestic environmental protection, adding that "each Party shall ensure that its laws and regulations provide for high levels of environmental protection and shall strive to continue to improve those laws and regulations." In other words, Mexico can choose lower levels of environmental protection, but it must enforce its laws to ensure that these standards are met.

Building institutional capacity, the Side Agreement created a centralized forum for environmental cooperation among the parties, establishing the North American Commission for Environmental Cooperation, or "CEC." An intergovernmental agency directed and funded equally by the three parties, the CEC is comprised of three organs–the Council, the Secretariat, and the Joint Public Advisory Committee. The Council is the CEC's political organ and its governing body. It is composed of one cabinet-level representative from each of the three parties: Canada's Minister of the Environment, Mexico's Secretary of Environment, Natural Resources and Fisheries, and the Administrator of the United States Environmental Protection Agency. The Council oversees implementation of the Agreement, directs the Secretariat, addresses disputes between the parties, and serves as a general forum for environmental cooperation among the parties. The Joint Public Advisory Committee (JPAC) serves as a formal mechanism by which NGOs and individuals may influence the decision making process of the CEC. The Agreement defines NGOs broadly to include "any scientific, professional, business, non-profit, or public interest organization or association which is neither affiliated with, nor under the direction of, a government." The JPAC is comprised of fifteen members, five appointed by each party.

To the surprise of many, the CEC has played an important role in publicizing and investigating cases of environmental violations or non-enforcement. The Side Agreement created two routes for the CEC to ensure parties were complying with NAFTA. Article 13 of the NAAEC authorizes the Secretariat to prepare a report "on any matter within the scope of the annual program" without Council approval, and on "any other environmental matter related to the cooperative functions of this Agreement" unless the Council objects by a two–thirds vote. If the Secretariat lacks expertise in the matter being examined, it must obtain the assistance of "independent experts of recognized experience in the matter" in the preparation of the report.

In 1995, for example, responding to a complaint from United States and Mexican NGOs, the Secretariat prepared a report evaluating the death of 40,000 migratory birds at the Silva Reservoir in Guanajuato, Mexico. With the cooperation of the Mexican government, the Secretariat sent an international team of scientists to investigate. The team determined that the deaths were caused by an outbreak of avian botulism. As a result of this discovery, the CEC worked with the Guanajuato government to clean up the Reservoir. A second research team has been formed to develop a better understanding of the causes and prevention of avian botulism. Note that the purpose of Article 13 is not to sanction parties but, rather, to draw attention to environmental problems and focus resources and expertise to remedy them.

The one explicit restriction on the scope of Article 13 is that the CEC may not report on "issues related to whether a Party has failed to enforce its environmental laws and regulations." The Agreement envisions these complaints being handled through the Article 14 citizen submission process. Article 14 of the Side Agreement creates a mechanism for citizens to file submissions in which they assert that a party is failing to effectively enforce its environmental law. The CEC Secretariat initially considers these submissions based on strict criteria requiring, among others, that the submission appears to be aimed at promoting enforcement rather than at harassing industry, provides sufficient information to allow the Secretariat to review the submission, and is filed by a person or organization residing or established in the territory of a party.

Once the Secretariat finds that a submission meets these criteria it will determine if a response is warranted from the party named in the submission. If so, the CEC prepares a "factual record," identifying specific instances of noncompliance and their causes. Finally, the CEC may offer technical assistance to parties found not to be in compliance or arbitrate disputes. This approach differs significantly from the antagonistic WTO dispute settlement process. Article 14 submissions, instead, rely on research, data analysis and dissemination, and publicity to encourage compliance with environmental laws. It also, in stark contrast to the WTO, permits stakeholders to participate in transnational legal processes.

Despite these benefits, the Secretariat has held tight reins on the citizen submission process. As of February, 2002, 33 submissions had been made under Article 14. Of these, only three factual records had been completed and released. Finally, Article 22 of the Side Agreement provides that if a party to the Environmental Side Agreement believes that another party has engaged in a "persistent pattern of failure" to effectively enforce its environmental laws as they pertain to goods traded in North Americe, it may request consultations with an eye to resolving the dispute. To date, neither Mexico, Canada, nor the United States has made use of this provision to complain that another government is not enforcing its environmental laws, presumably because one does not throw stones at a neighbor's glass house (particularly when you live in one, too).

C. Chapter 11

Despite its name, NAFTA is as much an investment as a trade agreement. The most controversial and unique part of NAFTA has been its "investor-state" provision in Chapter 11. Protections against expropriation have become common in investment treaties and, in principle, make good sense. There has been a longstanding concern among foreign investors over "expropriation," the taking over of local operations. In the 1950s, for example, a number of Middle Eastern countries nationalized foreign oil company assets, as Mexico had in 1938. Thus many investor agreements provide for compensation of private parties whose assets have been expropriated.

Chapter 11 introduces two important changes. First, it broadens the scope of offending actions. In particular, it provides compensation for direct expropriation and for measures "tantamount to nationalization or expropriation" of an investment. Rather than the traditional view of expropriation as a property transaction (your property is now the State's), Chapter 11 expands the range of potentially compensable actions to laws and regulations adopted by national, state, or provincial legislatures and agencies. Put in the context of the 5th Amendment to the Constitution, Chapter 11 recognizes regulatory takings (discussed *supra* at pages 64–68).

Second, trade and investment treaties have traditionally provided for the state of the national whose investment has been expropriated or otherwise injured to press the claim against the host state. Chapter 11, by contrast, allows a *private investor* to sue the host state directly for a claim that an investor right has been breached. On the positive side, this change removes diplomatic considerations from blocking the pursuit of legitimate claims for compensation. On the negative side, it literally opens the gate to private challenges and problems of harassment and nuisance suits.

The dilemma of Chapter 11 tracks that of U.S. takings jurisprudence. At a certain point, governmental actions that diminish property values must also provide compensation out of concerns of basic fairness. Private foreign investors should be accorded the protection warranted under customary international law, which includes "fair and equitable treatment" and "full protection and security." On the other hand, the NAFTA countries—indeed, all countries of the world—must be able to use their police power to regulate private property to protect public health and the environment, as well as to promote sustainable development, and they must be able to regulate without the fear that they will have to pay each polluter for such regulation. As Justice Holmes observed, if government had to compensate injured parties for *every* economic loss caused by regulation, government could not go on. While the stated goal of Chapter 11 is to ensure investor confidence, the result has been extremely controversial claims that, many argue, threaten to chill legitimate environmental protection measures.

Chapter 11's dispute settlement process is based on accepted international practice for commercial arbitration, a practice that bears little resemblance to domestic court procedure. As with the WTO, the panel of three arbitrators are chosen from trade and investment law experts (who usually do not have an environmental background). To ensure confidentiality of commercially sensitive information, both the pleadings and argument are kept secret unless otherwise agreed to by the parties. Since commercial disputes have traditionally only affected the parties at issue, lack of transparency has not been a major concern. The challenged state bears the burden of proof to show that the restricted product or activity is unsafe. The arbitration panel's decision is binding on both participants, with limited opportunities to appeal a decision.

As with the Tuna/Dolphin cases and the GATT, Chapter 11 was not viewed as a major concern to environmental protection until the first decision. In *Ethyl Corp. v. Canada*, a U.S. firm sued the Canadian government because of its decision to ban the import and inter-provincial transport of MMT, a manganese-based gasoline additive that could pose a significant health risk. There also was evidence that MMT damaged pollution control equipment in cars, and increased fuel emissions in general. Because there was inadequate data on the direct health risks of long-term exposure to the emissions, MMT could not be prohibited under Canada's Environmental Protection Act. As a result, the only way to prevent the use of MMT in Canada was to ban the import and inter-provincial transport of the substance. Ethyl Corporation, the only manufacturer of MMT, filed a notice of intent to arbitrate in April 1997, claiming violations of national treatment, minimum standards, performance requirements, and expropriation resulting in damages of $251 million. Even though MMT is not produced in Canada, Ethyl claimed that Canada acted in a discriminatory manner by banning the import of MMT without also banning domestic production or use. It argued that this discriminatory action reduced the value of a facility operated by Ethyl in Canada to blend MMT with other petroleum products, and that the ban was "tantamount to expropriation" of that facility. Ethyl's claim also included damages to their "good reputation" because of the ban on its product. The arbitration panel accepted jurisdiction, and shortly thereafter Canada settled the case, paying Ethyl $13 million for costs and lost profits. Canada also withdrew the legislation.

Canada's quick settlement caught the attention of lawyers, companies, and NGOs throughout North America. The attention turned to excitement on one part, and concern on the other, following the decision in *Metalclad*, the first investor-state claim to work its way through the appellate process. In that case, an Arbitral Tribunal determined that an Ecological Decree establishing a cacti reserve in Mexico (and revoking a permit to site a hazardous waste landfill) had expropriated the landfill owned by the U.S. investor, Metalclad. Mexico must pay compensation, the Tribunal concluded, because the local government had "failed to ensure a transparent and predictable framework for Metalclad's business planning and investment."

The most recent high profile Chapter 11 case is *Methanex Corporation v. United States*. On March 25, 1999, the Governor of the State of California issued an Executive Order that provided for the removal of MTBE from gasoline at the earliest possible date. MTBE is a gasoline additive that has raised concerns because it is highly soluble, moving readily through soil into groundwater. Drinking water tainted with even tiny amounts of MTBE gives off a strongly unpleasant odor. Exposure to MTBE has been linked to tumors and nervous system disorders in mice and rats. The U.S. EPA has classified it as a possible cancer-causing agent. Methanex Corporation, which manufactures an MTBE component, filed a notice of intent to arbitrate under Chapter 11. Methanex charged, among other things, that the measures taken by California were unfair and inequitable, not based on credible scientific evidence, went beyond what is necessary to protect any legitimate public interest, and would expropriate Methanex's business of selling methanol for use in MTBE in California. The complaint concluded that "This constitutes a substantial interference and taking of Methanex U.S. business and Methanex's investment in Methanex U.S. These measures are both directly and indirectly tantamount to an expropriation." Methanex has demanded $970 million in damages.

Beyond the size of the damage claim, NGOs are deeply concerned that the U.S. government, not California, is defending the case. Moreover, the limited Chapter 11 jurisprudence seems to suggest that the traditional takings exemption for so-called "police powers" doesn't apply. Methanex, for example, could never win its case in U.S. courts. Perhaps most important, even if Methanex loses its case, Chapter 11 challenges are raising serious concerns over chilling of environmental protection. A number of companies have written letters to state agencies and legislatures, threatening to bring Chapter 11 challenges if they restrict or ban certain substances. Some would counter these concerns, pointing out that frivolous nuisance suits are threatened all the time and the work of government goes on. Moreover, our elected representatives signed and ratified NAFTA, so charges that it is undemocratic hardly seem compelling. Interestingly, there has been a split in both the Clinton and Bush administrations over whether to amend Chapter 11 or not.

The EPA and Department of Justice have called for revisiting Chapter 11 while Commerce and Treasury have argued that its investor protections outweigh possible takings concerns.

IV.   The Trade in Chemicals

Modern industry and agriculture rely heavily on the production and use of synthetic chemical pesticides and fertilizers. Since 1945, international pesticide sales have doubled every decade to sales over $18 billion. Incidents of pesticide poisonings have doubled at roughly the same rate. Although pesticide use has been greatest in the industrialized countries of Europe, Japan, and the United States, the fastest growing market for pesticides is now in developing countries.

Although some pesticides pose significant health and environmental threats they may also offer significant benefits, particularly to developing countries. Pesticides are used to reduce the incidence of insect-borne human diseases and increase crop production through killing plant-eating insects and molds. Although banned in many countries, DDT is still used to battle vector-borne diseases in a number of developing countries such as malaria (which infests up to 500 million people per year), yellow fever, river blindness, and sleeping sickness. In the case of DDT, a debate has developed between Mexico—which still uses DDT to battle malaria—and Canada and the United States—which have banned DDT but still find significant levels as far north as the Great Lakes. The United States and Canada have pointed out that alternative mosquito insecticides are available, but Mexico contends that these are up to five–times more expensive than DDT and are acutely toxic, requiring extreme precaution in their application.

As the use of chemicals and pesticides has intensified, developed countries have become increasingly aware of the potential health and environmental problems and, in response, adopted advanced chemical management systems and regulatory structures to ban or severely restrict the use of certain chemicals within their countries. Although many pesticides and other hazardous chemicals may be banned for use in one country, they may still be exported to other countries. The legal trade of such chemicals presents several international concerns. While every country that imports pesticides has a registration program, generally requiring information on the pesticide's proposed use and efficacy, these programs are largely ineffective in those developing countries that lack the institutional capacity to make an informed decision on pesticide imports or on the proper management techniques after import. Not surprisingly, developing countries experience a high incidence of pesticide misuse, creating public health concerns as well as environmental harms to non-target species such as animals, birds, and insects

The sale of pesticides whose use is banned in the industrialized world to developing countries can lead to what has been labeled, "the circle of poison." The phrase refers to a pattern where hazardous pesticides are manufactured within a country where their use is either banned or severely restricted. As a result, the chemicals are exported for sale abroad. The foreign countries importing the pesticides use them on food crops that are then exported *back* into the country of manufacture and, in turn, end up on the dinner table and in school lunches. Hence the pesticides come "full circle," creating the circle of poison.

This trade is substantial. From 1992–1994, the United States shipped over 114,600 tons of banned pesticides. A study by the General Accounting Office in 1989 determined that the circle of poison warranted concern because of the EPA's poor monitoring of the content, quantity, and destination of exported, unregistered pesticides. The GAO concluded that the EPA "does not know whether export notices are being submitted, as required under FIFRA" and that "notices were not sent for three pesticides (out of four) that were voluntarily canceled [by the manufacturer] because of concern about toxic effects."[8]

In the United States, the Toxic Substances Control Act (TSCA, described in Chapter 6) contains provisions governing the export and import of chemicals.[9] If a chemical requires testing under the Act (i.e., if it may present an unreasonable risk of injury to health or the environment), exporters of the chemical "shall notify the Administrator [of the EPA] of such exportation or intent to export and the Administrator shall furnish to the government of such country notice of the availability of the data submitted to the Administrator ..."[10] TSCA permits exports of pesticides so long as "prior to export, the foreign purchaser has signed a statement acknowledging that the purchaser understands that such pesticide is not registered in the United States and cannot be sold in the United States...."[11] Similarly, the government may ban the import of chemicals if it is determined that its manufacture, processing, distribution in commerce, use, or disposal presents or may present an unreasonable risk of injury to health or the environment.[12]

The circle of poison presents a paradox. Why do developed countries allow banned pesticides to be exported if they may return on vegetables and fruit, and why do importing countries knowingly import banned pesticides? The answer is two–fold. First, each country's cost-benefit analysis is unique. A developing country may determine its overall

8. *As quoted in* Jefferson D. Reynolds, International Pesticide Trade: Is There Any Hope for the International Pesticide Trade: Is There Any Hope for the Effective Regulation of Controlled Substances', 13 J. Land Use & Envt'l L. 69 (1997).

9. 15 U.S.C. §§ 2601 et seq.

10. 15 U.S.C. § 2611.

11. 7 U.S.C. § 1360(a).

12. 15 U.S.C. § 2612.

interests are served best by using relatively more dangerous chemicals because, it believes, the cost of environmental harms or increased injury among farm workers is outweighed by the benefit in reducing insect-borne disease or increasing crop production. A developed country may rationally ban the same chemical if it has no malaria to control or other significant benefit to be gained from the chemical's use. If a developing country wishes to import a banned pesticide, it follows, it would be paternalistic for a developed country to forbid such transactions.

The second explanation for the export of banned chemicals is information or, more precisely, lack of information. The cost-benefit analysis described above is only possible if you assume countries have (1) accurate data available on which to base their policy decisions concerning harmful effects of the imported chemicals and (2) adequate institutional infrastructure to control imports, use, and disposal of pesticides. If, however, importing countries are not adequately informed of the potential harms of the chemicals, then their cost-benefit analysis will be inaccurately skewed in favor of importation. The key issues, then, are provision of accurate information and institutional capacity to act on it.

The international community has addressed the challenge of ensuring prior informed consent through a series of voluntary codes of conduct and guidelines, culminating in the binding Convention for the Application of Prior Informed Consent Procedure for Certain Hazardous Chemicals and Pesticides in International Trade (also known as the Rotterdam Convention) in 1998.[13] As of June 2001, 73 countries (including the United States) had signed the Convention and 15 had ratified. The Convention enters into force once 50 countries have ratified.

Generally speaking, the Convention bans the export of any chemicals listed on Annex III, unless the importing country has given its prior consent. Chemicals are listed on Annex III when they have been "banned" or "severely restricted" in the exporting country. The Convention uses a broad definition, including pesticides voluntarily withdrawn from the market. Banned chemicals include those that have been refused approval for first–time use or "withdrawn by industry either from the domestic market or from further consideration in the domestic approval process where there is clear evidence that such action has been taken in order to protect human health or the environment." Similarly, the definition of "severely restricted" includes chemicals with clear evidence of a human health or environmental concern.

To add a banned or severely restricted chemical to Annex III, the Secretariat must receive at least one notification from two of the seven designated regions. Upon receipt of a country's notification of banning or restriction, the Secretariat refers the pesticide to the Chemical Review

---

13.   38 I.L.M. 1 (1999).

Committee. The Chemical Review Committee then decides whether to propose that the Conference of Parties add the chemical to Annex III. The Convention also allows developing countries to short-cut the Annex III listing process for "severely hazardous pesticide formulations." These are pesticides that produce severe environmental or health effects within a short period from time of exposure.

For severely hazardous pesticide formulations, developing countries must submit information regarding the chemical's active ingredients, descriptions of incidents relating to the chemical, and the responses to these incidents. The Secretariat then looks into whether other countries have applicator or handling restrictions and whether any incidents have been reported in other countries. The Secretariat subsequently forwards this information to the Chemical Review Committee, which then decides whether to recommend that the Conference of the Parties include the chemical in Annex III. The Chemical Review Committee's decisions regarding both banned/severely restricted chemicals and severely hazardous chemical formulations must be approved by a consensus of the Conference of Parties. Thus, essentially each country has the power to veto the inclusion of a particular chemical.

Once a chemical is listed in Annex III, importing countries are notified and have nine months to review the listing and decide whether to import, exclude, or restrict future importation of the substance. Such decisions must respect the trade principles of most-favored nation (i.e., ban imports of the chemical from all States) and national treatment (a party choosing to exclude imports from another party may not produce the chemical or pesticide domestically). Once the importing party makes its decision and notifies the treaty secretariat, exporting parties must then take measures to ensure that exporters within its jurisdiction do not ship listed substances to parties that have chosen to exclude them.

Importantly, if the importing country has not responded after the nine–month review period, the exporting country must assume the importing country does *not* consent unless the chemical is registered in that country or has been previously used in that country. Exporting countries are also responsible for complying with technical assistance requirements. Article 16 of the Convention requires that parties "cooperate in promoting technical assistance for the development of the infrastructure and the capacity necessary to manage chemicals to enable implementation of this Convention." This provision has been criticized as too weak, because without adequate financial and technical assistance it is unlikely developing countries will have the resources to evaluate chemical risks, even with the information.

The Convention also applies to unlisted chemicals for which there has been domestic regulatory action. If a party bans or severely restricts an unlisted chemical, it must notify the Secretariat of these actions prior to the first export following the ban or restriction. If the importing country does not acknowledge receipt of this notification, the exporting country is required to send repeat notices. While these notification provisions are mandatory, the Convention includes no compliance mechanisms to enforce this provision.

*

PART IV

Natural Resources

CHAPTER 9

PROTECTING NATURAL RESOURCES

I. The Nation's Diminishing Resources

Much of America's history has been shaped by the nation's abundant natural resources and wildlife, from coastal fisheries and forested valleys to powerful rivers and deep aquifers. Yet our nation is losing many of its natural resources. As a result of land development and the introduction of exotic species, nearly 60 percent of the nation outside Alaska has lost its native vegetation. In large swaths of the country, ranging from the Central Valley of California to Texas to New England, less than a quarter of the land retains its natural vegetation. At the same time, more than half of the nation's wetlands have disappeared. A number of states have lost eighty percent or more of their wetlands. With growing water consumption, literally thousands of the county's waterways are totally drained of water at various points of the year. Other waterways turn into mere trickles. To store water for later use, the United States has dammed and flooded natural wonderlands like Glen Canyon and the Hetch Hetchy Valley. Loss of habitat, in turn, has led to a decline in species. One percent of United States species are presumed extinct, and about one–third are at risk of becoming extinct.

The nation also faces the depletion of resources that have been essential to its economic growth and well-being. The country's farm and range soil, for example, has lost some fifteen percent of its natural mineral content through erosion and poor agricultural management. In approximately half of the states, water users are pumping more groundwater from wells than nature is replenishing. Such groundwater mining ultimately can deprive regions of necessary irrigation water. The United States Geological Survey, for example, estimates that groundwater shortages will reduce irrigated acreage on the high plains of Texas by over 50 percent by the middle of this century. The National Marine Fisheries Service has classified about a third of the nation's marine fisheries as overfished. So-called "table fish," such as cod and tuna, which historical-

239

ly have provided the bulk of fish for restaurants and stores, are under the heaviest threat.

Hundreds of laws manage and protect United States natural resources—though not always effectively, as these statistics testify. While federal laws such as the Clean Air Act play the dominant role in regulating pollution, state governments provide the principal protection for many natural resources. State, not federal, law primarily controls how land is developed and used, how much water is withdrawn from rivers and underground aquifers, the pace of petroleum extraction, and the taking of wildlife and fresh water fish. The federal role in natural resource policy historically was limited to management of national forests, national parks, and the remainder of the federal public domain. In recent decades, however, the federal role has grown. The Magnuson–Stevens Act manages marine fisheries, including salmon fishing. The Coastal Zone Management Act provides for state-federal coordination in the conservation of coastal regions. As discussed below, the Endangered Species Act and section 404 of the Clean Water Act limit how various environmentally sensitive lands are used. The Endangered Species Act also restricts how much water can be taken from many of the country's rivers, streams, and aquifers.

This Chapter focuses on the three most important state and federal means of protecting environmentally sensitive land and water—the public trust doctrine, section 404 of the Clean Water Act, and the Endangered Species Act. The public trust doctrine provides that state governments own navigable waterways and tidelands in trust for the common use of the public. Beginning in the 1970s, environmental advocates turned to the public trust doctrine as one means of forcing the government to protect these and other resources against development threats. Section 404 of the Clean Water Act and the Endangered Species Act, in turn, are perhaps the most powerful federal laws added in the 1970s to the arsenal of natural resource protections.

II. The Public Trust Doctrine

Throughout history, the law has treated some resources as public commons that belong to all and are irreducible to private ownership. This concept forms the core of the traditional public trust doctrine. Under the Roman Institutes of Justinian, the ocean and its shores, as well as running water and air, were by the "law of nature" *res communes*, incapable of exclusive private ownership.[1] The codes or customs of most European countries subsequently reaffirmed this principle. In the United States, the Northwest Ordinance of 1787 incorporated the

1. J. Inst. 2.1.1.

axiom, declaring that the navigable waters of the Mississippi River "shall be common highways and forever free ... to the citizens of the United States."[2]

The most famous public trust case in the United States is *Illinois Central Railroad Company v. Illinois*.[3] In 1869, Illinois granted over 1,000 acres underlying Lake Michigan along the Chicago shore to the Illinois Central Railroad for harbor and commercial development. Four years later, Illinois changed its mind. The State sued to declare the original grant invalid, and the Supreme Court ruled in its favor, holding that the grant was either voidable or void *ab initio*. The reason, according to the Court, is that submerged lands are "different in character" from other governmentally owned lands. Navigable waterways are of special importance to the public, and the State holds title to the underlying lands "in trust for the people" so that "they may enjoy the navigation of the waters, carry on commerce over them, and have liberty of fishing therein freed from the obstruction or interference of private parties." Although the government might convey small parcels of submerged land to private parties where it would not injure the purposes of the trust, the government cannot convey an entire harbor without violating the public trust.

The public trust doctrine has evolved today in several states to provide environmental protection as well as public access and to cover a broader set of resources. California law illustrates the expansion. In *Marks v. Whitney*,[4] for example, Marks owned tidelands bordering Tomales Bay in Northern California. When Marks threatened to fill and develop the tidelands, a neighboring property owner whose access to the bay would have been blocked sued. The California Supreme Court held that, except in limited situations, the private owner of tidelands holds title subject to the state's public trust. Any member of the public, moreover, can bring a lawsuit to enforce the public trust and enjoin actions that would violate the trust. Most importantly, the purposes of the public trust "are sufficiently flexible to encompass changing public needs." According to the court, one of the most important purposes of the public trust today is to preserve tidelands "in their natural state, so that they may serve as ecological units for scientific study, as open space, and as environments which provide food and habitat for birds and marine life, and which favorably affect the scenery and climate of the area." Marks therefore could not fill or develop the tidelands on his property.

A decade later, the California Supreme Court held that the public trust doctrine also restricts the amount of water that can be withdrawn

2. Northwest Ordinance of 1787, 1 Stat. 50 (1789).

3. 146 U.S. 387 (1892).

4. 491 P.2d 374 (Cal.1971).

from navigable waterways.[5] For years, Los Angeles had diverted water from streams feeding Mono Lake, a large salt water lake in Eastern California that Mark Twain once described as a "solemn, silent, sailless sea," and exported the water over 200 miles to the city's residents. Because of the diversions, Mono Lake had shrunk by a third, and dropping water levels had exposed seagull rookeries to coyotes and other predators. The court concluded that the public trust doctrine applies as much to the waters themselves as to the lands underlying the water. It would do little good to prohibit landowners from filling a waterway if water users simply could suck the waterway dry. The state has a "duty" to protect the public's "common heritage of streams, lakes, marshlands and tidelands." Although the state can authorize people to divert water for domestic or economic use, it must "preserve, so far as consistent with the public interest, the uses protected by the trust." In subsequent proceedings, the California courts ordered Los Angeles to reduce its diversions by about two thirds until the lake level rises to a more acceptable level (a goal expected to take approximately twenty years).

Not every state has followed California's lead. Maine, for example, has decided that the public trust doctrine in that state protects only fishing, fowling, and navigation.[6] Efforts to expand the public trust doctrine, moreover, often have been controversial. When the Idaho Supreme Court tried to apply the public trust doctrine to water diversions, the Idaho legislature passed a law prohibiting the courts from applying the public trust doctrine to water rights or withdrawals.[7] An interesting (and unanswered) question is whether such legislation itself violates the public trust doctrine.

Some commentators have urged courts to use the public trust doctrine even more aggressively to protect environmental resources. Fearing that developers, timber companies, mining companies, and other commercial interests enjoy undue influence in many state legislatures (a fear supported by political science studies), these commentators have argued that the public trust doctrine is essential to safeguard the public's interest in preservation. Although *Illinois Central Railroad* dealt with navigable waterways, the Supreme Court in that case described the public trust doctrine as applying more expansively to "property in which the whole people are interested, like navigable waters and soils underneath them." Shouldn't the public trust doctrine therefore also apply today as a shield against threats to national parks, forests, wetlands, wildlife, and other environmental resources? Courts, however, have shown little interest in extending the public trust doctrine beyond

5. National Audubon Soc. v. Superior Ct., 658 P.2d 709 (Cal.1983).

6. See Bell v. Town of Wells, 557 A.2d 168 (Me.1989).

7. Idaho Code §§ 58–1201 to 59–1203.

its traditional amphibious setting, although one federal district court in the early 1970s suggested in dictum that national parks are subject to a common law public trust.

Critics of the public trust doctrine have argued that the courts are effectively legislating. The legal basis for the public trust has never been clear. If a legislature authorizes water diversions or sells environmentally valuable public lands, what gives the courts the authority to override the legislative judgment? Only constitutions generally trump legislative decisions, yet the few courts to have speculated on the genesis of the public trust doctrine have held that the trust flows from common law, not from state or federal constitutions.

III.   Protecting Wetlands

Many people might find it odd that the government protects "swamps" and "bogs," but wetlands such as these are crucial natural resources. Wetlands, which typically are defined as surface areas that are saturated or inundated with water long enough each year to support hydrophilic ("water-loving") vegetation, provide a variety of valuable services. To start, wetlands help protect waterways, and thus drinking water, from a variety of contaminants. Wetlands, for example, filter out nutrients and other contaminants from water running off of neighboring lands into a waterway. Studies indicate that wetlands retain 80 percent of the phosphorous and 89 percent of the nitrogen found in runoff. Forested wetlands also lower water temperature in hot summer months, reducing harmful algal blooms. In addition, wetlands reduce the risk of floods (which in an average year cause over $4 billion in damages and dozens of deaths). Wetlands act as natural sponges, soaking up water during peak runoffs and then releasing the water slowly over time. A 1993 study by the Illinois State Water Survey estimated that every one percent increase in wetlands along a stream corridor decreases peak stream flows by an average of almost four percent. A Wisconsin study found that watersheds consisting of 30 percent or more wetlands enjoy 60 to 80 percent lower flood-water levels compared to watersheds with no wetlands. By storing water during periods of high precipitation and then releasing the water during the dry season, wetlands also serve as natural reservoirs.

Wetlands also provide crucial habitat for migrating birds and other species. Approximately a third of the domestic species listed as endangered or threatened under the federal Endangered Species Act use wetlands as habitat. Half of the nation's migratory bird species use wetlands as nesting, migratory, or wintering areas. Wetlands also provide nursery or spawning habitat for 60 to 90 percent of the nation's commercial fish species. Because wetlands attract so much wildlife, they serve as an important source of recreation. Each year millions of people use wetlands for nature watching, hunting, hiking, and canoeing. In 1980, 55 million people spent $10 billion observing and photographing waterfowl and other wetlands species.

Wetlands, however, have been under threat for centuries. Hydrologic alterations such as dams and water diversions, urban development, new marinas and harbors, mosquito control programs, peat mining, and agriculture all have contributed over the last several centuries to a dramatic decline in wetlands acreage. In the 1600s, the lower 48 states enjoyed over 220 million acres of wetlands; today, fewer than 110 million acres remain. Both California and Iowa have lost nearly 99 percent of their wetlands. The wetlands that remain, moreover, are often degraded, reducing their ability to provide the valuable services described above.

A majority of states now safeguard their wetlands. The federal government, however, provides the principal protection. Since 1988, the United States has pursued a policy of no net loss of wetlands (although the nation still loses about 100,000 acres of wetlands each year). For historical reasons, the Army Corps of Engineers, which is the engineering wing of the Department of Defense, serves as the key regulatory agency. Federal wetlands regulation grew out of efforts to protect the navigability of the nation's waterways, and navigability was the bailiwick of the Corps. Although the federal EPA today plays an important supporting role (and even has the power to veto some Corps actions), the Corps still takes the lead.

A. Rivers & Harbors Act of 1899

The oldest federal regulatory authority over wetlands is section 10 of the Rivers & Harbors Act of 1899.[8] The principal purpose of the Act is to protect navigation. Section 10 thus prohibits anyone from dredging, filling, or otherwise altering or modifying "navigable waters" without obtaining a permit from the United States Army Corps of Engineers. To qualify for protection under this provision, a wetland must be truly navigable (either now or in the past) or be susceptible of navigation with reasonable improvements. The Act's protection also applies only up to the ordinary high water mark of a waterway. Some wetlands qualify for protection, in which case the Act provides quite broad protections against virtually any form of destruction or modification. Because most wetlands do not qualify for protection, however, section 10 generally serves only a secondary role in federal regulation of wetlands.

B. Section 404 of the Clean Water Act

Section 404 of the Clean Water Act provides the principal protection for wetlands.[9] Under section 404, no one can discharge dredged or fill

8. 33 U.S.C. § 403.
9. 33 U.S.C. § 1344.

materials into a wetland without obtaining a permit from the Army Corps of Engineers. Section 404 enjoys much broader jurisdictional reach than the Rivers & Harbors Act of 1899. Although section 404 again applies only to "navigable waters," the Clean Water Act defines this term as all "waters of the United States including the territorial seas."[10] As described below, courts have interpreted this definition to encompass wetlands that historically would not have been considered navigable. On the downside, however, section 404 regulates only a limited set of activities and contains a number of broad exemptions. While section 10 of the Rivers & Harbors Act restricts both dredging and filling of wetlands, for example, section 404 extends only to discharges of materials into the wetlands. As discussed in more detail below, section 404 also exempts various activities, including normal farming, ranching, and silviculture activities, from its requirements.

Over the past several decades, section 404 has become a legal battlefield as landowners have tried to limit its scope and environmentalists and governmental regulators have tried to stretch its reach as far as possible. Landowners have focused on the term "navigable waters" and argued that, as a matter of both constitutional power and statutory interpretation, section 404 does not apply to nonnavigable wetlands. Environmentalists and governmental regulators, by contrast, have argued that a large number of activities, including dredging, result in illegal "discharges" and thus require permits under section 404. Environmentalists and regulators also have urged courts to interpret the principal exemptions narrowly.

1.   What are "navigable waters"?

The constitutional basis for Congress' regulation of wetlands is the Commerce Clause. For most of the nation's history, Congress believed that its commerce power extended only to navigable waterways. For this reason, section 10 of the Rivers & Harbors Act and most other Congressional water legislation assert authority only over "navigable waters." When Congress drafted section 404 of the Clean Water Act, it used the same terminology. But in an effort to broaden the stretch of the Clean Water Act, Congress then defined the term "navigable waters" to mean the "waters of the United States." The result has been judicial confusion. If Congress meant to regulate all wetlands, why did it use the term "navigable" in section 404? But if Congress did not mean to regulate all wetlands, what is the relevant test for jurisdiction? As is often the case

---

10.   CWA § 502(7), 33 U.S.C. § 1362(7).

in environmental law, Congress was maddeningly obscure, leaving it to the courts and administrative agencies to make the jurisdictional decisions over section 404's breadth of coverage.

The Corps initially took the position that, despite the broad definition of "navigable waters" in the Clean Water Act, its jurisdiction under section 404 extended only to actually, potentially, or historically navigable waterways, which include few wetlands and virtually no freshwater wetlands. Environmental groups successfully challenged this narrow view of the Corps' jurisdiction in *Natural Resources Defense Council v. Callaway*.[11] After reviewing the legislative history of the Clean Water Act, the district court concluded that Congress intended to claim as much jurisdiction as its commerce powers permitted. Rather than appealing the decision, the Corps issued new regulations asserting jurisdiction over not only actually navigable waters, but also adjacent wetlands, interstate wetlands, and intrastate "wetlands, sloughs, prairie potholes, wet meadows, playa lakes, or natural ponds, the use of which could affect interstate or foreign commerce."[12]

The first jurisdictional question to reach the Supreme Court was whether section 404 applies to wetlands that are adjacent to navigable waterways but not themselves navigable. In *United States v. Riverside Bayview Homes, Inc.*,[13] the United States Supreme Court unanimously agreed that the Corps could regulate such wetlands. The Court's logic was simple. Given the broad statutory definition of "navigable waters," the Corps' assertion of authority over wetlands that are integrally connected to actually navigable waters is reasonable. The physical dividing line between navigable waterways and adjoining wetlands is often amorphous, and the federal government could not protect the quality of navigable waterways if it did not enjoy authority over adjacent wetlands.

In the 1990's, the question shifted to whether the Corps possesses authority over isolated wetlands that sit apart from any navigable waters. In its post-*Callaway* regulations, the Corps claimed that section 404's prohibitions extend to isolated wetlands that are the actual or potential habitat for migratory birds. Migratory birds fly across numerous states, and bird hunting involves significant interstate commerce. The Corps therefore believed that the Commerce Clause would cover wetlands meeting the "Migratory Bird Rule." Because over half of all migratory bird species use wetlands as habitat, the Corps also felt that the preservation of such wetlands is important to the protection of these birds.

11. 392 F.Supp. 685 (D.D.C.1975).   **13.** 474 U.S. 121 (1985).
12. 33 C.F.R. § 328.3(a); 40 C.F.R. § 230.3(s).

The Supreme Court granted review in *Solid Waste Agency of Northern Cook County v. United States Army Corps of Engineers*[14] (*"SWANCC"*) to decide whether the Clean Water Act extends this far and, if so, whether the act exceeds Congress' commerce power. The Court did not reach the constitutional question because it concluded, by a close 5–4 vote, that the Corps' Migratory Bird Rule exceeded the Corps' statutory authority. But constitutional concerns played a role in the Court's interpretation of the statute. "Where an administrative interpretation of a statute invokes the outer limits of Congress' power" or "push[es] the limit of congressional authority," there must be clear evidence that Congress intended to assert that authority. This is particularly true, according to the Court, where the interpretation would encroach on a "traditional state power," such as land use regulation. Given these constitutional concerns and Congress' express use of the term "navigable," the Court concluded that section 404 does not extend to wetlands with no connection at all to navigable waters.

A few cases also have dealt with the Corps' jurisdiction over artificially created wetlands. Although regulating artificial wetlands might seem odd or even counterproductive (since it might discourage landowners from creating new wetlands), artificial wetlands can serve the same important functions as natural wetlands, and their destruction can be equally problematic. At least one court has held that the Corps does not have jurisdiction over artificial wetlands that it has helped create through its own civil works (since otherwise the Corps could create jurisdiction for itself by steering water onto private lands) or that are not environmentally beneficial (since there is no evidence that Congress intended to regulate such wetlands).[15] Except in these limited situations, however, courts consistently have held that artificial wetlands are subject to section 404.[16]

2. *What is a "Discharge" of Material?*

Section 404 regulates only "discharges" of materials into wetlands. On the surface, this would suggest that section 404 regulates the filling of wetlands but not other significant threats to wetlands such as draining or dredging. The Corps, however, has tried to assert authority over many of these other threats by adopting a broad interpretation of the term "discharge." Under what was called the "Tulloch rule," for example, the Corps asserted jurisdiction over excavation and dredging operations if they led to *"any* redeposit of dredged material."[17] If someone scooped a bucket of a mud out of a wetland and even a drop of mud fell

---

14. 531 U.S. 159 (2001).

15. See United States v. Fort Pierre, 747 F.2d 464 (8th Cir.1984).

16. See, e.g., Leslie Salt Co. v. United States, 896 F.2d 354 (9th Cir.1990).

17. 58 Fed. Reg. 45,008 (Aug. 25, 1993) (emphasis added).

back into the wetland, the Corps could claim jurisdiction. In practice, this required virtually anyone planning to excavate or dredge a wetland to obtain a permit under section 404.

In *National Mining Association v. United States Army Corps of Engineers*,[18] the D.C. Circuit held that the Tulloch rule exceeded the Corps' statutory authority. To the court, it was absurd to imagine that Congress had intended the term "discharge" to extend to such activities. "Congress could not have contemplated that the attempted removal of 100 tons of [dredged material] could constitute an addition simply because only 99 tons of it were actually taken away." The Corps, however, has resisted the message of this decision. In response to the D.C. Circuit's decision, the Corps merely changed the words *"any* redeposit of dredged material" in its regulatory definition of "discharge" to the words "any redeposit of dredged material *other than incidental fallback.*"[19] The regulations, moreover, provide that the Corps and EPA "regard the use of mechanized earth-moving equipment to conduct landclearing, ditching, channelization, in-stream mining or other earth-moving activity in waters of the United States as resulting in a discharge of dredged material *unless project-specific evidence shows that the activity results in only incidental fallback.*"[20]

Not all courts have been as unreceptive as the D.C. Circuit to the Corps' jurisdictional claims. In *Borden Ranch Partnership v. United States Army Corps of Engineers*,[21] a California real estate developer purchased a large ranch with the intent to convert the ranch into vineyards and orchards and then subdivide it into upscale residential parcels. During rainy periods of the year, a shallow layer of impermeable clay formed vernal pools, swales, and other intermittent wetlands on portions of the ranch. Problems arose when the developer started to "deep rip" these areas to accommodate the deep roots of the vineyards and orchards. Deep ripping, in which tractors drag lengthy metal prongs through the soil, tears the clay layer and thus can destroy the wetlands. By a 2–1 vote, a three–judge panel of the Ninth Circuit Court of Appeals ignored the D.C. Circuit's *Tulloch* decision and held that deep ripping moves and redeposits soil and thus constitutes a "discharge." The Supreme Court granted review, but then affirmed by an equally divided vote without opinions.[22]

The legal dilemma in these cases is that, while section 404 applies literally only to "discharges," a variety of other activities can be equally if not more destructive of wetland services. Courts that apply section 404

18. 145 F.3d 1399 (D.C.Cir.1998).

19. 33 C.F.R. 323.2 (emphasis added).

20. Id. (emphasis added).

21. 261 F.3d 810 (9th Cir.2001).

22. Borden Ranch Partnership v. United States Army Corps of Engineers, 123 S.Ct. 599 (2002). Justice Kennedy did not participate, setting the stage for a 4–4 tie.

broadly, like the Ninth Circuit in *Borden Ranch*, focus on the environmental purposes of section 404 and try their best to manipulate the language of the Clean Water Act to accomplish those purposes. Courts like the D.C. Circuit in the *Tulloch* case take the language more literally.

Why did Congress not use more sweeping language like that found in the Rivers and Harbors Act? The reason may be simply historical: the Clean Water Act was concerned with pollution—and thus "discharges"—rather than with broader environmental problems. Whatever the reason, however, courts must continue to struggle with the inherent tension in section 404 between purpose and language.

3. *Special Exceptions*

Section 404 exempts a variety of activities from its permit requirements. Perhaps most important are the farming exceptions, which exempt "normal farming, silviculture, and ranching activities such as plowing, seeding, cultivating, minor drainage, harvesting for the production of food, fiber, and forest products, or upland soil and water conservation practices."[23] Also exempt is the "construction of farm or stock ponds or irrigation ditches."[24] These exceptions again demonstrate the political power of the agricultural community. The exempt activities often are no less harmful to wetland services than other forms of discharges, so the only justification is that farming is important enough to justify the loss of wetlands. Congress, however, placed a limit on the exemptions. Under what is known as the "recapture provision," even an otherwise exempt activity needs a permit if the activity would change the use of the land and either impair the "flow or circulation of navigable waters" or reduce the "reach of such waters."[25]

Whenever environmental regulations contain a "loophole," of course, members of the regulated community will try to squeeze through it. In the *Borden Ranch* case, for example, the developer argued that the deep ripping was exempt from section 404 because it was a "normal farming" activity like plowing. The majority in *Borden Ranch* held that the exemption did not apply because the developer was converting the land from wetlands to vineyards, triggering the recapture provision. Courts in general have been unsympathetic to farmers seeking to change wetlands into farmland. The legislative history of section 404 makes clear that, while Congress was willing to tolerate some harm to wetlands from farming activities, it did not intend to allow wholesale conversion of sizable amounts of wetlands into dry land.

---

23. CWA § 404(f)(1)(A), 33 U.S.C. § 1344(f)(1)(A).

24. CWA § 404(f)(1)(C), 33 U.S.C. § 1344(f)(1)(C).

25. CWA § 404(f)(2), 33 U.S.C. § 1344(f)(2).

4. The Permitting Process

The Clean Water Act provides little guidance regarding the appropriate standards for issuing a permit. Instead, section 404(b) instructs EPA to develop appropriate guidelines. Under these guidelines, anyone seeking a permit must show that

(1) there is no practicable alternative to the proposed activity that would have less impact on the aquatic ecosystem,

(2) the proposed activity will not have significant adverse impacts on aquatic resources;

(3) all "appropriate and practicable" mitigation will be employed, and

(4) the proposed activity will not violate other state or federal laws (such as the Endangered Species Act).[26]

Even if an activity would meet these specific requirements, the Corps also will scrutinize the activity under its own regulations to see if it would be "contrary to the public interest." In making this determination, the Corps will consider a broad range of factors, including the effect of the activity on fish, wildlife, water quality, flood control, recreation, and aesthetics.[27]

EPA's "no practicable alternative" standard has generated significant legal controversy. Although the presence or absence of practicable alternatives might seem a straightforward inquiry, whether something is a practicable alternative can depend on both *how* you define the purpose of the proposed activity and *when* you look to see if there is an alternative. Imagine, for example, that a developer plans to build condominiums along the waterfront of Rivertown. There might be many alternative sites if the purpose is simply to build condominiums, but no alternative site if the purpose is to build waterfront condominiums complete with a boat dock. Indeed, EPA's guidelines presume that there is a practicable alternative where a proposed land use "does not require access or proximity" to a waterway.[28] Similarly, a waterfront parcel down the road that does not involve wetlands might be a practicable alternative in 2002 when it is vacant and on the market, but not five years later when someone has bought and built a restaurant on the land.

Courts have been somewhat inconsistent in how they have determined the purpose of a proposed activity. According to the courts, the Corps must take into account how the *applicant* defines the purpose. If a resort developer sets out to build a resort with a golf course, for example, a resort without a golf course generally would not be a practicable

26. 40 C.F.R. § 230.10.
27. 40 C.F.R. § 320.4.

28. 40 C.F.R. § 230.10(a).

alternative.[29] But the applicant cannot "define a project in order to preclude the existence of any alternative sites and thus make what is practicable appear impracticable."[30] Nor does an alternative "have to accommodate components of a project that are merely incidental to the applicant's basic purpose."[31] Courts unfortunately have been less than clear about how the Corps should determine whether a project component, like a golf course, is or is not "merely incidental." As to timing, the one published opinion to consider the issue held that the Corps should determine whether alternatives were available at the time of "market entry." If alternative land sites were available when the applicant first started looking for a parcel to develop, the Corps should deny the permit even if the parcel is no longer available today.[32]

Another critical question is the adequacy of the proposed mitigation. The Corps' first preference is to avoid *any* negative impact on the wetland. If this is not possible, the Corps will look to see if the direct impact can be reduced. If the impact cannot be avoided or sufficiently minimized, the Corps will require the applicant to restore, enhance, or create other wetlands. This is known as "compensatory mitigation." The Corps prefers on-site mitigation to off-site mitigation and prefers that the applicant restore, enhance, or create the same general type of wetland as the wetland that is harmed. In evaluating such mitigation, the Corps favors restoration of prior wetlands over enhancement of low-quality wetlands and favors enhancement over the creation of new wetlands. In rare cases, the Corps even may accept protection of other existing wetlands as adequate mitigation, but this is the Corps' least favored option.

Determining compensatory mitigation on a permit-by-permit basis is not ideal. The resulting restoration and preservation efforts are often piecemeal and uncoordinated, and the costs of monitoring and enforcing the mitigation are high. For these reasons, the Corps has encouraged mitigation banking in which private or public organizations restore, enhance, or create wetlands on a coordinated basis in a region and use the mitigation "credits" to satisfy the 404 mitigation requirements for individual development projects. In private mitigation banks, developers themselves create and operate banks in order to generate credits for their future development plans. In commercial or public mitigation banks, third parties develop the bank and then sell or transfer the resulting credits to developers wishing to meet their 404 mitigation requirements. Today wetlands mitigation banking resembles a commodity market, with freewheeling, entrepreneurial wetlands banks offering

---

29. Sylvester v. Army Corps of Engineers, 882 F.2d 407 (9th Cir.1989).

30. Id.

31. Id.

32. See Bersani v. U.S. EPA, 850 F.2d 36 (2d Cir.1988).

for sale (and often profit) finished off-site wetlands as credits to anyone in need of mitigation for their 404 permits.

Despite its potential advantages, wetlands mitigation banking also poses several possible problems. First, unless the mitigation wetlands are of similar composition to the destroyed wetlands, the mitigation wetlands may not be able to provide the same level and type of ecosystem services (such as nutrient retention, habitat, or flood control) as the destroyed wetlands furnished. Indeed an alarmingly high percentage of mitigation wetlands fail to function effectively at all. More subtly, because the wetlands banks are rarely adjacent to the wetlands that are being destroyed, the ecosystem services provided by the mitigation wetlands will generally be of lower value for the simple reason that mitigation wetlands are built where land is cheap and, therefore, far from towns. For services to be valuable, however, they need to be delivered to people. The service of flood control, for example, is worth very little if the floods are not diverted from where people live.

5. General Permits

Of the approximately 100,000 activities each year that fall within the Corps' section 404 jurisdiction, only about 15 percent go through the full regulatory review process. The vast majority of the activities are covered by generic nationwide, regional, or programmatic permits known as "general permits." People seeking to engage in an activity covered by a general permit do not need to file individual applications and often do not even need to notify the Corps beforehand, so long as they comply with the conditions set out in the general permit.

To date, the Corps has issued over 35 nationwide general permits. Under section 404(e) of the Clean Water Act, the Corps is to issue general permits only if it determines that the authorized activities "are similar in nature, will cause only minimal adverse environmental effects when performed separately, and will have only minimal cumulative adverse effect on the environment." But in an effort to reduce administrative burdens on both it and applicants, the Corps often has pushed the limits of its authority to avoid full permitting review by issuing general permits. The most controversial general permit for many years was Nationwide Permit 26, which authorized the filling of up to three acres of isolated wetlands for commercial or residential purposes. Faced by mounting criticism that Nationwide Permit 26 was leading to significant cumulative reductions in wetland acreage, the Corps allowed the permit to expire in 2000, replacing it with Nationwide Permit 39, which authorizes the filling of only half an acre or less subject to significant restrictions and mitigation measures, including the maintenance of a vegetation buffer. Like Nationwide Permit 26, Nationwide Permit 39 can undermine the goal of "no net loss" because no compensatory mitigation is required.

6.   EPA Vetoes

Congress did not entirely trust the Corps, which historically has not enjoyed a good environmental record, to police the nation's wetlands. While awarding the Corps the principal permitting authority, Congress therefore asked EPA to develop the permitting guidelines. Congress, moreover, also awarded EPA veto power over the Corps' decisions. Under section 404(c), EPA can veto a permit if it determines, after public comments and notice, that the proposed discharge "will have an unacceptable adverse effect on municipal water supplies, shellfish beds and fishery areas (including spawning and breeding areas), wildlife, or recreational areas." EPA has used its veto authority only sparingly. As of 2000, EPA had vetoed only eleven of the 150,000 permits that the Corps had issued since 1979. But the ever-present threat of a veto almost certainly encourages the Corps to be vigilant in its protection of wetlands.

7.   Constitutional Takings Challenges

Section 404 has probably generated more takings challenges in the last decade than any other federal regulatory scheme. Many property owners who have been denied permits have sued, arguing that section 404 has taken their property by depriving them of any use of the protected wetlands in violation of *Lucas v. South Carolina Coastal Council*.[33] As discussed in Chapter 3, one major issue in these cases is whether the wetlands can be viewed in isolation in applying the *Lucas* test. Where the wetlands are part of a larger parcel of land owned by the plaintiff, courts have generally held that there is no taking because the plaintiff can still use the remaining land. However, where the remaining land is physically separate or when the wetlands were purchased separately, courts sometimes have found takings.[34] Another frequent question is whether the protected wetlands are truly worthless simply because the property owner cannot develop the wetlands under section 404. The wetlands often retain some modicum of value for recreational use or as open space or even a speculative investment.

C.   Incentive Programs

Just as in the pollution field, incentives often can be a more effective means than command and control regulations of protecting natural

---

33.   505 U.S. 1003 (1992). See p. 66 supra.

34.   See, e.g., Loveladies Harbor v. United States, 28 F.3d 1171 (Fed.Cir.1994).

resources. The federal government has created a number of important incentives for wetlands protection, all of which play a crucial role in helping the nation meet its goal of no net loss. The federal Swampbuster program, for example, denies specified agricultural benefits to farmers who convert non-exempt wetlands into farmland without complying with an approved wetlands conservation plan. Wetlands are exempt if they were previously converted or artificially created or can be farmed with minimal environmental impact. The Department of Agriculture estimates, based on the economics of the agricultural sector, that the Swampbuster program is preventing the conversion of over 200,000 acres of wetlands each year.

In the Swampbuster program, Congress is leveraging its existing farm subsidies to protect wetlands; the program costs the federal government nothing. In other cases, Congress uses tax dollars to encourage wetlands restoration and conservation. Under the Wetland Reserve Program (WRP), for example, the Department of Agriculture pays landowners who restore and protect wetlands on their property.[35] In most cases, the landowners provide the federal government with a permanent easement encumbering their wetlands. WRP currently protects almost a million acres of wetlands throughout the United States. The federal government also protects over 500,000 acres of privately-held wetlands through short-term conservation agreements entered into under the Water Bank Act of 1970.[36]

IV. The Endangered Species Act

Most scientists agree that the world is experiencing the highest rate of species extinction since dinosaurs died out sixty–five million years ago, although the exact size of the current extinction "crisis" is uncertain. Some scientists estimate that, at the current rate of extinction, only half of the world's existing species will survive to the end of this century. Even conservative estimates peg current species loss to be three or four orders of magnitude greater than the historical average. In the United States alone over the last century some sixty species of mammals and forty species of freshwater fish have died out.

Humans are the major cause of the current wave of extinctions. Through habitat degradation, introduction of exotic species, and over-hunting, humans threaten the continued existence of a growing number of species. Habitat destruction and modification are the major threats in the United States. Urban sprawl and such commercial land uses as farming, ranching, and silviculture reduce the amount of habitat usable

35. 16 U.S.C. § 3837.   **36.** 16 U.S.C. §§ 1301–1311.

by endangered species and fragment what habitat remains. Competition from exotic species for food and habitat is a growing threat. Some exotic species purposefully have been introduced into the United States, while others have smuggled in as uninvited guests on cargo ships, airplanes, and other objects. Overhunting and overfishing of species are of less importance than habitat destruction and exotics, but still threaten a significant number of species ranging from various runs of salmon to assorted species of freshwater mussels. Various species also face a variety of other threats, including pollution, automobiles, and natural disturbances.

The Endangered Species Act ("ESA") provides the strongest federal protection against species loss. As described in more detail below, the ESA flatly bans the hunting or killing of endangered species and protects against significant habitat loss. But the ESA is not a complete or perfect solution. The ESA does not effectively address the problem of exotic species. Indeed, no federal or state law currently provides a comprehensive and workable solution to this problem. More importantly, the ESA provides no protection to a species until that species is in serious danger of extinction. The ESA thus takes an "emergency room" approach to biodiversity. Rather than protecting species or ecosystems when they are healthy, the ESA waits until a species is on the brink of extinction. At that stage, however, saving the species is often very difficult. If a species already has lost virtually all of its habitat, for example, preserving the remaining habitat may not be sufficient to restore the species to its prior health. The remaining habitat, moreover, often is subject to strong development pressure.

Despite the ESA's limits, economic interests attack the ESA for going too far in protecting species. In many regions of the nation, the ESA restricts new land development, angering property owners and local governments. In the western United States, the ESA has reduced the amount of water that farmers and cities can divert from rivers and other waterways. The ESA also constrains the federal government's freedom to build dams and freeways, to develop timber, petroleum, and other natural resources, and to take a variety of other actions of importance to various political constituencies.

The Congress that passed the ESA in 1973 had no idea how controversial the law would become. No Senator and only four members of the House voted against the ESA. Most legislators thought that the ESA simply protected charismatic birds and megafauna, such as grizzly bears, bald eagles, and alligators, against hunters and poachers. Few newspapers thought that the ESA's passage was important enough even to report. But as discussed below, they were wrong. For all its failings, the ESA today is perhaps the most powerful natural resources law in the nation or, for that matter, in the world.

A major controversy is whether the ESA should balance the benefits of preserving a species against the economic costs of preservation. As you will see, cost plays only a marginal role in the direct implementation of the ESA's regulatory restrictions. Federal agencies, for example, cannot take any action that would jeopardize the continued existence of an endangered species or materially alter the species' "critical habitat," no matter how valuable the action would be to society. Where the habitat is located on private land, property owners cannot use their land in a way that would appreciably reduce the likelihood that the species will survive and recover, no matter how valuable the land use. This does not mean that cost is irrelevant. Congress has never provided the funds needed to ensure full recovery of endangered species under the ESA—reflecting an implicit judgment that other budgetary items are more important. Faced with significant regulatory costs, moreover, property owners and other interest groups have tried, sometimes successfully, to undermine or weaken ESA regulation through lawsuits, Congressional legislation, and political pressure. But the ESA's prohibitions do not provide for any explicit balancing of costs and benefits.

How much should society be willing to spend in order to protect and restore endangered species? To many people, the answer is "however much it takes!" Under some biocentric views of nature, species have an intrinsic right to exist and thrive, and humans have an obligation to respect that right. Many religions, moreover, believe that humans have an ethical obligation to be careful stewards of nature. When Congress threatened to weaken the ESA in the mid–1990s, then Secretary of the Interior Bruce Babbitt turned to the Bible, and particularly the story of Noah, for defense.[37] From these various perspectives, species have an infinite or incalculable value.

To many other people, however, the question is more utilitarian: how much are the endangered species worth to humans? Answering this question is difficult because many of the values are not readily measurable. Some endangered species, such as salmon, have an easily quantified value to humans as food, clothing, or some other commercially traded good. Others, like whales, might have an indirect commercial value as the focus of ecotourism. Most endangered species, however, do not have any significant commercial value, which is the principal reason they are endangered. Property owners and the government, seeing little direct market value from the species, prefer to devote the species' habitat to "more valuable" economic uses that are often incompatible with the species' continued existence.

37. The Bible unfortunately is a two–edged sword on this issue. For every passage that emphasizes the importance of stewardship, there are other passages that emphasize humans' dominion over non-human species.

When Congress passed the ESA in 1973, some members of Congress believed that we should preserve species for their potential genetic value in the development of pharmaceutical, industrial, or agricultural products. Indeed, one frequently cited House report concluded that the "value of this genetic heritage is, quite literally, incalculable ..... Who knows, or can say, what potential cures for cancer or other scourges, present or future, may lie locked up in the structures of plants which may yet be undiscovered, much less analyzed?"[38] Species do sometimes provide valuable drugs or genetic information. The oft-cited rosy periwinkle of Madagascar, for example, yielded cures for both lymphocytic leukemia and Hodgkin's disease. Economic studies, however, suggest that the expected value from saving any particular species is quite small, in part because the same genetic information or chemical compounds often will be found in multiple species. According to one study of the value for pharmaceuticals, only ten in 250,000 species, at best, are likely to produce commercially valuable discoveries, yielding an expected value per individual species of less than $10,000.

Turning to potentially greater values, biodiversity (which constitutes the overall community of organisms within a habitat and the physical conditions under which they live) provides a wide range of "ecosystem services" of immense importance to humans. These services include detoxification and decomposition of wastes, purification of air and water, generation and renewal of soil and soil fertility, pollination of crops and natural vegetation, control of harmful agricultural pests, support of cultural activities, and the provision of aesthetic beauty and pleasure. Economists estimate that the overall value of these services is immense, totaling in the trillion of dollars. The contribution of any individual species to these values, however, is typically uncertain and, in many cases, may be insignificant.

Many people, of course, value the preservation of even commercially worthless species—and this value must go into any utilitarian calculation of the value of protecting endangered species. Using the "contingent valuation methodology" or CVM (see page 34), some economists have tried to estimate such *nonuse values* by asking people in surveys how much they would be willing to pay to save a species. Most people report that they are willing to pay significant sums, even to save those species with little known commercial value. American residents have reported a "willingness to pay" ranging from $5–10 per household for some less known fish such as the striped shiner to $95 per household for more infamous and charismatic species such as the northern spotted owl. Many economists have questioned the accuracy of these numbers. As explained in Chapter 2, the survey results often appear to be inconsis-

38. H.R. Rep. No. 93–412, 93d Cong., 1st Sess. 4–5 (1973).

tent with basic economic principles and vary considerably with the exact questions asked. Some critics, moreover, suspect that people report high values not because they would be willing to pay that much but because they want the surveyor to think that they are moral and environmentally conscious. No matter what the deficiencies of CVM, however, it is the best means currently available to estimate nonuse values.

Two federal agencies split administrative responsibilities under the ESA. The Fish & Wildlife Service (FWS) within the Department of the Interior is responsible for protecting terrestrial and avian species and freshwater fish. The National Marine Fisheries Service (NMFS) within the Department of Commerce takes responsibility for marine species, including anadromous fish such as salmon. Interestingly, the only major debate within the Congressional conference committee that put the finishing touches on the ESA was how to allocate responsibility between these two agencies. Most observers believe that the FWS is more protective and proactive than NMFS, and occasionally policymakers propose returning NMFS to the Department of the Interior, where NMFS was part of the FWS prior to 1970. The odds on such a move, however, are currently slim to none. For convenience, the remainder of this chapter will refer to the FWS alone as the ESA implementing agency. Far more species fall within the FWS' jurisdiction so it is the principal agency. When you read "FWS," however, keep in mind that it can be either the FWS or NMFS depending on the species under protection.

A. Listing Species

The ESA protects only those species that are listed by the FWS as either *endangered* or *threatened*.[39] A species is endangered if the FWS finds that it is "in danger of extinction throughout all or a significant portion of its range."[40] A species is threatened if it is "likely to become an endangered species in the foreseeable future."[41] Congress created the "threatened" category both to provide some protection to species before they are on the very edge of extinction and as a "halfway house" for species on the road to recovery. For most purposes, the ESA provides the same protections to endangered and threatened species, although there are some differences under section 9 as discussed below.

Under section 4 of the ESA, the FWS can decide to list a species on its own initiative, or an individual or organization can petition to list the

---

39. There is one exception to this rule. If a species so closely resembles a listed species that it also requires protection, section 4(e) of the ESA authorizes the FWS to list the similar species even if it is not endangered or threatened.

40. ESA § 3(6), 16 U.S.C. § 1532(6).

41. ESA § 3(20), 16 U.S.C. § 1532(20).

species. When Congress passed the current ESA in 1973, the government already had listed 392 species under a prior version of the Act. Almost thirty years later, over 1800 species have been listed under the ESA, of which over 1250 are found in the United States. Of the listed domestic species, over 500 are animals and almost 750 are plants. About 80 percent of the U.S. species are listed as endangered, with the remainder categorized as threatened. All states, as well as the District of Columbia and Puerto Rico, host at least a handful of listed species. Listed species, however, tend to be found more often in those areas naturally high in biodiversity and threatened by significant habitat modification. Thus Hawaii has the most listed species (over 300), followed closely behind by California. Other states in the "top six" are Alabama, Florida, Tennessee, and Texas.

In deciding whether to list a species, the FWS sometimes must decide what is a *species*. If a flower is very similar to a known species but the flower appears to have slightly smaller petals, for example, is the flower a separate species? If two separate plant species combine to reproduce, is the resulting plant a new and distinct species or merely a hybrid? Unfortunately, the ESA does not define the term "species" or address these issues. In light of the ESA's silence and the FWS's expertise, courts have been very deferential to the FWS's judgment as to what constitutes a species. The issue is further complicated, however, by the fact that the ESA authorizes the FWS to list not only individual species but also *subspecies* and, in the case of vertebrates, *distinct population segments* that interbreed when mature. Because of their role as reservoirs of genetic diversity, the loss of some subspecies and local populations ultimately can endanger the species as a whole even if other populations currently are numerous; individual populations and subspecies, moreover, can be of ecological or aesthetic importance to a local region. The ESA, however, once again fails to define subspecies and distinct population segments, making the listing of subspecies and distinct populations ripe for controversy.

The ESA tries to keep economic and political considerations out of listing decisions. Under the ESA, the FWS must determine within 90 days of receiving a listing petition whether the petition presents sufficient evidence to pursue a full review of the species' status and must decide within a year of that determination whether to list the species. The FWS must list a species if it finds that "natural or manmade factors" make the species endangered or threatened. The FWS must use the "best scientific and commercial data available" and cannot consider the potential economic consequences of listing the species. In an effort to support the scientific basis for its decisions, the FWS also has adopted a peer review policy of seeking the expert opinions of outside specialists before making a listing determination.

Because listings require the application of scientific expertise, courts have been reticent to overturn the FWS's determinations. Courts review the substance of the determinations under the liberal "arbitrary and capricious" standard and overturn the decisions only where the agency has "failed to articulate a satisfactory explanation for its actions."[42] Courts also generally have resisted ordering the FWS to engage in additional scientific research before deciding whether to list a species, noting that the ESA only requires the FWS to consider the best scientific information "available."

The FWS, nonetheless, often faces significant pressure not to list a species. Where listings are likely to limit local development or other economic activity, property owners and other affected interests often threaten lawsuits or seek Congressional or White House intervention. Despite its strict deadlines and requirements, the ESA provides the FWS with a variety of ways to avoid listing a species. The FWS, for example, can conclude that it needs additional information to decide whether a species should be listed (although courts have warned that the ESA does not require "conclusive evidence" before a species should be listed[43]). Under the ESA, the FWS also can conclude that listing is "warranted," but that immediate listing of the species is "precluded" by higher listing priorities (i.e., the agency is too busy at the moment on other, more important listings).[44] As of mid–2002, over 250 species were languishing in this purgatory status of *candidate species*. At times Congress itself directly intervenes in the listing process. In 1995, for example, Congress imposed a moratorium on new listings for approximately a year.

The FWS also sometimes tries to avoid listings by asserting that other efforts to preserve a species provide adequate protection. The ESA explicitly permits the FWS, in deciding whether to list a species, to consider "efforts, if any, being made by any State ... or any political subdivision of a State ... to protect" the species.[45] Courts, however, have been skeptical of FWS reliance on state and local efforts unless those efforts are in place, enforceable, and comparable to protections provided under the ESA. In recent years, the FWS also has argued that it has the authority to consider all conservation efforts, including efforts being made by private entities.[46] This argument, which relies on a general provision of the ESA requiring the FWS to consider "other natural or manmade factors affecting [a species'] continued existence,"[47] remains untested.

42. Northern Spotted Owl v. Hodel, 716 F.Supp. 479 (W.D.Wash.1988).

43. E.g., Defenders of Wildlife v. Babbitt, 958 F.Supp. 670 (D.D.C.1997).

44. ESA § 4(b)(3)(B)(iii), 16 U.S.C. § 1533(b)(3)(B)(iii).

45. ESA § 4(b)(1)(A), 16 U.S.C. § 1533(b)(1)(A).

46. See Announcement of Draft Policy for Evaluation of Conservation Efforts When Making Listing Decisions, 65 Fed. Reg. 37102 (June 13, 2000).

47. ESA § 4(a)(1)(E), 16 U.S.C. § 1533(a)(1)(E).

B. Limits on Federal Agency Actions

Under section 7(a)(2) of the ESA, all federal agencies must consult with the FWS before taking any action that might affect either an endangered or threatened species and must insure that the action is not "likely" either (1) to "jeopardize the continued existence" of the species or (2) to "result in the destruction or adverse modification of [the critical] habitat of such species." As the Supreme Court emphasized in *TVA v. Hill*,[48] this mandate permits no consideration of cost. "The plain intent of Congress in enacting [the ESA] was to halt and reverse the trend towards species extinction, whatever the cost." According to the Court, "Congress intended endangered species to be afforded the highest priorities," adopting a policy which the House Report on the ESA described as the "institutionalization of . . . caution."[49] If written today, the House Report almost certainly would have spoken in terms of the precautionary principle (discussed earlier at pages 13–14).

TVA v. Hill is one of the most famous environmental cases of the twentieth century and offers a number of useful lessons. Environmentalists for years had been trying to block the Tennessee Valley Authority (TVA) from building the Tellico Dam. The dam promised little hydroelectricity or other benefits, yet would destroy the last free flowing stretch of the Little Tennessee River and flood a beautiful valley rich in farmland and sacred Indian sites. No law, however, proscribed a dam because its environmental costs outweighed its economic benefits. The National Environmental Policy Act, described in the next chapter, required TVA to examine the environmental costs but imposed no substantive mandates. Stopping the dam seemed a lost cause until an ichthyologist, shortly after the ESA was passed, discovered snail darters, a previously unknown species of perch about three inches long, just downstream from the dam site. After the species was listed as endangered, several individuals and a local environmental group sued under the ESA's citizen suit provision to enjoin the dam as a violation of section 7(a)(2).

The major issue in *TVA v. Hill* was whether the ESA required courts to enjoin a dam that was essentially complete and had cost almost $80 million. As noted, a majority of the Court concluded that Congress meant to forbid agency actions that jeopardized the continued existence of endangered species, no matter what the economic costs. Justices Powell and Blackmun dissented, arguing that the ESA did not apply to projects that already were underway when the Act was passed. Justice

---

48.   437 U.S. 153 (1978).

49.   H.R. Rep. No. 93–412, at 4–5 (1973).

Rehnquist also dissented, contending that, absent clear Congressional directives to the contrary, courts retain the equitable discretion to deny injunctions where the costs of the injunction would far outweigh the benefits.[50]

Congress responded to *TVA v. Hill* by creating an Endangered Species Committee, colloquially known as the God Squad because of its power to determine the fate of a species.[51] The God Squad is a cabinet-level committee, comprised of the Secretaries of Agriculture, the Army, and Interior; the Administrators of EPA and National Oceanic and Atmospheric Administration (NMFS's mother agency); the Chairman of the Council of Economic Advisors; and a state representative appointed by the President. At the request of any federal agency, state governor, or permit applicant, the God Squad can vote to exempt a federal action from section 7(a)(2) if it determines that there are no "reasonable and prudent alternatives," the benefits of the action "clearly outweigh" the environmental costs, and the action is of "regional or national significance."[52] In granting an exemption, the God Squad also can require "reasonable mitigation and enhancement measures."[53]

Congress expected that the God Squad would exempt the Tellico Dam, overturning the Supreme Court's decision. But the God Squad unanimously denied an exemption, finding that the dam was not worth completing even if one ignored the snail darter. Secretary of the Interior Cecil Andrus bemoaned that he hated "to see the snail darter get the credit for stopping a project that was ill-conceived and uneconomical in the first place." In 1980, Congress nonetheless exempted the Tellico Dam from the ESA in a rider to a military appropriations bill. Although TVA completed the dam and thus destroyed the snail darter's principal known habitat, other populations of snail darters were discovered later in the main stretch of the Tennessee River and a number of its tributaries. In 1984, the FWS upgraded the snail darter's status from endangered to threatened.

What are the lessons of *TVA v. Hill*? From a legal perspective, the main lesson is that agencies cannot use cost as an excuse for not complying with the requirements of section 7(a)(2). *TVA v. Hill* also teaches that, if Congress wants to exempt a project from the dictates of the ESA (or any other federal environmental statute for that matter), it better be clear. Subsequent to the discovery and listing of the snail

---

50. Although Justice Rehnquist failed to convince any other justice that the ESA permits courts to exercise equitable discretion in deciding whether to enjoin agency actions, he later convinced a majority that courts do retain equitable discretion in an injunction action under the Clean Water Act. See Weinberger v. Romero–Barcelo, 456 U.S. 305 (1982).

51. ESA § 7(e), 16 U.S.C. § 1536(e).

52. ESA § 7(h), 16 U.S.C. § 1536(h).

53. ESA § 7(h)(1)(B), 16 U.S.C. § 1536(h)(1)(B).

darter, Congress repeatedly had appropriated funds to continue constructing the Tellico Dam and, in reports accompanying the appropriation bills, declared that the ESA should not stand in the way of the dam. Noting that courts should be reticent to conclude that Congress has repealed a law by implication, however, the Court held that the appropriation bills did not exempt the Tellico Dam from the ESA. In a more recent lawsuit, the Ninth Circuit Court of Appeals held that a law authorizing the University of Arizona to build three telescopes on Mount Graham, even if the construction would jeopardize the continued existence of the endangered Mount Graham red squirrel, did not exempt construction of one of the telescopes at a slightly different location than that specified in the law.[54]

TVA v. Hill also demonstrates the immense importance of the ESA in protecting natural resources. The ESA is one of the few federal laws in the natural resources field with real teeth. NEPA, as discussed in the next chapter, is purely procedural. Environmental groups wishing to derail or modify a proposed federal action thus will look to see if the action might menace a listed species. Opponents of the ESA often accuse environmental groups of using the ESA for "ulterior" purposes. The opponents are correct that environmental groups often oppose federal actions for multiple reasons, of which harm to the listed species may be the least important. Unfortunately, there is no federal law outlawing federal actions that are, to use Cecil Andrus' phrase, "ill-conceived and uneconomical," so environmental groups often are forced to turn to the ESA for help. For better or worse, the ESA remains the strongest tool that environmental groups have to help shape natural resource policy in the United States.

The aftermath of *TVA v. Hill* also illustrates that, no matter what a statute might say, cost and politics are realities of regulation. Given the local political and economic support for the Tellico Dam, completion of the dam may have been inevitable. To date, the God Squad has exempted only two projects (and one of those exemptions was reversed).[55] But few agencies have requested exemptions, in large part because the FWS often finds ways to allow federal actions to proceed forward in the face of jeopardy determinations at only slight cost and inconvenience to the agencies and their constituents. Professor Oliver Houck of Tulane Law School studied 186,000 federal projects that the FWS and NMFS reviewed under section 7(a)(2) from 1987 through 1995. The FWS and NMFS required alterations or delays for less than three percent of the

54. Mount Graham Coalition v. Thomas, 53 F.3d 970 (9th Cir.1995).

55. See Portland Audubon Soc'y v. Endangered Species Comm., 984 F.2d 1534 (9th Cir.1993) (reversing an exemption for thirteen timber sales that would have jeopardized the endangered northern spotted owl). The only lasting exemption was for the Gray Rocks Dam, which jeopardized the endangered whooping crane.

projects and blocked less than 0.05 percent. Most of the mandated alterations, moreover, were minor and undemanding.[56]

Recall that an agency violates section 7(a)(2) if its action will either "jeopardize the continued existence" of a listed species *or* destroy or adversely modify a species' "critical habitat." While it seems obvious today, the dual-pronged strategy of protecting both a species *and* its habitat was an important innovation at the time of the ESA's passage. The ESA requires the FWS to designate a species' critical habitat at the same time that it lists the species, so long as the designation is "prudent and determinable."[57] Because the cost of determining a species' critical habitat can cost as much $500,000 and use scarce agency resources, however, the FWS typically chooses to postpone designating critical habitat. Indeed, at the end of 2002, the FWS had designated critical habitat for less than 15 percent of domestic listed species. Because cost is not a legitimate factor in deciding *whether* to designate critical habitat, the FWS generally argues that it does not have sufficient information to determine the critical habitat or that designation would be imprudent (e.g., because the designation would alert poachers and collectors where to find the endangered species and thus increase the risk to the species). This practice has put the FWS on a collision course with environmental groups, which believe that the designation of critical habitat is important in enforcing section 7(a)(2). In recent years, environmental groups have brought and won a number of important lawsuits to force the FWS to designate critical habitat.

In contrast to the decision of *whether* to designate critical habitat, the decision of *how much* and *which* habitat to designate as "critical" is one of the few situations where the ESA permits the FWS to consider cost. In deciding what is critical habitat, the FWS must take "into consideration the economic impact, and any other relevant impact, of specifying any particular area as critical habitat." The FWS can exclude an area from the critical habitat if the benefits of excluding the area outweigh the benefits of including it, unless the exclusion "will result in the extinction of the species concerned."[58] Forced by lawsuit to designate critical habitat but lacking the resources to do so, the FWS sometimes has responded by designating broad swaths of land. Property owners and local governments have responded by suing to exclude land on economic grounds. Until Congress gives the FWS sufficient funding to conduct full evaluations of critical habitat, the FWS is between a rock and a hard place. Try to put off the designations, and environmental groups will

---

56. Oliver A. Houck, The Endangered Species Act and Its Implementation by the U.S. Departments of Interior and Commerce, 64 U. Colo. L. Rev. 277 (1993).

57. ESA § 4(a)(3), 16 U.S.C. § 1533(a)(3).

58. ESA § 4(b)(2), 16 U.S.C. § 1533(b)(2).

sue. Try to err in favor of designating all potential habitat, and property owners will sue.

An important but open issue under section 7(a)(2) is the degree, if any, to which it applies to actions that jeopardize the continued existence of species outside the United States. The FWS originally issued a regulation providing that section 7(a)(2) applies to federal actions both inside and outside the United States. Under this regulation, if the U.S. Agency for International Development (AID) had loaned money to construct an overseas dam that would flood the habitat of a listed species, AID would have had to consult with the FWS under section 7. In 1986, however, the FWS changed its mind and issued a revised regulation requiring agencies to consult only with regard to actions taken in the United States or on the high seas.[59] Several environmental organizations sued to invalidate the revised regulation in *Lujan v. Defenders of Wildlife*,[60] but the Supreme Court found that the organizations did not have standing (see page 74). The validity of the regulation still remains untested. A related question is whether section 7(a)(2) applies to federal agency actions taken *in* the United States that affect species *outside* the nation's borders. That issue is currently before the courts in connection with federal water projects on the Colorado River that reduce the flow to the Colorado River Delta, an area of historically high biodiversity with a number of endangered species. The government argues that it need not comply with section 7(a)(2); environmentalists disagree. The government's position on these issues is weak. On its surface, section 7(a)(2) would appear to apply to all actions that jeopardize the continued existence of endangered species, no matter where the actions occur or the species live.

C. Private Violations

1. The Prohibition On "Takings"

Under section 9(a)(1) of the ESA, no one, public or private, can *take* an endangered species of fish or wildlife. The ESA defines "take" to include actions that "harass, harm, pursue, hunt, shoot, wound, kill, trap, capture, or collect" an endangered species. In many cases, this prohibition is easy to apply. If a poacher kills or traps an endangered grizzly bear or bald eagle, for example, he clearly violates section 9. But does a landowner violate section 9 if she cuts down trees that are potential habitat for the endangered red cockaded woodpecker or paves over a sand dune that is the habitat of the endangered Delhi sands flower-loving fly? Does a farmer violate section 9 if he withdraws water

---

59. 50 C.F.R. 402.1(a).   **60.** 504 U.S. 555 (1992).

from a river in which endangered salmon spawn? In 1981, the FWS issued a regulation providing that "significant habitat modification or degradation" that "actually kills or injures wildlife by significantly impairing essential behavioral patterns, including breeding, feeding, or sheltering," constitutes unlawful "harm" under section 9.[61] This regulation has generated more controversy than any other aspect of the ESA.

It is questionable whether the members of Congress who passed the ESA fully understood that section 9 might limit how private landowners use their property and how much water farmers and cities can withdraw from domestic waterways. No one mentioned the possibility during debate on the ESA. Indeed the House floor manager said that the ESA would address the problem of habitat destruction "by providing funds for acquisition of critical habitat" and by enabling the "Department of Agriculture to cooperate with willing landowners who desire to assist in the protection of endangered species, but who are understandably unwilling to do so at excessive cost to themselves."[62] In *Babbitt v. Sweet Home Chapter of Communities for a Great Oregon*,[63] however, the Supreme Court upheld the FWS regulation by a six to three margin. As the Court explained, the term "harm" normally means to cause hurt or damage and "naturally encompasses habitat modification that results in actual injury or death." Congress, moreover, intended to provide expansive protection for listed species and to define "take" in the "broadest possible terms." Congress also amended the ESA in 1982 to authorize "incidental take permits," described in more detail below, that would allow property owners to develop their property without violating section 9. Congress thus implicitly recognized that, absent such a permit, destruction or modification of habitat could violate section 9.

Although *Sweet Home* settled the validity of the FWS regulation, it left open numerous questions regarding the applicability of the FWS regulation. For example, does the regulation apply if timber companies cut down an old growth forest in which spotted owls live, if the owls fly away before the trees fall and thus are not killed? Would it matter if the owls have no place left to breed? Because the plaintiffs in *Sweet Home* had challenged the FWS regulation on its face rather than as applied to particular facts, the justices did not need to decide what actions would actually violate the regulation or what proof is necessary. All the justices in *Sweet Home*, however, agreed that habitat destruction or modification violates section 9 only when it "actually kills or injures wildlife." Everyone also appeared to agree that the injury or death must be "foreseeable" and not merely "accidental." Justice O'Connor, in a concurring opinion, further argued that traditional principles of "proxi-

61. 50 C.F.R. § 17.3.
62. 119 Cong. Rec. 30162 (1973).

63. 515 U.S. 687 (1995).

mate causation," including "considerations of the fairness of imposing liability for remote consequences," should apply.

In discussing foreseeability, Justice O'Connor suggested that one of the first cases to interpret section 9, *Palila v. Hawaii Dept. of Land and Natural Resources (Palila II)*,[64] was wrongly decided. In the *Palila* decisions, the State of Hawaii had permitted mouflon sheep to graze on state land that also was habitat for the endangered palila bird. The sheep prevented regeneration of mamane trees, upon which palilas depend for food, by eating the tree's seedlings. In *Palila II*, the Ninth Circuit found that this violated section 9 by impeding recovery of the palila population and ordered the State to remove the sheep. Justice O'Connor disagreed with the Ninth Circuit's conclusion. "Destruction of the seedlings did not proximately cause actual death or injury to identifiable birds; it merely prevented the regeneration of forest land not currently inhabited by actual birds."

Justice Scalia, in a dissenting opinion in *Sweet Home*, and Justice O'Connor, in her concurrence, also briefly sparred over the issue of whether habitat destruction that prevents wildlife from breeding violates the ESA. Both agreed that the ESA requires injury or death to *individual animals*, and not simply injury to the species. But Justice Scalia argued that breeding interference does not injure any animal (but merely keeps some animals from being born) and thus does not violate section 9. Justice O'Connor disagreed. Destroying an animal's breeding habitat, O'Connor urged, injures a living animal much like sterilizing it and also makes it more vulnerable to predators and pollutants.

A question that has arisen on a number of occasions since *Sweet Home* is whether a court can enjoin the destruction or modification of habitat prior to an actual injury or death. In *Sweet Home*, the Court stated that "the Government cannot enforce the § 9 prohibition until an animal has actually been killed or injured." Subsequent courts, however, have rejected this language as dictum and held that an injunction is appropriate where there is a "reasonable certainty" of "imminent" injury or death.[65]

The "takings" prohibition of section 9(a)(1) applies only to endangered species of fish or wildlife. Plants are protected by section 9(a)(2), which bans the removal, digging up, or destruction of endangered plants either on federal land or "in knowing violation of any law or regulation of any State or in the course of any violation of a State criminal trespass law." Neither section 9(a)(1) nor section 9(a)(2), moreover, directly applies to threatened species. Section 4(d) of the ESA authorizes the FWS to issue regulations for the protection of threatened species, and

---

64. 852 F.2d 1106 (9th Cir.1988).

65. E.g., Marbled Murrelet v. Babbitt, 83 F.3d 1060 (9th Cir.1996).

the FWS has used this authority to extend the protections of section 9(a)(1) to threatened species. In a few instances, however, the FWS has used its discretion under section 4(d) to exempt certain species, such as threatened salmon and steelhead, from some or all of the provisions of section 9(a)(1). Although the FWS has argued that other programs adequately protect these species, politics almost certainly has played a role here as it has in listing decisions and implementation of section 7.

2. *Incidental Take Permits*

To mitigate section 9's potential restrictions on the use of private property, Congress in 1982 authorized the issuance of *incidental take permits*. Under section 10(a) of the ESA, the FWS can permit an otherwise unlawful taking of a species if (1) the taking is merely incidental to an otherwise lawful activity (such as property development), and (2) the permit applicant has devised an acceptable *habitat conservation plan*, or *HCP*. The HCP must minimize the impact of the taking "to the maximum extent practicable," ensure that the taking will not "appreciably reduce the likelihood of the survival and recovery of the species in the wild," and be adequately funded.

As of December 2002, the FWS had approved over 400 HCPs and issued accompanying incidental take permits, covering an area of approximately thirty million acres and over 200 listed species. The FWS has issued most of the permits to individual property owners wishing to develop or otherwise use their land in a manner that might be construed to be a violation of section 9. A number of communities, however, have developed *regional HCPs* encompassing multiple property owners and, where relevant, multiple species. Such regional HCPs reduce the burden on individual property owners, who no longer need to apply to the FWS for individual permits, and also enable regions to take a more comprehensive and coherent approach to species preservation. In most cases, federal, state, and local governmental officials, property owners, and environmental representatives meet over a lengthy period of time to try to hammer out acceptable terms for regional HCPs.

Many environmental groups are skeptical of incidental take permits and HCPs. In their view, the FWS often does not know enough about the listed species to ensure that the HCPs will adequately protect the species. They also worry that political pressures, and the desire to show that the ESA can "work" without causing economic disruption, encourage the FWS to agree to weak HCPs. Environmental groups nonetheless have launched few legal challenges to incidental take permits. Until 1998, moreover, courts had never overturned a permit. As in other areas, courts deferred to the expert judgment of the FWS. In *Sierra Club v.*

Babbitt,[66] however, a district court in 1998 rejected incidental take permits that the FWS had issued for two high density housing developments in the habitat of the endangered Alabama Beach Mouse. In the court's view, the FWS had failed to show that the offsite mitigation funding proposed in the HCPs would reduce the impact on the mouse to the "maximum extent practicable." Whether *Sierra Club v. Babbitt* reflects a new willingness by courts to scrutinize HCPs remains to be seen.

3. Administrative Reform Efforts

Faced with increasing Congressional hostility to the ESA, the Clinton Administration in the mid–1990s adopted a number of administrative reforms designed to ease the impact of section 9 on private landowners. First, the FWS announced a new policy of identifying, at the time it lists a species, those activities considered likely or unlikely to violate section 9. This policy has helped reduce the uncertainties that landowners and water users faced in deciding whether their actions might violate section 9.

More important, and contentious, was the FWS' announcement of a *no surprises policy*.[67] Many landowners are willing to agree to land use restrictions so long as the agreement buys them certainty. Landowners, however, often feared that, even if the FWS granted them an incidental take permit, the government might later try to limit their land use even further if the government discovered that additional habitat or actions were necessary to preserve a species. The no surprises policy tries to provide landowners with greater certainty by promising landowners who receive incidental take permits that the government will pay for any new habitat or actions that might be needed to meet unforeseen circumstances. Several environmental groups have brought a legal challenge to the no surprises policy, arguing that it exceeds the FWS's authority by tying the government's hands in the event that additional actions are needed to protect a species. The lawsuit remains unresolved.

The FWS also decided to use *safe harbor agreements* to encourage landowners to enhance, restore, or create habitat on their property. Prior to the safe harbor program, the ESA often discouraged private landowners from aiding species through such actions. If a landowner tried to help a species by creating habitat on his property, the land would become subject to section 9's restrictions, and the landowner might never be able to develop the land or change his use of the land if endangered species populations became established. Under safe harbor

---

66. 15 F.Supp.2d 1274 (D.Ala.1998).

67. Habitat Conservation Plan Assurances ("No Surprises") Rule, 63 Fed. Reg. 8859 (1998).

agreements, the FWS agrees that, if a landowner voluntary enhances, restores, or creates habitat, the landowner is free to return the land to its initial condition at a later time without running into problems under section 9. The safe harbor program has been quite successful. In South Carolina, for example, landowners have enrolled almost 100,000 acres of land in a program designed to protect the red-cockaded woodpecker.

4. Criticisms of Section 9

Many property rights advocates strongly criticize section 9 for restricting the use of land and water without compensation. The criticisms fall into three general categories. First, critics argue that section 9 encourages landowners to destroy valuable habitat, harming rather than helping listed species. Because section 9 restricts the use of habitat but not other lands, landowners can avoid section 9 by making sure their land is not viable habitat. Nothing prevents a landowner from destroying habitat prior to the listing of a species. And although it is illegal, landowners sometimes can escape section 9's grasp after a listing by surreptitiously destroying habitat on their property before the government discovers the habitat. Although there is no reliable estimate of the extent of such evasive behavior, stories abound of property owners trying to escape section 9 by cutting down trees, plowing their fields, or otherwise altering their land to make it unappealing to listed species. The phenomenon is problematic enough to have its own acronym: "shoot, shovel, and shut up," or the Three–S Syndrome.

Second, critics argue that it is unfair to force a limited group of landowners to "bear the burden" of protecting listed species. To property owners whose land use is restricted under section 9, the fact that their land is habitat for a listed species seems like blind bad luck. A farmer whose land is habitat for an endangered burrowing rodent may have to stop plowing her fields, while a farmer five miles away is unaffected. A property owner may not be able to develop her land because an endangered butterfly lives there, while new residential subdivisions rise up just over the hill. The butterfly may be endangered, moreover, because neighboring landowners previously developed their land, drastically reducing the available habitat. Section 9, however, forces only the current landowner to help in preserving the species. Critics argue that everyone should contribute toward the preservation of the species. If habitat needs to be preserved, the public should purchase it. After all, critics argue, preservation efforts benefit all members of the public.

Finally, some critics urge that the costs to society of section 9 outweigh the value of the protected species. To these critics, stopping new development to save a sand fly or a fairy shrimp is absurd. This critique, of course, returns us to the debate over the value of endangered species, with which we began our discussion of the ESA.

5. Constitutional Takings Challenges to Section 9

Only a few property owners have brought constitutional "takings" challenges to section 9 or to equivalent state habitat protections. Section 9 has seldom prevented property owners from making *any* use of their land, so *Lucas v. South Carolina Coastal Council*[68] is generally not relevant. In *Tulare Lake Basin Water Storage District v. United States*,[69] however, the Federal Claims Court held that the ESA had physically "taken" the water rights of an irrigation district in violation of the Fifth Amendment by reducing the amount of water that could be delivered to the district in an effort to protect two listed species of fish—winter-run Chinook salmon and delta smelt. Most landowners who have challenged habitat preservation measures have argued that the government is authorizing "permanent physical occupations" of their land by the protected species and thus is interfering with a core property interest. In *Nollan v. California Coastal Commission*,[70] the Supreme Court held that states cannot authorize the public to cross someone's land without compensation, so shouldn't compensation be required if the ESA forbids a landowner from excluding endangered species? Courts have rejected the argument, responding in part that the two types of "occupations" are quite different. While *Nolan* involved an intrusion by strangers and thus was especially offensive, endangered species are not "strangers to their ... habitat."[71]

D. Recovery Plans & Other Provisions

Once a species is listed as endangered or threatened, the FWS also typically prepares a recovery plan for the species. The ESA does not set any deadline for the preparation of a recovery plan and indeed contemplates that the FWS will prepare a plan more expeditiously for some species than for others. Section 4(f) of the ESA provides that the FWS, in developing and implementing recovery plans, will give priority to those species that are "most likely to benefit" from a recovery plan, "particularly those species that are, or may be, in conflict with construction or other development projects or other forms of economic activity." The FWS does not need to prepare a recovery plan at all for a species if the FWS concludes "such a plan will not promote the conservation of the species." As of the end of 2002, the FWS had prepared recovery plans for almost 1,000, or approximately 80 percent, of the listed U.S. species.

The FWS has a variety of tools with which it can implement recovery plans. As already discussed, sections 7(a)(2) and 9 furnishes

---

68. 505 U.S. 1003 (1992). See p. 66 supra.

69. 49 Fed.Cl. 313 (2001).

70. 483 U.S. 825 (1987).

71. Southview Assocs. v. Bongartz, 980 F.2d 84, 95 n. 5 (2d Cir.1992).

valuable protections. Section 7(a)(1) also provides that all federal agencies shall, in consultation with the FWS, "utilize their authorities in furtherance of the purposes" of the ESA by "carrying out programs for the conservation" of listed species. Under section 5, moreover, the FWS has the authority to acquire needed land and water "by purchase, donation, or otherwise."

Recovery plans unfortunately often need funding, and Congress has never provided full funding. Each year, hundreds of species receive no funding. In deciding where to spend federal dollars, moreover, Congress appears to care more about a species' poster quality than about its relative uniqueness or ecological importance. Mammals, birds, and fish, for example, receive significantly more funding than reptiles, amphibians, invertebrates, and plants. From 1989 through 1991, ten species, virtually all of which were charismatic birds or megafauna, received half of all government funding for endangered species.

E.   Does the ESA Work?

The ultimate question, of course, is does the ESA work? Does the ESA help to protect species from extinction? The point of the ESA, after all, is not to list endangered species but to restore endangered populations so they can be taken off the list. As of the end of 2002, only 33 species had been "delisted." Seven of these species, moreover, were delisted because they are now extinct. Another 12 were delisted because of taxonomic revisions, new information, or changes in the ESA. The FWS and NMFS have delisted only 14 species because the species had sufficiently recovered to be removed from protection. Among these "success stories" are the American alligator, peregrine falcon, brown pelican, and gray whale.

Delistings, however, are not a good indication of success. Given the severe threats that species face when they are listed, one should not be surprised to find few species being taken off the list. Indeed, the fact that only seven species have gone extinct after being listed may be the best indication of success. In one of the few empirical studies of the effectiveness of the ESA, Professor Jeff Rachlinski also found that the status of a species improves the longer the species is listed as endangered or threatened.[72]

No matter how effective the current ESA, most policy analysts believe that the ESA could be improved. One major reform would be to provide protection for species at an earlier stage—before a species finds itself on the brink of extinction and before the regulatory options become

---

72. Jeffrey J. Rachlinski, Noah by the Numbers: An Empirical Evaluation of the   Endangered Species Act, 82 Cornell L. Rev. 356 (1997).

limited. Another reform would be to refocus the ESA on the general protection of biodiversity, perhaps through the protection of different types of ecosystems, rather than on the protection of individual species.

Efforts to amend the ESA in Congress unfortunately remain mired in controversy. Thankfully, the FWS has been able to implement important reforms at the administrative level. Agency reforms, such as the no surprises and safe harbor policies and the development of regional HCPs, have fundamentally changed the ESA, in many people's view for the better. These reforms also have acted as a political steam valve that has deflated calls to weaken the ESA.

*

PART V

Environmental Impact Statements

CHAPTER 10

The National Environmental Policy Act

Passed in 1969, the National Environmental Policy Act (NEPA) was the first major statute of the modern era of environmental law.[1] A trailblazer, NEPA took a fundamentally different approach than the patchwork laws that had preceded it and the more prescriptive national pollution statutes that would follow. NEPA does not seek to ensure environmental protection through technology-forcing standards or market instruments, nor does it mandate conservation of endangered species or wetlands. Rather, NEPA relies on information, forcing agencies to consider the environmental impacts of their proposed actions and alternatives. This approach reflects a New Deal faith in agency management—the belief that a bureaucracy will do the right thing if it considers the proper issues. Without question, NEPA's influence has been far-reaching, with its progeny in the statute books of 19 states and over 130 of the world's nations.

NEPA requires that all federal agencies create an environmental impact statement (EIS) on a "recommendation or report on proposals for legislation and other major Federal actions significantly affecting the quality of the human environment."[2] Preparing an EIS is a considerable undertaking. Occasionally reaching the size of a metropolitan phone book, the EIS analyzes the environmental impacts across a range of proposed actions. This analysis considers both unavoidable adverse impacts and mitigation alternatives. For example, concerned over the amount of traffic in Yosemite Valley, the National Park Service might propose closing parking lots in the Valley and creating a shuttle bus service. Before undertaking this action, the Park Service must first prepare an EIS that considers not only the environmental impacts from this approach but also the impacts from a range of other actions—perhaps charging additional car fees to enter the Valley, a light-rail system, a tradable permit system for entry, or doing nothing at all. While

---

1. 42 U.S.C. §§ 4321 et seq.

2. 42 U.S.C. § 4332(c); also known as NEPA Section 102(2)(c).

laying out the environmental impacts of all these options, an EIS is agnostic and leaves the final choice to the decisionmaker.

NEPA also created the Council on Environmental Quality (CEQ) to oversee the NEPA process and its implementation. Perhaps surprisingly, the CEQ does not have (nor does NEPA provide for) enforcement authority. In practice, enforcement has come through citizen suits under the Administrative Procedure Act and federal question jurisdiction. In simple terms, NEPA cases generally raise one of two questions—should the agency have prepared an environmental impact statement and, if so, was the EIS adequate? The general remedy for a NEPA violation is a remand to the agency to stay its proposed project until it prepares and considers a satisfactory EIS.

Perhaps surprisingly, there have been thousands of NEPA suits. It might seem strange that NEPA's seemingly innocuous requirement of preparing an EIS has led to more lawsuits than any other environmental statute. What purposes does this requirement serve, and why are litigants so eager to enforce it?

As described above, the fundamental goal of NEPA is to *educate* decisionmakers, ideally by sensitizing them to environmental issues and helping the agencies find easy, inexpensive means of mitigating environmental impacts. From an *advocacy* perspective, an EIS can provide a source of leverage for internal agency opposition. A study by the National Science Foundation in the 1980s, for example, concluded that EISs give agency personnel a tool "to resist political importunities to pursue environmentally harmful measures." Moreover, it provides information that can be used to fight an agency's decision in court, and the information is not easily dismissed. It's hard, after all, for an agency to explain why its own EIS is incorrect. In relying on the EIS, in some instances litigants may be able to show that an agency action is "arbitrary and capricious" under the Administrative Procedure Act. From a *political* perspective, the EIS can be used to educate the public and provide information that can be used to fight the decision through the legislature or voting booth. Finally, NEPA litigation can *delay* a project (particularly if the EIS must be done again), allowing time to organize opposition and, in some cases, making the project so costly that it expires on its own.

I. NEPA Grows Teeth

Calvert Cliffs' Coordinating Committee v. U.S. Atomic Energy Commission was the first significant decision that interpreted NEPA, and it provides a useful insight into agencies' lack of environmental concern at the time of NEPA's passage.[3] In complying with the statute, the Atomic

3. Calvert Cliffs' Coordinating Committee v. United States Atomic Energy Commission, 449 F.2d 1109 (D.C.Cir.1971).

Energy Commission fully acknowledged that NEPA requires a "detailed statement" to be "prepared" and to "accompany" the licensing application for a nuclear plant. And amazingly, this is exactly what happened. The agency's staff prepared an environmental impact statement on the license application, and it accompanied the license throughout the process. In a brilliant example of form over substance, though, *the statement was never read or considered by the licensing board.* It simply went along for the ride. In his opinion, Judge Skelly Wright stated that the whole point of NEPA is to ensure that environmental considerations are taken into account by agency decision makers. Thus, to survive judicial review, agencies must prove that they have fully considered the detailed environmental statement "at every important stage in the decision making process."

In decisions that followed, particularly *Strycker's Bay Neighborhood Council, Inc. v. Karlen*, courts have gone to great lengths to make clear that NEPA is a procedural rather than a substantive statute.[4] Once an agency has made a decision subject to NEPA's procedural requirements, the judge may only consider whether the agency was arbitrary and capricious in failing to prepare an EIS or consider the relevant environmental issues. The judge cannot make the substantive decision on behalf of the agency. So long as the agency complied with the NEPA process and fully considered the EIS, the decision must stand *even if* the agency did not choose the environmentally preferable option. As the legal realists made clear over 60 years ago, however, the distinction between procedural and substantive review quickly breaks down. After all, how can the court take a hard look to determine if the agency complied with NEPA's procedural requirements (i.e., whether it fully considered the relevant factors) unless the court assesses the agency's final decision (a substantive analysis)?

II.   When Must An Agency Prepare An EIS?

The logic behind preparation of an EIS is straightforward—a better informed agency will make better decisions. To conserve resources, time and avoid hassle, though, it's equally obvious why, given the choice, some agencies would prefer not to create an EIS that questioned its proposed action, at all. Recall that an EIS must be prepared for a "recommendation or report on proposals for legislation and other major Federal actions significantly affecting" the environment. The threshold questions for an agency deciding whether it must create an EIA, then, is (1) whether it is dealing with legislative recommendations or major

---

4. Strycker's Bay Neighborhood Council
Inc. v. Karlen, 444 U.S. 223 (1980).

federal actions and (2) whether the environmental impacts are significant.

Most of the legal skirmishing has been over federal actions rather than proposed legislation. In court decisions, federal actions have been interpreted to include a wide range of activities—such as approval of specific projects (e.g., construction of a road in a national park), approval of rules, regulations, and other official policies (e.g., adopting a new set of regulations for concessionaires in national parks), adoption of formal plans or programs to guide agency decisions (e.g., a plan to permit local rangers greater discretion over their parks), and permitting or funding of private projects (e.g., approval of a river crossing for a power line).

Of course, not all federal actions trigger NEPA. Some statutes, such as the Clean Air Act and parts of the Clean Water Act, exempt preparation of an EIS, and the EPA need not comply with NEPA in other instances where EPA's decision-making process is functionally equivalent to NEPA's requirements. (Why do you think the National Park Service has not been able to take advantage of the same "functional equivalent" exemption?) Decisions not to act do not trigger NEPA, either. Thus neither the decision by the Department of Interior not to stop a planned wolf kill by Alaska nor the decision by the Forest Service to stop a decades-long practice of using herbicides to control vegetation in a National Forest triggered NEPA. Finally, an agency may provide indirect support (e.g., funding for a local group that undertakes a project with environmental impacts). In determining whether indirect action should constitute a federal action under NEPA, courts have considered whether the action could exist absent the support of the federal government.

A. Major Actions

Deciding whether there is a federal action is a straightforward judgment in most instances, but it can become complicated when considering NEPA's qualifying adjectives—that the federal action be *major* and that it *significantly* affect the environment. One could certainly imagine a major federal action that does not cause a significant environmental impact (e.g., providing a congressman for the District of Columbia) but, for actions that are environmental, one cannot practically determine if an action is major solely by focusing on the resources involved and ignoring its impacts. Consider, for example, an application for a federal right-of-way so a private power line can cross a navigable waterway. The crossing of the waterway will, in itself, have little environmental impact. But construction of the 67 mile power line will have significant impacts, and cannot be built unless it crosses the waterway.[5] This looks like a

---

5. Winnebago Tribe of Nebraska v. Ray,
621 F.2d 269 (8th Cir.1980).

minor federal action with significant consequential impacts and is known as a "small handle" problem, when federal permission or funding is only a small (though necessary) part of a much bigger project. Does it require an EIS? Small handle cases go both ways, with some courts focusing on the impacts of the entire project made possible by federal activity (EIS required) and others just focusing on the federal activity (no EIS).

Agencies may try to avoid NEPA's reach by dividing up or "segmenting" projects. At the extreme, for example, consider how the Forest Service might try to avoid preparing an EIS for its decision to build a 20–mile road in a National Forest. This 20–mile road certainly would seem to be a major federal action significantly affecting the environment. But what if, instead, the Forest Service transformed the project into twenty separate decisions to build 1–mile roads? By segmenting, the agency can transform major projects into innocuous minor ones. In isolation, none of these one–mile roads will likely trigger the requirements for an EIS. In scrutinizing examples like this, therefore, courts have asked whether the separate segments have independent utility. If the road segment along mile 16 makes no sense without miles 17 and 15, then they must be considered together.

A related problem concerns attempts to divide up separate types of actions. Imagine, for example, that the Forest Service decides to build a small road into a timber harvest area but does not prepare an EIS because the road will not have significant impacts. Soon after, the Forest Service approves two timber sales in the area but does not prepare an EIS because the timber harvest will not have significant effects.[6] Should the road and timber sales be considered together in a joint EIS? "Connected actions" are interdependent parts of a larger action and cannot proceed unless other actions occur before or simultaneously. The timber sale cannot occur without the road, and the road makes no sense without the timber sales. As a result, the CEQ has stated that such actions must be considered together and many courts have ruled against such segmentation, stressing NEPA's role in having agencies consider broadly the impacts of its actions.

B. *Significantly Affecting the Human Environment*

In determining whether an action significantly affects the human environment (such as filling 30 acres of wetland), CEQ has directed agencies to consider the "context" and "intensity" of the proposed action. Put another way, the significance of the impact depends on the overall setting, particularly if it is in an environmentally sensitive or valued area. As a real estate agent would observe—location, location,

---

6. Marsh v. Oregon Natural Resources
Council, 490 U.S. 360 (1989).

location. In considering intensity, is the action controversial or does it involve uncertain effects? Are its impacts short or long term? Does it involve endangered species or critical habitat? The rules for determining significance are, by necessity, far from bright lines and ultimately require agencies to consider a range of factors in making a judgment call. Moreover, the impact must primarily be physical rather than social or economic. In *Metropolitan Edison v. People Against Nuclear Energy*, for example, prior to restarting the companion reactor at 3–Mile Island, the Nuclear Regulatory Commission performed an EIS that considered the effects of fog from cooling towers, the possibility of low-level radiation, and the danger of an accident.[7] Plaintiffs demanded that the EIS also consider the psychological trauma on the community of restarting the reactor. The court rejected this claim, stating that even if psychological injuries are genuine, they are too remote from challenged action. In other words, an EIS need not consider potential psychological harm caused by exposure to risk.

III. Timing

Unless it is obvious that an EIS must be prepared, agencies will often first develop a 10–15 page Environmental Assessment (EA). An EA operates as a quick and dirty review and, if it suggests no EIS is necessary, the agency will issue a FONSI (Finding Of No Significant Impact). This decision not to undertake an EIS can then be challenged in court as a challenge to a final agency action. If the agency proceeds to prepare an EIS, a draft EIS is distributed and made available for public comment for 45 days. The agency then prepares a final EIS as well as responds to categories of public comments. Once the EIS has been issued, there is a 30 day moratorium on agency action so that challenges can be filed. This timeline, however, says nothing about when the review process should commence.

To prove useful, an EIS must be considered before the agency decides on an action, early enough that it can meaningfully contribute to the decision making process. Otherwise it simply serves as a *post hoc* rationalization for a decision already taken. Equally, the agency must have something fairly concrete in mind, otherwise the scope of potential EISs would be limitless. CEQ has taken a pragmatic view of timing, acknowledging that, even without a formal report or recommendation, an agency proposal may exist in fact. CEQ regulations require preparation of an EIS when the agency commences developing a proposal. This is before a report or recommendation, but after mere contemplation or

---

7. Metropolitan Edison Co. v. People   766 (1983).
Against Nuclear Energy (PANE), 460 U.S.

study. In the context of connected actions, this means preparing an EIS before the first of the actions and assessing the cumulative impact. Challenging the timing of EIS preparation is difficult for outside parties because, without inside knowledge, they really cannot know the status of various initiatives under consideration and whether so-called proposals have already become *de facto* decisions. To provide a bright line standard, courts have required that preparation of an EIS commence "before irreversible and irretrievable commitment of resources."

Another way timing plays out is in the context of scope. The case, *Kleppe v. Sierra Club*, for example, dealt with coal development policy on federal lands in the Northern Great Plains area.[8] It was clear to most observers during the Ford Administration in the mid–1970s that there was an ongoing plan to lease major areas in the northern Great Plains region to coal mining interests, but there was no official plan or announcement. The Department of Interior prepared EISs for its national coal leasing program and for individual leases. The Sierra Club, though, sued to force Interior to conduct a regional EIS, arguing that the national EIS was too general and the project-specific EISs too narrow to assess regional impacts. Impacts were greatest at the regional level and it was here that the Sierra Club argued alternative approaches should be considered. The problem from Interior's perspective, the government responded, was that there were many levels of decisionmaking at which one could reasonably prepare an EIS, and it was unreasonable to demand an EIS at every level.

The Supreme Court sided with Interior, stating that an EIS is required only where there is an actual "report or recommendation on a proposal for major federal action." A comprehensive EIS is appropriate, the Court declared, when there are significant cumulative or synergistic environmental effects, but it is left to the discretion of agency when this is the case. In other words, the Court defers to agency discretion over the proper scale of analysis. In practice, agencies have addressed this through the practice of "tiering," preparing successive EISs from broad scale to smaller. Thus an agency often prepares a "programmatic EIS" on an overall project, considering cumulative effects and overall alternatives, and then prepares site-specific supplemental EISs as they become appropriate. By tiering, an agency does not have to consider general effects each time it prepares an individual EIS, and does not need to be comprehensive in its programmatic EIS.

IV. Adequacy of the EIS

The issues raised above formed the basis for much of the early NEPA litigation. Much NEPA litigation focuses, as well, on the question

---

8. Kleppe v. Sierra Club, 427 U.S. 390 (1976).

of whether the EIS is adequate. A standard EIS will include an explanation of the purpose and need for action, a full description of alternative actions, an assessment of the environmental impacts of these actions, and possible mitigation measures to reduce adverse impacts of the proposed actions. In taking a hard look at such an EIS, courts have focused on questions of alternatives, adequacy, uncertainty, and new information. As we shall see, this has resulted in four main legal strategies to consider in challenging the adequacy of an EIS—(1) the EIS did not set forth responsible opposing views or alternatives, (2) it was not compiled in objective good faith, (3) it would not permit the decision-maker to fully consider and balance the relevant factors, or (4) the fact-finding did not have a substantial basis in fact.

According to CEQ regulations, the requirement that an EIS evaluate alternative actions is the "heart" of the EIS. This forces comparative assessment of the impacts and benefit of each action and, hopefully, show the agency how it can achieve its objective in a less environmentally harmful manner. Obviously, though, there is an endless number of potential alternatives an agency could consider. To address this, courts have required that agencies consider an array of alternatives that fairly represent the *range* of alternatives. In *California v. Block*, for example, plaintiffs challenged the EIS informing the U.S. Forest Service's decision over which portions of a 62 million acre national forest should remain roadless and designated wilderness.[9] There was no lack of interest on the part of the public, and the Service's draft EIS drew 264,000 public comments. In its final EIS, the Service considered 11 alternatives, ranging from the extremes of all wilderness to no wilderness. So far, so good. In between the extremes, however, none of the alternatives considered allocating more than 33 percent of the roadless area to wilderness. In holding that this was inadequate, the Ninth Circuit emphasized that an agency need not consider every alternative or alternatives that are unlikely to be implemented for legitimate reasons but, equally, it must not ignore important alternatives or bias its evaluation by arbitrarily narrowing the range of options considered. While NEPA remains a procedural statute, this type of analysis skates a very close line to substantive review.

It goes without saying, but the quality of an EIS analysis is obviously subject to judicial review, as well. In practice, this means the agency has to address the issues seriously. In *Sierra Club v. U.S. Army Corps of Engineers*, for example, the Corps prepared an EIS for filling part of the Hudson River to build a highway.[10] The EIS described the area to be filled as a "biological wasteland," despite objections by EPA and the Fish

9. California v. Block, 690 F.2d 753 (9th Cir.1982).

10. Sierra Club v. United States Army Corps of Engineers, 701 F.2d 1011 (2d Cir. 1983).

& Wildlife Service. In requiring the Corps to prepare a supplemental EIS, the 2nd Circuit concluded that by ignoring the views of other expert agencies, and by not adequately compiling relevant data and analyzing it reasonably, the Corps had reached a "baseless and erroneous factual conclusion" that "cannot be accepted as a 'reasoned' decision." In most cases, though, wary of appearing to engage in substantive review, courts are reluctant to reverse agencies on this ground. Thus in *Sierra Club v. Marita*, plaintiffs sued the Forest Service, claiming that its EIS needed to employ an ecosystems approach based on advanced principles of conservation biology.[11] Despite the testimony of 13 distinguished scientists, the court rejected the plaintiffs' argument. According to the 7th Circuit, agencies must use "high quality" science and ensure the "scientific integrity" of their analysis. But they don't have to use any particular methodology.

As described in Chapter 2, scientific uncertainty is an unavoidable aspect of environmental decision making. This arises in the context of NEPA when agencies must decide what to do if there is insufficient information to predict the impacts of specific options. In particular, when do agencies have to conduct more research? CEQ Regulations require that an agency make "reasonable efforts" to obtain relevant information, but obtain information that is "essential" to a reasoned choice among alternatives unless the overall costs of doing so are exorbitant. In practice, this requires that agencies at least consider the tradeoffs between the costs of getting more information and the value of getting it. When possible, an agency should rely on credible scientific evidence and, if information is unavailable, admit that the effects are uncertain and unknown.

A related question is whether an agency must prepare a supplemental EIS when new information becomes available, perhaps significantly changing the range of impacts considered. Imagine, for example, that the area to be filled in the Hudson River really was a "biological wasteland." Soon after the filling of the river, though, a local fisherman caught an endangered species and it now appears that a population of the fish lives nearby. Must the Corps stop construction and prepare a supplemental EIS? Recall that NEPA's goal is to ensure the agency makes decisions based on complete information. Thus CEQ regulations require preparation of a supplemental EIS if "significant new circumstances or information relevant to environmental concerns" becomes available. As with other stages of the EIS process, this is subject to the rule of reason. Surely such a "post-decision" supplemental EIS is not necessary every time new information comes to light. Rather, an agency must look to the

---

11. Sierra Club v. Marita, 46 F.3d 606 (7th Cir.1995).

significance of the new information, its value to the decision making process, and how much of the federal action remains to be done.

NEPA also applies to international actions when there are impacts in the United States. In perhaps the most creative of all NEPA challenges, in *National Organization for the Reform of Marijuana Laws (NORML) v. U.S. Dep't of State*, NORML alleged that a U.S.-supported narcotics program in Mexico that sprayed herbicide on marijuana and poppy plants would have significant health effects (by Americans smoking the herbicide laden weed) in the United States and that an EIS must be prepared.[12] The government agreed to conduct an EIS. By contrast, an EIS is not required when environmental impacts occur *exclusively* in a foreign jurisdiction. The case law regarding environmental impacts in the global commons such as the high seas or Antarctica, though, is less clear. President Carter signed Executive Order 12114 in 1979, providing for analysis of environmental impacts abroad from major federal actions, including impacts in the global commons. The Order exempts, however, actions taken by the president or when national security is involved. Moreover, as with all Executive Orders, it does not create a cause of action and noncompliance cannot be challenged in courts. More recently, President Clinton required environmental reviews for major trade agreements.

V. Does It Work?

Determining the effectiveness of NEPA is hard to do. Unlike the Clean Air Act or Clean Water Act, where one can simply measure air quality or water pollution over time, measuring the influence of environmental information on agency decision making is no easy matter. At one extreme, the EIS could simply serve as a *post hoc* rationalization for decisions already taken—simply going through the bureaucratic motions. And there certainly is reason to fear that this may happen in some instances. After all, conflicts of interest run to the very core of NEPA. Placing agencies in charge of conducting an EIS that may challenge their proposed actions, some have commented, is like placing the fox as guard of the hen house. As Joe Sax has memorably commented on NEPA, "I think the emphasis on the redemptive quality of procedural reform is about nine parts myth and one part coconut oil." Given the concrete statutory mission of an agency with dedicated budgets, organized lobbies, and congressional pressure, on the one hand, and the requirements of NEPA to consider environmental impacts of a range of actions, on the other, one might reasonably be doubtful of NEPA's influence. After all,

12. National Organization for Reform of Marijuana Laws (NORML) v. United States   Dep't of State, 452 F.Supp. 1226 (D.D.C. 1978).

there have traditionally been few political reward for forests not cut or range lands not grazed.

Despite all these reasons to dismiss NEPA, it has achieved a great deal and continues to do so. Compared to the state of agency transparency at the time of its passage, NEPA has played an important role in opening agency decision making to the public. NEPA has provided constant pressure on agencies to broaden their missions to consider and adopt environmental values. And it has spurred agencies to modify proposals and mitigate adverse impacts.

The experience of the Atomic Energy Commission, preparing an EIS and refusing even to read it, simply could not happen today. Indeed the numbers bear this out. Courts issued 202 NEPA injunctions in 1977, yet only 3 in 1987. Environmental impact analysis has become a standard part of federal decision making. Moreover, mindful of what an EIS will likely show, many projects are dropped before even conducting an EA, thus escaping measurement. Talk to environmental group litigators about NEPA and many say it is critical in providing data on agency actions they could not otherwise obtain or use. Does NEPA ensure agency decisions will be environmentally responsible? No. But it does ensure they will be informed and, in a field with such strongly conflicting interests and values, that is no small feat.

*

TABLE OF CASES

References are to Pages.

---

*

INDEX

291

†